A Practical Introduction to Computer Networking and Cybersecurity

By

Bongsik Shin, Ph.D

To Yujin, who made this book possible

Preface

This book is for people who study or practice information technology, management information systems (MIS), accounting information systems (AIS), or computer science. In writing the book, it is assumed that readers are exposed to computer networking and cybersecurity for the first time. They are challenging subjects partially because of the constant rise and fall of related technologies and IT paradigms. As the title implies, much focus is placed on providing reader audience with practical as well as theoretical knowledge necessary to build a successful professional career. With the book's practical value, a number of my students told me that they were keeping it as a future reference.

If used for a class, the book of 12 chapters contains just about right amount of coverage for a semester or quarter. It balances introductory and fairly advanced subjects on computer networking and cybersecurity to furnish both technical and managerial knowledge. Although the writing is moderately dense, much effort has been placed on explaining sometimes challenging concepts in a manner that readers can follow through with careful readings.

No effort was spared in providing readers with real or quasi hands-on learning experience without necessarily relying on a computer lab. First, each chapter comes with practical exercises questions. In the class setting, they are good as individual or group assignments. Many of them are based on simulated or real cases, and take advantage of actual industry products and systems for a reader to better relate theories to practice. Second, there are a number of information-rich screen shots, figures, and tables in each chapter carefully constructed to enhance visual learning. Readers are encouraged to review each of them carefully to solidify learning.

In addition to the thorough technical details, managerial issues including network planning, design, and management are covered throughout the book from the practitioner's perspective to afford balanced learning. Besides, bearing in mind of the critical importance of cybersecurity in today's computer networks, implications of a networking technology on cybersecurity are discussed whenever appropriate. Lastly, two chapters are dedicated to introduce fundamentals of cybersecurity in terms of threat types and defense techniques.

Summary of Updates

This edition has several improvements over the previous one:

- With the rise of *Internet of Things,* a section is introduced (Chapter 1).
- The measures available to strengthen the security of Ethernet switches are expanded (Chapter 3).
- A section is newly created to provide a high-level understanding of the border gateway protocol (Chapter 6).
- The explanation of the data VLAN is expanded (Chapter 7).
- With the rapid progress in WiFi standards, Chapter 8 is updated throughout (Chapter 8).
- The explanation of Metro-Ethernet is replaced by Carrier-Ethernet reflecting technology advancement (Chapter 9).

- The cellular network section is added as a wireless WAN technology (Chapter 9).
- The explanation of WAN topologies (9.4.2) is dropped to avoid duplication (Chapter 9).
- The explanation of IPv6 is updated (Chapter 10).
- The firewall and DMZ section is expanded significantly to introduce different practical approaches in setting up the firewall (Chapter 12).

Instructor Support

If used for a class, the book comes with PowerPoint lecture slides, solutions of chapter exercise questions, a test bank, and additional hands-on assignments of practical values.

TABLE OF CONTENTS

xi

CHAPTER 1   FUNDAMENTAL ELEMENTS

1.1   INTRODUCTION

By definition, the computer network represents a collection of communication links (both wired and wireless) through which computers and other hardware devices exchange various types of data (or messages). A network can be as small as the one installed in a house and as big as the Internet that literally covers the entire planet. Naturally, the size of a particular network directly reflects the size of the place (e.g., building, campus) it is installed. The wireless and wired network links have become arteries of an organization (e.g., company, university) and the society, revolutionizing every facet of our life by allowing resource (e.g., CPU, storage) sharing and by facilitating exchange of data (e.g., texts, videos, sounds) in an unprecedented manner. *Throughout the book, 'data' and 'message' are used synonymously.*

With the rapid advancement of information and communication technologies (or ICTs), more devices are being attached to the computer network that has been mostly the playground of traditional computers. Among them are digital smart phones, high definition IPTVs, music and video game players, tablets such as iPads, electronic appliances, control and monitoring systems (e.g., security cameras, CCTVs, traffic signals), and a myriad of other wireless and wired devices. The rapid addition of numerous digital devices makes the network a much more dynamic, diversified, vulnerable, and complicated platform.

Besides the digital computer network, there are also other traditional network platforms that existed long before the digital revolution unfolding before us. They include radio/TV broadcasting networks and the telephone system infrastructure called *public switched telephone network* (PSTN). These traditional networks are, however, not the focus of this book.

Although the traditional network infrastructure (e.g., PSTN) and the digital computer network have evolved separately, their convergence has been taking place at a rapid pace. For instance, more voice calls are digitized and transported over the Internet. Think of the popularity of various Internet call services including Skype, Vonage, and Google Voice. The convergence is accelerating as the computer network has become a stable platform in handling both non-real time (e.g., email, web browsing) and real time (e.g., voice, live video) data traffic.

The prevalence of computer networks, meanwhile, poses a great deal of security threats to individuals, organizations (e.g., businesses, universities), and the government. The threats are getting more stealthy and sophisticated, and the consequences are becoming more damaging than ever before. Attackers and organized crimes have mounted various security breaches, and many ill-prepared victims (e.g., individuals, public/private organizations) have suffered dearly. With most attacks taking place in the network space, adequate preparations such as threat monitoring and prevention have become essential in the design and operation of a computer network. In a measure to enhance awareness of such threats, relevant security concepts are explained throughout the book in addition to having two dedicated security chapters. This chapter begins with fundamentals, essential to the understanding of computer networking. Main objectives of the chapter are to learn:

- Key elements of the computer network
- Methods used by network nodes to distribute data
- Directionality of data propagation in the computer network
- Network topology as the architectural layout of a computer network
- Classification of networks in terms of their scope
- Differences between subnetwork and internetwork
- Key measures of network performance
- Numbering systems including binary, decimal, and hexadecimal systems
- Addressing methods of network nodes and their differences

1.2 NETWORK ELEMENTS

The computer network is made up of various hardware and software components including hosts, intermediary devices, network links (or communication links), applications, data (or messages), and network protocols. As a demonstration, Figure 1.1 displays a simple network in which two *hosts* (PC and server) exchange data produced by an *application* (e.g., web browser, web server) in accordance with *protocols* as pre-arranged rules of communication over the two *network links* joined by an *intermediary device*. Each of the constituents is briefly explained.

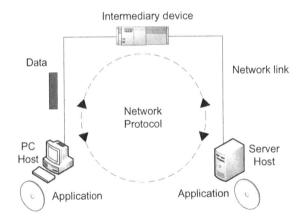

Figure 1.1 Key elements of a computer network

1.2.1 Host

The host in this textbook is defined as a data producing entity attached to a network and has been primarily a computer. Often times, hosts are also called *end devices, end systems,* or *end stations*. They have capability of accepting inputs (e.g., keyboarding, video feeds from a camera), process them, generate outputs in 1s and 0s, and store them. Processed data outputs may be digitized text, sound, image, video or any other multimedia content that can be transported over the computer network. The host is generally either a source or a destination of data in transit, and has been predominantly a general-purpose or high-performance computer (e.g., PC, laptop, mainframe, supercomputer). With continuous addition of non-traditional computing and communicating

2

devices to the network, host types are much more diversified these days. They include smart phones, personal digital assistants (PDA), video game consoles, home electronics and appliances, and other peripheral devices including network-enabled printers, copiers, and fax machines. When hosts exchange data over a network, their relationship is defined in one of two modes: client/server mode or peer-to-peer (or P2P) mode.

Client-Server Mode

In the client/server mode, a host acts as a dedicated client or server. The client host takes advantage of resources (e.g., files, storage space, databases, web pages, CPU's processing capacity) offered by servers. The server host generally has high performance capacity to quickly respond to resource requests from client hosts. In the early days, many programs (e.g., Microsoft Outlook for email) installed in the client host were tailored to a particular server application (e.g., Microsoft Exchange server). However, the web browser (e.g., Firefox, Google Chrome, Internet Explorer) has changed it all. The browser has become a universal program that allows a client host to communicate with many different servers (e.g., email, database, web servers) over the network. This paradigm of *one client application (web browser) to many server applications* has benefitted individuals and organizations tremendously. Above all, with the "thin" client in which the client host only needs a web browser to take advantage of various resources available from servers, organizations can control IT spending and significantly curtail efforts to maintain and upgrade programs on client hosts.

Peer-to-peer (P2P) Mode

Although network traffic is primarily the result of correspondence between designated clients and servers these days, there is also an alternative mode termed peer-to-peer networking in defining the relationship between communicating hosts. With P2P, there are no dedicated client or server hosts. The participating host behaves as both a client and a server concurrently in sharing resources. As an example, by joining P2P file sharing sites such as BitTorrent.com and Kazaa.com, my laptop can download multimedia files from other computers (client mode) and also makes files in its hard drive available to other computers (server mode) over the Internet. As another example of the P2P technology, today's operating systems such as Windows allow easy creation of a P2P network among participating computers, especially through the WiFi standard known as *WiFi Direct*.

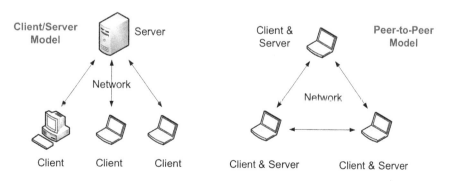

Figure 1.2 Client/server vs. P2P networking

Exercise 1-1

1. It is generally agreed that the client/server approach has many advantages over peer-to-peer. Explain why in terms of the following aspects. Search the Internet if necessary.
   a) Easier to maintain security protection of resources (e.g., data)
   b) Better accessibility to server resources
   c) Easier to back up server resources
   d) More cost effective in maintaining and upgrading server programs (or applications)
   e) Easier to add resources to meet growing demands

2. Create a simple private P2P network and conduct file swapping. For this, form a team of two students each with his/her own computer. Create a P2P network by connecting the two computers using a cable (e.g., crossover, USB transfer cable) or via WiFi connection. In addition to the cabling or WiFi link, P2P requires additional configuration (e.g., creation of workgroups on Windows). Once the configuration is complete, exchange files over the P2P network. If necessary, conduct Internet search to learn the setup procedure.

Network Interface Card

To be network enabled, a host is equipped with at least one network interface card (NIC), an electronic circuit board. Also called an *adaptor* or *LAN card*, the NIC is generally built into a computer these days and converts host-generated binary data into signals (e.g., electronic currents, lights, radio signals) and releases them to the network. The NIC also accepts signals arriving over the network, restores original data, and forwards them to the host's CPU for processing.

Many user computers have two NICs these days: one for cabled *Ethernet* LAN and one for *Wireless* (or WiFi) LAN to enable both wired and wireless networking as needed. Figure 1.3 illustrates a NIC card for Ethernet (left) and one for WiFi (right). You can observe that the Ethernet NIC has a *port* that allows physical connection of a computer to the wired network, but the wireless NIC (or WNIC) has only one or more antennas for radio communications. Each NIC comes with a unique address, called a physical or MAC address (to be explained).

Figure 1.3 Wired vs. wireless NIC (source: bargainhopping.com)

[Video Tour 1-1]   1. Wireless NIC installation in a laptop
                       2. NIC installation in a PC

1.2.2 Intermediary Device

Depending on its size, a network can have many different intermediary devices that conduct functions necessary to relay data between the source and destination hosts. Intermediary devices do not produce such data, but should transport them in an effective, reliable, and secure manner. Among the intermediary devices are *modems*, *firewalls*, *multiplexers*, *CSU/DSU*, *hubs* (or *multi-port repeaters*), *switches*, *routers*, *bridges*, and *wireless access points*. Their functional details are explained in other chapters, mainly in Chapter 3.

Hubs, bridges, wireless access points, and switches provide hosts (e.g., clients, servers) with interconnectivity "within" a network segment called a *subnetwork* (or subnet). Meanwhile, the router is used to tie different network segments (or subnetworks). The data forwarding activity (e.g., email delivery between two nodes) taking place within a subnetwork boundary is termed as *intra-networking* and that across two or more subnetworks enabled by routers is called *inter-networking* (Figure 1.4). In other words, hubs, bridges, wireless access points, and switches are intra-networking devices and routers are inter-networking devices. More on *intra-networking* versus *inter-networking* are in Section 1.6 of Chapter 1.

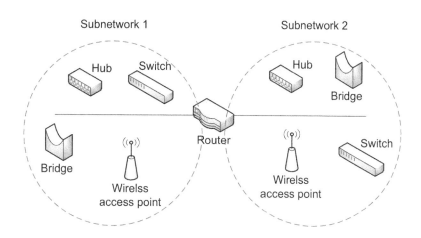

Figure 1.4 Intra-networking and inter-networking devices

Intermediary devices are distinct from each other in many different ways. For example, some devices (e.g., hubs) transmit data in half-duplex mode, whereas others (e.g., switches, routers) in full-duplex mode (more in Section 1.3). Some devices are hardware-driven in performing their primary functions, while others rely more on software capability. Software-enabled devices generally use a higher level of intelligence to conduct networking functions than hardware-enabled devices. Intermediary devices are also different in their processing speeds; capacity in data filtering and security provision; and addressing mechanism used to forward data. As with the host, the intermediary device also has one or more internal network cards with built-in ports (or interfaces) in order to join wireless or wired network segments. Because of the critical importance of intermediary devices in computer networking, Chapter 3 is dedicated to cover their structural and functional features in detail.

The term, *network node*, is used throughout the textbook as an inclusive concept that refers to an intermediary device or a host.

$$\text{Network nodes} = \text{intermediary devices} + \text{hosts (end devices)}$$

1.2.3 Network Link

The network link is a wired (or guided) or wireless (or unguided) link that enables data exchange between network nodes. To form the link, various communication media have been in use. Copper wires (e.g., twisted pairs, coaxial cables) and optical fibers made of extremely pure glass or plastic are predominant wired media these days. The earth's atmosphere becomes the medium of wireless communications. Various signals are utilized to transport data through the guided and unguided media: electronic signals for copper wires and coaxial cables, light signals for optical fibers, and radio/microwave signals in atmosphere. Details on the media and communication signals are explained in Chapter 4.

The network link can be either an *access link* or a *trunk link*. While the access link represents direct connectivity between a host (end station) and an intermediary device, the trunk link interconnects intermediary devices (e.g., router-router, router-switch, switch-switch) resulting in the extension of network span. The trunk link is a point-to-point connection and generally carries traffic coming from multiple access links. When two hosts exchange data through two or more intermediary devices, it takes one or more trunk links to complete the *end-to-end* data delivery (see Figure 1.5). Although no trunk link is necessary to create a small scale network such as the one in Figure 1.1, the majority of private and public organizations rely on it to form their enterprise networks.

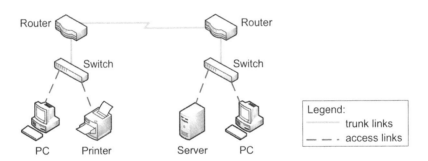

Figure 1.5 Access links vs. trunk links

Exercise 1-2: The hypothetical enterprise network of an organization in Figure 1.6 covers one main office and two remotely located branch offices. Each office has its own LAN (local area network) and the three LANs are interconnected by routers (R1, R2, and R3) over the three WAN (wide area network) links leased from a WAN service provider, AT&T.

1. How many hosts each LAN contains?
2. How many intermediary devices each LAN contains?

3. How many access links and trunk links are in each LAN?
4. What is the total number of access links and trunk links in the enterprise network?
5. How many network nodes are in the enterprise network?
6. What intermediary devices are used for intra-networking in each LAN?
7. What intermediary device is used for inter-networking?

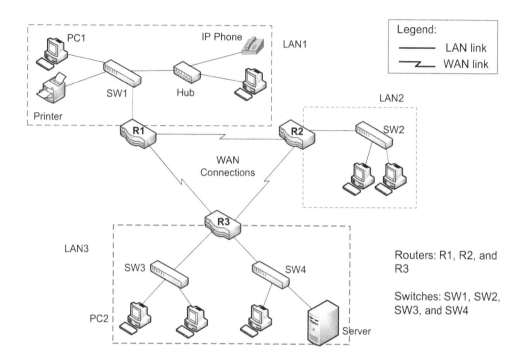

Figure 1.6 A hypothetical enterprise network

1.2.4 Application

The application (e.g., MS Outlook, web browser) represents a software program developed to support a specialized user task (e.g., email exchange, web surfing). Numerous applications have been introduced to support various tasks over the computer network. Many of them are designed to improve communications, which include those of email (e.g., Outlook, Thunderbird), instant messaging (e.g., Yahoo Messenger), and voice & video (e.g., Skype, Google Voice). Also, the web browser has become an extremely popular application on which numerous online services (e.g., social networking on Facebook, online banking, e-commerce storefront, cloud computing service from Amazon.com) are offered over the Internet.

Applications can be characterized from different angles, and their individual and organizational usage has important implications on the design of computer networks because of close tie between application types and requirements of network performance. For instance, there are:

7

- Applications that demand predictable or guaranteed network *reliability* (e.g., financial transactions)
- Applications that require predictable or guaranteed network *capacity* (e.g., video conferencing)
- Applications that cannot afford message *delay/latency* (e.g., audio conferencing, video streaming)
- Applications that are not real-time but requires responsive interactions (e.g., web browser, instant messaging)
- Applications with no particular requirement in network reliability, capacity, or delay (e.g., email)

1.2.5 Data/Message

Applications produce data (or messages) that need to be transported over the network. The data may be real-time or interactive audios/videos or such static contents as web pages and emails. In computer networking, produced data are packaged in discrete data units and they are delivered to the destination one by one. As a simple demonstration, imagine a network-enabled conversation between two persons and observe how their dialog is packaged into discrete data units and gets delivered (see Figure 1.7). The general name of each data unit is *packet*. Each packet contains source data and additional overhead information such as source and destination addresses necessary for its delivery. To better visualize the relationship between the source data and the packet, think of a letter (as source data) contained in an envelope with mailing addresses (as packet).

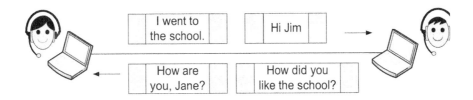

Figure 1.7 Transmission of discrete data units over a computer network

1.2.6 Protocol

The host application (e.g., web browser, email program) produces and exchanges data/messages according a *protocol* that contains a collection of detailed communication rules. For this, an application should have a built-in protocol. The application produces outgoing data and interprets incoming data strictly based on the set of rules defined by the protocol. The communication rules of a protocol are divided into two categories:

- Syntactic rules: Rules regarding the format of a message in its construction
- Semantic rules: Rules concerned with the meaning or interpretation of a message

For example, if a computer user enters *http://www.facebook.com* into the web browser's *URL*

(Uniform Resource Locator), the browser produces a simple request message according to the built-in *Hypertext Transfer Protocol*. Here, the request message has a format (syntax) similar to:

GET / HTTP/1.1
Host: www.facebook.com

so that the target host (www.facebook.com server) can understand/interpret its meaning (semantics). The semantics of above statements is '*Please send me the main page of www.facebook.com using the HTTP protocol, version 1.1.*' The request message thus produced is then dispatched to the target server.

Certain protocols are *standardized* so that hardware and software vendors can incorporate them into their own products. For example, HTTP is a standard protocol adopted by all web browsers (e.g., Firefox, Internet Explorer, Chrome) and web servers (e.g., Apache, Microsoft IIS). There are also numerous *proprietary* protocols developed by vendors exclusively for their own commercial products (e.g., the protocol embedded in Skype). Several standard protocols are introduced throughout the textbook.

1.3 MODES OF COMMUNICATION

This section explains methods network nodes utilize to distribute data and the directionality aspects of data exchanges.

1.3.1 Methods of Data Distribution

Data distribution methods between network nodes are largely divided into *unicasting, broadcasting,* and *multicasting.*

Unicasting

With unicasting, data exchange takes place between a single source and a single destination identified by their unique addresses. The destination may be located within the same network as the source or separated from the source across multiple networks. It was explained that the co-location of the source and the destination within a subnetwork takes intra-networking for data delivery. When the source and the destination are in different subnetworks, data delivery requires inter-networking (more in Section 1.6). Normally, the majority of messages produced by an application (e.g., email, web browser) are exchanged in the unicasting mode.

Broadcasting

Broadcasting results in the flooding of data from one node to all the other nodes within a network in a simultaneous fashion. In fact, we have been enjoying the broadcasting service daily by tuning into radio or TV channels. From satellites or earth stations, radio and TV companies broadcast signals that carry various contents (e.g., music, drama, reality shows). Such broadcasting is also widely used by computer networks for various reasons. A good example is WiFi.

Multicasting

Multicasting from a data source results in its concurrent delivery to a selected group of destinations. We have been using multicasting services extensively. For example, there are many web sites that offer audio or video streaming for live news, music, TV programs, movies, or videos over the Internet. These services rely on a multicasting protocol so that servers can stream multimedia contents to requesting clients concurrently. With increasing popularity of such on-demand multimedia-driven services, usage of multicasting will only grow.

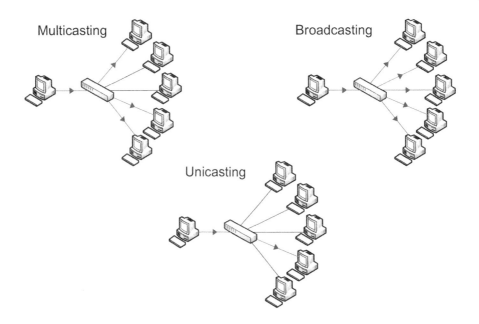

Figure 1.8 Unicasting, multicasting, and broadcasting

Although the demonstration in Figure 1.8 is made in the form of data distribution between hosts, intermediary nodes including switches and routers also take advantage of them to advertise supervisory information or to exchange information necessary to perform scheduled and unscheduled control functions.

1.3.2   Directionality in Data Exchange

Data flows between two network nodes can be one of three types in directionality: *simplex, half-duplex*, and *full-duplex*.

Simplex

With simplex transmission, data flows one direction only. Radio and TV broadcasting services are good examples. This mode of communication also exists between computers and their input devices such as keyboards. The simplex transmission, however, is not a prevalent mode in the computer network.

Duplex

In the duplex mode, data flows both ways between two network nodes and thus each node has capability of sending and receiving data. Duplex transmission is further divided into half-duplex and full-duplex modes.

Half-duplex: In this mode, only one party is allowed to transmit data at a time, and the other party should wait until its turn. For a good analogy of half-duplex communication, imagine the two-way traffic flow on a single lane railway. Another well-known technology example is walkie-talkie, a portable radio device with which two communicating parties take turns for speaking. Although used in the early generation of computer networking (e.g., hubs), it has been largely replaced by more effective full-duplex mode of communication these days.

Full-duplex: With full-duplex, data flows both directions simultaneously between two network nodes. For this, there are generally two channels established for a link (or circuit): one channel for each direction. It is like having double lanes for two-way traffic. The traditional telephone system has been using the full-duplex mode so that two parties on a circuit can talk and listen simultaneously. Most computer networks take advantage of the full-duplex technology these days.

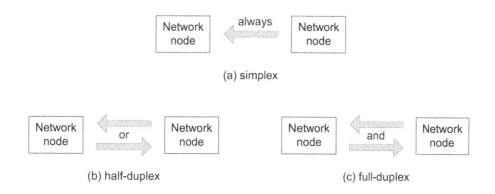

Figure 1.9 Simplex, half-duplex, and full-duplex transmissions

1.4   NETWORK TOPOLOGIES

Network topology is the physical layout of a network. The logical layout concept also exists, but we focus more on the physical placement of network nodes and links. The network topology, therefore, represents a design approach utilized to interconnect network nodes (intermediary devices and hosts). The physical layout can be understood in terms of the relationship between *intermediary devices* and *hosts,* between *hosts,* or between *intermediary devices.* Many different topologies including bus, star, ring, mesh, tree (hierarchy), and hybrid (e.g., bus-star) have been in use to arrange network nodes. Each topology has its own strengths and weaknesses, and the design process of an enterprise network should factor in various consideration elements unique to its circumstance. These include characteristics of *locations* (e.g., number of locations, degree of their distribution), *users* (e.g., number of users), *hosts* (e.g., number of onsite hosts), and *applications* (e.g., importance of reliability in message delivery).

1.4.1 Point-to-Point Topology

As the simplest topology, point-to-point establishes a direct connection between two nodes. There may be only two end nodes directly linked or more than two nodes between two end nodes making it an extended point-to-point connection (see Figure 1.10). The point-to-point link can be given dedicated capacity as in the case of the phone line between a house and a telephone company. The point-to-point connection can also be dynamically constructed and dismantled as needed. This dynamic formation occurs more often in the form of extended point-to-point topology. For example, a long-distance or an international call between two remote locations requires dynamic circuit formation through multiple switches.

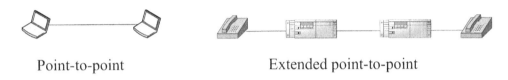

Point-to-point   Extended point-to-point

Figure 1.10 (Extended) point-to-point topologies

1.4.2 Bus Topology

In bus, end stations are tapped into the main transmission line, with a terminator device at each end of the main line absorbing data remaining in the network (Figure 1.11). Communications between any two stations, therefore, should be made via the backbone medium. Using the common line approach practically results in *broadcasting* of data in which transmissions from a station reach all the other stations on the network although there is only one intended receiver. This topology therefore allows only a single station to release data at a time to avoid transmission collisions. With its structural simplicity, bus works well for small networks. However, this topology is subject to traffic congestions when the network size grows with more stations attached. The early generation of Ethernet LAN was running on the bus topology, but its usage has mostly disappeared in the corporate world due to inherent limitations including unnecessary data broadcasting and cabling difficulties (e.g., installing the main line inside ceiling).

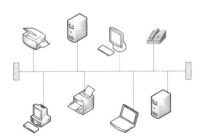

Figure 1.11 Bus Topology (LAN example)

1.4.3 Ring Topology

With ring topology, stations are attached to a backbone ring that may be copper wire or optical fiber. Depending on the technology standard, a network can have a single-ring or a dual-ring architecture that offers redundancy and therefore higher survivability from link failures. The ring network has technological advantages in handling high-traffic volume in a reliable manner. This topology also has strength in constructing long-haul networks. Despite the technological advancement and availability of ring-based standards for LANs such as Token Ring and FDDI (Fiber Distributed Data Interface), their acceptance has been dwarfed by more cost-effective Ethernet that runs on star (or extended star) topology. Ring topology, however, remains a popular choice in creating the high-speed WAN backbone with fiber optics (more details in Chapter 9).

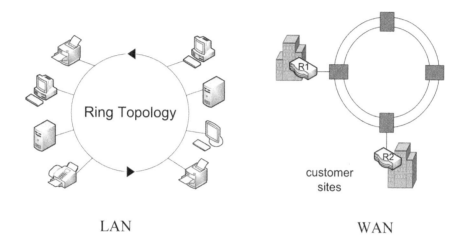

LAN   WAN

Figure 1.12 Ring Topology (LAN and WAN examples)

1.4.4 Star (hub-and-spoke) Topology

With star topology on a LAN, host stations are connected to a central intermediary device (see Figure 1.13). The topology has several advantages. Above all, the topology makes it is easy to add and remove a host station from the network and also to locate node and/or cable problems. It is also simple to expand the network scope by connecting more end stations. Ethernet LANs mostly run on this topology these days. With dominance of Ethernet as a wired LAN standard, there are many equipment options (e.g., cabling, ports, connection speeds) at a competitive price. As its main disadvantage, this topology is susceptible to a single point of failure in which a fault with the intermediary device brings down the network.

An enterprise can also adopt star topology to interconnect distributed branch LANs with WAN connections. In this case, the network node placed at the hub location (e.g., main office) mediates traffic between any other locations. You can observe that the WAN topology is determined by the relationship among intermediary devices such as routers rather than that between hosts and an intermediary device.

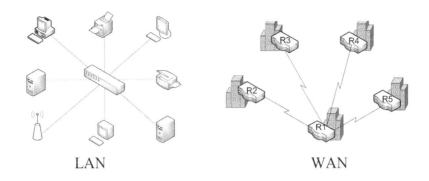

LAN   WAN

Figure 1.13 Star (Hub-and-spoke) topology (LAN and WAN examples)

1.4.5 Mesh Topology

Mesh topology is an arrangement in which all possible connections between network nodes are directly linked. This makes a network very reliable through extra redundancies in which one inoperable node does not drag down the entire network. The mesh network can be a sound option when the number of nodes is relatively small. For example, with three network nodes, there are only 3 connections required and 4 nodes takes 6 direct links. When the number of devices or locations increases, however, direct connections required increase exponentially making it less practical mainly due to inflated operational costs. Partial-mesh topology carries less links (thus less cost burden) than full-mesh but more links than star (hub-and-spoke), offering a certain degree of link redundancy that makes a network less vulnerable to link failures.

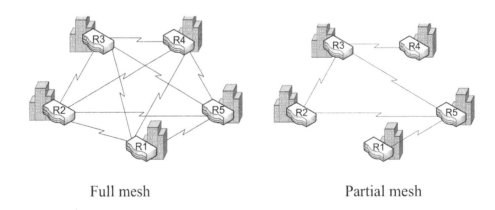

Full mesh   Partial mesh

Figure 1.14 Full mesh and partial mesh topology (WAN examples)

1.4.6 Tree (or Hierarchical) Topology

With tree topology, nodes are joined in a hierarchical fashion in which the one on top becomes a root node. There are, in general, at least three levels (two levels make a star topology) in the hierarchy with the number of nodes increasing at the lower level, making the overall structure like the Christmas tree. The tree structure is highly effective when many nodes (or locations) have to be interconnected using reduced direct links. This topology has been a popular choice in forming the backbone network of telephone service providers or Internet Service Providers (ISPs) to cover a large geographical area.

The tree approach is also frequently used to construct an enterprise network in which a large number of end stations are interconnected through the hierarchy of intermediary devices. For example, the LAN of a building may have a star-based network in each floor. Then, the multiple star networks from different floors can be linked to higher-speed devices to form a bigger network that covers the entire building. The hierarchical topology shares strengths inherent to the star network such as easy of network management and expansion. When a network has the tree structure, intermediary devices (e.g., switches) located at the higher level generally handle more traffic and thus should be more powerful (e.g., faster forwarding rate) than those at the lower level.

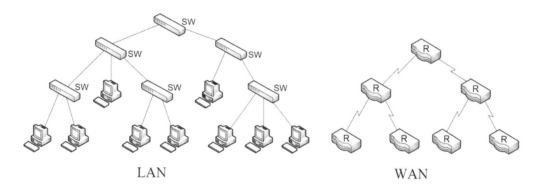

LAN   WAN

Figure 1.15 Tree/Hierarchical Topology (LAN and WAN examples)

When it comes to actual implementation, many corporate networks take the form of a hybrid structure in which more than one topology is combined. Taking a simple example, each direct link between two nodes in star, mesh, or tree topology becomes an instance of the point-to-point connection.

1.5   CLASSIFICATION OF NETWORKS

In terms of their spatial scope, computer networks are generally classified into four different types: Personal area networks (PAN), Local Area Networks (LANs), Metropolitan Area Networks (MANs) and Wide Area Networks (WANs). Each network category has widely accepted standard technologies.

1.5.1   Personal Area Network (PAN)

The PAN is a small network whose coverage is typically a few (up to 10) meters. It has been popularized with the introduction of such wireless standards as *Bluetooth, WiFi Direct, Zigbee,* and more recently *NFC (Near Field Communication)*. For instance, *NFC* technology is enabling people to make credit card transactions (e.g., tap-and-pay in a grocery store) using such smartphone systems as Apple Pay and Google Wallet. As another example, Bluetooth-enabled devices located in close proximity can exchange data without hard wiring. Among them are laptops, printers, wireless mouse and keyboards, smart phones, headsets and earphones, MP3 players, portable multimedia players, personal data assistants (PDAs), speakers and microphones, global positioning systems (GPS), digital cameras, video game consoles, video camcorders, and other hands-free devices.

Figure 1.16 Personal area network

1.5.2   Local Area Network (LAN)

The LAN, in general, covers a relatively confined area to interconnect hosts located within the physical boundary of an organization or a company. Its coverage scope is therefore larger than that of personal area networks. Size of the LAN varies considerably as it is determined by the size of an organization in a local area. For example, if a company occupies only a single floor of a building, the firm's LAN is limited to the floor. If an organization uses all floors of a building, its LAN covers the entire building.

The bigger network that interconnects LANs of multiple buildings within a university or corporate campus is also considered a LAN. The oversized LAN formed by joining LANs of multiple buildings is frequently termed as campus LAN or campus area network. The campus LAN's expanded scale makes its design and operation more challenging than ordinary-sized LANs. To create a campus LAN, smaller LANs are joined by high-speed intermediary devices (e.g., core routers or switches) in a hierarchical structure of multiple layers (see the tree topology in Figure 1.15).

As a simple example, imagine a relatively small-scale campus LAN of two buildings each with a fast core switch and two workgroup switches that attach computers to the LAN (Figure 1.17). The actual campus LAN can be far more complicated than the example, with many more high-speed intermediary devices interconnected. Details of LAN technologies are covered in Chapter 7 and 8 focusing on the dominant Ethernet and WiFi standards. As said, there is no one-size-fit-all definition of the LAN especially in its scope and, therefore, readers should interpret the term in its usage context.

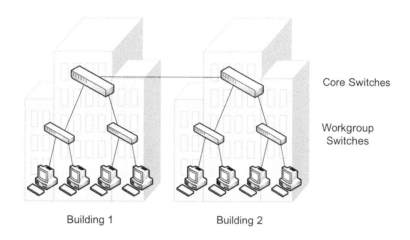

Figure 1.17 An illustration of campus LAN

1.5.3 Metropolitan Area Network (MAN)

The MAN is generally designed to cover a good-sized city, being considerably larger in its geographical span than the LAN. The MAN is used to interconnect LANs through land-based or wireless standards within a metropolitan area. Corporate clients also subscribe the MAN service to access the Internet. In general, *common carriers* (or simply *carriers*) such as telephone service providers (telcos) and Internet service providers (ISPs) have the ownership of MAN infrastructure.

Figure 1.18 demonstrates hypothetical MAN infrastructure of a carrier with high-speed cabling (e.g., 10 Gigabits/second) and fast intermediary devices in the Boston metropolitan area. It shows that, through the MAN, the three client site LANs can be interconnected and also send data to the Internet and to the carrier's WAN platform (called public switched data network or PSDN).

In the past, wide area network (WAN) standards such as Frame Relay were technology choices for the MAN infrastructure. However, with dominance of Ethernet as a LAN standard, the Ethernet-derived standard called *Metro-Ethernet* has become a popular choice for the MAN platform as well. Besides, with the prevalence of wireless networking, WiMax (or WirelessMAN) has been introduced as a broadband standard for wireless MAN service.

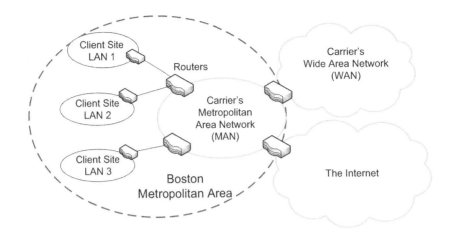

Figure 1.18 An illustration of MAN

1.5.4 Wide Area Network (WAN)

The WAN is designed to cover a state, a nation, or an international territory. It is, therefore, designed to interlink LANs including campus networks, MANs, or even smaller WANs. A client organization (e.g., university, company) creates its own private WAN connections by subscribing to the WAN service available from common carriers (e.g., Verizon) in order to tie its geographically distributed LANs. To offer the WAN service commercially, carriers install and maintain privately owned WAN infrastructure.

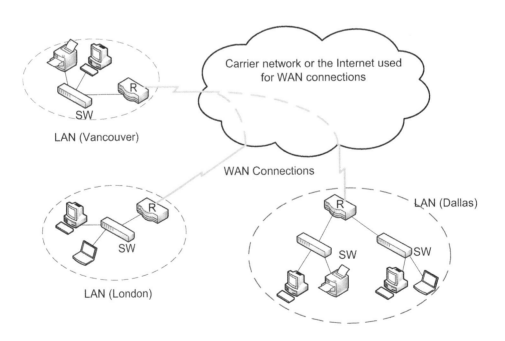

Figure 1.19 WAN links and an enterprise network

18

Separate from the carrier-owned WAN infrastructure, the Internet has become an extremely popular platform for WAN connections as well. The Internet itself is the largest global network of which no single company or nation has an exclusive ownership. For example, a carrier has its own Internet infrastructure but it makes up just a small fraction of the global Internet backbone. With Internet's ubiquity (covering the entire planet), flexibility (connect anytime and anyplace), and cost advantage (substantially cheaper than the private WAN service offered by carriers), more organizations are taking advantage of the Internet to create WAN connections. Many *enterprise networks* of companies are therefore composed of LANs (e.g., main and branch office LANs) joined by WAN/MAN connections (see Figure 1.19). Chapter 9 explains popular WAN services offered by carriers and Chapter 10 introduces the architectural side of the Internet.

1.5.5   Internet of Things (IoT)

With the prevalence of PANs, LANs, MANs, and WANs, a new paradigm called *Internet of Things* (or IoT) is unfolding. IoT is not a type of network, but represents a phenomenon in which numerous devices (e.g., cars, appliances, gadgets, electronics, mobile devices, security monitoring devices, health devices) automatically detect each other and communicate seamlessly to perform a host of routine and innovative tasks over the wired and wireless networks. Surely, the various network types explained above are the keys that will bring IoT to reality although its full-swing may be years away. The following scenario is constructed to depict how the emerging IoT is going to fundamentally transform the society through the transparent and automated connectivity among numerous computing and non-computing devices.

~~~~~~

Exercise 1-3: "Year 2025 in San Diego: Laura is a marketing manager of a large business insurance firm. Her daily schedule is loaded with both personal routines and job related activities. Today, she has to wake up at 6 am. There is a meeting scheduled at downtown and also a business flight to Los Angeles is scheduled at 12 pm. While her car self-drives to downtown, she is warned by her car's monitoring system that its brake pads are nearing their life span and the tire pressure is low. Her car also transmits the information to her maintenance shop for the monthly assessment and report. At one point, her car warns that the shortest path originally suggested has a sudden traffic jam caused by an unexpected accident and chooses an alternative path. It also senses weather conditions, adjusts internal temperature and humidity, activates the sun blind, and controls influx of polluted air.

After the brief meeting at downtown, she is on the road again for a short trip to Los Angeles to meet a key business partner. The electronic ticket purchased days ago has been stored in her Apple Watch. When she enters the Lindberg airport, the Watch initiates communications with the airport's customer support system (CSS) by sending the ticket information. Then, the CSS suggests the nearest entrance gate as well as a close parking lot for the flight. At the boarding gate, she taps her Watch to the side kiosk for boarding.

While flying, she checks the delivery status of the Xbox game she ordered two days ago. Her son has been asking for it for his birthday gift. Tracking the postal office database indicates that the game has been delivered to her office. Using her Watch, she also checks her son's current location and health conditions. Although he is with a caring nanny, she worries about her son who suffers from asthma. He wears a wrist-device for remote diagnosis and monitoring by her family doctor. On arriving in Los Angeles, she is directed by her Watch to pick a reserved rental car equipped with a smart chip that records usage time, location, travel distance, and other information for automated billing to the corporate account. After a short meeting with her boss to report the outcome of the Los Angeles trip, she heads home with her son's Xbox game.

It has been a long day for Laura. On the way home, she drops by a nearby grocery store for food shopping. When she grabs a shopping cart, its attached display greets her recognizing her membership and shows special discount items of the day. She also picks up an advertisement paper that has a full list of products in promotion. By placing her Apple Watch close to a particular product code, more details are displayed. Prior to shopping, she connects her home network to check the availability of food items and their conditions (e.g., expirations). With the check, the Apple Watch automatically develops a shopping list. As the Watch knows Laura's precise location enabled by the store-installed triangulation technology, it plots ideal routing through the store, saving her precious time in searching shopping items. With her busy schedule, she realizes that she might have to sign-up for the grocery store's auto-replenishment service that links her home network to the store's tracking system.

When Laura arrives home, information and data stored in her Apple Watch and the notebook computer is auto-synchronized with the home network's central server. Laura's health information (e.g., pulse rates) gathered by the Watch sensors is also synchronized with the home server's health assistant. Tonight, the health assistant analyzes gathered data and recommends her to see a doctor after recognizing abnormality in her pulsation for the past three days. With Laura's nodding, the health assistant makes an appointment with her family doctor's reservation system and transmits health data for doctor's review. When she replenishes groceries in the refrigerator, product information including their expirations is passed on to the central server. It is already ten o'clock. Before going to bed, she reads arrived messages including automatic diagnosis of her son's condition and an electronic report from the auto maintenance shop.

Class Discussion:
1. Discuss where and how PAN, LAN, MAN, and WAN technologies are used to realize IoT.
2. In the scenario, can you identify new business opportunities (called business models) that do not exist today? What about existing business models that may become less relevant or even obsolete in the future because of technology advancement?

1.6   SUBNETWORK VS. INTERNETWORK

Building on the explanation of intermediary devices in Section 1.2.2, the relationship among network, subnetwork (or subnet), and internetwork (or internet) is further clarified. In doing so, especially important is to clearly understand difference between network and subnetwork, and between network and internetwork. As stated in the beginning of this chapter, the network as a loosely defined term can span a small home, a university campus, a country, or even the planet. Section 1.5 classified it in terms of PAN, LAN, MAN, and WAN. In other words, depending on scope and design, a network can contain just one subnetwork or an internetwork (*i* as a lower-case character) with multiple subnetworks joined by one or more routers. Remember that the internetwork is a generic term different from the Internet (*I* as an upper-case character) we surf daily for web browsing (Details of the Internet architecture are covered in Chapter 10).

Figure 1.20 is a simple demonstration of LAN installed in a building in which two subnetworks are tied by a router to become an internetwork. When two computers exchange data across the two subnetworks, the data forwarding process becomes 'inter-networking'. As related, the difference between intra-networking and inter-networking was explained in Figure 1.4 in which a subnetwork contains various intermediary devices (e.g., switches, wireless access points) for intra-networking. In summary, Figure 1.20 shows a case where the company network is LAN that is also an internetwork containing two subnetworks.

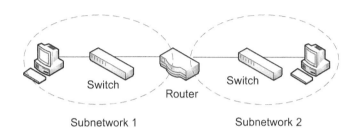

Figure 1.20 Scenario 1: A company's network

Figure 1.21 is another demonstration of a company network composed of two remotely located office LANs and one WAN link that enables data exchange between them. You can observe that each LAN contains only one subnetwork because delivering messages within the LAN boundary does not need router's help. This differs from Figure 1.20 in which one LAN consists of two subnetworks. Additionally, the WAN connection is considered a subnetwork (Although it may be 3,000 miles in length!). As a result, the enterprise network as a whole becomes an internetwork with three subnetworks. From the two scenarios, you can observe fluid relationships among the LAN/WAN, subnetwork, and internetwork boundaries.

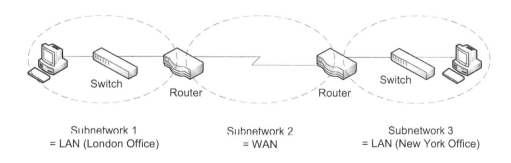

Figure 1.21 Scenario 2: A company's network

Exercise 1-4

1. Refer to Figure 1.6 and answer the following questions.
   a) How many subnetworks are there in each LAN?
   b) If PC1 in LAN1 sends a file to the printer in LAN1, is this inter-networking?
   c) If PC1 in LAN1 sends a request message to the Server in LAN3, is this inter-networking?
   d) If PC1 in LAN1 connects to IP Phone in LAN1, is this inter-networking?
   e) If PC2 and Server in LAN3 exchange messages, is this inter-networking?

2. Figure 1.22 is a small corporate network deployed in a building. It has three switches connected to the border router with built-in firewall capability to prevent intrusions from the Internet. Disregarding the connection between the firewall router and the Internet:
   a) How many LANs are there?
   b) How many subnetworks are there?
   c) If PC1 sends a message to E-mail Server, is this inter-networking?
   d) If PC1 sends a message to File Server, is this inter-networking?
   e) What is the intermediary device used for intra-networking?

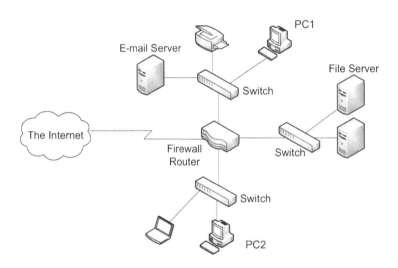

Figure 1.22 A hypothetical corporate network

1.7   MEASURES OF NETWORK PERFORMANCE

Network performance in effectively propagating host-produced data is a critical issue and much consideration should be given to optimize it during the stages of network planning, design, implementation, maintenance and upgrade. There is no shortage of stories that underscore the importance of adequate network performance, especially as it carries more real-time (e.g., voice calls, video streaming) and mission-critical applications (e.g., financial transactions). Many of the applications demand a certain degree of 'guaranteed' performance regardless of circumstance (e.g., traffic congestion). A number of measures are being used to indicate network performance from different angles, and those of *capacity* (or *speed*), *delay* (or *latency*), and *reliability* are among the most important ones.

1.7.1 Capacity

Network capacity (or speed) is represented by metrics of *data rate* as increasing factors of bits per second (or bps). Data rate is about how fast data flows in one direction from point A to point B (not the combined speed of both directions). Not to confuse between *byte* and *bit* metrics (1 byte is generally 8 bits) in which byte metrics are primarily for data storage or memory capacity, not network capacity. Table 1.1 summarizes metrics of data storage/memory capacity and network capacity.

Storage/Memory Capacity	Network Capacity in Data Rate
KB(Kilobyte) = 1000 bytes	Kbps (kilobits/sec) = 1000 bits/sec
MB (Megabyte) = 1 million bytes	Mbps (Megabits/sec) = 1 million bits/sec
GB (Gigabyte) = 1 billion bytes	Gbps (Gigabits/sec) = 1 billion bits/sec
TB(Terabyte) = 1 trillion bytes	Tbps (Terabits/sec) = 1 trillion bits/sec
PB(Petabyte) = 1 quadrillion bytes	Pbps (Petabits/sec) = 1 quadrillion bits/sec

Table 1.1 Metrics of storage vs. network capacity

Data types and data rate: Depending on the data type to be propagated, required data rate differs considerably in which plain text takes up the smallest capacity followed by audio and video. These days, much of network traffic is in the multimedia format that combines text, sound, image and video. To put things in perspective, Table 1.2 summarizes data rate necessary to transport audio and video data at different quality levels. MP3 and MPEC2 are popular compression standards used to encode audio and video data.

Type of content	Quality level	Data rate
Audio (MP3 encoding)	Telephone sound quality	8 Kbps
	AM sound quality	32 Kbps
	FM sound quality	96 Kbps
	CD sound quality	224-320 Kbps
Video (MPEC2 encoding)	DVD quality	5 Mbps
	HDTV quality	15 Mbps

Table 1.2 Data rates for audio and video contents

Exercise 1-5: Refer to Table 1.2. 8Kbps is data rate (each direction) necessary for a digitized telephone call. This means that, to have a two-way full-duplex call between two parties, it takes 16Kbps. How many calls can be made concurrently with the data rate necessary to transport just one HDTV channel?

The network's transmission capacity can be measured in terms of *Channel Capacity* and *Throughput*.

- **Channel Capacity**: It is the maximum theoretical data rate of a link and oftentimes referred to as *bandwidth* or *rated speed*. The channel capacity measured in data rate is a digital concept and bandwidth is an analog concept (More accurate technical definition of bandwidth is explained in Chapter 4). However, they are directly correlated in which the bigger the bandwidth, the bigger the channel capacity. Understandably, practitioners use them interchangeably.

- **Throughput**: It refers to actual data rate of a link. As a more realistic speed of a network link, it is usually slower than channel capacity due to a number of technical reasons including the effect of link distance, transmission interferences, and internal/external noises. For instance, the channel capacity of the popular WiFi LAN standard, 802.11g, is 54Mbps (see Chapter 8). However, its actual throughput gets substantially lower as the distance between two communicating nodes is increased.

1.7.2 Delay

Delay (or latency) represents the amount of time a network link takes to deliver data between any two nodes and is usually measured in milliseconds (or 1000th of a second). Delay can be measured in both one-way trip and round trip (a request and response cycle) between two points. For example, as in Figure 2.10 in Chapter 2, the *ping* utility program that tests if a particular target node is reachable measures latency based on the round-trip. In the figure, the ping request was issued four times by the source host and all of them were replied by the target host (209.131.36.158) with round trip latency of 26 ~ 29 milliseconds.

When computers exchange data, there are various delay sources. Imagine a hypothetical situation in which a person is trying to download the webpage of *www.facebook.com*. She/he will certainly experience delay until the webpage is displayed on the browser. Among the main sources of delay are:

- **Propagation delay**: It takes time for the signal carrying the webpage to travel between two remotely located hosts.

- **Delay at hosts**: The source host should internally process the user request before releasing it to the Internet. This includes conversion of the request into a packet (to be explained in Chapter 2) and then to an electronic signal (to be explained in Chapter 4) for propagation. When the request arrives at the destination host (*www.facebook.com* server), it also performs similar internal processing to ultimately produce a response packet and convert it to a signal for delivery.

- **Delay at intermediary devices**: Intermediary devices such as routers and switches mediate data transmissions between hosts, and the forwarding requires its own internal processing including the lookup of reference tables (e.g., routing tables, switch tables) and subsequent determination of the forwarding path. Also, when packets arrive at an intermediary device continuously, they are temporarily placed in its queue and the queuing delay rests on the amount of traffic the node should process.

Delay is especially a sensitive issue when a network is used by time-sensitive applications. In fact, with ever-growing popularity of real-time (or near real-time) multimedia applications such as video-on-demand and video-conferencing, more messages need to be propagated with little delay and oftentimes with guaranteed performance.

1.7.3   Reliability

This performance dimension is about a network's capacity to convey data in a stable manner. The reliability of data delivery is mildly or severely affected (1) when there are corrupted or lost data in the middle of their transmissions and (2) when a network experiences interruptions (e.g., node failures, link failures).

- **Corrupted or lost data:** Data corruption or loss takes place in a wide range of severity. It can be as small as a bit change (e.g., from 0 to 1) or as big as the moderation or loss of bit streams. There are a number of sources that trigger the reliability problem. Among them are crash of a network node, physical damage or cut of cabling, overflow of a network node's buffer space, power interruption or surge, and noise caused by various reasons (e.g., signal interference due to lightning, industrial noise, or crosstalk).

- **Network unavailability:** A network becomes unavailable when there is a node or link failure. Just as a computer crashes, an intermediary device can fail for several reasons including overload, a system bug in its built-in software, power interruption, succumbing to a malicious attack, and operational mismanagement. Also, the network link can be a source of trouble when it is accidentally damaged or when cabling between a node and a link is unstable. When a network itself becomes unavailable either entirely or partially due to the node or link fault, this limits network accessibility.

1.7.4   Quality of Service (QoS)

A concept closely associated with the dimensions of network performance is Quality of Service (shortly QoS). QoS represents the capability of a network in *guaranteeing performance* in terms of link capacity, latency, and reliability. It is particularly germane to the carrier's WAN service offered to business clients (e.g., e-commerce stores). In the early days, QoS was not such a critical issue for WAN connections as applications running on the network platform were not that sophisticated and mission critical. As more mission critical activities are taking place in the network space, QoS has become an important requirement to many businesses. For example, Amazon.com and eBay.com totally rely on the Internet for business transactions and they cannot afford even a few hours of service disruption as it translates into millions of dollars in lost revenue.

When a carrier offers QoS to a client firm, network performance should be guaranteed regardless of the circumstance (e.g., traffic congestion), especially for real-time and mission-critical applications. Of course, this performance guarantee is more costly to clients than non-QoS service. The carrier can achieve the enhanced service quality through such measures as data prioritization and reservation of link capacity. Businesses, however, may not need such QoS provision if the WAN link is mainly for emails and web surfing.

1.8   NUMBERING SYSTEMS

In this section, a review is made on three different numbering systems (i.e., binary, decimal, and hexadecimal) used to represent numeric values in the networking field. Although they are used altogether, there is a preference of one system over the others depending on the usage context. As we are already aware of, network nodes process various data types (e.g., texts, images, videos) in binary of 0s and 1s. Data in binary, however, is hard to comprehend for human beings and thus both decimal (with 10-base) and hexadecimal (with 16-base) numbering systems are also utilized for better readability. As such, translation between binary and decimal, and that between binary and hexadecimal constitute basic knowledge in studying computer networking, especially network addressing. Table 1.3 summarizes three numbering systems and their numerical base.

Numbering System	Number of Digits in Base	Digits
Binary	2	0 and 1
Decimal	10	0 through 9
Hexadecimal	16	0 through 9, A, B, C, D, E, and F (in which A=10, B=11, C=12, D=13, E=14, F=15)

Note: To differentiate decimal and hexadecimal values (e.g., decimal 5 vs. hexadecimal 5), hexadecimal values are indicated by either *0x* prefix or *h* suffix. For example, *0x*3256 means that 3256 is a hexadecimal value. With 16 base, hexadecimal is more efficient than decimal in expressing binary combinations.

Table 1.3 Numbering systems used in computer networking

1.8.1   Translation: Binary vs. Decimal

The translation between binary and decimal is explained based on the unit of 8 bits as it becomes the building block of 32bit IP addresses. For example, an IP address of 123.45.56.89 is equivalent to 01111011. 00101101. 00111000. 01011001. Let's practice the binary-decimal conversion using an example of 8-bit binary (01011010) and its equivalent decimal (90) values.

(1) Binary (01011010) to decimal (90) conversion

    a. First, determine the decimal position value of each binary bit using the *power-of-two* computation.

b. Once decimal position values are in place, add up the decimal values of non-zero binary positions. In the example, the summation of 64, 16, 8, and 2 becomes 90.

Initial binary combination (8bits)	0	1	0	1	1	0	1	0
Power of two	2^7	2^6	2^5	2^4	2^3	2^2	2^1	2^0
Decimal position values	128	64	32	16	8	4	2	1
Add decimal values of non-zero binary positions		64		+16	+8		+2	=90

(2) Decimal (90) to binary (01011010) conversion

Decimal position values	128	64	32	16	8	4	2	1
a. Find the largest decimal position value that is less than or equal to 90.	128	[64]	32	16	8	4	2	1
b. Obtain the remainder value	Difference between 90 and 64 = 26							
c. Find the largest decimal position value that is less than or equal to the remainder value 26.	128	64	32	[16]	8	4	2	1
d. Obtain the remainder value	Difference between 26 and 16 =10							
e. Find the largest decimal position value that is less than or equal to the remainder value 10.	128	64	32	16	[8]	4	2	1
f. Obtain the remainder value	Difference between 10 and 8 = 2							
g. Find the largest decimal position value that is less than or equal to the remainder value 2.	128	64	32	16	8	4	[2]	1
h. Obtain the remainder value. As the remainder becomes 0, stop here.	Difference between 2 and 2 = 0							
i. Binary numbers corresponding to the parenthesis values above are 1s and the others are 0s.	0	1	0	1	1	0	1	0

Note: 01011010 (8 bit) is identical to 1011010 (7 bit). The demonstration above is based on 8-bit combination.

Exercise 1-6
1. Convert decimal values 38, 110, 192, and 255 to their 8-bit binary counterparts.
2. Translate the following 8-bit binary blocks to their corresponding decimal values.
   01100001   11110110   11100011   10100010

1.8.2 Translation: Binary vs. Hexadecimal

Hexadecimal digits are used to represent the MAC or physical address (see Network Interface Card in Section 1.2.1). Each MAC address is 48 bits (see Section 1.9.2) and they are converted to 12 hexadecimal digits (each hex digit is equivalent to 4 bits). The following demonstration, therefore, focuses on the conversion between a hexadecimal digit and its equivalent 4 binary bits.

The conversion takes nothing but the translation between a hexadecimal's decimal value and its corresponding 4 bits. For example, the hexadecimal digit 'A' is equivalent to decimal '10', which in turn translates into 1010 in binary using the same conversion method in Section 1.8.1. Summary of the computational procedure is:

Hexadecimal		Decimal		Binary
A	=>	10	=>	1010
A	<=	10	<=	1010

Reversely, to translate a binary bit 'stream' into its corresponding hexadecimal values, the bit stream should be divided into 4 bit blocks first. Then, convert each 4-bit unit into its corresponding decimal value and subsequently find its hexadecimal equivalence. Recall that A=10, B=11, C=12, D=13, E=14, F=15. As an example, for the binary bit stream 10010110100010101101:

1. Creation of 4 bit blocks: 10010110100010101101 becomes 1001.0110.1000.1010.1101.
2. Conversion of each block into a decimal value: 1001.0110.1000.1010.1101 becomes 9.6.8.10.13.
3. Conversion of each decimal value into a hexadecimal equivalence: 9.6.8.10.13 becomes 0x968AD.

Exercise 1-7

1. Convert 0x17AB to its binary counterpart.
2. Convert the following hex digits to binary bits with each hex digit representing 4 binary bits.
   0xABCDEF   0x34A57   0x12DF01   0x78ADC
3. Convert the binary stream, '10110110100011100001' to hex with each hex digit representing 4 binary bits.
4. If the physical address of a computer's network card (NIC) is
   001001100111100010101011010111000100100010001101,
   what is its corresponding hexadecimal address?

1.9   NETWORK ADDRESSING

Just as postal addresses are necessary to deliver snail mails, network nodes transport data relying on standardized address information. So, allocation of addresses to hosts and intermediary devices, their configuration, and subsequent management are activities fundamental to adequate operation of computer networks. In this section, network addresses currently in use are characterized in terms of permanency, accessibility, and privacy dimensions.

1.9.1 Characterizing Network Addressing

- **Permanency (Temporary vs. Permanent)**

Network addresses can be either *temporary* (or *dynamic*) or *permanent* (or *static*). The temporary address is dynamically assigned to a station and can be reclaimed and reassigned to another station if unused by the station for a certain period of time. Such temporary address is typically allocated to a station during its start-up process (as a related concept, the DHCP standard is explained in Chapter 2 and 10). The permanent address, meanwhile, is either printed on a node's network card (e.g., MAC address) by the device manufacturer or manually set up (e.g., IP address) in a computer system. The manual assignment of a permanent IP address is generally applied to a server computer or intermediary device.

- **Accessibility (Local vs. Global)**

As for the accessibility dimension, addresses can be either *locally* or *globally* accessible. Local addresses are only recognized within a subnetwork and therefore they are only used for intra-networking. The MAC address printed on a host's network card (NIC) is an example of the local address. Meanwhile, the global address is recognized universally and therefore is utilized for packet forwarding beyond a local network (or subnetwork) boundary, enabling inter-networking. IP is the global addressing standard.

- **Privacy (Public vs. Private)**

IP addresses are divided into *public* and *private* addresses. Packets containing public addresses can be forwarded to the destination host over the Internet. Whereas, the private address, as the term implies, is used only within an organization or a home network. In other words, the packet with a private address is deliverable to a destination node located within the same organizational or home network boundary, but not outside. The usage of private addresses offers heightened security as internal nodes are invisible from public probing and spying. Many organizations rely on private IP addresses to protect their internal networks and also to be flexible in address allocation to internal hosts and intermediary devices (More details of public and private IP addresses are explained in Chapter 5).

Two different address schemes are used *concurrently* for computer networking: MAC (Media Access Control) and IP addresses.

1.9.2 MAC Address

The network interface card (NIC) of a computer has at least one MAC address assigned to it. The MAC address is also known as a physical or hardware address because it is permanently printed on a NIC and thus cannot be changed (although it can be spoofed or masked using software). The NIC for Ethernet or WiFi as two most dominant LAN standards uses a MAC address of 48 bits, which is burned into the NIC's *Read Only Memory* (ROM). When a node is started, its MAC address is copied into the NIC's *Random Access Memory* (RAM) to enable the node's networking function.

As stated, the 48-bit MAC address is presented to people as a 12 hexadecimal digits, with each digit representing four binary bits. The MAC address in hex is written in one of three formats:

- o 01-35-A7-BC-48-2D (two hex digits separated by '–')
- o 01.35.A7.BC.48.2D (two hex digits separated by '.')
- o 0135.A7BC.482D (four hex digits separated by '.')

Out of 12 hexadecimal digits, the first six becomes an *Organizationally Unique Identifier* (OUI). The OUI indicates a NIC card's manufacturer and is assigned by *IEEE* (*Institute of Electrical and Electronics Engineers*), a leading standard-setting organization responsible for LAN standards (e.g., Ethernet, WiFi). The remaining six digits represent a combination uniquely allocated to each NIC. With this allocation scheme, no two NICs share the same MAC address.

Exercise 1-8: Conduct Internet search to locate OUIs of technology powerhouses including Cisco, Apple, Intel, and Microsoft. Observe how many different OUIs are owned by each company.

1.9.3   IP Address

IP addressing is another addressing scheme. As explained, the temporary IP address is dynamically allocated to a host station whenever it issues a request during the initial startup and therefore has an expiration. Whereas, the permanent IP address allocated to a host (e.g., server) stays with it so that the host provides the intended service without interruptions. Whereas the MAC address is a physical address, the IP address is a logical address because it does not bind to a node physically.

There are two different IP standards: IPv4 (version 4) and IPv6 (also known as IP next generation or IPng). IP addresses based on IPv4 dominate network space now. The IPv4 address consists of 32 bits that are translated into a combination of 4 decimal values (e.g., 127.232.53.8). The IP address is composed of network and host identity parts. For example, in 172.232.53.8, 172.232 and 53.8 may represent the network and host identities respectively. With knowledge of IP addressing fundamental in understanding computer networking, the entire Chapter 5 is dedicated to this topic.

1.9.4   Pairing of MAC and IP Addresses

To be able to exchange data over the network, a host station needs a pair of MAC and IP addresses. Figure 1.23 illustrates the one-to-one pairing (or binding) of MAC and IP addresses. In the case of intermediary devices, the pairing relationship is a little different and will be explained in Chapter 3.

It is natural to raise a question of why a host needs pairing of a MAC and an IP. A rather simple answer is that MAC is for intra-networking and IP is for inter-networking. In other words, within a subnetwork, the MAC address of a destination host is all it takes in delivering packets from a source station. When a packet has to cross multiple subnetworks (for inter-networking) before reaching the ultimate destination, its IP address needs to be continuously referenced by the router(s) on the way. The somewhat complicated logic behind the concurrent usage of both addressing systems is explained in Chapter 2 and Chapter 3.

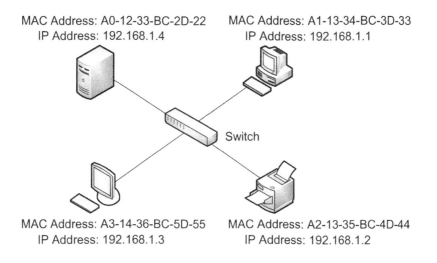

MAC Address: A0-12-33-BC-2D-22
IP Address: 192.168.1.4

MAC Address: A1-13-34-BC-3D-33
IP Address: 192.168.1.1

Switch

MAC Address: A3-14-36-BC-5D-55
IP Address: 192.168.1.3

MAC Address: A2-13-35-BC-4D-44
IP Address: 192.168.1.2

Figure 1.23 Pairing of MAC and IP addresses

Exercise 1-9: Find out the MAC and IP addresses of your computer by typing *ipconfig /all* for Windows and *ifconfig* for Linux/Unix at the command prompt. As shown in Figure 1.24, today's computers are generally equipped with two MAC addresses, one for Ethernet NIC and another for WiFi NIC. At one point, only the MAC address in usage is associated with the host's IP address. Based on Figure 1.24, answer below questions.

1. What is the computer's current IP address?
2. How many NICs and MAC addresses the host station has?
3. What are their MAC addresses and why there is more than one MAC address?
4. Who are the manufacturers of the NICs?
5. It shows that the WiFi LAN's MAC address is bound to the IP address, 192.128.1.2. What does that mean?

Other items in Figure 1.24 including autoconfiguration, subnet masks, default gateway, DHCP servers, and DNS servers are explained throughout the textbook.

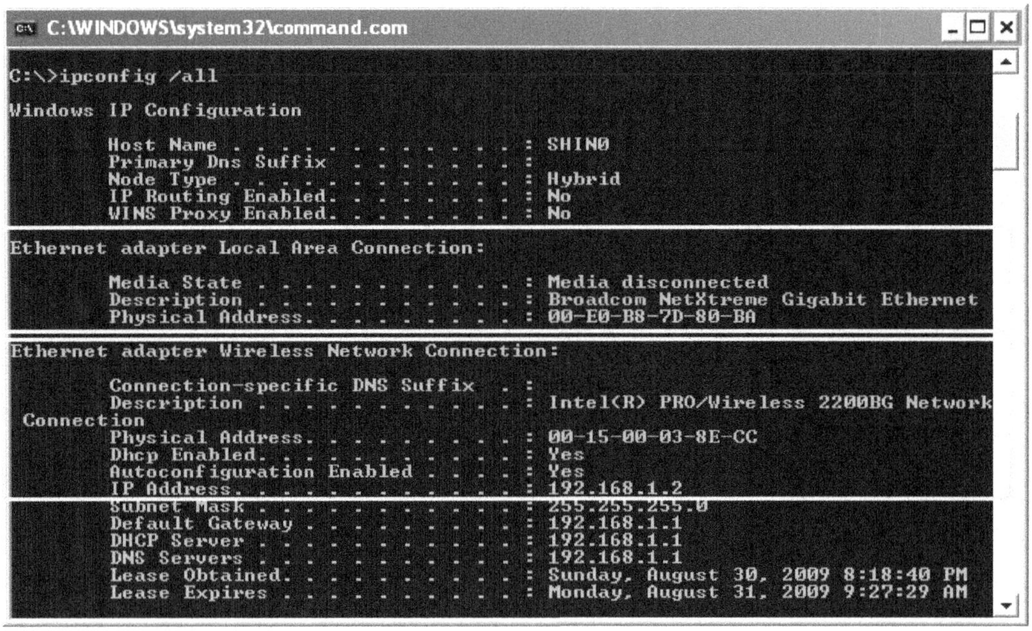

```
C:\WINDOWS\system32\command.com                                    _ □ ×

C:\>ipconfig /all

Windows IP Configuration

        Host Name . . . . . . . . . . . . : SHIN0
        Primary Dns Suffix  . . . . . . . :
        Node Type . . . . . . . . . . . . : Hybrid
        IP Routing Enabled. . . . . . . . : No
        WINS Proxy Enabled. . . . . . . . : No

Ethernet adapter Local Area Connection:

        Media State . . . . . . . . . . . : Media disconnected
        Description . . . . . . . . . . . : Broadcom NetXtreme Gigabit Ethernet
        Physical Address. . . . . . . . . : 00-E0-B8-7D-80-BA

Ethernet adapter Wireless Network Connection:

        Connection-specific DNS Suffix  . :
        Description . . . . . . . . . . . : Intel(R) PRO/Wireless 2200BG Network
Connection
        Physical Address. . . . . . . . . : 00-15-00-03-8E-CC
        Dhcp Enabled. . . . . . . . . . . : Yes
        Autoconfiguration Enabled . . . . : Yes
        IP Address. . . . . . . . . . . . : 192.168.1.2
        Subnet Mask . . . . . . . . . . . : 255.255.255.0
        Default Gateway . . . . . . . . . : 192.168.1.1
        DHCP Server . . . . . . . . . . . : 192.168.1.1
        DNS Servers . . . . . . . . . . . : 192.168.1.1
        Lease Obtained. . . . . . . . . . : Sunday, August 30, 2009 8:18:40 PM
        Lease Expires . . . . . . . . . . : Monday, August 31, 2009 9:27:29 AM
```

Figure 1.24 IP configuration of a host station (MS Windows)

KEY TERMS

access link
application
binary
bits per second (bps)
Bluetooth
broadcasting
bus topology
campus network
capacity
channel capacity
circuit switching
client-server computing
command line interface
data rate
decimal
delay
duplex
end device
end station
end system
enterprise network

full-duplex
half-duplex
hexadecimal (HEX)
hierarchical topology
host
hub-and-spoke topology
ifconfig
intermediary device
internet
Internet
Internet of Things (IoT)
Inter-networking
intra-networking
IP address
ipconfig
IPv4
IPv6
latency
local area network (LAN)
logical address
MAC address

mesh topology
message
metropolitan area network
(MAN)
multicasting
Near Field Communication
(NFC)
network
network interface card (NIC)
network link
network node
networking device
organizationally unique
identifier (OUI)
peer-to-peer computing
permanent (or static) address
personal area network (PAN)
physical address
point-to-point topology
protocol
quality of service (QoS)

random access memory
(RAM)
read only memory (ROM)
reliability
ring topology
semantic rule
simplex
star topology

subnetwork (subnet)
syntactic rule
temporary (or dynamic)
address
throughput
topology
tree topology
trunk link

unicasting
wide area network (WAN)
WiFi
WiFi Direct
wireless NIC (WNIC)
Zigbee

CHAPTER REVIEW QUESTIONS

1. The _____ represents physical arrangement of network nodes.
A) network layout
B) network domain
C) network topology
D) network architecture
E) network blueprint

2. Choose an ACCURATE statement regarding the relationship between hosts, intermediary devices, and network nodes.
A) Hosts are intermediary devices.
B) Hosts are also called networking devices.
C) Intermediary devices are divided into network nodes and hosts.
D) An intermediary device is either a network node or a host.
E) Network nodes include intermediary devices and hosts.

3. Which topology is used widely when network redundancy is important to prepare for node or link failures?
A) point-to-point
B) partial mesh
C) star
D) bus
E) hub-and-spoke

4. Star topology is also known as:
A) ring
B) partial mesh
C) full mesh

D) bus
E) hub-and-spoke

5. Which is an access link?
A) router – router link
B) switch – switch link
C) switch – router link
D) web server – switch link
E) hub – switch link

6. The OUI (organizationally unique identifier) is an element of _____.
A) MAC addresses
B) public addresses
C) IP addresses
D) global addresses
E) local addresses

7. The *throughput* of a network
A) represents the speed guaranteed by a service provider.
B) describes the strength of a signal.
C) is interchangeably used with *rated speed*.
D) represents the maximum capacity of its cabling.
E) represents its actual speed.

8. Packets are produced and exchanged according to meticulously defined rules of communication. These rules are implemented in _____.
A) protocols
B) messages

C) network links
D) applications
E) data

9. Choose an INCORRECT statement regarding the network link.
A) Copper wires and optical fibers are popular wired media these days.
B) Network links are divided into access and trunk links.
C) Creating a computer network needs to have at least one trunk link.
D) The access link provides connectivity between a host and an intermediary device.
E) The trunk link interconnects intermediary devices.

10. The *campus network* is a type of _____.
A) local area network
B) metropolitan area network
C) personal area network
D) wide area network
E) wireless network

11. What is the binary correspondence of hex digits 'B301'?
A) 1110001100000001
B) 1011001100000001
C) 1001001100010001
D) 1011001100101001
E) 1011001100100101

12. Select an ACCURATE statement on network addressing.
A) MAC addresses of a university's PCs are the same in their first 6 hex digits.
B) The primary usage of the MAC address is for inter-networking.
C) The IPv4 address is longer in its length than the MAC address.
D) An IP address should be permanently assigned to a host station.
E) A host station should have a MAC and an IP address for networking.

13. Which is TRUE regarding the MAC address?
A) It is a permanent address.
B) It is stored in the computer's random access memory (RAM) in 8 hex digits.
C) It is dynamically provided by a designated server to requesting stations.
D) It is determined by a computer's operating system.
E) Two computers can own the same MAC address.

14. Which 3 terms are used interchangeably as metrics of network performance?
A) channel capacity, bandwidth, throughput
B) channel capacity, throughput, flow
C) reliability, accuracy, availability
D) channel capacity, bandwidth, rated speed
E) reliability, accuracy, latency

15. When the laptop, wireless mouse and keyboard, smart phone, and digital camera are interconnected to exchange data, they are using a _____ standard:
A) WAN (wide area network)
B) PAN (personal area network)
C) NFC (near field communication)
D) LAN (local area network)
E) MAN (metropolitan area network)

16. Which is a legitimate MAC address?
A) ab-01-cd-ef-23-45
B) ab-01-cd-ef-23-4
C) ab-01-cd-ef-23
D) ab-01-cd-ef-2
E) ab-01-cd-ef

17. Switches within a network are interconnected by ___.
A) protocols
B) peer-to-peer links
C) trunk links
D) channels
E) unicasting

18. Network nodes include _____.

A) intra-networking and inter-networking devices
B) intermediary devices and end stations
C) intermediary devices and network links
D) intermediary devices and networking devices
E) end devices and network links

19. Which is NOT NECESSARILY an accurate description of the intermediary device?
A) It has at least one built-in network card.
B) It also becomes a network node.
C) It always operates in the full-duplex mode.
D) It relies on addressing to exchange data.
E) It is for either intra-networking or inter-networking.

20. Which is a right sequence of data rate metrics from the smallest to the largest?
A) Kbps - Mbps - Pbps - Gbps - Tbps
B) Tbps - Pbps - Kbps - Mbps - Gbps
C) Kbps - Gbps - Mbps - Tbps - Pbps
D) Kbps - Mbps - Gbps - Tbps - Pbps
E) Kbps - Mbps - Gbps – Pbps - Tbps

21. There are many web sites that offer audio or video streaming of TV programs and movies over the Internet. These services generally rely on the _____ technology.
A) unicasting
B) anycasting
C) multicasting
D) broadcasting
E) dualcasting

22. Three main sources of network latency (or delay) include:
A) propagation delay, delay at hosts, and delay of server processing.
B) propagation delay, delay at hosts, and delay at intermediary devices.
C) delay at intermediary devices, delay at hosts, and delay of client processing.
D) delay of application processing, propagation delay, and delay at hosts.
E) delay of server processing, delay at intermediary devices, and delay at hosts.

23. Key indicators of network performance include _____.
A) delay, cost, and reliability
B) capacity, reliability, and accessibility
C) capacity, reliability, and cost
D) delay, capacity, and reliability
E) reliability, delay, and accessibility

24. The following message is produced by the web browser according to the

_____ .
   "GET / HTTP/1.1
   Host: www.facebook.com"
A) semantic rule
B) lexicon rule
C) syntactic rule
D) message rule
E) link rule

25. Which statement CORRECTLY describes network topology?
A) Tree: All network nodes are either a hub or a spoke.
B) Bus: All nodes of a network are directly connected.
C) Hierarchy: Host stations are connected to the main transmission line.
D) Star: All locations connect to a central site and thus the network is susceptible to a single point of failure.
E) Full mesh: It is a cost effective approach in creating a highly reliable network with redundancy.

CHAPTER 2   ARCHITECTURES AND STANDARDS

2.1   INTRODUCTION

This chapter explains concepts of network architecture, layer, standard and protocol, and their relationships. The concepts are highly abstract and can pose a considerable challenge in their comprehensions. Nonetheless, they are so fundamental to computer networking and thus introduced in the early part of this book. *You are encouraged to go through the entire chapter several times to better grasp the concepts and their relationships.*

First of all, communications between network nodes demand execution of many predefined functions (or activities). If just one of the functions is not properly performed, nodes will either misunderstand or be unable to understand each other. The many functions can be grouped in terms of their native similarities. The *standard architecture* in computer networking is a multi-layered framework (also known as a reference model) that *broadly* defines primary network functions to be performed in each layer. Once the layers and layer functions are defined in the form of *standard architecture*, then more specific *standards* (primarily in the form of protocols) intended to undertake the layer functions are introduced in each layer. The layer approach of the standard architecture offers distinct benefits; especially, changes of a software or hardware standard within a layer can be made independently of standards in other layers.

Given the general description of relationships among the standard architecture, layer, and standard, main objectives of this chapter are to understand:

- TCP/IP and OSI standard architectures
- Different types of the protocol data unit (PDU)
- Primary functions of application, transport, internet, data link, and physical layers
- Key standards (mostly in the form of protocols) of each layer
- Explanation of key networking protocols including:
    - IP and ICMP at the internet layer
    - TCP and UDP at the transport layer
- Software/hardware components of a host that implement layers
- The encapsulation and de-encapsulation process between layers

2.2   TCP/IP vs. OSI ARCHITECTURES

2.2.1   Standard Architecture

TCP/IP and OSI (Open Systems Interconnection) are two dominant standard architectures. TCP/IP was introduced for the Internet. The organization called *Internet Engineering Task Force* (or IETF) is responsible for crafting the TCP/IP architecture and its standards. IETF, as an international community of network designers, operators, vendors and researchers, maintains a number of working groups that develop *Request for Comments* (or RFC), the document of a particular TCP/IP-related project. Some RFCs become official TCP/IP standards after going through maturation stages and final ratification by IETF. The list of working groups and RFCs are available at the IETF's website (www.IETF.org).

OSI is another standard architecture from *International Organization for Standardization* (or ISO), an international standard setting body being represented by many national standard organizations including ANSI (*American National Standards Institute*) from USA. Both TCP/IP and OSI standard architectures define network functions in terms of two slightly different layer structures in which TCP/IP defines 4 functional layers and OSI has 7 layers (see Figure 2.1). OSI further divides TCP/IP's application layer functions into those of application, presentation, and session layers. Also, you can observe that OSI separates TCP/IP's subnet layer into data link and physical layers.

In practice, standards introduced for OSI and TCP/IP complement each other rather than compete. The majority of popular standards at the application, transport, and internet (or network) layers are from TCP/IP and OSI standards rule the data link and physical layer. As a result, the five-layer hybrid architecture composed of application, transport, internet, data link, and physical layers is widely used by practitioners. The hybrid structure also becomes the basis of my explanations throughout this book.

As shown in Figure 2.1, the key task of the application layer is to enable application-to-application communications (e.g., 'web browser – web server', 'email client – email server'). The transport and internet layers are primarily designed to support inter-networking across subnetworks and the remaining two bottom layers (i.e., data link and physical layers) are to carry out intra-networking activities within a subnetwork.

For necessary inter-networking and intra-networking, nodes (hosts and intermediary devices) conduct many different layer functions. Host computers implement all five layer capabilities, but intermediary devices perform only a subset of five layers. For example, traditional *switches* conduct data link and physical layer activities, and *routers* are designed to undertake internet, data link and physical layer tasks (more details are in Chapter 3).

TCP/IP	OSI	Hybrid	Layer	Key Tasks
Application	Application	Application	5	Application-application Communications
	Presentation			
	Session			
Transport	Transport	Transport	4	Packet delivery across subnetworks (inter-networking)
Internet	Network	Internet	3	
Network Access (or Subnet)	Data link	Data link	2	Packet delivery within a single subnetwork (intra-networking)
	Physical	Physical	1	

Figure 2.1 TCP/IP and OSI layers

2.2.2 Standard and Protocol

As said, each layer defines networking functions to undertake and these functions are formalized as *standards*. Given that a layer is responsible for a number of pre-determined functions (or activities), it comes with standards. Certain layers (i.e., application and physical layers) have a lot more standards than other layers (i.e., internet and transport layers). Some of the well-known standards in each layer are summarized in Table 2.1 and they are explained throughout the book. The standards are implemented in the form of software or hardware.

Application	• SMTP (Simple Mail Transfer Protocol)
	• HTTP (Hypertext Transfer Protocol)
	• DNS (Domain Name System)
	• DHCP (Dynamic Host Configuration Protocol)
Transport	• TCP (Transmission Control Protocol)
	• UDP (User Datagram Protocol)
Internet	• IP (Internet Protocol)
	• ICMP (Internet Control Message Protocol)
Data link	• LAN standards (e.g., Ethernet, WiFi)
	• WAN/MAN standards (e.g., Frame Relay, Metro-Ethernet)
Physical	• Network cabling standards (e.g., Twisted pair, Optical fiber)
	• Port/interface standards (e.g., RJ-45, Serial port, Parallel port)
	• Transmission technology standards (e.g., Modulation, Multiplexing)

Table 2.1 Select standards in each layer

As a subset of *standards*, there are many *protocols* that are implemented in software. Each protocol contains a number of communication rules to be followed by network nodes to be able to exchange data (refer to Section 1.2.6 regarding syntactic and semantic rules). HTTP in the application layer, TCP in the transport layer, and IP in the internet layer are among the well-known protocols. The physical layer includes numerous hardware-related standards (see Table 2.1), but they are not called protocols.

2.2.3 Protocol Data Unit (PDU)

The host computer should have all layer functions built-in for networking. All layers except the physical layer produce discrete message units called *Protocol Data Units* (PDUs) when two hosts communicate. This means that there are application layer PDUs, transport layer PDUs, internet layer PDUs, and data link layer PDUs. The transport-, internet-, and data link layer PDUs are called *segments/datagrams, packets,* and *frames* respectively (see Table 2.4). The application layer PDU (or APDU), however, does not have a designated name.

To be more specific, once an APDU containing user data (e.g., email) is created in the application layer, this triggers successive formation of segment (or datagram), packet, and frame. Then the frame that is still in 0s and 1s are turned into a signal for transmission. When the signal arrives at the destination host, there will be a reverse process (frame -> packet -> segment (or datagram) -> APDU). This continuous procedure that enables exchange of application data is demonstrated in Figure 2.22 in the name of encapsulation and de-encapsulation (more in Section 2.10).

In the meantime, Chapter 1 briefly introduced only the *packet* concept and you may wonder why. In a nutshell, the ultimate goal for computer networking is effective and reliable delivery of *packets* between hosts (end stations). You should be able to see why if you fully comprehend Figure 2.3.

The PDU is a selective combination of *data, header,* and/or *trailer* fields. The data field is where the original data such as email, voice or video is placed. To transport the original data within the data field, additional overhead information is included in the header and/or trailer. A standard protocol such as TCP and IP produces PDUs in one of three different formats (see Figure 2.2):
    (1) PDUs with a header, a data field, and a trailer
    (2) PDUs with a header and a data field only
    (3) PDUs with a header only
The header and the trailer added before and after the data field are further divided into several sub-fields to include information pre-defined (e.g., source and destination addresses).

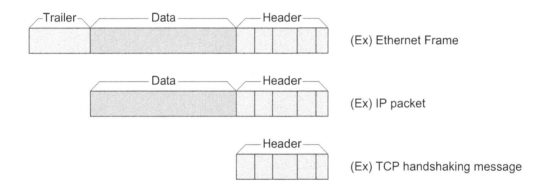

Figure 2.2 Three formats of protocol data units

2.3 LAYER FUNCTIONS – BIG PICTURE

Key layer functions are explained in this section. Comprehending primary responsibilities of each layer poses a considerable challenge when a student is exposed to this concept for the first time. To make it somewhat easier to visualize the role of each layer, let's use a real-life scenario in which a *business letter* (an analogy of the application PDU) is exchanged between Jayne and Brian living in two distant cities (Figure 2.3).

Assume that the following will take place sequentially:
    1. Jayne writes a business letter in English.
    2. Before mailing it, Jayne calls Brian to say that the business letter is going to be mailed and to ask Brian for a return call upon receiving it. Brian agrees to confirm the receipt.
    3. The letter is sealed in an envelope with Jayne's and Brian's mailing addresses and placed in the mailbox.
    4. Jayne's mail is transported to a local post office by a mailman's vehicle. At the local office, the mail is sorted out according to its destination address and shipped to a regional post office by a bigger postal truck. The same mail sorting is repeated a few times before it reaches the destination local post office.

5. From the local post office, a mail carrier delivers Jayne's mail to Brian in the mail truck.

In that scenario, there is a resemblance between the delivery processes of Jayne's postal mail and the IP packet:

1. The business letter written by Jayne = Application layer function (writing a mail)
2. The Jayne's call to Brian to notify the incoming letter and Brian's acknowledgement of its receipt = Transport layer function (handshaking and acknowledgement)
3. Enveloping the letter with mailing addresses = Internet layer function (IP packet development)
4. Sorting the Jayne's mail by a post office = Internet layer function (IP packet routing decision)
5. Mail transportation in a vehicle = Data link layer function (IP packet delivery)

Basically, the ultimate goal of a computer network is to safely deliver IP packets (e.g., Jayne's letter in an envelope) between communicating hosts. Given that, data link layer technologies (e.g., Ethernet, WiFi) merely represent different transportation mechanisms (e.g., trucks, airplanes) available to deliver IP packets. The term, intra-networking, represents IP packet delivery by a transportation mechanism such as WiFi within a subnetwork boundary (step 5 above). Meanwhile, packet development and sorting (step 3 and 4 above) are key inter-networking activities. Pay close attention to the details of Figure 2.3 that compresses much information.

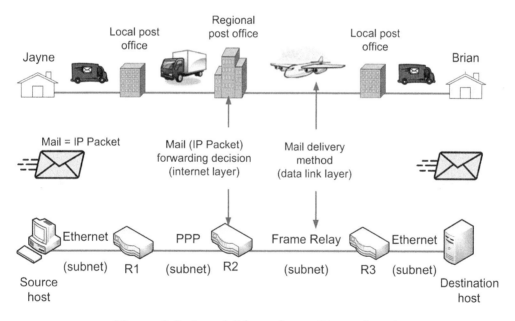

Figure 2.3 A real-life analogy of layer functions

With that understanding, let me begin explanations of the physical layer (layer 1) going up to the application layer (layer 5). Whereas the physical layer primarily deals with hardware standards, the internet, transport, and application layer standards are implemented in software.

2.4 PHYSICAL LAYER (LAYER 1)

The physical layer (layer 1) is responsible for data signaling between nodes through wired (e.g., fiber optics, copper cables) and wireless (e.g., atmosphere) media. Physical layer functions are, therefore, implemented in such hardware devices as networks cards (or NICs) that convert data link layer frames into *electronic, radio,* or *light signals* for propagation. The frame produced in the data link layer is a bit stream of 1s and 0s, and they should be encoded into signals to travel through a network. The conversion process is called *signaling*. Figure 2.4 offers a simple demonstration of electronic signaling in which a binary bit stream of '10110' is converted to an electronic signal. The high electronic state represents a 0 bit and the low state indicates a 1 bit.

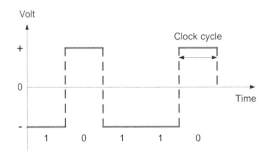

Figure 2.4 An illustration of signaling

Depending on the transmission medium used to connect network nodes, electronic signals (through twisted pairs and coaxial cables), light signals (through optical fibers), or radio signals (through atmosphere) are produced and propagated. A number of conversion methods between bit streams and signals have been introduced as industry standards. In fact, much more sophisticated encoding methods than the one in Figure 2.4 are used these days to transport bit streams faster. Also, LAN and WAN links use different signaling methods with varying characteristics (e.g., signal shapes, signal strengths). More details of signaling are explained in Chapter 4.

~~~~~~

Exercise 2-1: Imagine an enterprise network with three LANs and three WAN connections as in Figure 2.5. Assume that WAN connections are lines leased from a WAN provider such as AT&T.

1. How many LANs and WAN connections are in the enterprise network (exclude the Internet connection)?
2. How many physical links exist between PC1 and Server1 assuming that packets go through R1 and R3?
3. Assume that Laptop1 is communicating with PC2 through the R3-R1-R2 route. How many physical links (including the wireless connection) are there for the end-to-end connection?
4. Do you think the signaling features (e.g., shapes, strengths) are identical between the SW1–Hub link and the R1-R2 link?

Note 1: SW1 = Switch 1, R1 = Router 1, WAN links are called serial lines.
Note 2: Although each WAN connection is shown as a direct line for the sake of simplicity, in

reality, it takes more than one physical link to connect two remotely separated routers (e.g., R1 and R3). The WAN details are explained in Chapter 9.

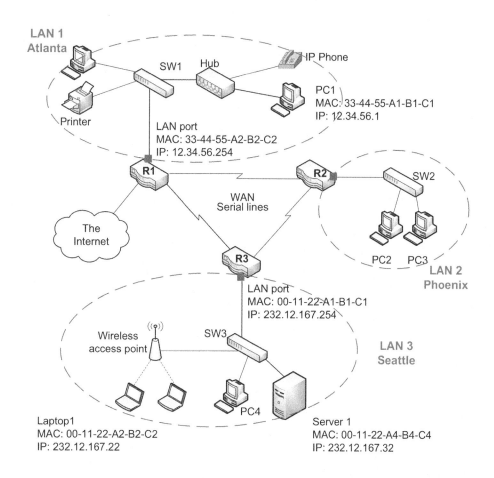

Figure 2.5 An enterprise network and physical layer links

For signaling between two nodes to work without errors, many physical-layer technologies have to be standardized so that hardware products from different manufacturers remain compatible as long as they comply with the standards. Below are examples of the physical layer details that have to be standardized (see Figure 2.6).

- Properties of signals (e.g., signal strengths, digital vs. analog signaling)
- Properties of ports that process signals (e.g., number of pins/holes, port speeds)

The correspondence of physical layer standards to the real life scenario is not shown in Figure 2.3. Standard details of vehicle parts (e.g., tires) that enable a vehicle operational are equivalent to the physical layer standards.

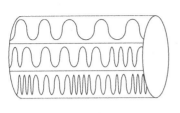

Cable

Signal multiplexing   Port / Interface

Figure 2.6 Select physical layer standards

2.5   DATA LINK LAYER (LAYER 2)

The data link layer standard (e.g., Ethernet, WiFi) performs IP packet transportation between nodes located within a subnetwork. Thus, this layer is responsible for intra-networking (e.g., between two neighboring post offices, between a house and a post office in Figure 2.3). In the following sub-sections, the data link concept is explained in the LAN and WAN contexts.

2.5.1. LAN Data Link

Frame and Switching

In Chapter 1, it was stated that intra-networking relies on one or more intra-networking devices such as switches and wireless access points. In other words, when the delivery of an IP packet between two nodes (e.g., host-to-host) is done without going through a router, it is termed as intra-networking (see Figure 1.4). For intra-networking, the IP packet produced in the internet layer is turned into a frame and gets delivered (Referring to Section 2.2.3, *frame* is the PDU produced in the data link layer). This process is termed packet *encapsulation* (to be explained in Figure 2.22). The delivery of frames for intra-networking is called *switching* and switching within a subnetwork is carried out purely based on MAC addresses. For this, each frame's header should contain 48 bit source and destination MAC addresses (refer to Section 1.9.4).

Link Types

As an example, Figure 2.7 (LAN3 of Figure 2.5) demonstrates a situation in which PC4 is transmitting an IP packet (encapsulated within a frame) to Server1 and the switch SW3 relays the frame based on its destination MAC address. In this situation, the logical path between the two hosts (PC4 and Server1) via SW3 becomes one data link.

As a somewhat different example, think of a situation in Figure 2.7 where PC4 sends an IP packet (encapsulated within a frame) beyond the subnetwork boundary through the router (R3). The packet should first reach R3's LAN port (Fa0/1) before it is routed to another network via R3's other port. In this situation, the logical path from PC4 to the R3's LAN port (Fa0/1) becomes a data link as well.

44

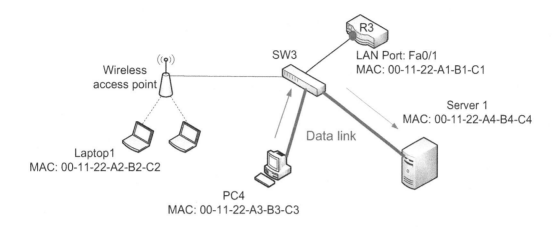

Figure 2.7 Use of MAC addressing for intra-networking

Technology Standard(s)

A data link generally relies on one standard LAN technology (e.g., Ethernet). There are also times when more than one standard technology is used to form a data link for intra-networking. It is generally when an organization relies on both Ethernet and WiFi for its network infrastructure. Using Figure 2.7 as an example, the data link between Laptop1 and Server1 relies on both Ethernet (between Wireless access point and Server1) and WiFi (between Laptop1 and Wireless access point) standards. In this case, the wireless access point does the conversion between Ethernet and WiFi frames (more details in Chapter 8). Despite the difference in the frame structure, Ethernet and WiFi, as two dominant data link standards for LAN, use the same 48 bit MAC addressing.

Single Active Delivery Path

Remember that, within a subnetwork, only a single delivery path (therefore only a single data link) becomes active between any two nodes. This is true regardless of how many host stations and intermediary devices are in the subnetwork. Although many subnetworks have more than one *physical* path available between two nodes to provide network redundancy and survivability, intermediary devices (especially switches) can figure out redundant paths and disable them to ensure that only a single data link path becomes available between any two stations at one point (more details in Chapter 7).

Frame's MAC Addresses

A frame's source and destination MAC addresses do not change while traveling within a subnetwork even if it goes through multiple intermediary devices. For instance, when Laptop1 sends a frame to Server1, the frame's source MAC (00-11-22-A2-B2-C2) and destination MAC (00-11-22-A4-B4-C4) addresses remain the same while it is forwarded by the wireless access point and SW3.

Exercise 2-2: Refer to Figure 2.7 and answer questions.

1. How many data links can be formed from Laptop 1 and list them?
2. How many data links can be formed from PC4 and list them?
3. How many of the data links identified in question 1 involve more than one intermediary device?
4. How many of the data links identified in question 2 involve more than one intermediary device?
5. If Server1 sends a frame to R3's LAN port (Fa0/1), what are its source and destination data link layer addresses? Do the addresses change while the frame passes through SW3?
6. If Laptop1 sends a frame to the router R3's LAN port (Fa0/1), what are its source and destination data link layer addresses? Do the addresses change while the frame passes through the wireless access point and SW3? Hint: Remember that both Ethernet and WiFi use the same 48 bit MAC addressing.

2.5.2   WAN Data Link

Although the data link concept has been explained in the LAN context previously, it applies to WAN connections as well. As an illustration, refer to Figure 2.5. In the enterprise network composed of LANs and WAN connections, assume that a packet from PC1 to Server1 should go through R1 and R3. Then, the packet travels through 3 different data links separated by 2 border routers of R1 and R3.

*   Data link #1:   Connectivity from PC1 to R1
*   Data link #2:   Connectivity from R1 to R3
*   Data link #3:   Connectivity from R3 to Server1

You can observe that Data link #1 and Data link #3 are formed inside LANs, but Data link #2 is a WAN connection. In Figure 2.5, therefore, each of the three WAN connections between routers becomes a data link. Data link #2 between R1 and R3 may be separated by a few thousand miles. Regardless of the distance, it is still a data link to the enterprise network. Data links use different technology standards in enabling the end-to-end (e.g., PC1 and Server1) connection. For instance, Data link #1 and Data link #3 may be on the Ethernet LAN and Data link #2 may be a leased line running the PPP (Point-to-point Protocol) WAN standard.

As previously explained, the data link address is necessary only for intra-networking. Thus, when an IP packet from PC1 travels to Server1, a frame that encapsulates the IP packet is created only for intra-networking on Data link #1(PC1 to R1). In forwarding the IP packet, R1 creates a new frame for intra-networking only on Data link #2 (R1 to R3), and this is repeated by R3 for the delivery of the IP packet to Server 1 on Data link #3. Creating a new frame in each subnetwork encapsulating the same IP packet resembles the real life scenario of Figure 2.3 in which the transportation vehicle (= frame) changes in each hop to ultimately deliver the Jayne's enveloped letter (= IP packet) to Brian.

Exercise 2-3: Refer to Figure 2.5 and answer questions.

1. How many different data links can be formed from IP Phone and list them?
2. How many different data links can be formed from PC1 and list them?
3. How many of the data links identified in question 1 involve more than one intermediary device?
4. How many of the data links identified in question 2 take more than one intermediary device?
5. Assume that IP Phone is calling Laptop1, and the call connection is established via R1 and R3. How many data links are there for the end-to-end connectivity?
6. Assume that Laptop1 is connecting PC2 through the R3-R1-R2 route. How many data links are there for the end-to-end connectivity?
7. If PC1 sends an IP packet to Server1, what are the source and destination MAC addresses of the initial frame and the last frame that contain the IP packet? Do the data link addresses change on the way to Server1?
8. If an IP packet from PC1 travels to Server1 via R1 and R3, how many different frames are formed during the trip?
9. If an IP packet from PC1 travels to Server1 via R1 and R3, what would be the source and destination MAC addresses of the frame when it arrives at Server1?
10. If an IP packet from PC1 travels to Laptop1 via R1 and R3, how many different frames are formed to complete the journey? Remember that WiFi and Ethernet have different frame structures.

~~~~~~

2.6   INTERNET LAYER (LAYER 3)

This layer conducts *inter-networking* functions, especially creation of IP packets and their routing decision across multiple subnetworks conjoined by one or more routers. Whereas *switching* of frames in the data link layer has a single active delivery path between two nodes within a subnetwork, *routing* of packets presumes a multitude in the delivery path between the source and destination nodes. Packet routing in layer 3 is therefore a more complicated and process intensive processing than frame switching in layer 2. The internet layer is responsible to undertake several principal and supplementary functions to support inter-networking. They are:

(1) Creation of IP packets and their routing decision
(2) Perform supervisory functions

2.6.1   Packet Creation and Routing Decision

The internet layer's main responsibility is to develop IP packets containing application data and route them to destinations through multiple subnetworks.

- *Creation of IP packets*: Packets have a predefined structure including data (e.g., web pages) and header fields as shown in Figure 2.2 and Figure 2.8.
- *Routing decision of IP packets*: Presuming multitude in delivery path between the source host and the destination host of an IP packet, the router makes its forwarding decision so that the packet can ultimately reach the destination host.

Packet Creation

There are currently two versions of the internet protocol (IP) standard: IPv4 and IPv6. Although IPv6 represents a significant enhancement over IPv4 in various aspects, the Internet is still dominated by the IPv4 standard for packet development and transportation (more details of IPv6 are in Chapter 10). Figure 2.8 shows the IPv4's packet structure and a brief explanation of each header field is provided.

Bit 0   Bit 31

Version 4 (= 0100)	Header Length (4 bits)	Diff-Serv (8 bits)	Total Length in Octets (16 bits)	
Identification (16 bits)			Flags (3 bits)	Fragment Offset (13 bits)
Time to Live (8 bits)		Protocol in the Data field (8bits)	Header Checksum (16 bits)	
Source IP address (32 bits)				
Destination IP address (32 bits)				
Options (if any)			Padding	
Data Field				

Note: Each row represents 32bits. As in Figure 2.2, field information is transmitted sequentially. For example, the *Identification* field follows the *Total Length in Octet* field. Their display in multiple layers above is simply due to limited space. The header is 20 bytes in length excluding *Options* and *Padding* and the data field (can be thousands of bytes) is significantly longer than the header although shown only as a single row.

Figure 2.8 IPv4's packet structure

- Version 4 (always 0100): It indicates that IPv4 is used to create the packet.
- Header length (4 bits): It specifies header size.
- Diff-Serv (8 bits): It is designed to offer priority for real-time data (e.g., video streaming) to enhance the quality of network service.
- Total length in Octets (16 bits): It tells the size of an entire packet.
- Identification (16 bits): This information is used to identify fragments of an IP packet if it is broken into smaller pieces prior to their transportation. These days, the fragmentation of an IP packet is avoided by end nodes during the initial negation process and thus usage of this field is limited.
- Time to Live (TTL) (8 bits): As a counter, it defines the maximum number of routers a packet can pass through. If the packet does not reach the destination before the TTL counter reaches 0, the packet is dropped by a router.
- Protocol in the Data field (8bits): It specifies the protocol data unit (PDU) contained inside an IP packet's data field. For example, ICMP = 1, TCP = 6, and UDP= 17.
- Header Checksum (16 bits): This field is used for detecting an error in the header (e.g.,

changed bits). Any IP packet with an error in the header should be removed because it can affect network performance (e.g., confuse routers). The internet layer does not reproduce the dropped packet as it is a responsibility of the transport layer.

- Source & destination IP address (32 bits each): The fields include 32 bit IP address information necessary for packet delivery.

Packet Routing Decision

The internet layer is also responsible for deciding a packet's *routing path* over an internetwork (including the Internet). For instance, Figure 2.5 shows one selected routing path between PC1 and Server1 in which IP packets go through R1and R3. Alternatively, the R1- R2 - R3 route also exists. When a packet from PC1 takes the R1 – R3 route to reach Server1, the R1's *next hop router* becomes R3. The routing decision by a router is, therefore, all about determining which next hop router should get an IP packet so that it ultimately reaches the destination host. The routing decision of an IP packet is, therefore, made by each router the packet passes through, but not by any other intermediary devices designed for intra-networking.

Here, bear in mind that the source and destination addresses of an IP packet stay unchanged while it crosses multiple subnetworks. For example, a packet issued by PC1 in Figure 2.5 carries the source IP address of PC1 and the destination IP address of Server1; and the IP addresses remain the same during the end-to-end journey through 3 different subnetworks. The constancy of IP addresses is what makes them different from data link addresses that remain unchanged only within a subnetwork boundary.

Here is a little bit more about the mechanism of packet routing decision. For packet routing, a router maps the destination IP address of an arriving packet to the *routing table* maintained in its memory, finds the best path en route to the destination network, and forwards the packet to the next hop router (more details of packet routing decision in Chapter 6). For its transportation, the packet is encapsulated within a frame. As stated, the use of a packet's IP addresses to cross subnetworks (inter-networking) in order to reach the target host is what differentiates *routing* from MAC address-driven *switching* that moves a frame within the boundary of a subnetwork (intra-networking).

2.6.2 Perform Supervisory Functions

The internet layer also conducts important supervisory functions. The *Internet Control Message Protocol* (ICMP) is the protocol designed to exchange supervisory packets in this layer. There are many different usages of ICMP including diagnosis of connectivity between two network nodes and reporting of transmission errors (e.g., target host unreachable) back to the data source. The ICMP protocol produces its own PDU that is delivered to the destination node within the IP packet's data field to perform the intended task (see Figure 2.9).

Type, Code, and *Checksum* are three common fields included in all ICMP PDUs and what goes in the *Others* field rests on the *Type* field.

- The *Type* value indicates the supervisory function of a particular ICMP PDU. Among the heavily used are 0 (echo reply), 3 (destination unreachable), and 8 (echo request).

- The *Code* value provides additional information regarding the *Type* value. For example, if the Type value is 3 (destination unreachable), then the Code value explains the reason.
- *Checksum* is the error detection code that is computed over the entire ICMP PDU.

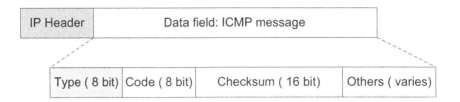

Figure 2.9 The structure of an ICMP packet

Among various supervisory functions (refer to *www.iana.org*), *Ping* and *Traceroute* are most well-known and further explained next.

Ping (Type value = 8 in Figure 2.9)

Ping (= *echo request*) is an important utility in testing and troubleshooting network links and nodes. With it, a host station or router transmits *echo requests* to a target node to check its availability and network connectivity. For example, entering *C:\>ping www.yahoo.com* at the command prompt produces ping requests destined to the Yahoo web server. If the Yahoo server is active and is configured to respond to the *echo request*, it will reply back with *echo responses* (Type value=0). The response has two meanings: (1) the server is up and running and (2) the link between the two communicating nodes works properly.

```
C:\WINDOWS\system32\cmd.exe                                    - □ ×
C:\>ping www.yahoo.com

Pinging www-real.wa1.b.yahoo.com [209.131.36.158] with 32 bytes of d

Reply from 209.131.36.158: bytes=32 time=29ms TTL=56
Reply from 209.131.36.158: bytes=32 time=28ms TTL=56
Reply from 209.131.36.158: bytes=32 time=27ms TTL=56
Reply from 209.131.36.158: bytes=32 time=26ms TTL=56

Ping statistics for 209.131.36.158:
    Packets: Sent = 4, Received = 4, Lost = 0 (0% loss),
Approximate round trip times in milli-seconds:
    Minimum = 26ms, Maximum = 29ms, Average = 27ms
```

Figure 2.10 A demonstration of pinging

Although intermediary devices especially routers respond to pinging, most server hosts are configured to ignore it these days out of security concerns such as denial-of-service attacks (see Chapter 11). Figure 2.10 is a demonstration in which the Yahoo server (www.yahoo.com) is pinged four times from the author's residence. Below is a brief description of key information elements in Figure 2.10:

- 209.131.36.158: The yahoo server's IP address
- *bytes=32*: The ICMP packet is 32 bytes long.
- *time=29ms*: The round trip delay (latency) between the source and the destination is 29 milliseconds.
- *TTL=56*: Time-To-Live (see the description of Figure 2.8). TTL=56 means that the returning echo reply packets had a TTL field value of 56. If the Yahoo server set the initial TTL value to 64, it means that each echo response packet passed through 8 routers (64-56 = 8) on the way.

Traceroute (Type value = 30 in Figure 2.9)

As another useful utility program that runs on ICMP, *traceroute* shows a packet's routing path and delay while traversing the Internet. The function is activated by slightly different commands depending on the operating system (e.g., *tracert* in Windows, *traceroute* in Linux). Tracing the routing path becomes possible as each router along the way responds to the ICMP request. For example, Figure 2.11 demonstrates the result of *C:\>tracert -d www.yahoo.com* issued to reach the Yahoo web server (209.131.36.158). The command issues the echo request 3 times to each and every router (shown as a hop number in the first column) on the way to the destination host. Next three column values (e.g., 2ms, 2ms, and 1ms for the first router) indicate round-trip time (in milliseconds) taken to receive echo responses. The last column indicates each responding router's IP address.

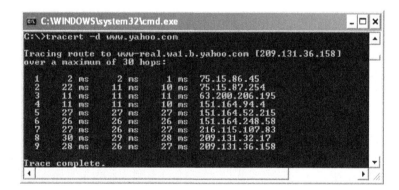

Figure 2.11 A demonstration of *tracert*

Exercise 2-4

1. Visit the website *www.arin.net* and use the 'SEARCH Whois' function to find the company that owns each of the 9 IP addresses in Figure 2.11. You can observe that the last is the IP address of www.yahoo.com.
2. Ping first three nodes (routers) to observe delay time and compare it with the results of *tracert*.

2.7 TRANSPORT LAYER (LAYER 4)

Broadly speaking, the primary responsibility of this layer is to maintain 'reliability' of data exchange between two end stations (hosts). The transport layer functions are, therefore, implemented in end stations, but not in intermediary devices. As related, this layer is charged with three functions:

(1) Provision of data integrity
(2) Session management
(3) Port management

Transmission Control Protocol (TCP) and *User Datagram Protocol* (UDP) implement the functions. The functions (1) and (2) are particularly relevant to TCP, and (3) is performed by both TCP and UDP.

2.7.1 Provision of Data Integrity

The transport layer is responsible to maintain the integrity of application layer data exchanged between end stations. This is achieved by two different mechanisms available through TCP: *error control* and *flow control*.

Error Control

The error control is intended to detect and correct transmission errors (e.g., change or loss of data). TCP utilizes *acknowledgement* for error control (see Figure 2.12). To that end, a host station that receives error-free application data returns an acknowledgement to its sender. If there is no acknowledgement from the destination host, the source host retransmits the application data presuming that there has been a transmission error. Although the actual mechanism of the acknowledgement-based error control is more complicated, the details are not elaborated here.

Flow Control

Flow control is used to regulate the transmission speed between two hosts with different processing capacity so that one party is not overwhelmed by the other's transmission onslaught. The key mechanism of *flow control* is through the *Window Size* field (see Figure 2.12) in which one party basically tells the other party how many bytes (or octets) of data can be sent without receiving an acknowledgement. The Window size shrinks whenever a party releases data and if it reaches 0 then the sender should halt transmissions until an acknowledgement from the receiver node returns. The receiver host's acknowledgement results in the expansion of the Window size, which allows the sender host to resume data transmissions. You can tell that the receiver host can intentionally hold the acknowledgement to slow down data flows.

TCP and Data Integrity

TCP mandates both error control and flow control between two hosts, and thus is ideal for user applications that need to exchange large files reliably. Among the application layer protocols are *Simple Mail Transfer Protocol* (SMTP), *File Transfer Protocol* (FTP), and *Hypertext Transfer Protocol* (HTTP). TCP, therefore, becomes a *reliable protocol* that makes use of the acknowledgement to improve dependability of communications between hosts. Achieving such reliability, however, incurs significant overhead because of (1) the process burden for end hosts to produce acknowledgements and (2) the additional consumption of network capacity to deliver acknowledgements.

As previously stated, the PDU formed by TCP is called a *segment*. Figure 2.12 displays the segment's header fields. A segment is born when an application-layer PDU is passed down to the transport layer and appended by a TCP header. The application-layer PDU is placed in the data field of the resulting segment, a data *encapsulation* process.

Unlike the ordinary segment that has both a header and a data field, there is also a segment that contains only an acknowledgement. That segment has a header but no data field as the acknowledgement information is contained in the header (refer to Figure 2.2).

Bit 0   Bit 31

Source Port #(16)			Destination Port #(16)	
Sequence Number (32 bits)				
Acknowledge Number (32 bits)				
Hdr Len (4)	Reserved (6)	Flags (6)	Window Size (16)	
TCP Checksum (16)			Urgent Pointer (16)	
Options (if any)				PAD
Application PDU				

Figure 2.12 TCP segment

Below are brief descriptions of TCP header fields:
- *Source port* and *destination port* indicate the sending and receiving applications of data contained inside a segment.
- *Sequence number* is a unique identifier assigned to a segment to be transported. When multiple segments are released by a sending host, the receiving host recognizes their correct sequence based on the numbering information.
- *Acknowledgement number* is used to acknowledge one or more TCK segments received.
- *Window size* is for flow control.
- *Flags* are for additional control functions such as session establishment (handshaking) and session termination.
- *Checksum* is for detecting a possible transmission error within a segment (error detection).

UDP and Data Integrity

UDP is a transport layer protocol alternative to TCP. UDP's main concern is not maintaining the integrity and reliability of application layer data as TCP does. UDP is therefore an *unreliable protocol* that does not perform flow control and error control. Figure 2.13

53

demonstrates simplicity of the UDP protocol data unit (called *datagram*) and its header structure. With the absence of *reliability* features, UDP reduces the workload of source and destination hosts, and also does not burden the network with acknowledgement traffic. This simplicity and efficiency makes UDP an ideal transport protocol for real time data produced by voice over IP, video conferencing, online gaming, and multimedia streaming that cannot afford delays by having the acknowledgement overhead. For such real-time applications, avoiding latency is more important than ensuring integrity of exchanged data.

Bit 0   Bit 31

Source port (16 bits)	Destination port (16 bits)
Length (16 bits)	Checksum (16 bits)
Data (Application PDU)	

Figure 2.13 UDP datagram

Except TCP, most protocols in other layers are *unreliable* as they have no built-in procedure to perform the detection and correction of transmission errors by themselves. This is fine because even if transmission errors (e.g., dropped IP packets) occur in other layers, TCP in the transport layer can find and fix them (But UDP does not do it).

2.7.2 Session Management

Session vs. No-Session

When two hosts try to exchange application layer data over a network, two different options exist depending on the application type.
- Handshaking (for session establishment) should be done between two end-nodes prior to data exchange. It represents a mutual agreement between hosts to exchange data.
- Alternatively, the source host can release application data to the destination host without handshaking. In this mode, there is no need for the source to seek an approval (or agreement) from the counterpart before releasing data to the network.

When the handshaking is needed between two end hosts, TCP is used. As it establishes a session (or handshaking) before hosts engage in data exchange, TCP becomes a *connection-oriented* protocol. Meanwhile, UDP is a *connection-less* protocol with which the source releases application-layer data without having a formal handshaking process. *Connection-orientation* and *reliability* of a protocol go hand-in-hand. For example, TCP is a connection-oriented and reliable protocol but UDP is a connection-less and unreliable protocol.

Session Establishment & Termination

To enable the handshaking process by TCP, the TCP Header's *Flags* field (see Figure 2.12) includes *SYN, ACK*, and *FIN* bits: *SYN* for initial handshaking, *ACK* for acknowledgement, and *FIN* for the termination of handshaking. By setting each of the three field bits either 0 or

1, two hosts can convey their intentions of handshaking or handshaking termination. For example, a source host sets SYN=1 to show its intention for handshaking (or session establishment) with a target host. The *ACK* bit is used only for handshaking or handshaking termination, and thus should not be confused with *Acknowledge Number* that confirms arrival of application data.

Figure 2.14 demonstrates that exchanging application data between two hosts based on TCP is composed of:
1. *Session establishment* through three-way handshaking of:
   (a) SYN => (b) SYN+ACK => (c) ACK
2. Exchange of application layer data (e.g., web pages)
3. *Session termination* through four-way correspondence of:
   (a) FIN => (b) ACK => (c) FIN => (d) ACK

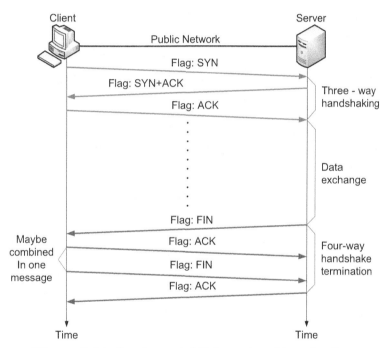

Figure 2.14 Session establishment and termination

What Happens in Real Setting?

To better relate the session establishment in Figure 2.14, a university web page (www.sdsu.edu) is demonstrated. Figure 2.15 shows that, to display the webpage on a browser, it has to download several objects including the main text page and several JPEG and GIF image files. To download an object, one TCP session is established. During a TCP session, sometimes just one TCP segment is enough to transport a target object. Other times, multiple TCP segments are used to deliver one oversized object (e.g., object 2 in Figure 2.15) using fragmentation within a TCP session. There are at least 4 image files in Figure 2.15 and their downloading takes at least 4 different TCP sessions. The TCP sessions are established in

55

parallel to load the web page faster. It is not difficult to see that each TCP session incurs a considerable processing and network overhead. The new HTTP standard is designed to reduce the number of sessions necessary to download files needed to construct a web page.

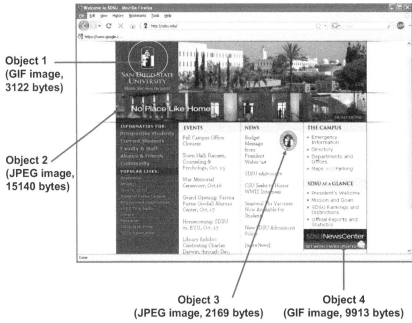

Object 1
(GIF image,
3122 bytes)

Object 2
(JPEG image,
15140 bytes)

Object 3
(JPEG image, 2169 bytes)

Object 4
(GIF image, 9913 bytes)

Figure 2.15 Objects of a web page and TCP sessions
(Source website: www.sdsu.edu)

Additional Notes

Many application-layer protocols (e.g., HTTP, SMTP) require TCP-enabled handshaking at the transport layer. Once a logical connection (or session) is established by TCP, two hosts start to exchange application data (e.g., web pages, emails). Handshaking is not a guaranteed process, though. For example, when a server host is too tied up with handling existing sessions, it may not accept additional handshaking requests or it may take too long to respond. The failure of handshaking results in the display of such error message as in Figure 2.16.

Figure 2.16 Notification of failed TCP handshaking

2.7.3 Port management

Another important transport layer function is port management (Be careful, the port here has nothing to do with the physical switch or router port). TCP and UDP identify an application by its unique 16-bit port number in the range of 0 through 65535 (see Figure 2.12 and 2.13). For example, when a TCP segment arriving at a host carries 80 in its destination port field, it is forwarded to the host's HTTP server application (see Table 2.2).

Port Types & Ranges

Port numbers are divided into three groups: *well-known, registered,* and *private* ports.
- Well-known Ports (0 through 1023): They are mainly used to indicate *standard* server application protocols. Table 2.2 summarizes some of the well-known port numbers allocated for standard application layer protocols.

Protocols	Function	Server Port
Telnet	Remote access	23
FTP	File transfer	20,21
SMTP	E-mail transfer	25
DNS	Domain name service	53
DHCP	Dynamic IP address provision	67,68
HTTP	Web server access	80
HTTPS (HTTP over SSL)	Secure web server access	443

Table 2.2 Well-known server ports

- Registered Ports (1024 through 49151): These port numbers are intended to identify proprietary applications such as MS SQL (1433) and MSN Messenger (1863).
- Private/Dynamic Ports (49152 through 65535): They are for ad hoc assignment of a client (not server) port.

Source vs. Destination Port

The *source port* and *destination port* fields (see Figure 2.12 and Figure 2.13) indicate the sender's application (e.g., HTTP web browser) and the receiver's application (e.g., HTTP web server) respectively. Generally, the client tries to connect to the server to obtain available resources (e.g., web pages, databases, video files, emails), making the former a source and the latter a destination. In doing so, the client host randomly chooses a source port number, termed *ephemeral port*. Meanwhile, a well-known server port number (see Table 2.2) is placed in the destination port for correspondence. Subsequently, the same port numbers will be re-used throughout a session.

As for the ephemeral port number, although *Internet Engineering Task Force* (IETF) recommends that it be chosen from the private/dynamic port range, operating systems from different vendors are not necessarily programmed to conform to the guidance, sometimes making a selection from the registered port range.

Exercise 2-5

1. Find out the IP address of a particular web server using the *nslookup* command (e.g., C:\>*nslookup www.yahoo.com*). Assume that the IP of *www.yahoo.com* is 11.22.33.44. Try *http://11.22.33.44* and *http://11.22.33.44:80* (or *www.yahoo.com:80*). What happens?
2. What happens when you try http://11.22.33.44:70 (or *www.yahoo.com:70*) or any port other than 80? Explain the result.

Socket

The IP packet arriving at an end station should be adequately handed over to the target application. As an example, imagine that a person's laptop is concurrently running multiple user programs including Firefox (for HTTP web browsing), MS Outlook (for SMTP email), and Skype (for proprietary VoIP). When an IP packet containing an email message arrives at the laptop, how does it know that the email should be forwarded to MS Outlook, not Firefox or Skype?

It uses *socket* information that combines an IP address and a port number assigned to an application. Therefore:

A socket = An IP address: A port number

By combining an IP address and a port number, a host can direct incoming data to a right application. Figure 2.17 demonstrates a client socket (20.20.20.1:50000) and a server socket (30.30.30.1:80). You can observe that the port number is a critical information piece in correctly forwarding arrived data to the target program.

To be more specific, if TCP is used in the transport layer, a socket is assigned to each session of an application to correctly forward exchanged data to the right session. This means that an application can be associated with multiple sockets, each assigned to a particular TCP session established. For example, referring back to Figure 2.15, the web page results in at least 4 different TCP sessions and thus as many different combinations of source and destination sockets.

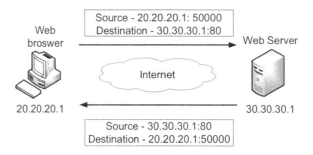

Figure 2.17 A demonstration of sockets

Exercise 2-6: Operating systems let computer users view the list of TCP connections and sockets with the *netstat* utility. The command *C:\>netstat –n*, for example, displays active TCP connections.

1. Figure 2.18 displays a partial screenshot of *C:\>netstat –n* after visiting a particular web site with a browser. The output has four columns: protocol, source socket, destination socket, and status (e.g., established). Based only on the screenshot information:
   a) How many different sessions are established by visiting the particular web site?
   b) How many different source sockets are used to establish the sessions?
   c) What is the port range assigned to source sockets?
   d) How many different destination sockets are shown in the sessions?
   e) What is the server port used by the destination socket?
   f) Find out the server name of 130.191.8.198 with the *nslookup* command.

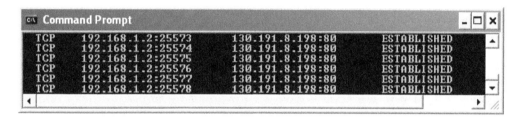

Figure 2.18 TCP sessions and sockets

2. Conduct the following activities.
   a) Open up a web browser and a command line prompt concurrently.
   b) In the browser's URL, enter different websites of your choice and then observe the changes of session and socket information by issuing *C:\>netstat –n* at the command prompt.

2.8 APPLICATION LAYER (LAYER 5)

In this layer, the client and server programs installed in host computers exchange data using a built-in protocol. For example, *Firefox* and *Internet Explorer* are client programs and communicate with web-server programs (e.g., MS IIS, Apache) using HTTP to download web pages. As another example, the email client (e.g., MS Outlook) and server (e.g., MS Exchange) programs exchange emails based on the built-in standard protocol such as SMTP (Simple Mail Transfer Protocol).

On receiving instructions from computer users (e.g., click hyperlinks, send emails), these protocols produce *Protocol Data Units* (PDUs) to be dispatched to target computers. Numerous application-layer protocols have been developed and Table 2.3 lists some of the well-known ones. There are important application layer protocols (especially *DHCP* and *DNS*) that are not tied to a particular user program but perform functions fundamental for the computer to be a host machine. DHCP (Dynamic Host Configuration Protocol) is a standard protocol that dynamically allocates IP addresses to requesting computers (primarily user devices). DNS (Domain Name System) is a protocol that provides mapping between host names (e.g., www.michigan.edu) and their IP addresses. More details of HTTP, DHCP and DNS are explained in Chapter 10 while explaining the Internet infrastructure.

Types	Applications programs	Standard protocols embedded
User application oriented	Email	SMTP(Simple Mail Transfer Protocol) POP3 (Post Office Protocol 3)
	Conferencing	IRC (Internet Relay Chat)
	Remote file transfer	FTP (File Transfer Protocol)
	Remote access	SSH (Telnet, Secure Shell)
	World Wide Web	HTTP (Hyper Text Transfer Protocol)
	Network management	SNMP (Simple Network Management Protocol)
	Voice over IP (Internet calls)	H.323
Common service oriented	Mapping between IP address and host name	DNS (Domain Name System)
	Provision of temporary IP addresses	DHCP (Dynamic Host Configuration Protocol)

Table 2.3 Well-known application layer protocols

2.9 LAYER IMPLEMENTATION

As stated, a host computer performs all five layer functions internally. In this section, software and/or hardware elements responsible for conducting layer functions are explained.

2.9.1 Application Layer

Most protocols in this layer are built into user applications. There are also application layer protocols such as DNS and DHCP that are not necessarily tied to a particular user application, but play a critical role in enabling networking. To observe all active applications in Windows, for example, pressing *Ctr-Alt-Del* key combination will bring up the *Windows Task Manager* (see Figure 2.19). It shows the list of applications and processes. Processes are instances of an application program and an application can have one or more associated processes.

2.9.2 Transport and Internet Layers

The programs that execute transport and internet layer protocols including TCP, UDP, and IP are embedded in the operating system. Figure 2.20 demonstrates the TCP/IP configuration panel of Windows OS.

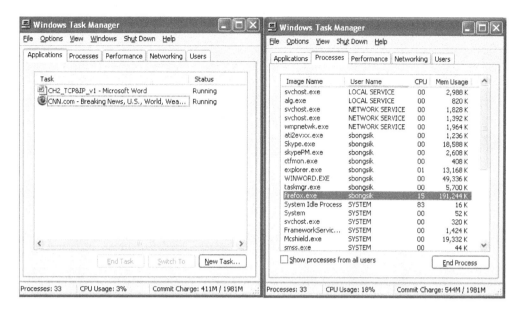

Figure 2.19 Applications and Processes in Windows Task Manager

2.9.3 Data link and Physical Layers

Data link and physical layer functions of a host are built into the *network interface card* (NIC). In other words, the NIC implements a data link protocol such as Ethernet or WiFi, and interfaces with the transmission medium (e.g., twisted pair, optical fiber) through a physical port such as RJ-45 (WiFi does not need a connecting port). The host OS communicates with the NIC through device driver software. In summary, exchanging application-layer data (e.g., email) entails connectivity of "user application <-> operating system <-> NIC" within a host.

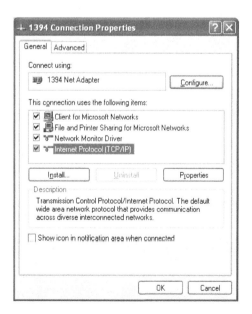

Figure 2.20 TCP/IP configuration in Windows

61

For the exchange of application-layer data, the PDU (protocol data unit) is produced at each layer except the physical layer, and passed between layers. Table 2.4 summarizes key layer functions, their implementation places, and the name of PDUs produced in each layer. It is again highlighted that *all five layer functions are performed within a host computer, but only a subset of five layers are implemented in intermediary devices.*

Layers	Key Functions	Implementation of layer functions	PDU name
Application	Application-to-application Communication	Applications (e.g., browser)	No designated name for PDUs
Transport	Host-to-host (or end-to-end) handshaking and flow/error control	Operating system (e.g., Windows)	Segment, Datagram (e.g., TCP segment, UDP datagram)
Internet	Packet creation and routing decision across an internetwork	Operating system	Packet (e.g., IP Packet)
Data link	Frame creation and switching within a subnetwork	Network interface card (NIC)	Frame (e.g., Ethernet frame)
Physical	Generating signals to encode frames and their physical delivery	Network interface card (NIC)	No PDUs produced.

Table 2.4 Key layer functions and their implementation

Figure 2.21 demonstrates what happens inside the host computer in processing application-layer data (e.g., email) initiated by a user. Intermediary devices such as switches and routers have their own operating systems (e.g., Cisco's Internetwork Operating System) and NICs for networking. The intermediary device, however, has no application-layer functions because its role is to relay host-generated data through the network.

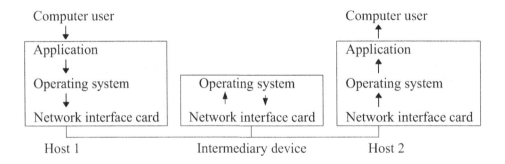

Figure 2.21 Hardware/software components of network nodes

2.10 LAYER PROCESSING

This section explains how different standard layers of a network node work together to successfully produce and transport data. Basically, the delivery requires continuous repetition of *encapsulation* and *de-encapsulation* activities through the layers as in Figure 2.22. Whenever encapsulation takes place in a layer, a new PDU is created based on the upper layer's PDU. The production of an application PDU (in the application layer), therefore, triggers the generation of PDUs in the transport, internet, and data link layers for which an upper layer PDU is encapsulated within the next lower layer PDU.

Figure 2.22 illustrates a scenario in which a request message is produced by the web browser and processed through the layers to ultimately reach its target web server program in the destination host:

1. Application layer: The HTTP request (application PDU) is produced in the application layer. The application PDU is, then, passed down to the transport layer.

2. Transport layer: For encapsulation, a TCP header is added to the HTTP PDU, and the combined entity becomes another PDU, *segment*. The TCP segment, then, is moved to the internet layer.

3. Internet layer: The TCP segment is appended to an IP header (another encapsulation) resulting in a PDU, *packet*. The packet is then handed over to the data link layer.

4. Data link layer: The IP packet becomes a data link PDU or *frame*, when it is appended by a data link header and trailer, another encapsulation process. Unlike the upper layer PDUs that has only the header, data link frames generally have both the header and the trailer. This is because data link is the last layer that defines a PDU before its transmission by the physical layer, and thus the header and trailer indicates a frame's boundary.

5. Physical layer: The frame (in 0s and 1s) coming down from the data link layer is translated (or encoded) into an electronic, light, or radio signal and released to a wireless or wired network.

Once the signal arrives at the destination host, the reverse process takes place in which the header and/or the trailer in each layer's PDU are removed (de-encapsulation process) and the remaining portion is pushed up to the next upper layer. As a result of the repeated de-encapsulation, the web server program in the application layer receives only the browser's original request message and processes it.

Although Figure 2.22 demonstrates what happens only in two end stations, intermediary devices also perform encapsulation and de-encapsulation to forward application-layer data. Figure 2.23 describes a situation in which an application PDU from the source host goes through two switches (layer 2 devices) and one router (layer 3 device) before it reaches the destination host. It indicates that whenever a physical-layer signal arrives at a switch or router port, de-encapsulation and re-encapsulation take place as a part of the forwarding routine.

63

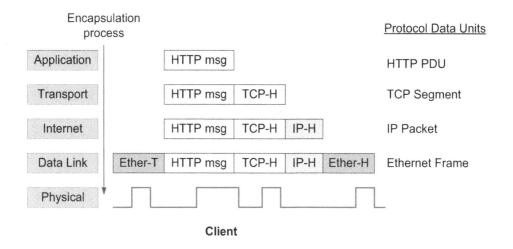

Client

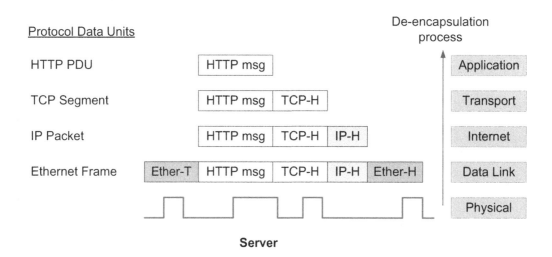

Server

Figure 2.22 PDU encapsulation/de-encapsulation

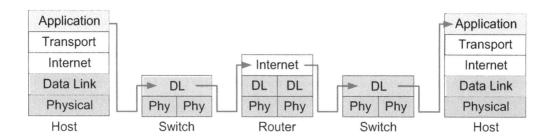

Figure 2.23 Layer processing by intermediary devices

As a demonstration, Figure 2.24 gives a closer look of encapsulation/de-encapsulation by a router based on a scenario in which the router interconnects Ethernet LAN and PPP (Point-to-Point) WAN. The two data link layer standards are not compatible (e.g., different frame structures and signaling methods) and the router provides necessary frame conversion through de-encapsulation

64

and encapsulation. Let us see how it works. When an Ethernet frame arrives at a LAN port, the router removes (de-encapsulates) the Ethernet frame's header and trailer, and then moves the remaining IP packet to the internet layer. The router's internet layer, then, conducts such functions as routing path decision of the packet and decreases the packet header's TTL (time to live) value by 1 (revisit Figure 2.8). Then, the packet is handed over to the data link layer in which the router encapsulates the IP packet in a PPP frame for transportation over the WAN connection. As can be seen, routers should support popular LAN (e.g., Ethernet) and WAN (e.g., PPP) protocols to bridge heterogeneity of data links.

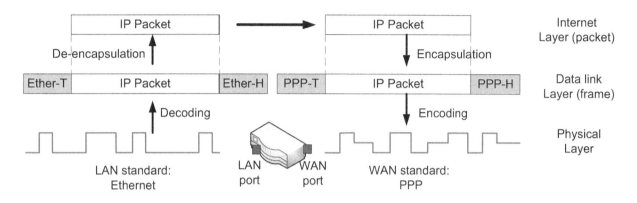

Figure 2.24 Packet de-encapsulation/encapsulation by router

Exercise 2-7

1. Assume that a router interconnects two Ethernet LANs in the data link layer and it is forwarding a HTTP message (browser request) from one subnetwork to another. Develop a drawing similar to Figure 2.24 that shows the internal de-encapsulation/encapsulation process.

2. The switch is a layer 2 device for intra-networking (see Figure 1.4). When a frame containing a HTTP message arrives at a switch port, what de-encapsulation/encapsulation should take place for its relay? Develop a drawing similar to Figure 2.24 to show the internal process.

KEY TERMS

application layer	data integrity	error control
acknowledgement (ACK)	de-encapsulation	FIN
checksum	destination port	flags
connection-less	Domain Name System (DNS)	flow control
connection-oriented	Dynamic Host Control	frame
data link layer	Protocol (DHCP)	handshaking
datagram	encapsulation	header

Hyper Text Transfer Protocol (HTTP)
International Organization for Standardization (ISO)
Internet Control Message Protocol (ICMP)
Internet Engineering Task Force (IETF)
internet layer
internet protocol (IP)
netstat
Open Systems Interconnection (OSI)
optical fiber
packet
physical layer
ping
port

private/dynamic port
protocol
protocol data unit (PDU)
registered port
reliable connection
Request for Comments (RFC)
routing
segment
session
signaling
Simple Mail Transfer Protocol (SMTP)
socket
source port
standard architecture
standards
subnetwork
switching

SYN
TCP/IP
time to live (TTL)
traceroute
trailor
Transmission Control Protocol (TCP)
transport layer
twisted pair
uniform resource locator (URL)
unreliable connection
User Datagram Protocol (UDP)
well-known port
window size field
Windows Task Manager
wired media

CHAPTER REVIEW QUESTIONS

1.   The standard _____ is a framework that broadly classifies network functions into layers.
A) topology
B) architecture
C) platform
D) reference
E) protocol

2.   All layers of a standard architecture have their own protocol data unit (PDU) except the _____ layer.
A) application
B) transport
C) internet
D) data link
E) physical

3.   An email message goes through encapsulations in the sequence of _____ before it is released to the network.
A) segment–packet–frame
B) segment-frame-packet
C) frame-segment-packet

D) packet-segment-packet
E) packet-frame-segment

4. Which two layer functions are generally built in an operating system such as Windows and Linux?
A) physical and transport layers
B) transport and internet layers
C) internet and data link layers
D) physical and internet layers
E) transport and data link layers

5. The socket is/represents:
A) a group of applications providing similar services.
B) used to indicate a range of available ports on a server.
C) the combination of an IP address and a port number.
D) the combination of an IP address and an application-layer protocol.
E) the combination of an IP address and a session identification.

6. Which statement is true?
A) IP is a connection-oriented protocol.
B) UDP is a reliable protocol.
C) IP is a reliable protocol.
D) TCP is a reliable protocol.
E) TCP is a connection-less protocol

7. The TCP port is used to:
A) prioritize a service request.
B) forward a service request to a specific application.
C) identify a sender's IP address.
D) translate a domain name into an IP address.
E) identify a sender's MAC address.

8. The ____ bit in the TCP header is used to request handshaking.
A) FIN
B) ACK
C) SYN
D) CON
E) SEQ

9. Which is NOT accurate in terms of layer functions?
A) application layer - to establish sessions (or handshaking)
B) transport layer - to provide message (or data) integrity
C) internet layer - to execute packet routing
D) data link layer - to conduct frame switching
E) physical layer - for actual transportation of frames in signals

10. Which layer function(s) is/are implemented in the network interface card?
A) physical layer only
B) data link layer only
C) physical layer and data link layer
D) physical layer, data link layer, and internet layer
E) physical layer, data link layer, internet layer, and transport layer

11. _____ most likely depend(s) on UDP in the transport layer.
A) E-mails
B) Internet surfing with a web browser
C) Online credit card authorization for Internet shopping
D) File transfer with FTP (File Transfer Protocol)
E) Three-way video conferencing over the Internet

12. Port numbers have to be included in the header of _____.
A) packets only
B) datagrams only
C) segments only
D) segments and datagrams
E) packets, segments, and datagrams

13. TCP and UDP are compared. Which is CORRECT?

Protocol	TCP	UDP
A) Defined layer	transport	internet
B) Require handshaking	Yes	Yes
C) Require acknowledgement	Yes	Yes
D) Burden on communicating hosts	Low	Low
E) Burden on the network	High	Low

14. The TTL (time to live) value in the IP packet's header indicates a maximum number of _____ a packet can go through before reaching the destination:
A) switches
B) routers
C) hosts
D) networks
E) circuits

15. At the command prompt, "C:\>nctstat -n" can be issued to
A) check available host stations within a network.
B) list of sockets with TCP sessions.
C) check the subnetwork address of a host.

D) find the DNS server address of a host.
E) locate the DHCP server address of a host.

16. Choose a CORRECT statement.
A) A standard protocol should define either semantics or syntax, but not both.
B) The term standard is used interchangeably with architecture.
C) The semantics of a protocol is about how to interpret PDUs exchanged.
D) A reliable protocol detects transmission errors but does not correct them.
E) All standard protocols of the application layer are reliable protocols.

17. Assume that an email should cross three subnetworks for its delivery to a destination host. How many different packets are produced along the way?
A) 0
B) 1
C) 2
D) 3
E) 4

18. The IP packet is encapsulated within the _____ to travel to the destination node.
A) application message
B) TCP segment
C) UDP datagram
D) frame
E) ICMP packet

19. If a host computer develops a TCP segment with 80 as the source port and 54399 as the destination port, the host is most likely a(n) _____.
A) client PC
B) DHCP server
C) webserver
D) e-mail server
E) DNS server

20. Choose a CORRECT statement on port numbers.

A) For a Windows host, 55953 becomes a well-known port number.
B) Port numbers are divided into well-known and unknown ones.
C) If a Linux machine sends a TCP segment with source port 45780 and destination port 7200, then the host must be an email server.
D) Well-known port numbers are generally assigned to server applications.
E) Well-known port numbers are also called ephemeral port numbers.

21. When the command "*C:\ping www.yahoo.com*" is issued by a client PC, the two hosts (the PC and yahoo web-server) communicate based on _____ protocol in the internet layer:
A) ICMP (Internet control message protocol)
B) UDP (User datagram protocol)
C) ARP (Address resolution protocol)
D) HTTP (Hyper text transfer protocol)
E) SNMP (Simple network management protocol)

22. The end-to-end error control and flow control are performed in the _____ layer.
A) application
B) internet
C) transport
D) data link
E) session

23. Choose a mismatch between a standard and its corresponding layer.
A) ICMP = internet layer
B) Ethernet = data link layer
C) Digital signaling = physical layer
D) Domain Name System (DNS) = application layer
E) Dynamic Host Configuration Protocol (DHCP) = internet layer

24. Which PDU type generally has a header and a trailer?

A) data
B) segment
C) packet
D) frame
E) bit

25. When the command *tracert*
www.gmail.com is issued, at least two
protocols would have to be use to obtain
information shown in the screenshot. What
are they?
A) DHCP and UDP
B) HTTP and DHCP
C) DNS and ICMP
D) DNS and HTTP
E) ARP and HTTP

Note: "-d" in "tracert –d" is to display only
the IP address of responding routers, not
their host names.

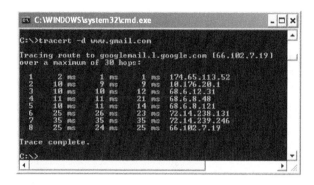

CHAPTER 3   INTERMEDIARY DEVICES

3.1   INTRODUCTION

There are many different intermediary (or networking) devices designed to enable packet exchange between end stations. Among them are *hubs, bridges, switches, routers, modems, firewalls, multiplexers, channel service unit/data service unit* (CSU/DSU), and *wireless access points* (or AP). The primary responsibility of hubs, bridges, switches, routers, and APs is packet forwarding in LANs and WANs. The others perform more specialized functions including the production and propagation of electronic and light signals over the WAN connection (e.g., modems, CSU/DSUs), provision of network security (e.g., firewalls), and bundling/unbundling of data from multiple transmission sources (e.g., multiplexers). This chapter explains the 'general purpose' intermediary devices including hubs, bridges, switches, and routers with more emphasis on switches and routers that dominate today's network infrastructure. Other specialty function-devices are covered throughout the book.

The primary objectives of this chapter are to learn:
- Intermediary devices and their operational layers
- The operating system of an intermediary device and its primary functions
- General properties of
  - Hubs
  - Bridges & Wireless Access Points
  - Switches
  - Routers
- Differences between switching and routing concepts
- Address Resolution Protocol (ARP)
- Collision domain
- Broadcast domain

3.2   INTERMEDIARY DEVICES

3.2.1   Operational Layers

Table 3.1 summarizes popular intermediary devices in terms of standard layers they belong to. Among them, layer 3 switches and their technical details are generally beyond the scope of this book but they will be briefly visited in this chapter.

Layers	Intermediary (or Networking) Devices
Application	
Transport	
Internet	Routers, Layer 3 switches
Data Link	Bridges, Wireless Access Points, Switches
Physical	Hubs (Multiport Repeaters)

Table 3.1 Intermediary devices and their standard layers

Intermediary devices implement functions below the transport layer (see Figure 2.23). This means that they do not understand PDUs from the application and transport layers. For example, the router is an internet layer device and the ordinary switch runs in the data link layer. Intermediary devices except those of physical layer (e.g., hubs, repeaters) have an operating system and a majority of them allow people to access it through *Command Line Interface* (CLI) and/or *Graphical User Interface* (GUI). As an example, Cisco's proprietary operating system is called *Internetwork Operating System* (shortly IOS) and the company uses IOS for both switches and routers.

Generally, the operating system of a switch/router has features to support specialized networking functions. Through CLI and GUI, one can change the system configuration of a device. This includes manual addition of switch/routing table entries, interface/port management (e.g., IP assignment to ports, port activation, shutting down ports), and setting up device and port security (e.g., password protection). Because of its functional specialization, the operating system of an intermediary device is relatively small. For example, the file size of Cisco's IOS is smaller than 100 Megabytes while Microsoft Windows is at least several Gigabytes.

With the compact size, the operating system of an intermediary device can be stored in the non-volatile *flash memory* that affords much faster access in reading files and also does not lose its content even if the device shuts down. When a switch or router is powered on, the operating system in the flash memory is copied into its *Random Access Memory* (RAM) during the boot up process. This is somewhat different from traditional computers whose operating systems (e.g., Windows, Linux) are stored in the hard disk and copied into the volatile RAM during the initial boot up.

3.2.2 Operating System Access

As stated, to configure parameters of an intermediary device, its operating system needs to be accessed through CLI (e.g., see Figure 3.1) or GUI. For instance, two router manufacturers, Cisco and Juniper Networks, have their GUI tools called *Security Device Manager* and *J-Web* respectively. GUI is more user-friendly as interactions with the operating system are primarily through a web browser, and thus it allows quick and intuitive configurations, monitoring, and troubleshooting of an intermediary device. As a simple example, Figure 8.23 and 8.24 in Chapter 8 demonstrates the GUI-based access of a wireless router's operating system. CLI is, however, preferred by many IT professionals especially in deploying and maintaining enterprise-class intermediary devices because it offers more flexibility and control. When CLI is preferred, the operating system can be accessed through two different ports: console port or regular LAN/WAN port (see Table 3.2).

Port	Accessing the OS of an intermediary device
Console port	<ul><li>A host station directly connects to the console port using a console cable. The console port is a dedicated connection port for device management.</li><li>With no IP configuration initially, the intermediary device is not accessible through the network. At this point, the direct cabling from a host station is the only option to access its OS.</li><li>The host workstation uses a terminal program (e.g., HyperTerminal program for Windows) to access the OS.</li></ul>

	▪ Once in the system, an IP address can be assigned for remote access and also the login name and password should be set up so that only authorized people can access the OS.
LAN or WAN port	▪ Once an intermediary device is set up with an IP address through the console port, the device is networking ready. ▪ Then, such remote access program as Telnet, SSH (Secure Shell), or web browser can be used to access the system over the network to change configurations. ▪ In this mode, a host station can access the OS through its regular LAN or WAN port (not the console port) by signing in with the legitimate login and password (see Figure 3.16). ▪ Telnet uses plaintext and is vulnerable to eavesdropping. SSH is the telnet's secure version that encrypts all communications.

Note: Although a layer 2 device, a switch can be given an IP address for remote access of its OS over the network. The IP address assigned is, therefore, purely for device management and it has nothing to do with switching of layer 2 frames. No device is network enabled without an IP address assigned.

Table 3.2 Accessing the OS of an intermediary device

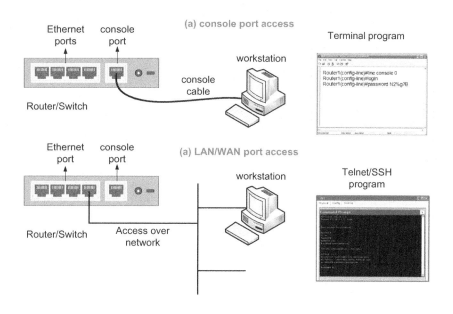

Figure 3.1 Managing an intermediary device

~~~~~~

Example: Cisco's IOS & access protection

Cisco's router/switch uses the following commands to set up a password protection from

73

unauthorized access to its OS.

Commands used	Meaning of each command
line console 0	To set up an access privilege of the console port
login	Access to the system requires login.
password N2%g7B	The access password is *N2%g7B*.

Figure 3.2 demonstrates the entrance of three commands in succession. Once set up, a person should know the password to access the router/switch's OS in order to manage the device.

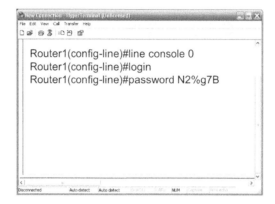

Figure 3.2 Protecting OS of an intermediary device

3.3 HUB (MULTI-PORT REPEATER)

The hub is a purely physical device that accepts incoming signals that carry frames, regenerates signal strength and shape, and repeats their propagation to connected ports. This pure physical layer device, therefore, does not need an operating system. On receiving a frame, the hub broadcasts it out to all connected ports except the entry port. Then, the end station that has a matching destination MAC address copies the frame into its NIC memory and processes it and the other hosts drop the frame because of MAC address mismatch. With its relay function, the hub is also known as a *multiport repeater*.

Because of the hub's indiscriminate broadcasting behavior, only a single host can release the frame at a time no matter how many hosts are connected to a hub. This *shared media* environment that allows restricted network access results in ineffective usage of network capacity. Because of the broadcasting, hub ports operate in the *half-duplex mode* in which frames flow only one direction at a time. As a result, if a port has 10Mbps capacity, actual speed in each direction (sending and receiving circuit) reduces to about 5Mbps due to the waiting time.

Using the hub, the network becomes more vulnerable to *collisions* when more than one host releases frames accidently. The risk gets higher as the number of hosts attached to the network grows and collisions result in lower throughput and higher latency in data delivery. Naturally, a network's scalability (or expandability) is limited when hubs are utilized. When the hub is deployed, host NICs attached to it activate the *CSMA/CD* (Carrier Sense Multiple Access/ Collision Detection) protocol to control network (or media) access. It is a mechanism designed to avoid frame collisions in the *shared media* environment and to remedy if collisions take place (CSMA/CD is explained later).

As another major drawback, host stations are more exposed to security risks due to frame broadcasting and relative ease of its interception. For example, when the NIC of a station is in the *promiscuous mode*, it copies all arriving frames and processes them even if there is mismatch between their destination MAC addresses and the NIC's MAC address. It is not difficult to see that, although used for a good cause (e.g., monitoring traffic for network management), the *promiscuous mode* option can be easily abused by an ill-minded person. In the enterprise environment, hubs have been replaced by switches due to the drawbacks, especially weak security and ineffective use of available network capacity. Hubs have built-in RJ-45 or USB ports to connect host stations.

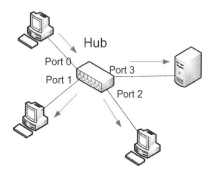

Figure 3.3 A small hub-based network

3.4 BRIDGE & WIRELESS ACCESS POINT

The bridge is a layer 2 device designed to divide the network into smaller manageable segments. Network segmentation is important to resolve growing pains of a network. Bridges, switches, and routers all can segment a network into more manageable sizes and control the flow of unnecessary traffic from one segment to another. The hub, however, is not a segmentation device because of its inability to filter frames.

The bridge examines the MAC address of every frame arriving at its port, and either passes or filters it based on information stored in its *bridge table* (see Figure 3.4). The bridging process is highly intuitive; that is, in the unicast mode, if the destination address of an incoming frame is in the same network segment then the frame is filtered (blocked). In Figure 3.4, for instance, if PC1 sends a frame to PC2 in the same network segment, the bridge also gets the frame as it is broadcasted by the hub. On receiving the frame, the bridge refers to its bridge table and decides that the destination MAC address of PC2 connects to the same port Fa0/0 (belonging to the same segment) and thus filters the frame.

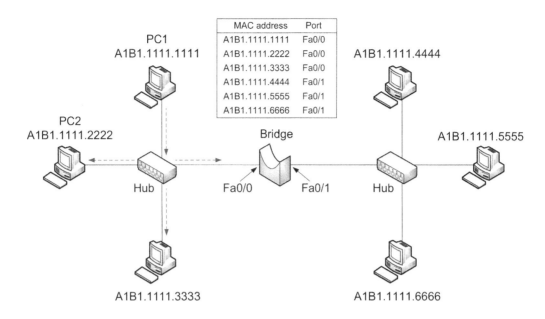

MAC address	Port
A1B1.1111.1111	Fa0/0
A1B1.1111.2222	Fa0/0
A1B1.1111.3333	Fa0/0
A1B1.1111.4444	Fa0/1
A1B1.1111.5555	Fa0/1
A1B1.1111.6666	Fa0/1

Figure 3.4 An example of bridge table

Frame filtering between segments has an effect of improving network response time by reducing unnecessary traffic flow. However, if a frame is broadcasted (instead of unicasting) by the source host, the bridge relays the frame through all ports rather than blocking it. As a result, although the bridge does a good job of isolating unicast traffic, it is unable to contain the flow of broadcasted frames to other segment(s). The traditional bridge (e.g., Figure 3.4) is less used these days because switches that dominate today's LANs have the same filtering capacity.

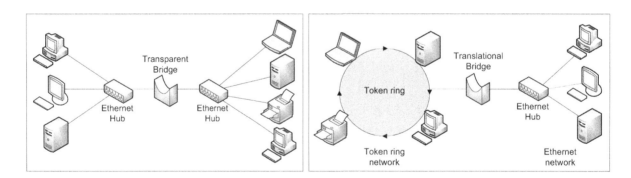

Figure 3.5 Transparent vs. translational bridges

Bridges are either *transparent* or *non-transparent* (Figure 3.5). *Transparent bridges* interconnect network segments running the same standard (e.g., Ethernet). Being transparent, thus, means that the bridge simply relays frames as they are without changing their structure. When network segments running on different standards (e.g., Ethernet, Token Ring) are bridged, the *non-transparent bridge* is used. It is also termed as *translational bridge* because it has to translate the format of frames before they are handed over from one segment to another.

76

The *AP* or *hotspot* is the most prevalent form of the translational bridge. With ubiquity of WiFi networks, APs that provide connectivity between Ethernet (wired segment) and 802.11 WiFi (wireless segment) are omnipresent. Ethernet and WiFi have their own frame formats with different information fields and APs are responsible for their translation. More details of APs are explained in Chapter 8.

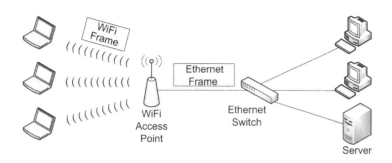

Figure 3.6 WiFi Access Point as translational bridge

Exercise 3-1: Imagine a hypothetical network in which a wireless bridge with two ports (say Fa0/0 and Fa0/1) connects two hubs (Hub A to Fa0/0 and Hub B to Fa0/1). The 'indirect' connectivity of bridge ports to hosts is captured in the bridge table below. Remember that the MAC addresses are in hexadecimal.

End stations	MAC address	Port
1	1100.0000.1111	Fa0/0
2	1100.0000.2222	Fa0/0
3	1100.0000.3333	Fa0/0
4	1100.0000.4444	Fa0/1
5	1100.0000.5555	Fa0/1

Decide what the bridge does to incoming frames and complete the table. The following is the description of each column:
- Filter/Forward: Decide if the frame is going to be filtered or forwarded by the bridge.
- Output port: What is the port through which a frame will be forwarded?
- Receiving hosts: Which host(s) gets the frame, although it may not be picked up and processed?

Hint: When the destination address of a frame is composed of all 1s (in other words, 48 ones) or is not found in the bridge table, the frame is broadcasted.

Source MAC address	Destination MAC address	Filter or Forward	Output Port	Hosts receiving the frame
1100.0000.1111	1100.0000.2222			
1100.0000.1111	1100.0000.4444			
1100.0000.5555	1100.0000.4444			
1100.0000.3333	FFFF.FFFF.FFFF			
1100.0000.4444	1100.2B22.4A4C			
1100.0000.5555	FFFF.FFFF.FFFF			

3.5   SWITCH

3.5.1   General Features

The switch is the most popular intermediary device used *to form data links between host stations*. Although there are switches designed for different LAN and WAN standards (e.g., Ethernet, Frame Relay), the focus here is the Ethernet standard that dominates wired LANs these days. A switch comes with a number of RJ-45 ports for twisted pair connection and, depending on the model, has additional high-speed ports for fiber links. Each port is given a permanent MAC address. For instance, the one in Figure 3.7 has 24 ports of RJ-45 with 24 different MAC addresses.

Unlike the hub that broadcasts frames to all ports, the switch forwards an incoming frame only to the port that directly or indirectly (via other switches) leads to its destination host. This one-to-one correspondence between an input and output ports (e.g., a frame arriving at port #1 exits through port #16) curtails network congestion considerably and eliminates frame collisions within a subnetwork. If two frames are launched concurrently destined to the same host, the switch places one frame in the waiting queue until the delivery of the other frame is completed. A switch can have a queue assigned to each port or alternatively have a common queue shared by all ports.

Figure 3.7 Ethernet switch – external view (not an actual product)

With *one input port-to-one output port* connectivity, the switch allows simultaneous formation of multiple data links with each link transmitting frames in the *full-duplex* mode between two host stations. For the full-duplex connectivity, a switch port keeps two separate circuits, each dedicated for inbounding or outbounding traffic. In the 'switched LAN' (LAN formed by Ethernet switches), the collision detection function (CSMA/CD) built in the host's NIC is not activated as there are no frame collisions. Also, neighboring switches auto-negotiate to decide link speed and duplex mode (either full-duplex or half-duplex). Although it relies on unicasting in the regular mode, the switch does broadcasting and multicasting as needed.

There are several terms commonly used to indicate switch capacity.

- *Port density*: Number of ports available on a switch (e.g., 24 ports)
- *Wire speed*: Maximum data rate (speed) of a switch port (e.g., 100Mbps, 1Gbps)
- *Forwarding rate*: Combined data rate of all switch ports. For instance, a switch with ten 100 Mbps ports has the forwarding rate of 1000 Mbps.

- *Aggregate throughput*: This is an actual data rate that can be pushed through a switch at any moment. A majority of LAN switches have an *aggregative throughput* that is considerably lower than its corresponding *forwarding rate* because of their internal architecture. For instance, a switch with a forwarding rate of 1000 Mbps may have an aggregate throughput of 600 Mbps only.

- *Non-blocking vs. blocking*: When the *aggregate throughput* of a switch can match its *forwarding rate*, the switch is non-blocking because all ports can concurrently achieve their highest transmission speeds without being constrained by the internal architecture. In reality, most switches are *blocking*. For example, a switch with *forwarding rate* of 1000 Mbps and *aggregate throughput* of 600 Mbps has 60 percent (600/1000) non-blocking capacity.

Exercise 3-2: Refer to the switch in Figure 3.7 in which each port can auto-sense 10/100/1000 Mbps transmission speeds.

1. What is the switch's port density?
2. What is the switch's wire speed?
3. What is the switch's forwarding rate?
4. Assume that the switch can attain aggregate throughput equivalent to 80 percent of its forwarding rate. What is its aggregate throughput? Is this switch non-blocking?
5. Can the aggregate throughput of a switch be higher than its forwarding rate? Why or why not?

3.5.2 Switch Port

Switches dominate Ethernet LANs. The switched Ethernet is physically wired in a star topology where the switch is used as a central concentrator to which host stations are attached. The switch port is a part of the electronic circuit board, *LAN card*, which is similar to the host station's NIC. Each port comes with an identifying name, a MAC address, and wire speed. There is no universal convention of port naming and vendors have their own way of naming. As an example, Table 3.3 shows one naming approach for a switch with 24 Fast Ethernet ports and 2 Gigabit Ethernet ports. Here, 0/3 means that 0 is a bay number and 3 is a port number recognized by the operating system. As can be seen, each switch port is given a unique data link layer MAC address. The switch's operating system understands both full and abbreviated port names in Table 3.3 and thus can be used interchangeably for configuration.

Switch ports come in several speeds including Ethernet (10Mbps), Fast Ethernet (100 Mbps), and

Gigabit Ethernet (1000 Mbps). Some switches have ports that support only a single speed and other switches have mixed port speeds (e.g., 100 Mbps Fast Ethernet + 1Gbps Gigabit Ethernet). Many switches come with ports that can dynamically adjust their speeds (e.g., 10/100/1000 Mbps) matching those of connecting hosts. For the matching, the host's Ethernet NIC and the switch port negotiate the highest speed that both parties can support by exchanging a set of bits (not an ordinary frame) in advance. This process is called auto-negotiation and is defined by an IEEE standard. As stated, some switches support only twisted pair connectivity and others support more than one cabling options (e.g., twisted pair and optical fiber).

Port full name	Abbreviation	MAC address
FastEthernet0/1	Fa0/1	0005.B119.6A01
FastEthernet0/2	Fa0/2	0005.B119.6A02
----	----	-----
----	----	-----
FastEthernet0/23	Fa0/23	0005.B119.6A03
FastEthernet0/24	Fa0/24	0005.B119.6A04
GigabitEthernet1/1	Gi1/1	0005.B119.7C03
GigabitEthernet1/2	Gi1/2	0005.B119.7C04

Table 3.3 Switch port naming (an example)

3.5.3   Switch Table

Switch Table Entries

The switch forwards incoming frames referring to entries in its *switch table*. The switch table stores MAC addresses of directly and indirectly connected *hosts* and their *exit ports* (see Table 3.4). Besides MAC addresses and exit ports, the switch table maintains additional information such as *address type* and *Virtual LAN* (VLAN). The address type field indicates whether an entry is *static* (manually entered) or *dynamic* (automatically obtained through its own learning process).

With the static entry method, a network administrator can maintain more control in switch management (e.g., security) by deciding which hosts can be attached to the intermediary device. Static entries stay in the switch table until they are manually removed. Despite the advantages, the manual addition of entries is a time consuming process and poses difficulties in network management especially when the network gets bigger. In contrast, the automatic addition of entries through the dynamic self-learning process lacks the benefits of better control and security, but becomes a more accurate (i.e., no human errors) and cost effective (e.g., less human intervention) solution. As for the VLAN field, all switch table entries belong to what they call *default VLAN* initially. The VLAN concept is explained in Chapter 7. Among the fields, the MAC address and exit port columns are fundamental in understanding the concept of frame switching.

Destination MAC Address	Exit Port	Address Type	VLAN
0002.584B.16E0	FastEthernet0/1	Static	1
00B0.D0F3.47AC	FastEthernet0/2	Static	1
00C1.4AC7.23D2	FastEthernet0/3	Dynamic	1
00B0.D045.963A	FastEthernet0/3	Dynamic	1

Table 3.4 Demonstration of a switch table (an example)

Switch Learning

As stated, entries exemplified in Table 3.4 can be dynamically added to the switch table based on *switch learning*. Let's take a look at a scenario.

1. When an Ethernet frame (let's say, source: A1B1.1111.1111 and destination: A1B1.1111.2222) arrives at a switch port, Fa0/10, the switch searches its switch table to find an entry that matches A1B1.1111.2222.
2. If the entry is found, then the switch releases the frame through the entry's exit port.
3. If the entry is not found, then the switch broadcasts the frame to all ports except the port, Fa0/10.
4. In doing step 3, the switch learns that the source MAC address, A1B1.1111.1111, is either *directly* or *indirectly* connected to its Fa0/10 port, and updates the pairing information (A1B1.1111.1111 and Fa0/10) to its switch table.
5. This learning and updating of table entries takes place continuously until the table has complete information.

In many networks (more specifically subnetworks), several switches are interlinked. In this situation, the switch table lists only host *MAC address* and *exit port* pairs. As a result, depending on network topology, an exit port can be paired to only one host MAC address or alternatively to multiple host MAC addresses. For instance, in Figure 3.8, the SW1's switch table has an entry that pairs Fa0/2 with A1B1.1111.1111 (i.e., *one port-to-one MAC address*). As for the *one port-to-multiple MAC addresses*, Fa0/1 is connected ultimately to four different hosts (A1B1.1111.3333, A1B1.1111.4444, A1B1.1111.5555, and A1B1.1111.6666) via SW2 and SW3. Observe that the SW1's switch table does not contain any information regarding SW2 and SW3. SW1 is only concerned about host computers ultimately connected through SW2 and SW3.

Exercise 3-3: Complete the SW 3's switch table in Figure 3.8.

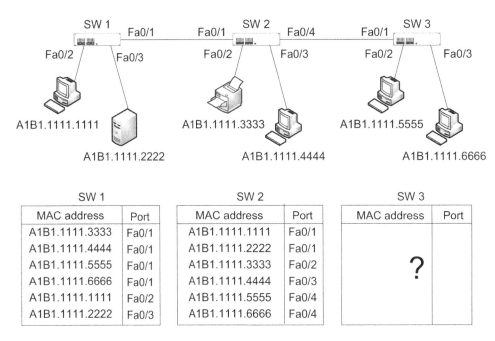

Figure 3.8 Switch tables

Aging of Entries

The entries *dynamically* added to a switch table have aging time (e.g., 300 seconds) that they can stay in the switch table without being referenced. When the aging time of an entry expires, the switch considers that the entry's MAC address is inactive and removes the MAC address-exit port pair from the switch table.

Aging time can be manually specified on a switch. In configuring aging time, a network administrator should consider the following factors. If it is set too short, this will result in premature removal of MAC addresses (including legitimate ones) from the switch table. This premature dropping can result in more broadcasting of frames by the switch, negatively affecting network performance. With longer aging time, meanwhile, the switch table can retain more inactive MAC entries (e.g., turned off computers) and this can adversely affect the learning and updating process of the switch table. As stated, the static entry remains in the switch table permanently unless manually dropped and is therefore not affected by the aging.

Exercise 3-4: Refer to the hypothetical network in Figure 3.9. Assume that each switch has six Fast Ethernet (100 Mbps) ports and all entries of the switch table are dynamically added.

Then:
1. Assign a MAC address of your choice to each host station.
2. Assign a MAC address to each LAN port of a switch (refer to Table 3.3).
3. For each switch, determine switch ports that link hosts or other switches.
4. Develop a switch table for each of the five switches. The switch table should list MAC address-exit port pairs.

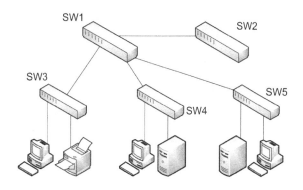

Figure 3.9 A hypothetical switched LAN

3.5.4 Switch Types

Non-Managed vs. Managed Switches

Switches are either non-managed or managed. The non-managed switch is relatively a simple and inexpensive device that does not allow any modification of its configuration and is literally put into production as it is. It, therefore, has only limited features such as auto-negotiation of data transfer speed and transmission mode (e.g., half-duplex vs. full-duplex).

In contrast, the managed switch allows manual configuration of switch functions through the interface with its operating system. Among available functions are login and password setup to control device accessibility, configuration of port security, activation of built-in supervisory protocols, creation of virtual LANs, and other management functions (e.g., backup of system files). Deploying the managed switch in a switched LAN, therefore, requires relevant knowledge for its initial setup and subsequent management.

As stated, switches are layer 2 devices that use only MAC addresses to make forwarding decisions of incoming frames. However, the managed switch is assigned an IP address by a network administrator so that it can be remotely accessed through such programs as web browser, telnet (remote access utility), and SSH as a secure version of telnet (see Table 3.2 and Figure 3.1). When a switch is given an IP address, it is only for its remote management of configuration through the network and has nothing to do with the switch's main function of frame forwarding that relies on MAC addresses. Recall that switches are layer 2 devices, not layer 3.

Store-and-Forward vs. Cut-Through Switches

In terms of the frame forwarding approach, a switch can take either *Store-and-forward switching* or *Cut-through switching*.

- Store-and-forward switching: When a frame begins to arrive at a port, the switch waits until the entire frame becomes available for forwarding (or switching). During the waiting, the frame is temporarily stored in a queue. Once the entire frame becomes available, it conducts such routines as error detection using the frame's *frame check sequence* (FCS) and the validation of frame length. If a transmission error is found, the frame is dropped. Otherwise, the switch forwards it according to the switch table information.

- Cut-through switching: When a frame begins to arrive at a port, the switch does not wait until the entire frame becomes available. Instead, the switch begins to forward the frame as soon as information (e.g., destination MAC address) necessary for switching becomes available. This approach reduces latency (or delay) in frame delivery; however, the switch is unable to perform such routine functions as detection of transmission errors and frame length validation. In this mode, therefore, defective frames are relayed to destination hosts where host NICs conduct error detection to remove faulty frames. When a defective frame (thus the packet contained in its data field) is dropped by the destination node, the sender's TCP detects and corrects the error by retransmitting the dropped packet.

Some switches are designed to change between the two alternative modes in which they use cut-through switching when the transmission error rate remains below a threshold level, but shift to the store-and-forward mode otherwise.

Symmetric vs. Asymmetric Switches

The switching speeds of available ports on a switch can be either symmetric or asymmetric. With symmetric switching, all ports of a switch use the same delivery speed such as 100Mbps. When traffic is more evenly distributed throughout a network, symmetric switching makes sense. For instance, a small network may be running on the peer-to-peer relationship in which the host computer acts as a client and a server simultaneously. With no dedicated servers, traffic flows are not concentrated on particular hosts. The peer-to-peer computing, though, is not a popular choice in enterprises these days.

In asymmetric switching, switch ports take advantage of different transmission speeds. For example, a switch can have a combination of 100 Mbps Fast Ethernet and 1 Gbps Gigabit Ethernet ports, or it can have 10/100/1000 Mbps auto-sensing ports. Asymmetric switching is necessary when network traffic is centered on one or more ports. For instance, in the client-server computing environment, client computers access resources available from dedicated servers such as email-, web-, database-, and collaboration servers. Naturally, much network traffic is directed at servers and the switch ports that link servers should be able to relay data at a faster rate than those connecting client computers. Otherwise, the server links can become bottlenecks that negatively affect overall network performance. A majority of enterprise-class switches use asymmetric switching because of their flexibility in handling concentrated traffic (see Figure 3.10).

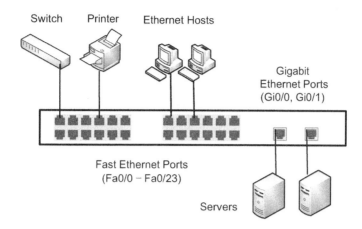

Figure 3.10 Demonstration of an asymmetric switch

Besides using the asymmetric switch, *link aggregation* is another solution to augment throughput of a particular link. Link aggregation (also known as *bonding* or *trunking*) enables bundling of two or more physical links between switches or between a switch and a host (primarily server). More on link aggregation is explained in Chapter 7.

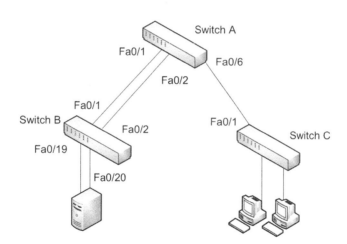

Figure 3.11 A switched network with link aggregation

Layer 2 vs. Layer 3 Switches

Traditional switches operate at layer 2 (data link layer) performing frame forwarding based only on MAC addresses. The layer 3 switch (or multi-layer switch) can behave differently from its layer 2 counterpart. The layer 3 switch port (or interface) can be flexibly configured either as a traditional layer 2 switch port (with only a MAC address assigned) or as a router port (with a MAC and an IP address paired). With an IP address assigned to a switch port, the layer 3 switch is capable of forwarding Ethernet frames based on IP addresses and also perform basic

IP-based routing, basically acting just like a router. For instance, multiple subnetworks can be joined by the layer 3 switch for inter-networking.

As another unique aspect of the layer 3 switch, its layer 3 functions are built into hardware and thus it processes packets faster than traditional routers whose layer 3 functions are implemented in software (see TCP/IP in Chapter 2). Hardware-based processing is simply faster than that based on software and this explains the popularity of layer 3 switches for internetworking within an enterprise or a campus.

However, the layer 3 switch is not designed to entirely substitute the router because it lacks some router functions. Most notably, its support for WAN connections and advanced routing protocols is considerably weaker than the router. For example, you can observe that there is no WAN serial port in Figure 3.12. Layer 3 switches are widely used in place of pure routers within the boundary of an enterprise or a campus network. Bear in mind that, unless the term *layer 3 switch* is used, the switch is a layer 2 device.

Figure 3.12 An Ethernet layer 3 switch

Fixed, Stackable, and Modular Switches

There are several switch types differing in their structural design:
- With the *fixed port switch*, what you see is what you get because ports cannot be added or changed (see Figure 3.7 for an example).
- With the *stackable switch*, multiple switches can be stacked on top of the other and they, as a whole, function as one oversized switch with many ports. The stacked switches are conjoined by high-speed cables in daisy chain mode.
- The *modular switch* comes with one or more slots that can accept a line card (or module) with multiple ports. Figure 3.13 demonstrates a core switch with several modules, each with multiple ports.

The decision of which switches to deploy on a network rests on various technical and non-technical (e.g., budget) considerations. Among the technical factors are:
- Required speed and media of NIC necessary to support computers in place
- Number of switch ports necessary

- Need for connection redundancy
- Growth potential of an enterprise network
- Switch types already in place
- Role of the switch to be deployed (e.g., workgroup, distribution, or core switch)
- Other functional features such as security

Power supply   Management ports   Ethernet LAN ports

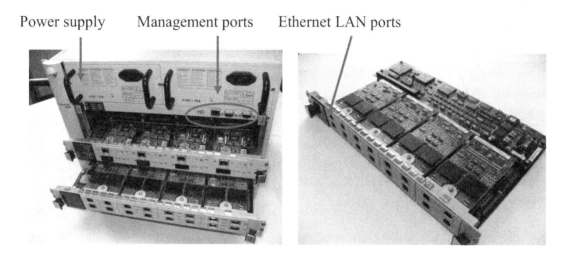

Figure 3.13 A modular core switch and multi-port switch card

[Video Tour 3-1]   1. An example of the modular switch
                                2. An example of the stackable switch

Power over Ethernet (PoE)

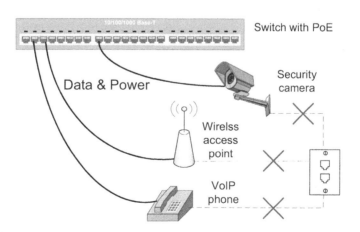

Figure 3.14 Power over Ethernet

Some switches offer *Power over Ethernet* (PoE) capability. With its technology details standardized by IEEE802.3, PoE enables a switch to use Ethernet LAN cables not only to transmit data signals but also to supply electric power to connecting nodes such as wireless access points (APs), VoIP phones, and web cameras. Using PoE enabled switches, the planning and deployment of these network nodes becomes more flexible without being constrained by the access to power sources. The PoE-enabled switches are generally costlier than the ones with no PoE capability.

[Video Tour 3-2] How to add the PoE function to any Ethernet switch?

3.5.5 Security Issues

Safeguarding Switch Ports

It is essential that only qualified computers are allowed to join intermediary devices to secure a network. Given the dominance of Ethernet switches for wired LANs, allowing uncontrolled access to switch ports by any computer can pose a grave security threat to an enterprise. To neutralize such risk, IT staff should use managed switches to block unauthorized access to the network.

To improve network security, the operating system of a managed switch can be instructed to allow only one or more legitimate MAC addresses on a port and to automatically shut down the port if an unauthorized computer attempts to join. This will prevent a network from such risks as *footprinting* and *reconnaissance* (gathering data regarding network environment), stealth access to other computers, and direct attacks such as *MAC address flooding* (more details in Chapter 11) by an intruder.

As another measure to further network security, it is a good practice to manually shutdown all unused ports of a switch. This can be done by issuing simple commands. For example, the port Fa0/1 of a Cisco switch is manually turned off by issuing *'interface fa0/1'* and *'shut'* consecutively at the command prompt. Such switch setup to safeguard a network from potential hostile threats is possible with managed switches.

Port Mirroring

Managed switches come with a *mirror port* for network management. Frames going through some or all regular ports of a switch can be copied to its mirror port so that network traffic can be monitored by the computer attached to the mirror port. Imagine the situation in which an attacker finds a way to connect to the mirror port of a switch and observes all frames (and inside packets) passing by. It highlights the importance of securing physical access to switches and switch ports.

3.6 ROUTERS

3.6.1 Two Primary Functions

The router that conducts routing decision of IP packets for inter-networking is another key intermediary device. Among the router's primary functions are:

Routing Table Development and Its Update

The router develops and maintains a routing table as the reference table for packet forwarding decisions. Entries in a routing table can be manually created and also dynamically added by the router itself based on information obtained from other routers. For dynamic updates of routing table entries, routers periodically advertise relevant information using such protocol as *Open Shortest Path First* (OSPF). The details are explained in Chapter 6.

Packet Forwarding

The ultimate task of a router is IP packet routing (or forwarding). On receiving an IP packet, the router examines its routing table entries to determine the optimal delivery path and forwards the packet to the destination. Routers interconnect subnetworks when each subnetwork runs a particular LAN (e.g., Ethernet, WiFi) or WAN (e.g., PPP, Frame Relay) standard (revisit Chapter 1 and 2 on intra-networking and inter-networking). Depending on the size, each subnetwork may include multiple layer 2 switches with a number of workstations and servers attached. The subnetwork separated from other subnetwork(s) by a router becomes a *broadcast domain,* a constraining boundary of packet broadcasting (more details in Section 3.10). In other words, the router generally does not relay broadcasted IP packets and therefore becomes a dividing point between broadcast domains.

3.6.2 Router Components

Physically, the router is a computer specialized in IP packet forwarding across subnetworks. It has all essential hardware and software elements that we see inside a computer. These include:

- Central processing unit (CPU)
- Memory: Read Only Memory (ROM), Random Access Memory (RAM), Non-volatile flash memory
- Operating System: A vendor may choose to store OS in the non-volatile flash memory for faster access and transfer to RAM.
- System bus that moves data between system elements
- Various ports (interfaces) including:
  - LAN ports (e.g., Fa0/1) mainly for Ethernet including Fast Ethernet and Gigabit Ethernet
  - WAN ports (e.g., Serial0/0) for serial lines such as T-1 and DSL links.
  - Console port for direct access to OS for system configuration and management (see Figure 3.1).

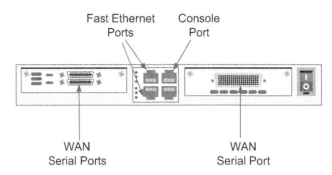

Figure 3.15 Router ports (not an actual product)

The drawing in Figure 3.15 demonstrates a router with Fast Ethernet LAN ports and serial WAN ports. The router's LAN ports generally use the RJ-45 connector that is also heavily used by Ethernet switches. Although not included in the figure, a router can have high speed LAN ports for optical fibers. Different choices are available for WAN serial ports and Figure 3.15 demonstrates two of them. The serial WAN ports are primarily used for enterprise class routers. Many routers marketed for homes and small businesses also adopt RJ-45 (in place of serial ports) for the WAN port that is wired to a cable or DSL modem for Internet connectivity.

3.6.3 Router Ports & Naming

Many routers are modular in which, besides built-in LAN and WAN ports, additional modules (i.e., LAN or WAN cards with one or more ports) can be installed in the expansion slot(s). The WAN card is called a *WAN interface card* (or WIC) as opposed to *network interface card* (or NIC) for LAN. The router's WIC comes with various serial ports as in Figure 3.15. Each router port connects to a subnetwork and thus no two ports of a router should be on the same subnetwork. There is no universal convention in naming router ports (interfaces) and vendors have their own preferences in the naming.

〰〰〰〰〰〰〰〰〰〰〰〰〰〰〰〰〰〰〰〰〰〰〰〰〰〰〰〰〰〰〰〰

Example: Cisco router's port naming

Just as with Cisco switches, Cisco routers use the naming approach of "*media type slot#/port#*" in which Ethernet LAN and serial WAN are representative media types. Assuming that a router comes with built-in (fixed) ports and additional expansion slots, the built-in ports are considered to be in slot 0 (rather than 1). The LAN or WAN card installed in an expansion slot has one or more ports and a particular port of a slot is identified as a "*slot#/port#*" combination. For instance, the first port of slot 0 includes such naming as Serial0/0 or FastEthernet0/0, and the second port of slot 0 can have naming such as Serial0/1 or FastEthernet0/1. As another example, FastEthernet1/0 and FastEthernet1/1 indicate the first and second Fast Ethernet ports in slot 1. Depending on the router model, the port naming is further extended to represent a combination of "*slot#/subslot#/port#*" (e.g., Serial0/0/0). The Cisco's operating system, IOS, recognizes the pre-assigned port names.

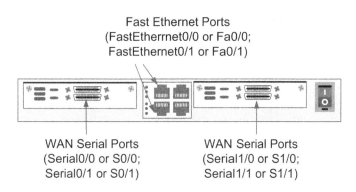

Fast Ethernet Ports
(FastEtherrnet0/0 or Fa0/0;
FastEthernet0/1 or Fa0/1)

WAN Serial Ports
(Serial0/0 or S0/0;
Serial0/1 or S0/1)

WAN Serial Ports
(Serial1/0 or S1/0;
Serial1/1 or S1/1)

Figure 3.16 Cisco's LAN and WAN port naming (not an actual model)

The router's LAN port such as FastEthernet0/1 or GigabitEthernet1/1 should be configured with a pair of MAC and IP addresses for it to be operational. It is because LAN is a *point-to-multipoint* setup in which a computer can have many possible destinations within a subnetwork, making it necessary to use unique MAC addresses for intra-networking. Meanwhile, the serial WAN port needs an IP address but not unique source/destination MAC addresses because of the *point-to-point* (i.e., There is only a single possible destination from a source) nature of a WAN connection. For this reason, the pairing between an IP address and a MAC address applies only to the LAN port, but not to the WAN port. The WAN frame also has data link address fields, but they are literally space fillers, containing values (e.g., all ones) of little meaning.

The router port may be in the *Up* or *Down* state and the former is an indication that the port is ready for packet exchanges. For a LAN/WAN port to be in the *Up* state, it should be given a unique IP address to be activated. Besides, the router connects to a WAN link (e.g., T-1 line) through the external device called a CSU/DSU (*Channel Service Unit/Data Service Unit*) unless the CSU/DSU function is built into the router. In the WAN link, the CSU/DSU does what the DSL/Cable modem does for the home network (more details in Chapter 4).

Exercise 3-5: A command is issued to a router and it displayed summary information of port status as in Table 3.5 (It is not a routing table). Answer the following questions.

1. How many LAN ports are there and what is their speed?
2. How many WAN ports do you see?
3. How many LAN and WAN ports are ready for networking?
4. Why does the serial port not have a MAC address?
5. Can FasEthernet0/1 have an IP address, 192.168.2.1/24?
6. Can FasEthernet0/2 have an IP address, 192.168.4.1/24?
7. How many different subnetworks are currently interconnected by the router?
8. Up to how many different subnetworks can be interconnected by the router?

Interface(port)	Link Status	IP address	MAC address
FastEthernet 0/0	Up	192.168.2.10/24	0001.34AB.1234
FastEthernet 0/1	Down	<not set>	0001.3464.A23C
FastEthernet 0/2	Down	<not set>	0001.3486.B18A
Serial 0/0	Up	192.168.5.10/24	
Serial 0/1	Down	<not set>	

Table 3.5 A hypothetical summary of router ports

3.6.4 Router Configuration

As explained, the router exists to perform IP packet routing (i.e., inter-networking across multiple subnetworks). To enable this, the router also develops and continuously maintains a routing table, a reference table for packet routing decisions. In addition, the router supports a variety of other functions for adequate network management and protection. They are conveniently divided into basic and advanced features.

Basic Features

- Router naming (e.g., R1)
- Setting up a password to allow protected access to operating system
- IP assignment to LAN/WAN ports and their activation
- Manual entry of static routing paths to the routing table
- Activation of a protocol that enables dynamic construction and update of the routing table (more details in Chapter 6)

Advanced Features

Depending on the product, a router also supports other advanced tasks primarily designed to enhance security of the computer network. Among them are:

- *Access control list* (ACL) to control inbound and outbound traffic flows by filtering packets based on such information as IP addresses and TCP/UDP ports (more details in Chapter 12)
- *Network address translation* (NAT) that performs conversion between internally used *private* IP addresses and externally shown *public* IP addresses to shield internal hosts from public views (more details in Chapter 5)
- Provision of dynamic (or temporary) IP addresses to requesting stations by activating the DHCP server function (more details in Chapter 10)
- *Virtual Private Network* (VPN) to support secure WAN connections between two remote locations over the Internet (more details in Chapter 10)
- *Intrusion Prevention System* (IPS) to detect possible attacks mainly coming from outside and prevent (e.g., drop suspicious packets) them from affecting the internal network

- *Security auditing* that examines current router setup, detects potential threats to the router and associated networks, and recommends configuration changes to neutralize the threats.

3.7   SWITCHING VS. ROUTING

In this section, differences between *switching* (by switches) and *routing* (by routers) are revisited (see Chapter 2) in more detail. Again, relating switching to intra-networking and routing to inter-networking makes their conceptual and technical differences easier to comprehend. Both switching and routing are intended to move application data from the source to the destination, possibly through multiple intermediary devices and trunk links. The fundamental reason for conducting switching and routing is that creating a full mesh network that directly interconnects all host stations is neither practical nor cost effective.

The key differences between switching and routing are summarized in terms of:
1. Data link layer vs. internet layer
2. Connection-oriented vs. connection-less
3. Single delivery path vs. multiple delivery paths

Review Chapter 2's Sections 2.5 and 2.6 to better relate the following summary.

Data Link Layer vs. Internet Layer

While the data link layer is responsible for frame *switching* within a single subnetwork (thus intra-networking) based on MAC addresses, the internet layer is responsible for packet *routing* decision relying on IP addresses to forward packets across subnetworks (thus inter-networking) joined by routers. Routing performed in the internet layer is therefore conceptually distinct from switching that takes place in the data link layer. Here, the route can be understood as the *end-to-end delivery path of an IP packet formed through multiple subnetworks*.

Connection-Oriented vs. Connection-Less

With switching for intra-networking, the logical delivery path between two nodes is pre-determined no matter how many intermediary devices are involved to form the path. Once decided, the logical switching path between any two hosts does not change unless there is an inordinate development (e.g., switch failure) that makes it difficult to use the same path. Keeping the same delivery path between two hosts makes switching a connection-oriented undertaking. Meanwhile, the routing path of a packet between two end nodes situated in different networks is not necessarily pre-determined, but can be dynamically decided by each router. For forwarding decision of a packet, the router refers to its routing table that periodically updates the network's changed conditions (e.g., traffic congestion in an area). This makes the packet routing decision a dynamic and connection-less process (more to come in Chapter 6).

Single Delivery vs. Multiple Delivery Paths

There is only a single *active* delivery path at a time between any two nodes in switching. In fact, many organizations maintain redundancy of the physical path between two nodes for intra-networking. In other words, it is possible to have a partial mesh topology among intermediary devices within a subnetwork (see Section 1.4.5 in Chapter 1). However, switches have a built-in routine called *spanning tree protocol* that figures out the path redundancy and erases it, allowing only a single data link to be active between any two nodes at a time.

As for routing, it assumes availability of multiple end-to-end active paths between any two communicating nodes for inter-networking and naturally requires a process to determine an optimal delivery route of the packet. For this, the router makes a forwarding decision for each arriving packet by mapping its destination IP address to the routing table. Relatively speaking, simplicity of switching decision (because there is only one active delivery path) makes it significantly faster than routing decision.

3.8   ADDRESS RESOLUTION PROTOCOL

3.8.1   Background

Transportation of application data across subnetworks requires that switching (based on MAC addressing) and routing (based on IP addressing) go hand-in-hand (revisit Chapter 2, Section 2.10). For this, the host's LAN port should have MAC and IP addresses coupled (see Figure 1.24) so that the IP address becomes a vehicle to forward packets between subnetworks (inter-networking) and the MAC address is used to move frames within a subnetwork (intra-networking).

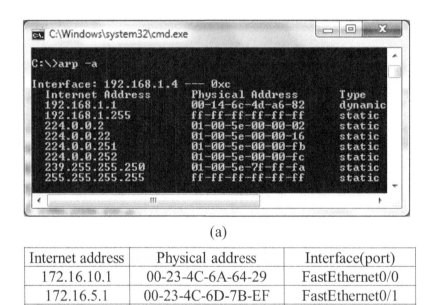

(a)

Internet address	Physical address	Interface(port)
172.16.10.1	00-23-4C-6A-64-29	FastEthernet0/0
172.16.5.1	00-23-4C-6D-7B-EF	FastEthernet0/1
172.16.7.1	00-23-4C-2C-8A-DE	FastEthernet0/2

(b)

Figure 3.17 Sample ARP tables of host (a) and router (b)

The *Address Resolution Protocol* (ARP) request is issued when the MAC address of a node (e.g., a host station, a router port) needs to be obtained based on its IP address. For instance, assume that a source host (192.168.10.1) has to deliver a frame to a target host (192.168.10.2) within a subnetwork (192.168.10.x). In this situation of intra-networking, the *frame* should contain the target host's MAC address in the frame header for its delivery. If the source host finds the target host's IP and corresponding MAC addresses in its own ARP table (or ARP cache), the mapping between them becomes straightforward. Figure 3.17a shows a sample ARP table of a host obtained by the *C:\>arp –a* command. You can observe that the host computer's ARP table only contains IP addresses and corresponding MAC (or physical) addresses. The router's ARP table (Figure 3.17b) has one more column that indicates the exit port (interface) of a target MAC address. This additional exit port information is required because, unlike the host station that belongs to only one subnetwork, the router is designed to connect several subnetworks simultaneously.

When the mapping information between an IP and a MAC is not available in the ARP cache, the source node has to broadcast an ARP request. Continuing the example above, the source host (192.168.10.1) can broadcast an ARP request asking '*Hello, what is the MAC address of the IP host 196.168.10.2?*' On receiving it, the target host (196.168.10.2) returns its MAC address to the requesting node (192.168.10.1). The source host, 192.168.10.1, then updates the mapping information on its ARP cache and dispatches the frame with the newly obtained MAC address in the destination address field.

Exercise 3-6

1. Refer to Figure 3.17. What is a key difference between the host's and router's ARP tables?
2. Refer to Figure 3.17(a). Assuming that the network address is 192.168.1.x, explain the entries "192.168.1.255 ff-ff-ff-ff-ff-ff" and "255.255.255.255 ff-ff-ff-ff-ff-ff" in their meanings.
3. Refer to Figure 3.17(b) and answer the following questions.
   a) How many different subnetworks the router is interconnecting?
   b) Can we tell from the ARP table if the router has a WAN connection? Why or why not?
4. Does the layer 2 switch need to maintain an ARP table for frame switching? Why or why not?

3.8.2 ARP Usage Scenarios

There are different situations in which ARP is utilized by a source node (a host station or router) to learn the MAC address of a target node.

- The source and destination hosts are in the same subnetwork (Figure 3.18) – The source host learns from a packet's destination IP address that the target host is in the same subnetwork. An ARP inquiry is broadcasted by the source when it does not know the target's MAC address and the source uses the returned MAC address to create a layer 2 frame.

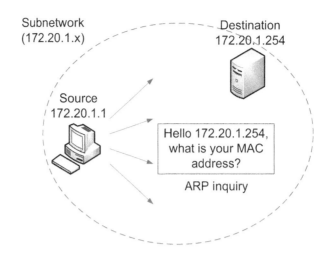

Figure 3.18 Scenario 1: host to host ARP inquiry

- The source and destination hosts are in two different subnetworks joined by a router (Figure 3.19) – The source host learns from a packet's destination IP address that the target host is not in the same subnetwork and the packet has to be directed to the router *R* for further forwarding. The source broadcasts an ARP inquiry to learn the MAC address of the router's LAN port, Fa0/0, and uses the returned MAC address to create a layer 2 frame.

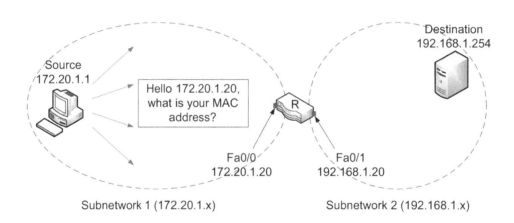

Figure 3.19 Scenario 2: host to router ARP inquiry

- A router forwards a packet to another router when the source and destination hosts are not in neighboring networks (Figure 3.20) – R1 learns from a packet's destination IP address that the target host is not in the same subnetwork and the packet has to be directed to R2 for further routing. R1 broadcasts an ARP request to obtain the MAC address of R2's Fa0/0 and uses the returned MAC address to create a layer 2 frame.

96

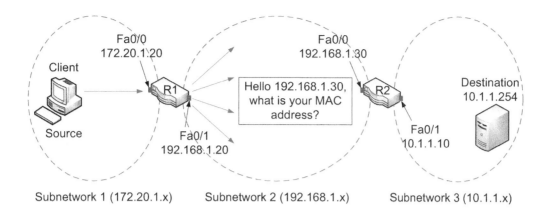

Figure 3.20 Scenario 3: router to router ARP inquiry

- A router sends a packet to its destination host when they are in the same subnetwork (Figure 3.21) – Router *R* learns from a packet's destination IP address that the target host is in the same subnetwork as its port Fa0/1. Router *R* broadcasts an ARP request to obtain the MAC address of the destination host and uses the returned MAC address to create a layer 2 frame.

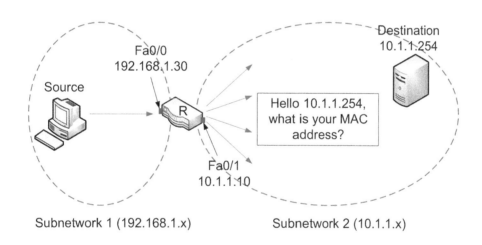

Figure 3.21 Scenario 4: router to host ARP inquiry

Exercise 3-7: Process view of packet delivery

How do DNS and ARP work together in delivering a packet? To understand the procedure, assume that the browser of a PC (192.168.1.1 with 192.168.1.x as the network ID) is trying to send an HTTP request to the web server, *www.whitehouse.gov* (let's say 123.45.67.89). Then, the following activities take place in succession for the PC to successfully release the HTTP request. Think logically and fill out the blanks.

1. The PC's browser produces a HTTP request destined to the web server

(*www.whitehouse.gov*) on receiving the user input, but the PC does not know the web server's IP address initially.

2. The PC sends an inquiry to a designated _____ server to learn the *www.whitehouse.gov*'s IP address.

3. The _____ server returns the IP address of the _____ server to the PC.

4. The PC creates a packet with the sender's IP address ( ) and the receiver's IP address ( ) included in its header.

5. From the *www.whitehouse.gov*'s IP address, the PC realizes that the target server is not in the PC's subnetwork and, therefore, the packet should travel beyond the subnetwork boundary.

6. The PC already knows the router port (called default gateway) that leads to other networks. Assume that the default gateway is (192.168.1.250). The PC (192.168.1.1) and the default gateway (192.168.1.250) are in the same subnetwork and therefore the packet delivery between them becomes a _____ activity.

7. For the delivery of the packet containing the HTTP request, the PC should use the _____ address of the default gateway (192.168.1.250).

8. The PC already knows the default gateway's IP address (provided by a DHCP server during the boot up) but the PC does not know the default gateway's _____. This triggers broadcasting of a(n) _____ inquiry by the PC.

9. On receiving the _____ inquiry, the default gateway (192.168.1.250) responds by sending its _____ address to the PC.

10. The PC updates the default gateway's IP and MAC address pairing to its _____ table. Then, it creates a data link layer PDU called a _____ by adding the PC's and the default gateway's MAC addresses to the packet and sends it directly to the default gateway to embark a long journey to the *www.whitehouse.gov* server.

3.9 CHOICE OF INTERMEDIARY DEVICES

Given many differences between the switch and the router, which is a better choice in designing an enterprise network? '*Switch when you can, route when you must*' has been the general rule of thumb. However, things have changed because the layer 3 switch with router capacity is also used widely as an alternative to the traditional router. In deploying layer 3 switches, user stations and servers are attached to traditional layer 2 switches and one or more layer 3 switches interconnect layer 2 switches in a hierarchical fashion (see Sections 1.4.6 and 3.5.4).

The router still plays an important role within an enterprise network. For example, the router (called border router) becomes a gateway to the Internet. Also, when an enterprise network is formed by several LANs remotely separated, the border router on each LAN provides connectivity of the LANs over WAN links.

Router and switch technologies are continuously evolving and many technical and non-technical factors should be assessed to choose them for deployment. Among the consideration factors are cost, manageability, port throughput/speed, LAN/WAN data link standards (e.g., Ethernet) supported, security features, and future expandability (e.g., availability of expansion slots).

Table 3.6 summarizes addressing requirement of three intermediary devices: hubs, switches, and routers. It is re-emphasized that each LAN port (e.g., FastEthernet0/1) of the router is given a MAC address, but its WAN port (e.g., Serial0/0/0) does not need a MAC address. Unlike LAN's point-to-multipoint link, the WAN connection is a point-to-point link which makes unique addressing of the WAN port meaningless. The WAN frame that carries an IP packet still has data link layer address fields in the frame header, but they are generally filled with a pre-determined value such as all 1s (see Chapter 9).

Device	Port/Interface	
	MAC address	IP address
Hub (multi-port repeater)	No	No
Switch (Ethernet)	Yes	No
Router	Yes (for a LAN port)	Yes
	No (for a WAN port)	

Table 3.6 Port addressing of intermediary devices

3.10   COLLISION VS. BROADCAST DOMAINS

The concepts of collision domain and broadcast domain are explained in this section. Understanding their definitions and differences is important because they have implications on the choice of intermediary devices and architecting an adequately performing enterprise network.

3.10.1 Collision Domain

The *collision domain* represents a network segment within which only a single node is allowed to transmit at a time because multiple outstanding frames from different sources result in collisions. The collision occurs because all hosts within a collision domain share the hardwired or wireless medium. Within a subnetwork, the switch performs the role of dividing collision domains. In other words, the switch is able to contain frame collisions to a collision domain and prevent them from triggering collisions in other collision domains. The switch uses *buffering* to prevent collisions. As an example of buffering, when the three PCs (PC1, PC2, and PC3) concurrently release frames destined to the printer in Figure 3.22, the switch allows the flow of a frame from a PC while buffering the other two PCs' frames in its memory to avoid collisions.

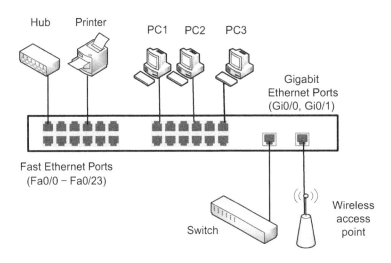

Figure 3.22 Switch as a collision domain divider

Collision Domain Types

Now knowing that the switch is a collision domain divider, let me explain how it forms different types of collision domains. Figure 3.23 demonstrates a scenario in which there are four collision domains separated by a switch. They are:

- **Collision Domain 1** formed by the direct connection between an end node (e.g., printer) and a switch port. It is a simple but prevalent collision domain type. In this domain, only one bit stream (e.g., between PC1 and Printer1) is allowed to flow at a time and those from other sources (e.g., from LT1 to Printer1) are buffered by the switch to avoid collisions. The link between Server1 and the connecting switch port is another collision domain of this type.

- **Collision Domain 2** formed by the direct link between two switch ports or between a switch port and a router port. As is the case with Collision Domain 1, only one bit stream (e.g., between PC1 and Server1) is allowed to flow through the link at a time and those from other sources (e.g., from LT1 to Server1) are buffered to avoid collisions.

- **Collision Domain 3** in which three computers are connected to a switch port through the Ethernet hub. As a physical layer repeater device, the hub broadcasts incoming frames and therefore no more than one frame should be outstanding within the domain to prevent collisions (refer to Section 3.3). To ensure this, data transmissions to the hub are controlled by the CSMA/CD standard implemented in each computer's NIC.

- **Collision Domain 4** formed by the wireless access point (AP), its associated computers, and its connection link to a switch port. The AP is placed so that computers in the domain can access the network through the wireless link. The AP allows only a single host to transmit data at a time regardless of how many host stations are within the domain. This is because wireless communication is natively broadcasting and concurrent signal propagations by more than one host result in frame collisions. To prevent collisions, WiFi devices (e.g., AP, wireless NIC) rely on the media access control protocol called CSMA/CA. It is slightly different from Ethernet's CSMA/CD. More details of WiFi including CSMA/CA are explained in Chapter 8.

Collision Domain and Network Design

One important principle of network design is to avoid the formation of collision domains to the extent possible because they negatively affect network performance. However, in many situations, especially WiFi networks that rely on wireless access points (APs), collision domains cannot be avoided. In that case, creating smaller collision domains (e.g., putting more APs) can relieve side effects. Before closing this section, it is again underscored that each switch port becomes a dividing point of the collision domain.

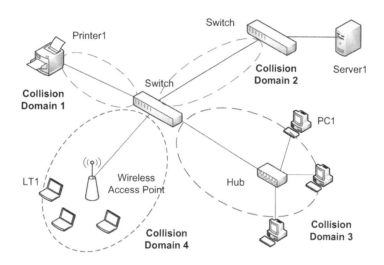

Figure 3.23 Types of collision domain

CSMA/CD

The CSMA/CD standard for Ethernet is explained regarding the procedural mechanism it uses to control network access within a collision domain to ensure that only one host is allowed to release the frame at a time (e.g., Collision Domain 3 in Figure 3.23). As stated, CSMA/CD is implemented in the host computer's NIC and only activated when it connects to a hub. The CSMA/CD rule is summarized below:

All host stations attached to an Ethernet hub *listen* to network activities.

IF: There is ongoing traffic in the network,
    THEN: Other host stations have to wait until the current transmission is over.

ELSE: Any host station can release frames based on first come first served. Although only a single host is allowed to access the media, there is always a possibility that more than one host starts transmitting data simultaneously, resulting in collisions. The chance of collision grows as more hosts are attached to the hub.

IF: A collision takes place,
   THEN: There is a natural increase in signal amplitude coming from the hub beyond the normal level and thus the *collision detection* function of host NICs spots the collision and sends out a jamming signal to indicate all hosts to stop transmissions to resolve the situation.

All host stations, from that moment, wait for a random amount of time before listening to the network activity again. The NIC's built-in algorithm gives hosts different random back-off times. When there is no traffic after the random waiting, any station can release frames based on first come first served.

3.10.2 Broadcast Domain

The broadcast domain of a network defines the scope within which a node's (i.e., a host or an intermediary device) data broadcasting can reach. Hubs, bridges, and switches relay broadcasted frames to all nodes attached to them. This means that whenever a device of this type is added to an existing network, the broadcast domain's scope grows. The difference between layer 1(hubs) and layer 2 (bridges and switches) devices is that, while the former does not even know about broadcasting in progress because it mechanically relay frames, the latter at least can tell broadcasting because they understand the meaning of a frame carrying all 1s (48 bits) in the destination MAC address field. Unlike layer 1 and layer 2 devices, routers generally do not relay broadcasted messages and therefore each router port sets the boundary of the broadcast domain (see Figure 3.24).

There is a catch here in terms of the relationship between the switch and the broadcast domain. As stated, the layer 2 switch does not divide broadcast domains in its ordinary usage. In other words, the subnetwork itself becomes a broadcast domain. However, by configuring so-called *virtual LANs* (or VLANs), a switch can segment the subnetwork into smaller broadcast domains. That is, when VLANs are created on a switch, each VLAN itself becomes a broadcast domain. This means that, by defining VLANs, several broadcast domains can be formed within Broadcast Domain 1 and also within Broadcast Domain 2 in Figure 3.24. The details are covered in Chapter 7.

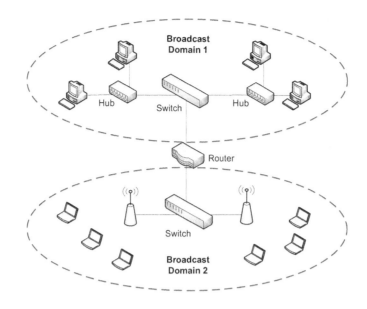

Figure 3.24 Two broadcast domains

When a node broadcasts a message, the host's NIC that receives the message generally does not have the capability to process it, and thus forwards it to the computer's CPU (central processing unit) for processing in the upper layer. Remember that the NIC only performs layer 1 (physical layer) and layer 2 (data link layer) functions (see Chapter 2). Protocols that rely on broadcasting to convey their messages are generally defined above the data link layer and thus they are beyond the NIC's handling. For example, DHCP (Dynamic Host Configuration Protocol) at the application layer and ARP (Address Resolution Protocol) at the internet layer take advantage of broadcasting. Broadcasting, therefore, not only multiplies traffic volume on the network but also becomes a process burden on the host's CPU.

Now it becomes clear that, depending on the choice of intermediary devices, the scope of the collision domain and of the broadcast domain is determined, which conveys varying implications on network performance. Table 3.7 summarizes the role of key intermediary devices in defining the collision and broadcast domains.

Intermediary devices	Layer	Collision domain divider?	Broadcast domain divider?
Hubs	1	No	No
Wireless access points	2	No	No
Bridges	2	Yes	No
Switches	2	Yes	No (Yes with VLANs)
Routers	3	Yes	Yes

Table 3.7 Dividers of collision and broadcast domains

Exercise 3-8

1. Discuss relationships among subnetwork, collision domain, and broadcast domain (Assume that virtual LANs are not created on the switch).
   a) Can the scope of a subnetwork be equal to that of the collision domain, why or why not?
   b) Can the scope of a subnetwork be equal to that of the broadcast domain, why or why not?
   c) Can the collision domain and the broadcast domain equivalent in their scope, why or why not?

2. Imagine the following four hypothetical networks. Identify collision domains and broadcast domains in each network.

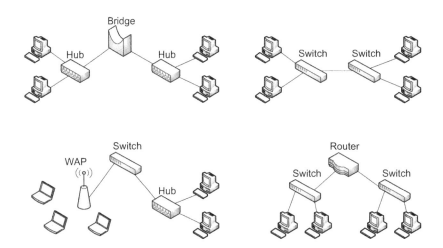

KEY TERMS

access control list (ACL)
address resolution protocol
aggregate throughput
aging time
asymmetric switch
blocking switch
bonding
bridge
bridge table
broadcast domain
Carrier Sense Multiple Access
/ Collision Detection
(CSMA/CD)
collision
collision domain
command line interface (CLI)

connection-less
connection-oriented
console port
CSU/DSU
cut-through switch
denial of service (DOS)
exit port
fixed switch
flash memory
forwarding rate
frame check sequence
graphical user interface (GUI)
hub
hyperterminal
intrusion prevention system
layer 2 switch

layer 3 switch
line card
link aggregation
MAC address flooding
managed switch
media access control
mirror port
modular switch
multiport repeater
multlayer switch (MLS)
network address translation
networking devices
non-blocking switch
non-managed switches
port density
port mirroring

104

power over Ethernet (PoE)
promiscuous mode
random access memory
RJ-45 port
router
secure shell (SSH)
security auditing
stackable switch

store-and-forward switch
switch learning
switch table
switches
symmetric switch
telnet
terminal mode
translational bridge

transparent bridge
trunking
virtual LAN (VLAN)
virtual private network
WAN interface card (WIC)
wire speed
wireless access point

CHAPTER REVIEW QUESTIONS

1. The wireless access point connects two different LAN standards, generally Ethernet and WiFi. Then, it must be a type of _____.
A) router
B) hub
C) bridge
D) gateway
E) switch

2. When a host station's NIC is connected to a hub, the link should use ___ transmission.
A) half-duplex
B) full-duplex
C) partial duplex
D) simplex
E) partial simplex

3. Which is correctly pairing an intermediary device with the standard layer it operates?
A) hub: layer 2 device
B) switch: layer 3 device
C) bridge: layer 2 device
D) router: layer 2 device
E) repeater: layer 2 device

4. What protocol is used to find the MAC address of a computer based on its IP address?
A) HTTP (Hypertext Transfer Protocol)
B) TCP (Transmission Control Protocol)
C) ARP (Address Resolution Protocol)
D) IP (Internet Protocol)
E) CSMA/CD Protocol

5. Which may NOT constitute an advanced router function?
A) Access control list for packet filtering
B) Network address translation between private and public IPs
C) Provision of dynamic IPs to requesting stations using DHCP
D) Intrusion detection and prevention
E) Automatic assignment of an IP address to the router port (interface)

6. Which of these may be adequate naming of a router's WAN port?
A) FastEthernet0/0
B) Console port
C) Auxiliary port
D) Serial0/0
E) Fiber0/1

7. Choose a CORRECT statement about the switch.
A) The switch cannot be assigned an IP address.
B) The switch is also known as a multi-port repeater.
C) The switch port mostly operates in the full-duplex mode.
D) The risk of frame collisions gets higher as the number of hosts attached to a switch increases.
E) CSMA/CD is used to avoid frame collisions when a network is running on switches.

8. Which intermediary device defines the boundary of a broadcast domain?
A) switch
B) repeater
C) hub
D) router
E) modem

9. When switching and routing are compared:
A) Both switching and routing are data link layer concepts.
B) Networks relying on switching can be more vulnerable to a single point of failure than those relying on routing.
C) Both switching and routing are internet layer concepts.
D) Switching is connection-less (no pre-determined delivery path between two hosts), but routing is connection-oriented in forwarding user data.
E) Both switching and routing presume availability of multiple active delivery paths between two hosts.

10. The media access protocol, CSMA/CD, is activated by the host station when it is connected to a _____.
A) switch
B) hub
C) bridge
D) either a switch or a hub
E) router

11. A switch has eight gigabit LAN ports. What aggregate throughput is needed to give the switch 100 percent non-blocking capacity?
A) 6.4 Gbps
B) 8.0 Gbps
C) 8.4 Gbps
D) 4.0 Gbps
E) 3.2 Gbps

12. The screen shot below must be a partial view of_____.
A) a host's ARP table
B) a router's routing table
C) a DNS table
D) a host's routing table
E) a switch's switch table

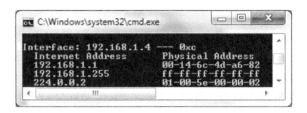

13. Which protocol uses broadcasting?
A) Simple mail transfer protocol (SMTP)
B) Hyper text transfer protocol (HTTP)
C) Transfer control protocol (TCP)
D) Address resolution protocol (ARP)
E) Internet control message protocol (ICMP)

14. The router uses ARP _____.
A) to notify its presence when it becomes active
B) to notify that it will become inactive soon
C) every time it forwards an IP packet to a host (e.g., web server)
D) whenever it has to broadcast an IP packet
E) when it needs to forward an IP packet to another router whose MAC address is not available

15. A switch has eight gigabit LAN ports. What is its *wire speed* and *forwarding rate*? Also, what *aggregate throughput* is needed to give the switch 80 percent non-blocking capacity?
A) 1 Gbps, 8 Gbps, 6.4 Gbps
B) 1 Gbps, 1 Gbps, 8 Gbps
C) 1 Gbps, 16 Gbps, 1.6Gbps
D) 2 Gbps, 16 Gbps, 6.4 Gbps
E) 2 Gbps, 8 Gbps, 8 Gbps

16. Cut-through switching is when:
A) all switch ports use the same wire speed.
B) switch ports have different wire speeds.
C) the switch forwards a frame without waiting for its arrival in its entirety.
D) there is no switch learning or aging.
E) switch ports have different throughputs.

17. The difference between *asymmetric* and *symmetric* switches is judged by _____.
A) accessibility to the operating system
B) available port speeds
C) number of ports
D) expandability of port density
E) operational layers (e.g., layer 2 vs. layer 3)

18. The _____ restricts frame delivery between two host stations to a single path?
A) modem
B) switch
C) router
D) layer 3 switch
E) CSU/DSU

19. Imagine a hypothetical network on which a wireless bridge with two ports (say 0 and 1) connects two hubs (Hub A to port 0 and Hub B to port 1). The connectivity of five host computers to the bridge ports is summarized below. Remember that the MAC addresses are in hexadecimal.

End stations	MAC address	Port
1	1100.0000.1111	0
2	1100.0000.2222	0
3	1100.0000.3333	0
4	1100.0000.4444	1
5	1100.0000.5555	1

Which entry in the *Filter* or *Forward* column of the bridge table is CORRECT?

Source MAC address	Destination MAC address	Filter or Forward
1100.0000.1111	1100.0000.2222	A) Forward
1100.0000.1111	1100.0000.4444	B) Filter
1100.0000.5555	1100.0000.4444	C) Forward
1100.0000.3333	FFFF.FFFF.FFFF	D) Filter
1100.0000.2222	1100.0000.4444	E) Forward

20-21: A system administrator issued a command to a network node and it displayed summary information shown below.

Interface	IP address	MAC address
Fa 0/0	192.168.2.10/24	0001.34AB.1234
Fa 0/1	<not set>	0001.3464.A23C
Fa 0/2	<not set>	0001.3486.B18A
Serial 0/0	192.168.5.10/24	0001.3412.B23A
Serial 0/1	<not set>	

20. What kind of network node should it be?
A) router
B) switch
D) bridge
D) hub
E) server

21. Among the highlighted items in the table, which entry must be an INCORRECT one?
A) FastEthernet 0/0
B) 192.168.2.10/24
C) 0001.3464.A23C
D) 0001.3412.B23A
E) Serial 0/1

22. Choose a CORRECT statement about the operating system of an intermediary device.
A) Hubs and repeaters need an OS to function.
B) The switch's OS does not allow modification of its port security.
C) The router's OS is about the same size as Windows or Linux developed for personal computers.
D) The router's OS is generally stored in the non-volatile flash memory.
E) When the router is powered on, the OS stored in its hard disk drive is copied into the RAM.

23. Imagine a 50% non-blocking Ethernet switch with 24 ports, each port with a speed of 100 Mbps. What can be the switch's aggregate throughput?
A) 24 ports
B) 100 Mbps
C) 200 Mbps
D) 1200 Mbps
E) 2400 Mbps

24. How does the layer 3 switch differ from the layer 2 switch?
A) The layer 3 switch has more ports than the layer 2 switch.
B) The layer 3 switch has more throughput than the layer 2 switch.
C) The layer 3 switch has better network management capability than the layer 2 switch.
D) The layer 3 switch port can be either a switch port or a router port.

E) The layer 3 switch port has higher security than the layer 2 switch port.

25. How many collision domains do you see in the figure?
A) 2
B) 3
C) 4
D) 5
E) 6

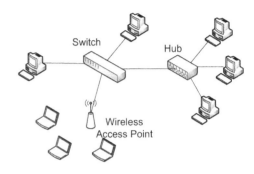

CHAPTER 4   ELEMENTS OF DATA TRANSMISSIONS

4.1   INTRODUCTION

This chapter explains technology elements and their standards necessary to physically propagate data-carrying signals over wired and wireless networks. Technology concepts introduced in this chapter, therefore, belong to the physical layer of the TCP/IP and OSI architectures. Despite that the concepts are highly hardware-driven, they still form fundamental knowledge in understanding computer networking. The objectives of this chapter are to learn:

- Digital and analog signaling
- Signaling devices (modems and CSU/DSU)
- Modulation including frequency and amplitude modulations
- Concepts of bandwidth, baseband, and broadband
- Synchronous transmission vs. asynchronous transmission
- Multiplexing technologies including frequency division and time division multiplexing
- International standards in digital speed hierarchies
- Networking media with focus on twisted pair and optical fiber
- Structured cabling system and its subsystems

4.2   DATA TRANSMISSION ELEMENTS

Data in various formats (e.g., texts, images, audios, videos) are produced by many different sources including computers, people, video cameras, and smart phones. The source data are either digital or analog. As an example of the digital format, text data produced by computer keyboarding is stored as a combination of 0s and 1s. As for the analog format, such source data as human voice, audio, and video take wave shapes that continuously vary rising and falling in intensity with an infinite number of states in the wave.

Regardless of whether the original data are digital or analog, they are represented and processed by the computer or any other digital device (e.g., smart phone) in 1s and 0s. This requires conversion between non-binary data contents and binary bit streams. The term, *data encoding*, represents the translation process from source data (e.g., videos) to their corresponding bit stream and *data decoding* is the reverse process. The data encoding and decoding process is generally the responsibility of application programs (e.g., Skype for VoIP) running in the application layer.

The focus of this chapter is not data encoding and decoding taking place in the application layer, but technical elements in the physical layer necessary to transport computer-produced binary bit streams over the wireless (unguided) or wired (guided) network. The propagation of bit streams over the network can be in digital or analog signals and this requires another conversion process, *signal encoding* (or *signaling*) in the physical layer. You can observe that *encoding* and *decoding* are generic terms referring to any kind of transformation or conversion from one format to another (see Figure 4.1).

Signals produced in the physical layer should be patterned in a way to embed the binary computer data according to standard rules of conversion. Two different approaches are used to convey a bit stream: digital signaling and analog signaling (see Figure 4.1). Here, the signals may be electronic pulses, light pulses, or radio waves that travel over wired (e.g., optical fibers, twisted pairs) or wireless (e.g., earth's atmosphere) media. Methods of converting (or encoding) bit streams into signals are standardized so that hosts and intermediary devices from different manufacturers can generate, transport, and process signals according to the common encoding/decoding rules.

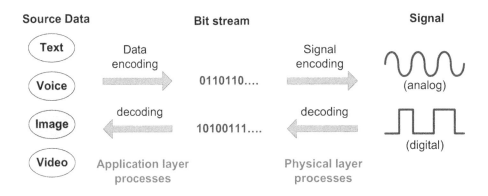

Figure 4.1 Data encoding/decoding vs. signal encoding/decoding

4.2.1   Digital Signaling

Widely used in networking (especially with wired media), digital signaling represents binary bits produced by a computer in two or more discrete signaling *states*. There are two different digital signaling approaches: on/off signaling and voltage signaling (Figure 4.2 and Figure 4.3).

On/off signaling

On/off signaling is mainly used for bit transmissions over optical fibers. With on/off signaling, the light source (e.g., lasers) of the fiber optic system rapidly switches between on and off states to transmit bits according to the exact timing of clocked cycles. A good analogy of the on/off signaling is the practice of turning a flash light on and off for communications between two sailing ships in the ocean.

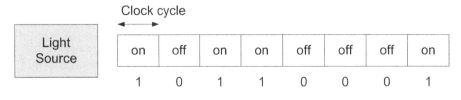

Figure 4.2 On/off digital signaling

Voltage signaling

Voltage signaling is another digital signaling method primarily used by traditional copper wires such as twisted pairs and coaxial cables to transport digitized source data. To represent binary bits, different voltage states that sustain the same signal strength during a clock-cycle are used. At the end of each clock cycle, the voltage state may abruptly change to another state to reflect another bit or bit combination.

Depending on the signaling standard, there may be two voltage states with each state indicating either 0 or 1 (Figure 4.3a). Or, there may be more than two voltage states so that each state represents two or more data bits. For example, Figure 4.3b shows that when there are four voltage states, a state can convey (or encode) two bits of data in one clock cycle because the four states can reflect different combinations of two bits: 00, 01, 10, and 11. In other words, each of the four voltage states can uniquely identify a two bit combination. Several digital signaling standards have been introduced to carry multiple bits with one signal state, making it more effective in transporting bit streams for high-speed networking.

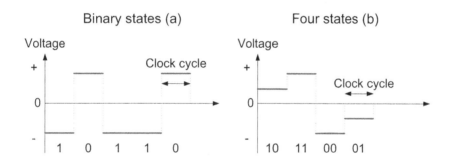

Figure 4.3 Voltage digital signaling

Exercise 4-1: If a signal state of a certain voltage strength is designed to carry 3 bits, how many different voltage states should be there in the signaling system? How about 4 bits or 5 bits?

Often times, the LAN/WAN technology such as Ethernet has its own signaling standards in the physical layer. Select methods of digital signaling are shown in Figure 4.4 for demonstration. As can be seen, the three standards (*NRZ – None Return to Zero*, *Manchester Encoding*, and *Differential Manchester Encoding*) use different rules in converting the same bit stream, resulting in discrepant effectiveness of data transmissions (Their conversion rules are not explained here).

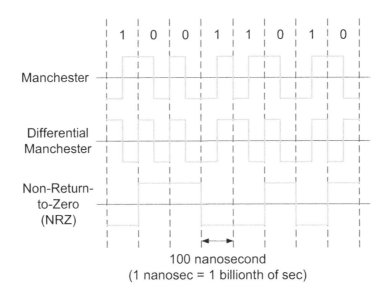

Figure 4.4 Select standards of digital signaling

Challenge Question: In Figure 4.4, can you figure out data conversion rules of the three different signaling methods?

4.2.2 Analog Signaling

Properties of Analog Signal

In analog signaling, the properties of continuously varying electromagnetic waves are used to embed bit stream data. As seen in Figure 4.5, an electromagnetic wave has several key properties: *amplitude, frequency, phase,* and *wavelength*.

- *Amplitude* represented by such metric as *voltage* is an indication of signal strength (the highest point of a wave).

- *Frequency* represents the number of cycles a wave has in every second. When a wave has one cycle per second, its frequency is 1 Hertz (or Hz). Key frequency metrics are summarized in Table 4.1. As an example, the human voice takes a continuous (analog) wave form and has frequency typically ranging between 300 Hz and 3400 Hz. The magnitude of frequency decides a signal's pitch in which higher frequency results in higher pitch.

- *Wavelength* represents distance between two adjacent peaks of a wave. Wavelength is inversely proportional to frequency: the higher the frequency, the smaller the wavelength. Depending on the frequency of an analog signal, its wavelength varies significantly (e.g., the size of a football field or of a molecule).

112

Unit of frequency	No. of cycles/second
hertz (Hz)	1 cycle
kilohertz (kHz) = 1000 Hz	1000 cycles
megahertz (MHz) = 1000 kHz	1 million cycles
gigahertz (GHz) = 1000 MHz	1 billion cycles
terahertz (THz) = 1000 GHz	1 trillion cycles

Table 4.1 Hierarchy of frequency metrics

- *Phase* represents the relative position of a signal point on a waveform cycle and is measured by an angular degree within the cycle. Figure 4.5 demonstrates 5 different angular degrees or phases (0^0, 90^0, 180^0, 270^0 and 360^0) of the first cycle.

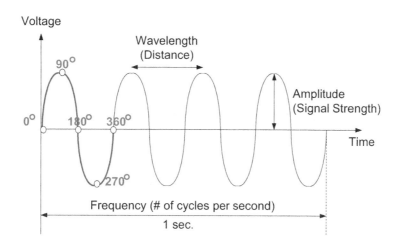

Figure 4.5 Analog signal and parameters

Modulation

In analog signaling, the parameter values of *frequency, amplitude*, and *phase* are varied (sometimes alone and other times in combination depending on the standard signaling method) to encode digital data. The process of altering analog signal characteristics to codify source bit data is called modulation. When the frequency, amplitude, or phase attributes of an analog signal is altered to embed bit stream data, it is called *frequency modulation, amplitude modulation*, or *phase modulation* respectively. There are also modulation techniques available when source data are analog (e.g., AM radio broadcasting, FM radio music), resulting in *analog data-to-analog signal* conversion. But, our main interest is the transportation of digital bit streams produced by computers and other digital devices, and therefore the coverage focuses on the modulation of digital bit streams to analog signals.

As an example, Figure 4.6 demonstrates amplitude modulation and frequency modulation. With amplitude modulation in Figure 4.6a, different amplitudes of an analog signal are used to differentiate source values of 0s (e.g., low amplitude) and 1s (e.g., high amplitude). You can observe that the frequency remains the same and only the amplitude changes reflecting source bits. With frequency modulation, different signal frequencies are applied to represent 0s and 1s. In Figure 4.6b, for example, 0s and 1s can be indicated by a low (e.g., 4000Hz) frequency and a high (e.g., 8000Hz) frequency respectively. Recall that each bit interval is precisely controlled by the clock cycle of a network node.

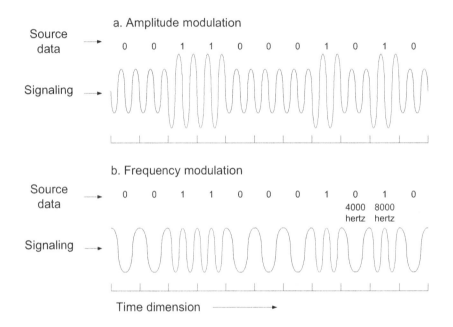

Figure 4.6 Amplitude modulation and frequency modulation

4.2.3 Signaling Devices

The main question in this section is what devices conduct such digital and analog signal encoding and decoding to move application-layer data over the network. Wired LANs, including the dominant Ethernet, primarily take advantage of digital signaling these days. The network interface card (or LAN card) of host stations and intermediary devices is responsible for the production and transmission of digital signals such as those in Figure 4.4. Meanwhile, WiFi that depends on radio waves uses analog signaling.

Just as with LANs, wide area network (WAN) connections also use both digital (e.g., T-1 lines) and analog (e.g., satellite links) signaling to transport bit stream data. There are two different device types that enable WAN signaling: CSU/DSUs *(Channel Service Unit/Data Service Units)* for digital signaling and Modems *(Modulator demodulators)* for analog signaling.

Modem and Analog Signaling

Dial-up, DSL *(Digital Subscriber Line)*, and Cable services enable an individual/business client to access the carrier's private WAN platform or the Internet over the local access line (e.g., telephone or cable lines). With relatively higher speeds than the conventional dial-up connection, DSL and Cable links are considered *broadband access service*. In the US, the Federal Communications Commission (FCC), which regulates interstate and international telecommunications, officially recognizes 4Mbps down and 1Mbps up as broadband speeds. With the continuous upgrade in network infrastructure, however, FCC may raise the threshold of a broadband service to 25Mbps down and 3Mbps up.

Here, the responsibility of dial-up, DSL, and Cable modems is to conduct necessary translations between digital and analog signals. The modem uses such technology as amplitude or frequency modulation to convert a computer's digital signals to analog signals necessary for transmissions.

(a) **Dial-Up Modem:** The dial-up modem takes advantage of the traditional telephone infrastructure (called *Public Switched Telephone Network* or PSTN) to transport computer-produced data. The computer's NIC port releases digital signals and they are converted to analog signals by the dial-up modem for transmissions through the phone line's voice channel in the frequency range of 0-4000 Hz (Figure 4.7). This conversion is necessary because the carrier's (e.g., AT&T) traditional PSTN infrastructure processes only analog signals of that frequency range coming from the local telephone line.

Once computer data transported through the voice frequency channel (0-4000 Hz) of the phone line arrives at a carrier's switching office, they are directed to the Internet instead of the PSTN backbone. Using analog signaling through the limited voice frequency range (0-4000 Hz) restricts the maximum speed of the dial-up connection to 64kbps (DS0 speed), unless other measure including data compression is used to boost the transmission speed.

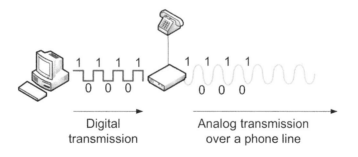

Figure 4.7 Data transmissions with a dial-up modem

(b) **DSL and Cable Modems:** Unlike the dial-up modem that utilizes a single voice channel (0-4000 Hz) to transport both voice and data (thus allowing either voice or data service at a time), DSL takes advantage of separate voice and data channels occupying different frequency ranges of the phone line. This approach eliminates the need of channel sharing by voice and data traffic, and thus affords simultaneous access to the telephone line and the Internet. Furthermore, there are two separate data channels for simultaneous flows of upstream and downstream traffic. *DSL modems* generally take advantage of analog signaling (see Figure 4.9b) to transport digital source data as well as telephone calls, making the naming somewhat confusing to readers.

There are several variants of DSL and they are largely divided into two groups: symmetric (SDSL) and asymmetric (ADSL). Unlike SDSL that offers the same channel speed in both upstream and downstream channels, ADSL has a downstream channel capacity larger than that of upstream allowing faster downloading of files from the Internet (see Figure 4.12). Similar technical approaches apply to Cable service in which the cable capacity (or bandwidth) is divided into several frequency channels to transport voice, Internet traffic (data), and cable TV concurrently.

CSU/DSU and Digital Signaling

Unlike the modem that provides compatibility between digital and analog signals at the physical layer, the *CSU/DSU* (Channel Service Unit/Data Service Unit) converts a digital signal generated by the customer premise equipment (e.g., routers) to another digital signal format required by the WAN/Internet access link. Therefore, unlike dial-up and DSL modems that connect to an analog circuit (i.e., traditional telephone line), the CSU/DSU is used when the access link runs a digital circuit such as T-1 or T-3 line.

Figure 4.8 demonstrates a situation in which the CSU/DSU translates the digital signal coming from the border router's WAN port to another digital signal format required by the T-1 access line. The CSU/DSU comes with different standard ports such as V.35. Many routers' *WAN interface card* (WIC) has a built-in CSU/DSU and thus these routers do not need a separate external CSU/DSU for WAN connectivity.

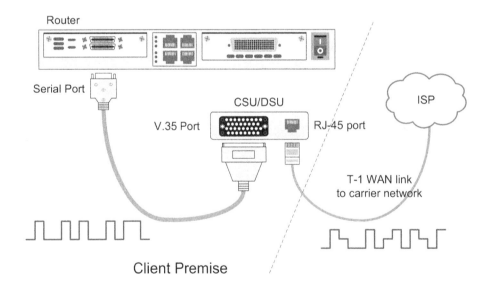

Figure 4.8 External CSU/DSU

[Video Tour 4-1] More about CSU/DSU

Table 4.2 summarizes this section's explanation on source data types, signaling methods, select standard conversion methods, and popular devices that perform the conversion.

Input	Output	Select conversion Standards	Conversion devices
Digital signal	Digital signal	• Manchester • Differential Manchester • Non-Return-to-Zero	CSU/DSU
Digital signal	Analog signal	• Amplitude Modulation • Frequency Modulation • Phase Modulation	Dial-up, DSL, and Cable modems

Table 4.2 Signaling and conversion devices

4.2.4   Bandwidth and Related Concepts

Bandwidth

In its technical definition, bandwidth represents the frequency range *between the highest and the lowest frequencies supported by a channel or a medium*. Wired (or guided) and wireless (or unguided) media including copper wires, optical fibers, and radio waves have their frequency ranges. For example, if the frequency of a radio channel ranges between 30 kHz and 300 kHz, its bandwidth becomes 300 kHz – 30 kHz = 270 kHz. As another example, given that human voice generally ranges 300 Hz through 3400 Hz, its bandwidth is 3400 Hz -300 Hz = 3100 Hz.

Bandwidth is therefore an analog concept that directly relates to a channel's or medium's frequency range (see Figure 4.5). It is an important concept in computer networking because the digital capacity of a medium or channel is a direct function of its bandwidth - the larger the bandwidth, the bigger the capacity in bits per second (bps). For this reason, industry practitioners have been using bandwidth and digital capacity (or speed) interchangeably. As related, there are significant differences in bandwidth between communication media (e.g., between optical fibers and copper wires) and this explains a large discrepancy in their data rates.

Baseband and Broadband

Baseband and broadband mean digital signaling and analog signaling respectively. With baseband (or digital) transmission, only one digital signal flows at a time using the full bandwidth of a medium to transport data (see Figure 4.9a). Today's wired computer networks generally take advantage of the baseband technology. For example, the early generation of Ethernet with 10Mbps speed relied on Manchester Encoding (see Figure 4.4) to translate a digital bit stream into a digital signal that uses the entire bandwidth of the copper cable. When multiple sources of data are to be combined (or multiplexed) and transported concurrently based on the baseband technology, so-called *Time Division Multiplexing* (TDM) is utilized (see Figure 4.9a for heads up). More details of TDM are explained shortly.

When the broadband (or analog) transmission is utilized, several frequency channels can be created within a cable or a channel of the medium to transport multiple analog signals concurrently through separated frequency ranges (see Figure 4.9b). Frequency channels can carry different data types such as text, voice, and video. Naturally, the wider the bandwidth of a medium or a channel, the more channels or sub-channels can be accommodated allowing concurrent flows of multiple data streams.

Cable TV services, for instance, primarily rely on the broadband technology to feed multiple TV channels along with Internet traffic and telephone calls. Also, DSL that transports both voice (telephone calls) and data (Internet traffic) concurrently is another example of the broadband transmission. When multiple sources of data are pulled together and transported concurrently over the network based on the broadband technology, *Frequency Division Multiplexing* (FDM) is utilized. More details of FDM are to be explained.

To confuse matters further, the term *broadband* is also used to indicate a high speed connection as opposed to *narrowband*. For instance, DSL, Cable, and T-1 are generally considered broadband technologies and, meanwhile, the dial-up connection with its maximum speed of 64 kbps (without using compression) is regarded as a narrowband technology. There is, however, no agreed bandwidth that separates broadband from narrowband although 200 kbps generally becomes a threshold for a broadband service.

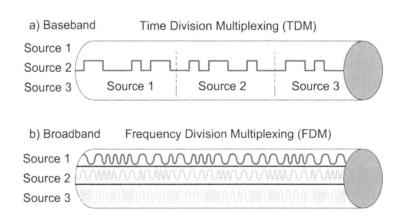

Figure 4.9 Baseband vs. broadband transmissions

4.2.5 Synchronous vs. Asynchronous Transmissions

Asynchronous Transmission

Digital bits can be moved either asynchronously or synchronously. With asynchronous transmission, each character (7 or 8 bits in ASCII) becomes a unit of delivery (Figure 4.10a). Its focus is on safely conveying one alphanumeric character at a time. For this, each character is added by the *start* (indicating the starting point), *stop* (indicating the ending point), and *parity* (for error detection) bits. If a character uses 7 bit ASCII, the delivery of each character takes 10 bits after adding the 3 overhead bits. With the large 30% overhead (3/10 bits), asynchronous transmission is ineffective and its usage in computer networking has been largely limited to low speed circuits such as those connecting a computer to a terminal, keyboard, and modem.

Synchronous Transmission

With synchronous transmission, each message unit is essentially a long string of characters rather than a single character (Figure 4.10b). In Chapter 2, for example, it was explained that there are three different types of the protocol data unit (PDU) (see Figure 2.2). The data link layer PDU (or frame) generally includes the header, data and trailer sections. The maximum size of the data field (also called a payload) and overhead varies depending on the technology standard. The Ethernet frame, for instance, can contain up to 1500 bytes in the data field with the maximum overhead (header and trailer) size of 26 bytes. With synchronous transmission, therefore, a number of data characters are transported in their entirety within a single PDU. Computer networking these days mostly relies on synchronous transmission.

When the PDU with bundled data characters is transported (of course, in the form of digital or analog signal), its delivery becomes more effective than asynchronous transmission. For instance, unlike the 30 percent overhead of asynchronous transmission, the overhead of synchronous transmission becomes much smaller (generally less than 5%) consuming less bandwidth to move the same amount of data. The start, stop, and parity bit functions of asynchronous transmission are also built into each PDU for synchronous transmission. For instance, with the Ethernet frame, these functions are realized through bits included in such fields as *preamble, start frame delimiter* and *frame check sequence* (more details in Chapter 7).

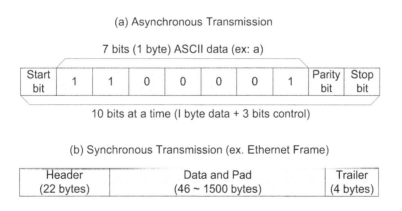

Figure 4.10 Asynchronous vs. synchronous transmissions

Exercise 4-2: Using information in Figure 4.10, compute the Ethernet frame's overhead in terms of percentage and compare it with that of asynchronous transmission. Assume that the Ethernet's data field contains the maximum number of characters possible.

4.2.6   Multiplexing

Multiplexing is another fundamental and important physical layer technology that is heavily used in modern networks. Multiplexing represents the process of combining signals (either analog or digital) from multiple sources to channel them over a single shared line or circuit. When multiple signals are merged and transported over a single line or channel, each signal takes up a portion of the available bandwidth. The multiplexer device performs multiplexing and the de-multiplexer separates combined signals.

Main benefits of multiplexing are:
- It dramatically increases effectiveness in capitalizing network capacity.
- It cuts the number of necessary links or circuits between two points.
- It lowers the cost of networking without sacrificing performance.

Several advanced multiplexing technologies have been developed and many of them are derived from the fundamental technologies of *frequency division multiplexing* (FDM) and *time division multiplexing* (TDM). Although already explained in Figure 4.9 without formally introducing them, FDM and TDM are further elaborated here.

Frequency Division Multiplexing (FDM)

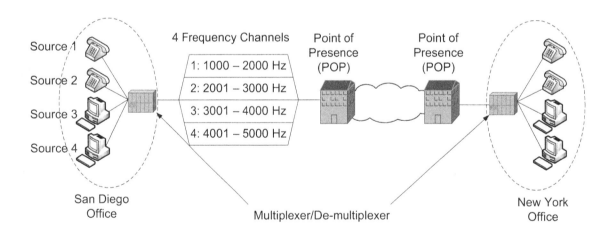

Figure 4.11 Frequency Division Multiplexing

For FDM, the line or channel bandwidth available is divided into several, non-overlapping frequency ranges and a data source (e.g., IP phone, computer) is assigned to one of the available frequency ranges so that multiple data sources share the line or channel capacity for concurrent network access. As the data source takes advantage of a pre-assigned frequency range, analog signaling is used (Remember that frequency is an analog concept). Analog signals from different data sources do not interfere with each other when they occupy different frequency ranges (see Figure 4.9b and Figure 4.11).

FDM Example: ADSL

As an example, ADSL (short for Asymmetric Digital Subscriber Line) as a popular broadband (fast) service creates three non-overlapping channels through a telephone line: one (0 ~ 4kHz) for the traditional *plain old telephone service* (POTS) and the other two channels (around 20kHz ~ 1MHz) for *upstream* and *downstream* data traffic. This multiplexing allows simultaneous flows of voice and data signals over a twisted pair cable (see Figure 4.12). The three separate channels, though, consume a small fraction of the twisted pair's entire bandwidth. For example, category 6 twisted pair cable has the bandwidth of 250MHz (see Table 4.5) and you can observe that the three channels are taking up less than 1 % of the available capacity.

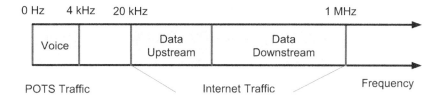

Figure 4.12 Frequency usage with the ADSL modem

With DSL's FDM, both voice traffic and data traffic are transported concurrently between the carrier's *central office* and the customer premise. At the *central office*, the signals are decoupled. Then, voice traffic is forwarded to the traditional *public switched telephone network* while data traffic is channeled to the Internet (Figure 4.13).

As another example of FDM, Cable TV service providers divide the bandwidth of a coaxial cable into at least three different frequency ranges: one for TV channels, one for voice service, and one for Internet access. Clients may subscribe to all three services at a discounted rate or a subset of the three available services.

Time Division Multiplexing (TDM)

TDM uses the entire bandwidth of a line for the transmission of a single digital signal that aggregates data from multiple sources (e.g., phones, computers). For this, inputs from data sources are interwoven one after the other within a frame that is transmitted every certain time interval regulated by the clock speed (see Figure 4.9a, Figure 4.14, and Figure 4.16). The frame, therefore, contains multiple time slots with each slot containing data from a transmitting source. Here, the term 'frame' is used to indicate a physical transmission unit produced when digital data from multiple data sources are combined (or multiplexed). This assemblage process is literally a mechanical procedure. For this reason, the frame produced by a multiplexer (a layer 1 device) is fundamentally different from the frame constructed in the data link layer by a LAN/WAN standard such as Ethernet. Once the physical layer frame is assembled, it is directly injected into the network for transmission, making multiplexing a physical layer technology.

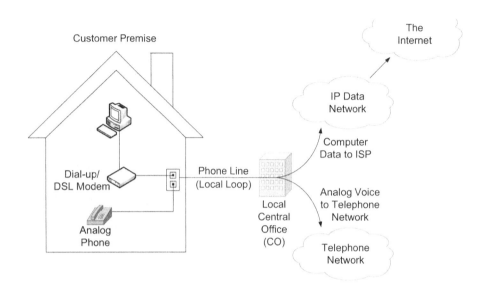

Figure 4.13 Internet connection with DSL

Two different approaches are used in utilizing available time slots of a frame: *synchronous TDM* and *statistical TDM*. With synchronous TDM, each data source is assigned a dedicated time slot of the frame. If there is no incoming data assigned to a particular time slot, the frame is released leaving the time slot empty. The number of data sources, therefore, equals the number of time slots in the frame. Figure 4.14 demonstrates synchronous TDM in which each frame carries data from four different sources in every clock cycle of the multiplexer. With the dedication of a time slot (therefore network bandwidth) to a data source, synchronous TDM does not result in transmission delays.

Statistical TDM (see Figure 4.15) is designed for more effective utilization of frame capacity. To that end, available time slots of the frame are dynamically allocated to incoming traffic on a first-come-first-served basis. Without committing a particular time slot to a particular source, Statistical TDM can serve more data sources than the number of available time slots because chances are that not all sources release data simultaneously. That way, Statistical TDM increases occupancy of available time slots. However, you can also observe that if more sources than available time slots transmit data at the same time, delay becomes inevitable.

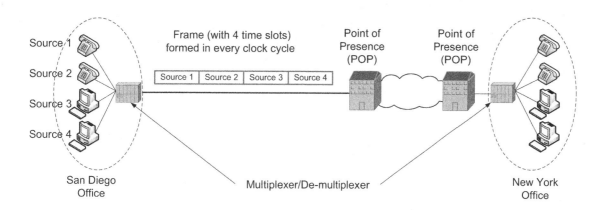

Figure 4.14 Synchronous Time Division Multiplexing

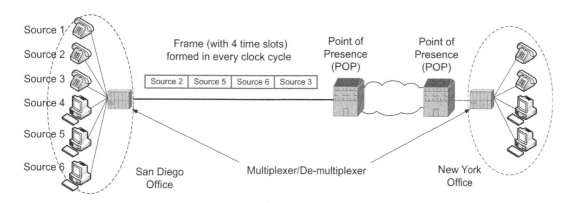

Figure 4.15 Statistical Time Division Multiplexing

TDM Example: T-1 Line

T-1 offered on the twisted pair or optical fiber is a popular service that connects a local network to the Internet or to other remote locations (e.g., branch offices) geographically dispersed. Using digital signaling, it achieves the data rate of 1.54Mbps and can convey both voice and data traffic. T-1 uses the physical layer *frame*, a discrete unit of bit stream produced in every clock cycle by bundling bits from several data sources.

Let's look into the details of how TDM is performed by the T-1 multiplexer. Each T-1 physical layer frame has 24 time slots (for 24 different voice and/or data sources) in which each slot can carry 8 bits (or 1 byte). As there are 24 slots in each frame, the size of a frame becomes 193 bits (24 x 8 bits/slot = 192 bits +1 bit overhead = 193 bits). The T-1 multiplexer quickly scans data sources in every clock cycle to fill up the time slots and the completed frame is dispatched. If a particular data source does not produce bits, its assigned time slot remains empty. With T-1, 8000 frames are produced per second, effectively reaching the speed of 193 x 8000 = 1.54 Mbps. Alternatively, the T-1 capacity may be used for data transmission only using its entire bandwidth of 1.54Mbps as a single channel without having time slots.

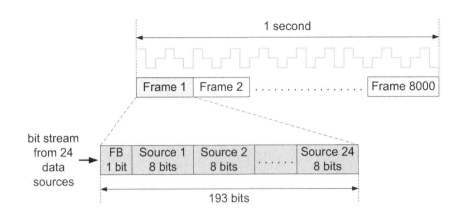

Figure 4.16 Time Division Multiplexing with T-1

Exercise 4-3

1. What is the data rate of each source (e.g., computer, IP phone) assigned to a time slot in Figure 4.16?
2. Given that 8000 frames are produced per second, what is the time interval of each frame produced in Figure 4.16?

Spread Spectrum

A more advanced and complex form of multiplexing, called *spread spectrum*, is heavily used for today's wireless networking including WiFi and cellular-phone networks. There are several spread spectrum standards including *Orthogonal Frequency Division Multiplexing* (OFDM), a type of frequency division multiplexing. Although their technical details are beyond the scope of this book, *spread spectrum* offers faster data rates than traditional Time Division or Frequency Division Multiplexing techniques. Popular WiFi standards including 802.11g and 802.11n rely on OFDM.

4.2.7 Digital Speed Hierarchies

Multiplexing by multiplexers (e.g., T-1 multiplexer) is conducted according to a standard hierarchy of digital speeds. *Digital Signal* (DS) and *Optical Carrier* (OC)/*Synchronous Transport Module* (STM) provide two different digital speed hierarchies. DS was introduced when cabling options for the computer network were mainly copper wires such as twisted pairs and coaxial cables. The OC/STM hierarchy specifies a set of channel speeds on fiber optic networks.

Digital Signal (DS)

DS0 at 64Kbps is the base speed of the Digital Speed (DS) hierarchy. 64Kbps represents the digital data rate produced when a single voice call (that is analog) is digitized by the standard conversion method called *Pulse Code Modulation* (PCM). Then, the capacity of higher-level digital channels is, therefore, decided by the multiples of DS0 (64kbps). For example, DS1 combines (or multiplexes) 24 DS0 channels achieving the data rate of 1.54 Mbps. You should be able to relate why the T-1 line is designed to provide DS1 data rate and supports up to 24 channels of 64kbps. DS speeds, therefore, represent the number of digitized phone calls (equivalent to DS0) that can be transported simultaneously. Table 4.3 summarizes the hierarchy levels, their corresponding speeds, and the number of voice channels supported.

Digital Signal (DS) hierarchy	Digital data rate	# of voice channels
DS0	64 kbps	1
DS1	1.54 Mbps	24
DS1C	3.15 Mbps	48
DS2	6.31 Mbps	96
DS3	44.74 Mbps	672
DS4	274.17 Mbps	4032

Table 4.3 Digital Signal (DS) hierarchy

Optical Carrier/Synchronous Transport Module

The digital speed hierarchies of *Optical Carrier* (OC) (as the North America standard) and *Synchronous Transport Module* (STM) (as the ITU-T international standard) define various channel speeds on the fiber optic network. With the huge bandwidth of an optical fiber, the base speed of the OC hierarchy starts at 51.84 Mbps (OC1) and higher OC levels are the multiples of OC1. For example, OC12 is about 622 Mbps (12 channels of 51.8 Mbps). For STM, the base (STM1) speed is equivalent to 3 OC1s (about 156 Mbps) and higher level STMs are multiples of STM1. You can observe that, although OC and STM are two different standards, there is correspondence between their hierarchy levels (see Table 4.4). Also, there is contiguity from the DS hierarchy to the OC/STM hierarchies. For instance, the OC1 data rate is the result of multiplexing 28 DS1 channels.

Select OC/STM Levels	Digital Speed	Note (OC vs. DS)
OC1	51.84 Mbps	28 DS1(1.54Mbps)
OC3 / STM1	155.52 Mbps	3 OC1s / 84 DS1s
OC12 / STM4	622.08 Mbps	4 OC3s / 336 DS1s
OC48 / STM16	2.48 Gbps	16 OC3s / 1344 DS1s
OC192 / STM64	9.95 Gbps	64 OC3s / 5376 DS1s

Table 4.4 OC/STM hierarchy – select speeds

4.3   NETWORKING MEDIA

Copper wires (twisted pairs and coaxial cables), *optical fibers*, and the earth's *atmosphere* (for wireless networking) are dominant media types these days. This section covers two most important media for wired (or guided) networking: twisted pairs and optical fibers. As explained, all details about networking media such as their physical properties, signal and transmission characteristics, and interfaces/ports and connectors are standardized at the physical layer.

These networking media differ in many ways including:
- Transmission characteristics including
  - Susceptibility to noise and interference
  - Signal propagation effects including signal attenuation and distortion
  - Bandwidth supported
- Physical properties (e.g., size, flexibility, number of wires, ease of installation)
- Cost of purchase, setup, maintenance, and operation
- Security of data in transition

With their varying characteristics, each medium has its right place when it comes to the design and deployment of a network.

4.3.1   Propagation Effects

All media have propagation effects especially in the form of signal *attenuation* and *distortion*.

Attenuation

Attenuation means that the strength or intensity of a signal (e.g., electronic currents, lights, radios) traveling through the media gets weaker as it progresses, and the rate of attenuation differs depending on the medium type. The light signal propagating through the optical fiber has the lowest attenuation rate. It can propagate a few miles without restoring its shape and strength. The electrical signal moving through the copper wire has much faster attenuation than the optical fiber's light signal. As a result, the effective distance of twisted pair cabling between two network nodes, generally up to 100 meters, is considerably shorter than that of the optical fiber. Wireless communication, meanwhile, has the steepest signal attenuation compared to guided or wired media.

Distortion

Distortion refers to the fact that a signal's original shape cannot be maintained when it propagates because of several reasons, including signal attenuation, added noise, and transmission interferences. The longer a signal travels, the more distortion takes place. If there is too much distortion, the receiving node may not recognize the signal pattern or it might misinterpret the meaning embedded, resulting in a transmission error.

In digital signaling where there is only a limited number of signal *states* (e.g., Figure 4.17 has 4 states), the network node can better recognize and reproduce the original signal even if there is a certain degree of distortion and attenuation. In contrast, the reproduction of an analog signal is much more challenging because of difficulties in separating the original signal pattern from any noise added during its propagation. The relative ease of restoring digital signals makes digital transmission a better choice for retaining the integrity and quality of data (e.g., music) being transported.

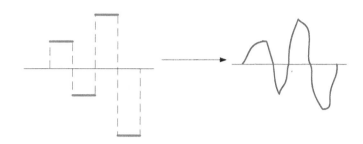

Figure 4.17 Attenuation and distortion effects of digital signaling

4.3.2 Twisted Pairs

UTP vs. STP

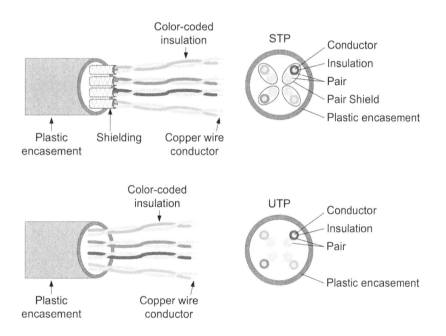

Figure 4.18 STP versus UTP

The twisted pair is an ordinary copper wire that uses electrical currents to encode data. With low cost, high durability, and easy installation, it has become a popular choice for network cabling. Twisted pairs are either unshielded or shielded (Figure 4.18). The *shielded twisted pair* (STP) has an extra metal shield over copper pairs to further protect signals inside from

127

external noise and, thus, can support higher data rates. The STP, however, has not been successful in the marketplace because its advantages over the *unshielded twisted pair* (UTP) generally do not compensate higher cost. The UTP simply satisfies performance requirements of most local networks. Naturally, STP's usage has been limited to atypical situations such as very high speed connectivity (e.g., 10Gbps) and presence of significant noise sources in the installation area.

Cable Structure and Categories

The twisted pair is composed of 8 copper wires with two copper wires twisted around one another to become a pair (see Figure 4.18). Thus, each UTP/STP cable has four twisted pairs inside. The twisting has an effect of canceling out external noise known as *electromagnetic interference* (or EMI). For example, each pair of the *category 5* (or CAT5) UTP cable is twisted 3 times per inch. More twisting results in reduced interference and noise (better protection from EMI), and thus improved signal quality.

Twisted pairs come in different categories including CAT5, CAT5e (CAT5 enhanced), CAT6, CAT6a, CAT7, and CAT7a. Though all copper wires, they differ in such technical properties as the number of twists per foot, copper purity, electrical resistance, bandwidth, and type of insulation. Some categories use UTP while others rely on STP to be able to handle very high data rate in a reliable manner. Given that there are four twisted pairs inside (Figure 4.18), some categories utilize one pair for sending and another pair for receiving, but other categories take advantage of all four pairs (two pairs for each direction) to support faster transmission speeds. Twisted pairs in higher categories offer better quality and support higher bandwidth, and thus are adequate for faster connections (see Table 4.5 and Table 4.7). For instance, although the same twisted pairs, CAT7a has bandwidth 10 times higher than CAT5, making the former ideal for high speed digital transmissions. Twisted pair cabling is prevalent in Ethernet LANs and in the traditional telephone system, especially local access lines.

Categories	Bandwidth (Approx.)
CAT5	100 MHz
CAT5e	100 MHz
CAT6	250 MHz
CAT6a	500 MHz
CAT7	600 MHz
CAT7a	1000 MHz

Table 4.5 Twisted pair categories and supported bandwidth

Twisted-pair Patch Cable

Twisted-pair *patch cables* (or *patch cords*) are used to link network nodes located within a few meters from each other and can be in the *straight-through* or *cross-over* mode.

Figure 4.19 UTP patch cable with RJ-45 connectors

On both ends of the patch cable, 8 wires are connected to 8 pins of the RJ-45 plug in which pin 1 and pin 2 are for transmitting and pin 3 and pin 6 are for receiving. With the straight-through cable, pin 1 and pin 2 of both ends are directly connected and so are the receiving pins 3 and 6. With the direct link of the same pins, the straight-through cable is designed to relay signals from one node to another node. On the other hand, the crossover cable directly connects transmitting pins (1 and 2) of one end to the receiving pins (3 and 6) of the other end and vice versa. Oftentimes, the crossover cable has a red sheath to differentiate it from the straight-through cable that comes in several colors including yellow, blue, and grey.

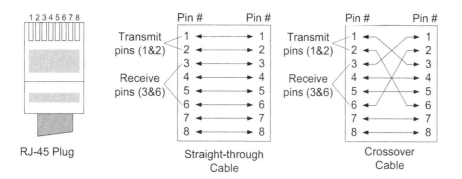

Figure 4.20 RJ-45 connector and pin pairing of a patch cable (10/100 Mbps cable)

Straight-through cables are used to interconnect different node types such as:
- Switch --- Router
- Hosts (clients/servers) ---- Switch
- Wireless access points ---- Router

Connecting two similar devices requires the crossover cable. For example, two computers can exchange data (without intermediary nodes) by directly linking their NICs with the crossover cable. Also, crossover cables are necessary to join:
- Switch --- Switch

129

- Router --- Router
- Host (server) --- Router (yes!)

It may sound somewhat odd that the crossover cable is used for 'host --- router' connectivity. As a matter of fact, they are considered similar devices in the networking field. Although linking a host (mostly server) directly to a router is not a prevalent practice, it certainly is an option. Why are hosts and routers regarded as similar devices? Unlike the switch port that has only a MAC address, both the host's NIC port and the router's LAN port require the pairing (or binding) of IP and MAC addresses to function (see Figure 1.23 and Section 3.6.3).

These days, manufacturers offer intermediary devices whose ports can auto-sense the attached node and the type of cabling, and internally adjust its configuration automatically. This function, called *Medium Dependent Interface Crossover* (MDIX), makes the choice of crossover versus straight-through cable irrelevant and thus reduces the risk of disconnection between network nodes due to cabling mismatch.

~~~~~~

Exercise 4-4: Imagine a hypothetical LAN with various network nodes and UTP connections as in Figure 4.21. Decide the patch cord type (either straight-through or crossover) that should be used for each link. Assume that the nodes do not come with MDIX capability.

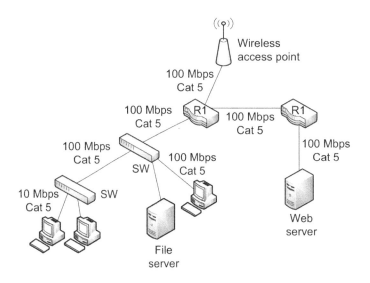

Figure 4.21 A hypothetical LAN

~~~~~~

[Video Tour 4-2] How to make an Ethernet patch cable?

4.3.3 Optical Fibers

The fiber optic cable has emerged as a medium of choice for high speed networking. Over the last two decades, optical fibers have replaced most of the copper lines for WAN and Internet backbone links, dramatically lowering communication costs. Also, fibers are increasingly replacing copper cables for the trunk links of LANs and campus networks.

Unlike twisted pairs and coaxial cables made of copper that transport data in electronic currents, optical fibers take advantage of light pulses to transmit data through the core made of extremely pure glass. The light transmitter device, primarily *laser*, switches on and off rapidly according to a clocked cycle to send digital bits (see Figure 4.2). The signaling method is analogous to turning a flashlight on and off to exchange Morse codes that convey a message; but the laser can do the altering of on and off at an amazing speed, several billions of times per second.

Advantages

The optical fiber enjoys several advantages over the copper wire, and some of them are summarized here:

- Bandwidth: It has huge bandwidth. A single fiber strand can transmit billions of bits per second. If the advanced multiplexing technology called *Dense Wave Division Multiplexing* is applied to inject a number of light signals concurrently into one fiber strand, this can boost its data rate to terabits per second.

- Security: Light signals are more difficult to tap without disrupting them than electrical currents and therefore are ideal for the link that needs heightened security.

- Lower interference: Electrical currents in neighboring copper wires can interfere with each other and wire twisting is used to reduce the interference. But, light signals traveling through multiple fibers do not interfere with each other even when they are bundled, resulting in better quality of data delivered.

- Low attenuation: The fiber optic cable can carry signals much longer than the copper wire before their reproduction becomes necessary due to the propagations effects (e.g., attenuation). According to the IEEE's recommendation, the maximum segment length of the twisted pair between two nodes is generally limited to 100 meters to maintain signal integrity. Meanwhile, the effective segment length of fiber stretches several miles. Telecom service providers place signal repeating/reproduction equipment in every 40 to 60 miles on long haul fiber lines.

- Cost effectiveness: Several miles of fiber can be manufactured more economically than the copper wire of equivalent length. Also, unlike copper wires that rely on high-voltage electrical transmitters, optical fibers can use low-power transmitters because signals degrade much more slowly.

Physical Structure

Physically, the optical fiber has a cylindrical structure composed of three elements: *core, cladding*, and *protective jacket* (Figure 4.22). Core and cladding are mostly made of glass. The core, especially, uses glass with extreme purity to preserve the integrity of the light signals.

Cladding is designed to keep light signals from escaping the glass core, creating the effect of a mirrored tube that reflects lights back into the tube. As a result of the mirroring, lights traveling through the core bounce at shallow angles, staying within the core.

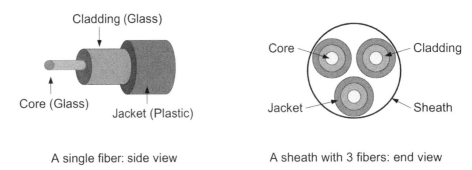

A single fiber: side view   A sheath with 3 fibers: end view

Figure 4.22 General structure of optical fiber (simplified views)

Single-Mode vs. Multi-Mode

The fiber optic cable is either *single-mode* or *multi-mode* (Figure 4.23). The single mode fiber is very thin in its core with a diameter typically less than 10 microns (1 micron is one millionth of a meter). With the narrow core, light signals in the single mode fiber travel in a straight line (therefore only one mode of propagation). The multi-mode fiber has a larger core diameter at around 50/62.5 microns, making it considerably cheaper to produce than the single-mode fiber. With the relatively large diameter, the multi-mode fiber allows light signals to travel through the core in different angles (thus multi-modes in propagation). But this does not mean that the multi-mode fiber has a larger transmission capacity than the single-mode counterpart. Multi-mode and single-mode have nothing to do with data rates, especially in a short range.

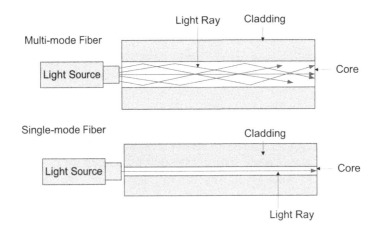

Figure 4.23 Optical fibers: single mode vs. multi-mode

When light pulses from a source travel in different modes through the multi-mode fiber, their arrivals at a destination may not be in sync. This problem of arrival gaps, called *modal dispersion*, gets worse as the travel distance extends further, increasing the chance of transmission errors or miscommunications between communicating nodes. Modal dispersion, thus, restricts the effective segment length of multi-mode fibers substantially shorter than that of single-mode fibers, making the former adequate for LANs but not for WANs. Modal dispersion is not a significant issue for the single mode fiber as there is only one mode in signal propagation. Carriers (e.g., AT&T) deploy WAN and Internet backbone links using the single mode fiber.

[Video Tour 4-3] Splicing fiber optic cable

Table 4.6 compares the single mode and multi-mode fibers.

Comparative dimensions	Multi-mode fiber	Single-mode fiber
Usage for networking	Popular for LAN	Popular for Carrier WAN (LAN standards also available)
Max segment length	200~300 meters	Several kilometers or miles
Cable cost	Significantly lower than single-mode fibers	Significantly higher than multi-mode fibers
Core diameter in micron (one millionth of a meter)	50 ~ 62.5 micron	8 ~ 10 micron
Propagation effect	Higher modal dispersion	Less modal dispersion
Select standards for LAN-cabling	1000BASE-SX 10GBASE-SR	1000BASE-LX 10GBASE-LR

Table 4.6 Multi-mode vs. single-mode fibers

Fiber Patch Cable

To link closely placed network nodes, the full-duplex patch cord with two fiber strands can be used. Different optical fiber connectors have been introduced and Figure 4.24 demonstrates a fiber patch code with a particular connector at each end.

[Video Tour 4-4]   1. Fiber optic patch cable
                        2. How to make a fiber patch cord?

Figure 4.24 Optical fiber patch cord and connectors
(source: tecratools.com)

4.3.4 LAN Cabling Standards

Ethernet is a dominant wired LAN standard and this section explains its standard cabling options defined at the physical layer. Ethernet's three most popular speed standards are Fast Ethernet (100 Mbps), Gigabit Ethernet (1 Gbps), and 10-Gigabit Ethernet (10 Gbps). 100-Gibabit Ethernet has been announced as well. In each of the speed categories, several cabling standards are available for both twisted pairs and optical fibers.

The cabling standards are expressed by combining *rated speed, signaling method* (*baseband* for digital signaling and *broadband* for analog signaling), and *cable type* (twisted pair or optical fiber). For example, as one of the most popular Fast Ethernet options, the 100BASE-TX cabling standard has the following specs:

- 100 means the transmission speed of 100 Mbps.
- BASE means baseband (or digital) signaling.
- TX means the unshielded twisted pair (UTP) that is category 5 (CAT5) or higher

As explained, the twisted pair cable such as CAT5 has 4 pairs inside but uses only two pairs for Fast Ethernet (100 Mbps): one pair for sending and another for receiving data. This results in two remaining pairs unused. Gigabit Ethernet, however, uses all four pairs; each pair operates in the full-duplex mode transmitting at 250Mbps each direction to achieve the aggregate rate of 1Gbps.

Ethernet speed standards	Select physical layer standards	Speed & Cabling	Minimum UTP categories recommended
Fast Ethernet	100BASE-TX	100Mbps/ UTP	CAT5
Fast Ethernet	100BASE-FX	100Mbps/ fiber	
Gigabit Ethernet	1000Base-T	1000Mbps/ UTP	CAT5e/CAT6
Gigabit Ethernet	1000BASE-SX	1000Mbps/ fiber	
10 Gigabit Ethernet	10GBASE-T	10Gbps/ UTP	CAT6a/CAT7
10 Gigabit Ethernet	10GBASE-SR	10Gbps/ fiber	
100 Gigabit Ethernet	100GBASE-SR10	100Gbps/ fiber	

Table 4.7 Ethernet's physical layer standards

In LANs, UTP cabling still dominates access links between host stations and access (or workgroup) switches. However, the optical fiber is popular for trunk links that interconnect core (backbone) and access switches. Several physical layer standards based on the optical fiber have been introduced to support different data rates (e.g., 100 Mbps, 1 Gbps, 10 Gbps, 100 Gbps). Table 4.7 summarizes select Ethernet standards available. You can observe that both UTP and fiber cabling options are available to support various speed options. However, the fiber has become a preferred medium for high speed links.

4.4 STRUCTURED CABLING

4.4.1 Background

With its importance in practice, the *structured cabling* concept is explained in this section. In a nutshell, network cabling undertaken in accordance with published standards is called structured cabling. The published standards specify recommended practices on all aspects of network cabling including cabling types available, effective segment distance of a cable type, connectors, installation requirements, and testing methods of installed cables. For structured cabling, it is important to use nationally and internationally standardized media, connection interfaces, and layout.

As widely adopted, EIA/TIA568 defines a set of standards for planning and implementing structured cabling. EIA/TIA568 standards include:
- 568-B.1: Commercial cabling standards – general requirements
- 568-B.2: Components of the twisted pair cable system
- 568-B.3: Components of the optical fiber cable system

EIA/TIA568 has been superseded by the international standard, ISO/IEC 11801.

By complying with the structured cabling principle, an organization can enjoy several benefits:
- It reduces initial costs of network implementation.
- IT staff can respond quickly and cost-effectively to changing needs of network infrastructure because they face fewer problems in hardware compatibility.
- Network reliability and performance is ensured.
- The network can better support broadband applications in the future.

4.4.2 Structured Cabling System

The *structured cabling system* of a building includes cabling, voice and data network components, and other building system components (e.g., safety alarms, lights, security access, energy systems), implemented according to the standard principles of high-performance structured cabling. The structured cabling system divides the cabling infrastructure of a building into six segments called subsystems:

[1] Work area
[2] Horizontal cabling
[3] Wiring closet (or Intermediate Distribution Facility - IDF)
[4] Backbone cabling
[5] Main equipment room (or Main Distribution Facility - MDF)
[6] Building entrance facility

Figure 4.25 demonstrates a general layout of the six subsystems within a building of three floors. For demonstration, the figure focuses on the data networking side. However, remember that the telephone system including telephones and telephone switches (called private branch exchange or PBX) is also an integral part of the structured cabling system.

[1] **Work area**: The work area subsystem covers structured cabling between wall plates of a room and various end devices attached to them including computers, wireless access points, telephones, and network printers.

[2] **Horizontal cabling**: The horizontal cabling subsystem connects wall plates of a room to the wiring closet. The subsystem is, therefore, pre-installed in the building structure and enables physical connectivity of end devices in the work area to intermediary devices (generally switches) placed in the wiring closet. The popular cabling choice is 100Mbps UTP or optical fiber.

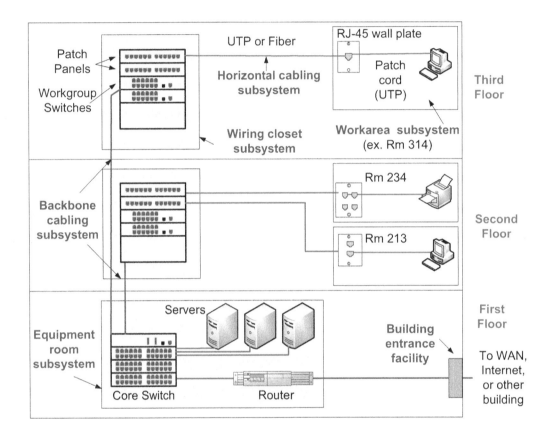

Figure 4.25 Structured cabling system and subsystems

Through horizontal cabling, each room on a floor is cabled to a patch panel installed in the wiring closet. The patch panel comes with many network ports (primarily RJ-45 ports) and enables easy connectivity between a switch of a wiring closet and end stations distributed throughout the floor. Each occupied port of a patch panel is labeled for easy identification of its assigned room. For example, Figure 4.27 demonstrates that the host stations in 3 rooms (i.e., Room1, Room2, and Room 3) are joined by the workgroup switch via the 12 port patch panel. You can observe that patch cords are used to link the patch panel's ports and the switch ports.

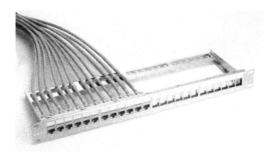

Figure 4.26 A Cat 6 patch panel (source: excel-networking.com)

[Video Tour 4-5] How to punch down a 24 port patch panel?

[3] **Wiring closet**: The wiring closet located on a floor is the cross-connection point of horizontal cabling and backbone cabling that leads to the main equipment room. The wiring closet houses one or more intermediary devices (e.g., workgroup switches) available for host stations in the adjacent work area. There is no limit to the number of wiring closets installed on a building floor and the decision largely rests on the floor plan. The wiring closet houses a rack that mounts intermediary devices such as patch panels, switches, and routers (see Figure 4.29). The rack mounting and concentration of intermediary nodes reduces the length of patch cables that interconnect them and simplifies cable management.

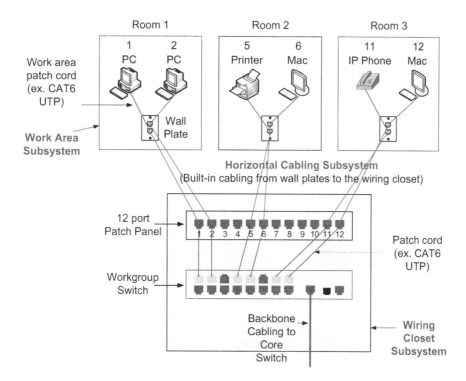

Figure 4.27 Work area, horizontal cabling, and wiring closet subsystems on a floor

137

For a simple demonstration of the structured cabling concept, let me use an EIA/TIA recommendation in coupling the horizontal, work area, and wiring closet subsystems with UTP cabling. The standard suggests that:

- The maximum horizontal distance between a patch panel and wall plates is 90 meters (297 feet).
- Patch cables used in the wiring closet and work area can be up to 6 meters (20 feet) each, but the combined length may not exceed 10 meters (33 feet).
- The overall length between an end node (e.g., computer) in the work area and a switch in the nearby wiring closet may not exceed 100 meters (330 feet), which represents the combined length of 90 meters and 10 meters above. This structured cabling guidance thus reflects the UTP's maximum segment length of 100 meters.

[Video Tour 4-6] Wiring (or telecommunication) closet and patch panel.

[4] **Backbone cabling**: Backbone cabling (or vertical cabling) ties wiring closets, the main equipment room, and the building entrance facility (see Figure 4.25) together. Backbone cabling runs through floors to cross-connect them. As trunk links (not access links), backbone cables require a larger capacity than horizontal cables do because the former transport much data traffic that enters or leaves a building. Also, end stations of a work area depend on the backbone cabling to access servers located outside the work area (e.g., another floor, main equipment room). To accommodate the large bandwidth consumption, backbone cabling primarily relies on optical fibers running Gigabit or 10 Gigabit Ethernet these days.

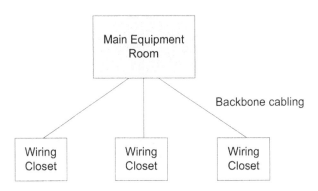

Figure 4.28 Connectivity between wiring closets and main equipment room

Although unclear in Figure 4.25 that shows the general layout of subsystems, backbone cabling takes advantage of the hierarchical topology (see Figure 4.28) to interconnect wiring closets and the main equipment room.

[5] **Main equipment room**: The main equipment room houses routers, telecom devices (e.g., private branch exchanges or PBXs), and core switches that interconnect workgroup switches in wiring closets (see Figure 4.29). The main equipment room is generally located on the first floor of a building (see Figure 4.25) and is the termination point of backbone cabling to which wiring closets are attached. Some firms may choose to place the room on a higher floor out of

138

such concern as flooding. The router in the equipment room becomes a gateway to the WAN or Internet connection outside of the building. If the building belongs to a campus network, the router may connect to other campus facility. Many organizations also choose to house enterprise-level servers in the main equipment room to directly link them to core switches.

[6] **Building entrance facility**: The building entrance facility is a dividing point between external and internal cabling of a building. It becomes a junction point to the campus backbone or a demarcation point that couples the building's internal network with a WAN carrier's or ISP's local link(s). The building entrance facility connects to the equipment room (see Figure 4.25). As a concept similar to the building entrance subsystem, the demarcation point of a house is demonstrated in Figure 9.2.

Figure 4.29 A wiring closet (L) and main equipment room (R)
(sources: tennexcom.com, web.engr.oregonstate.edu)

KEY TERMS

100-Gibabit Ethernet	copper wire	multiplexing (FDM)
10-Gigabit Ethernet	crossover cable	gigabit Ethernet
amplitude	CSU/DSU	horizontal cabling subsystem
analog signaling	decoding	intermediate distribution
asymmetric DSL (ADSL)	demodulation	facility (IDF)
asynchronous transmission	dense wave division	main distribution facility
attenuation	multiplexing	(MDF)
backbone cabling subsystem	digital signal (DS)	medium dependent interface
bandwidth	distortion	crossover (MDIX)
baseband	encoding	modal dispersion
broadband	equipment room subsystem	modem
building entrance subsystem	Fast Ethernet	modulation
central office (CO)	frequency	multi-mode fiber
coaxial cable	frequency division	on/off signaling

optical carrier (OC)
parity bit
patch cable (patch cord)
patch panel
phase
plain old telephone service (POTS)
public switched telephone network (PSTN)
shielded twisted pair (STP)
single-mode fiber

spread spectrum
start bit
statistical time division multiplexing (STDM)
stop bit
straight-through cable
structured cabling
structured cabling system
symmetric DSL (SDSL)
synchronous TDM
synchronous transmission

synchronous transport module (STM)
T-1 line
time division multiplexing (TDM)
unshielded twisted pair (UTP)
voltage signaling
wavelength
wiring closet subsystem
work area subsystem

CHAPTER REVIEW QUESTIONS

1. Choose a FALSE statement regarding the wiring (or telecommunications) closet.
A) It is a connecting point between horizontal cabling and backbone cabling.
B) It houses intermediary devices to connect end stations in the adjacent area.
C) It has one or more patch panels that are normally rack-mounted.
D) It is generally located on the bottom floor of a building.
E) It simplifies cable management within a building.

2. The fiber optic cable uses _____ signaling. (Choose the most specific one.)
A) multiple-level voltage
B) two-level voltage
C) on and off
D) analog
E) electronic

3. Which represents key properties of the analog wave?
A) bandwidth, amplitude, frequency
B) frequency, wavelength, bandwidth
C) wavelength, frequency, amplitude
D) attenuation, amplitude, wavelength
E) attenuation, amplitude, frequency

4. Which signal conversion device is placed between the border router and the T-1 WAN line, if any?
A) codec
B) CSU/DSU
C) switch
D) digital converter
E) modem

5. Which link needs cross-over cabling (assume MDIX not available)?
A) switch – router
B) user PC – switch
C) server – switch
D) wireless access point – router
E) switch – switch

6. DS0 represents the unit speed of a voice-grade channel. Then, its speed must be:
A) 64 kbps
B) 128 kbps
C) 32 kbps
D) 45 kbps
E) 10 kbps

7. Structured cabling is achieved in a building when
A) voice and data communications depend on digital signaling.
B) network nodes are interconnected in the 'star' topology.
C) the trunk links utilize optical fibers.

D) the cabling is designed to integrate voice and data traffic.
E) the cabling is conducted according to published standard practices.

8. The advantage of optical fibers over twisted pairs is NOT:
A) higher bandwidth
B) better security
C) lower interference
D) higher attenuation
E) longer signal propagation

9. The number of twists per foot, copper purity, electrical resistance, and insulation type are properties that determine:
A) the category of a twisted pair.
B) the mode of an optical fiber (single mode vs multi mode).
C) the type of a patch cable.
D) the category of an optical fiber.
E) the type of a twisted pair (cross-over vs. straight-through)

10. Which is INCORRECT about digital speed hierarchies?
A) DS (digital signal) is an international standard.
B) STM (Synchronous Transport Module) is the international standard of digital speed hierarchy for optical fibers.
C) The base speed of DS is 1.54 Mbps and higher speeds are its multiples.
D) OC (optical carrier) is the North American standard for optical fibers.
E) The base speed of OC is 51.84 Mbps and higher speeds are its multiples.

11. When the number of possible voltage states doubles in digital signaling,
A) one more bit can be additionally sent per clock cycle.
B) two more bits can be additionally sent per clock cycle.
C) the effective data rate is increased by 50%.

D) the effective data rate is reduced by 50%.
E) the number of bits sent per clock cycle remains the same.

12. Six components (or subsystems) of the structured cabling system do NOT include
A) main equipment room.
B) backbone (vertical) cabling.
C) telecommunications (or wiring) closet.
D) horizontal cabling.
E) cross-connect cabling.

13. The straight-through cable should be used to connect two nodes EXCEPT:
A) switch --- router
B) PC ---- switch
C) wireless access points ---- router
D) server ---- switch
E) server ---- router

14. The T-1 line combines multiple signals using _____ for their concurrent deliveries.
A) frequency division multiplexing
B) time division multiplexing
C) wavelength division multiplexing
D) dense wave division multiplexing
E) code division multiple access

15. Patch panels are used widely in the _____ to intermediate connections between end stations and switches.
A) building entrance
B) wiring closet
C) backbone cabling area
D) work area
E) switch room area

16. The access (or workgroup) switch is generally placed in the _____.
A) wiring closet subsystem
B) work area subsystem
C) horizontal cabling subsystem
D) backbone cabling subsystem
E) equipment room subsystem

17. When multi-mode and single-mode fibers are compared:
A) Multi-mode supports full-duplex transmissions, but single-mode does not.
B) Multi-mode is more reliable than single-mode in maintaining signal integrity.
C) Single-mode is easier to multiplex than multi-mode.
D) Multi-mode is adequate for LANs and campus network, but not for WANs.
E) Multi-mode has higher capacity than single-mode.

18. Choose a CORRECT statement in comparing baseband and broadband transmissions.
A) Baseband allows the flow of only a single data type (e.g., texts) at a time.
B) Baseband is slower than broadband.
C) Wired computer networks (e.g., Ethernet) primarily rely on broadband transmissions.
D) With baseband, several frequency channels can be created within a cable.
E) Using broadband, analog signals can travel through a cable concurrently.

19. The _____ is used to make a physical connection between two closely placed network nodes.
A) parallel cord
B) patch cord
C) conversion cord
D) horizontal cord
E) vertical cord

20. When light signals travel in different modes (angles) through the fiber optic cable, they may not reach the destination in exact time interval, this is _____.
A) multimode transmission
B) propagation conversion
C) modal bandwidth
D) modal dispersion
E) optical interference

21. Modulation is used when
A) a node produces text data/signal and the delivery channel relies on analog signaling.
B) a node produces sound data/signal and the delivery channel relies on digital signaling.
C) a node produces digital data/signal and the delivery channel relies on analog signaling.
D) a node produces digital data/signal and the delivery channel relies on digital signaling.
E) a node produces digital or analog data/signal and the delivery channel relies on digital signaling.

22. The main equipment room subsystem
A) is a demarcation point between the internal network and an ISP network.
B) is typically located on the top floor of a building.
C) houses workgroup switches that directly connect user stations.
D) is the termination point of backbone cabling.
E) is the ending point of horizontal cabling.

23. The transmission power of a signal weakens as it progresses. This is called _____.
A) attenuation
B) distortion
C) interference
D) withdrawal
E) dispersion

24. Which is CORRECT regarding the fiber optic cable?
A) The cable's properties are defined at the data link layer.
B) The cable does not require repeaters to boost signal strength.
C) Carriers normally use multi-mode fibers to develop their backbone infrastructure.
D) It uses light signals to move data.

E) It is the most popular medium for the access link that connects a host to a switch.

25. The following figure shows the process of _____ in data transmissions?
A) frequency division multiplexing
B) amplitude modulation
C) frequency modulation
D) statistical time division multiplexing
E) time division multiplexing

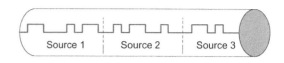

CHAPTER 5   IP ADDRESS PLANNING AND MANAGEMENT

5.1   INTRODUCTION

This chapter is designed to cover the fundamentals of IP addressing based on the IPv4 standard. Understanding IP addressing is crucial for the IT specialist to manage a network. The task of allocating IP addresses to network segments and nodes can be done relatively easily by depending on a software tool these days. Having relevant knowledge, however, is very important for effective planning, management, and upgrade of network infrastructure at an organization.

It was previously stated that the IPv4 standard uses a 32-bit address (e.g., 10000000.00000010.00000111.00001001) to uniquely identify a network node. Due to the lengthy nature of binary bits, we use the dotted decimal format (ex 129.131.12.10) in which one decimal value reflects an 8 bit combination. With the 32 bit structure, the entire address space of IPv4 ranges between 0.0.0.0 (all 0s in binary) and 255.255.255.255 (all 1s in binary).

With only 32 bits, however, IPv4 is unable to create enough address space to accommodate growing global demands, especially due to the rapid addition of mobile devices to the Internet. Already *Internet Assigned Numbers Authority* (IANA) that oversees the global allocation of IP address space announced in 2011 that its own IPv4 space was fully consumed. Nonetheless, IPv4 addressing still dominates corporate networks and the Internet, and will continue to do so for a while. IPv4 becomes the focus of this chapter and IPv6 as the next generation IP standard is explained in Chapter 10.

The objectives of this chapter are to learn:
- IP governance: who allocates IP space by what mechanism?
- The general structure of the 32 bit IP address
- Classful IP allocation scheme
- Classless IP allocation scheme
- IP address ranges assigned for special purposes
- IP subnetting
- Subnet mask
- IP supernetting
- Management of IP address space at an organization

5.2   GOVERNANCE OF IP ADDRESS SPACE

The IP address is composed of network identification (or network address) and host identification (or host address) parts. The network identification indicates a particular organization (e.g., firm, college, ISP). The host identification is assigned to a network node. Network addresses are allocated in a delegated manner by *Internet Assigned Numbers Authority* (IANA) (http://www.iana.org/). Being responsible for global coordination of IP space, IANA delegates available network address space to *Regional Internet Registries* (RIRs). There are currently five RIRs in the world:

- AfriNIC for the Africa region   (http://www.afrinic.net/)
- ARIN for North America   (https://www.arin.net/)
- APNIC for the Asia Pacific Region   (http://www.apnic.net/)
- LACNIC for Latin America   (http://www.lacnic.net/en/)
- RIPE NCC for Europe, the Middle East and Central Asia   (http://www.ripe.net/)

In the past, the request for an IP address block was directly submitted to a registry by a client organization. Once obtained, the organization retained the ownership of the granted IP block pretty much permanently. All that has changed and now Internet Service Providers (ISPs) play a central role in the management of IP address space and its allocation to requesting organizations. For this, large ISPs (e.g., AT&T) obtain IP blocks from Regional Internet Registries and divide them into smaller chunks for allocation to clients (e.g., small ISPs, business firms, schools). Individuals and small businesses, meanwhile, obtain a network address from their ISPs. Figure 5.1 demonstrates the top-down delegation of IP space. In the RIR website such as *http://ws.arin.net/*, you can find the ownership of a particular network address.

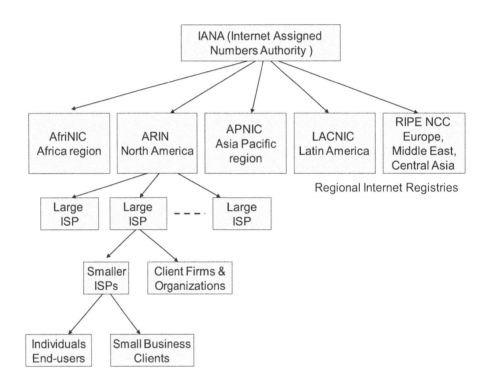

Figure 5.1 Delegation of IP address space

5.3 STRUCTURE OF THE IP ADDRESS

5.3.1 Binary vs. Decimal Value Conversion

IP addressing is a challenging concept and, above all, one should be comfortable with the relationship between binary and decimal values. So let's start with a brief review of the binary – decimal value conversion covered in Chapter 1. Table 5.1 enables quick mapping between them and thus becomes handy when you delve into the task of IP address planning and allocation.

Binary position (8 bits)	8th	7th	6th	5th	4th	3rd	2nd	1st
Decimal place values	128	64	32	16	8	4	2	1
Cumulative decimal values (Cumulate from left to right)	128	192	224	240	248	252	254	255

Table 5.1 Binary vs. decimal value conversion table

~~~~~~

Review Exercise 5-1: Make necessary translations between binary and decimal IP addresses.

IP Address	Binary or decimal correspondence
101.150.11.51	
156.230.15.251	
22.131.49.31	
223.100.31.76	
11001010.10001010.00110110.11110000	
10010010.11001101.10111110.00000011	
11001000.00011000.11101011.10101010	
10100000.01111000.11000001.00110011	

~~~~~~

5.3.2 Structure of the IP Address

As stated, an IP address is composed of at least two parts: network ID (or network address) and host ID (or host address) parts (Figure 5.2). In this chapter, the term *network* is used as an identifier of an organization (e.g., company, university). For instance, if an organization's network ID is *195.112.36.x* with *x* being any value for a host ID, the network address can also be expressed as *195.112.36.0.* It becomes obvious that, as more bits are allocated for the network ID, fewer bits are available for the host ID.

Generally, an enterprise network is broken into smaller segments of subnetworks (or shortly subnets) as explained in previous chapters. Subnets can be created according to physical (e.g., locations, buildings, floors) and/or logical (e.g., departments or workgroups of a business, colleges of a university) boundaries of an organization. The segmentation of a network into subnets requires that each subnet be uniquely identified. The network ID cannot be changed as it represents an organization's official public address. Then, the only available option to create subnets is to split the host ID field into two parts: one for the host ID and the other for the subnet ID. Often times, this division is considered *borrowing* bits from the host ID field to create subnet IDs (see Figure 5.2). The creation of subnets adds further hierarchy to the structure of an IP address. More details of subnet creation are explained later.

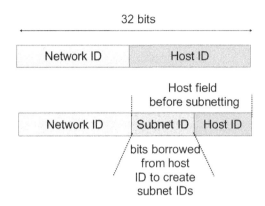

Figure 5.2 IPv4 address (without and with subnet ID)

5.4 CLASSFUL IP – LEGACY

The network ID can be assigned under the classful or classless scheme. This section briefly explains the classful allocation of IP space that was adopted in the early days of the Internet, but is defunct now due to its inefficiency. Despite, having a general idea is useful because classful network IDs are still owned by many organizations, sometimes traded between firms for financial gains. Also, protocols (e.g., routing protocol) designed for the classful IP scheme are still out there. For that reason, the classful IP scheme is briefly explained in this section.

Under the classful scheme, the network ID allocated to an organization (e.g., business, university) belongs to one of *class A* (8-bit network ID), *class B* (16-bit network ID), or *class C* (24-bit network ID) types.

5.4.1 Class A Network

In the early days, very large firms were given a *class A* network status in which the first octet (8 bits) out of 32 bits becomes a network ID and the remaining 3 octets (24 bits) constitute a host ID. The network ID cannot be changed as it becomes a unique identification of an organization in the Internet. When a company is given a class A network status, it can create about 16.7 million unique host IDs using the remaining 24 bits (2^{24} =16.7 million). No company or non-profit organization in the world should need 16.7 million IP addresses to run its network, subsequently resulting in much waste of IP space. This fact alone highlights how ineffective the classful IP system was.

With the class A network, the first bit of 8 bit network ID is fixed at *0* and the next 7 bits uniquely determine a particular organization. It means that the first 8 bits of a class A network fall anywhere between 00000001 and 01111110 (00000000 and 01111111 are reserved for special occasions).

When the 24 host ID bits are added to the first 8 bits, this results in 32-bit address space ranging:
00000001.00000000.00000000.00000000 ~ 01111110.11111111.11111111.11111111.

148

The binary range is equivalent to the decimal range of:
$$1.0.0.0 \sim 126.255.255.255.$$
According to this allocation system, only 126 firms (1 through 126) in the world can belong to the class A network. If an organization owns the class A network ID of 125, for instance, the 32-bit IP addresses available for its network ranges 125.0.0.0 through 125.255.255.255.

5.4.2 Class B Network

The Class B network was assigned to large public/private organizations including business firms and universities. It uses the first 16 bits for the network ID and the remaining 16 bits for the host ID. With a 16-bit host ID, the class B network can create up to 2^{16} (about 65500) host addresses. The first two bits of a class B network ID starts with *10* and therefore the next 14 bits represent the unique network ID of an organization. In binary, therefore, the first 16 bits of a class B network fall anywhere between 10000000.00000000 and 10111111.11111111 (or 128.0 $\sim$ 191.255 in decimal).

When 16 host ID bits are added to the first 16 network ID bits, this results in the 32-bit address range of class B networks:
$$10000000.00000000.00000000.00000000 \sim 10111111.11111111.11111111.11111111.$$
This translates into the decimal range of:
$$128.0.0.0 \sim 191.255.255.255.$$
If an organization belongs to a class B network ID of 130.191, for instance, the 32 bit IP addresses that can be assigned within the network ranges 130.191.0.0 through 130.191.255.255.

5.4.3 Class C Network

Class C network IDs were intended for small or mid-sized public/private organizations. The Class C network uses the first 24 bits for a network ID and the remaining 8 bits for a host ID. The Class C network starts with *110* bits, followed by 21 bits (total 24 bits) as a unique identifier of an organization. 8 bit host ID limits the total number of hosts within a network to $2^8 = 256$ (Strictly speaking, 256 - 2 =254 hosts to exclude all 0s and 1s for special usage). The first 24 bits of a class C network, therefore, should fall anywhere between
$$11000000.00000000.00000000 \text{ and } 11011111.11111111.11111111.$$

When 8 host ID bits are added to the first 24 network ID bits, this results in 32-bit address space ranging:
$$11000000.00000000.00000000.00000000 \sim 11011111.11111111.11111111.11111111$$
The binary range is equivalent to the decimal value range of:
$$192.0.0.0 \sim 223.255.255.255.$$

If an organization has a class C network ID of 192.10.10.x, for instance, IP addresses that can be assigned within the network ranges 192.10.10.0 through 192.10.10.255.

There are also *class D* and *class E* IP ranges that were introduced for special occasions such as multicasting. Table 5.2 summarizes classful IP ranges. You can observe that the possible number of nodes with an IP address at an organization is $2^n - 2$, where n = number of host bits. The two (all 1s and all 0s) are excluded from counting as they are for special occasions such as packet broadcasting.

Class	Initial bit(s)	Network ID	Host ID	Possible number of nodes	IP address range
A	0..........	8 bits	24 bits	2^{24}-2 = about 16.7 million	0.0.0.0 ~ 127.255.255.255
B	10........	16 bits	16 bits	2^{16}-2 = 65,534	128.0.0.0 ~ 191.255.255.255
C	110.......	24 bits	8 bits	2^8-2 = 254	192.0.0.0 ~ 223.255.255.255
D (Multicast)	1110.....	N/A	N/A	N/A	224.0.0.0 ~ 239.255.255.255
E (Reserved)	1111.....	N/A	N/A	N/A	240.0.0.0 ~ 255.255.255.255

Table 5.2 Classful allocation of IP space

Many businesses and universities still own the IP space allocated according to the classful scheme. As an example: San Diego State University owns two network IDs belonging to this class (use *www.arin.net* for IP address search): 130.191.0.0 and 146.244.0.0

The classful IP system was designed when nobody expected such a spectacular growth of the Internet and it turned out to be too wasteful of available IP space. For example, there was a report that less than 5 % of classful IP space allocated has been actually used. Facing the looming depletion of IPv4 space, the *classful* assignment has been replaced by the *classless* IP scheme.

5.5   CLASSLESS IP - TODAY

With the classless IP, the network ID is not necessarily multiples of an octet (i.e., 8 bits, 16 bits, or 24 bits) as the classful scheme does. For example, the first 13 bits can represent a network ID and the remaining 19 bits a host ID. The identification of a network address gets more complicated when it is not divided by an 8 bit block. In this case, it is better to work with binary digits to figure out the network address. Let's take 123.45.56.89 with the first 13 bits network ID as an example. From Table 5.1, the 32 bit binary combination of 123.45.56.89 becomes:

01111011. 00101101. 00111000. 01011001.

Here, the first 13 bits (01111011.00101) is the network ID. Therefore 32 bit network address becomes:

01111011. 00101000.00000000.00000000

(Thirteen bits network ID + Nineteen 0 bits for host ID).

Now, converting it back to corresponding decimal values results in the network address of

123.40.0.0. Recall that, although the classless IP does not assign the network ID in one or more 8 bit units, the conversion between binary and decimal values always has to be made in the 8-bit block that results in 4 decimal values separated by dots.

The network ID bits under the classless IP system ranges anywhere between 13 and 27 bits. Depending on its size, a network can have as small as 30 ($= 2^5$-2) host IP addresses with the 27 bit network ID or over 500,000 ($= 2^{19}$-2) host IPs with the 13 bit network ID.

~~~~~~

Exercise 5-2

1. You are given IP addresses of four computers. What are network addresses the four computers belong to? Show them in the decimal format.
   - 123.45.56.89 (with 14 bit network ID)
   - 123.45.56.89 (with 18 bit network ID)
   - 123.45.56.89 (with 19 bit network ID)
   - 123.45.56.89 (with 21 bit network ID)

2. Compute the maximum number of host IP addresses available for each network above. Keep in mind that two IPs (all 1s and all 0s in the host ID field) are excluded from the counting as they are set aside for designated functions such as packet broadcasting.

3. Visit *www.arin.com* (internet registry for North America) and search IP space allocated to well-known enterprises (e.g., Google, Microsoft, IBM, AT&T) using its *search* function.

~~~~~~

5.6   SPECIAL IP ADDESS RANGES

Within the entire IP space of 0.0.0.0 through 255.255.255.255, certain address ranges are designated for special functions including *loopback, broadcasting & multicasting*, and *private IP*. They are explained in this section.

5.6.1   Loopback (127.0.0.0 ~ 127.255.255.255)

The loopback IP is a special function a network node can use to send *packets addressed to itself*. The packet with a loopback address as the destination is, therefore, directed back to the source station before it is released to a connected network. Loopback is a very useful function in two different ways: (1) internal testing of the TCP/IP stack; and (2) offline testing of an application.

Internal Testing of TCP/IP Stack

Loopback can be used to check if a host's own TCP/IP protocol stack is working properly and if its IP address is adequately tied to its network card (NIC) and MAC address. For instance, you can issue a ping request such as *c:\>ping 127.0.0.1* (or c:\>ping localhost). In this case, the ping packet does not physically leave your computer, but is re-routed to the computer's receiving end of the TCP/IP stack by the NIC. Although the IP range 127.0.0.0 ~

127.255.255.255 is reserved for the loopback function, 127.0.0.1 is primarily used. *Localhost* is the *domain name* of the loopback IP address and therefore has the same effect as 127.0.0.1. More details of domain names are explained in Chapter 10. In Windows OS, the pairing information between a loopback address (e.g., 127.0.0.1) and its corresponding domain name, *localhost,* is stored in the *hosts* file (refer to Figure 10.20).

Exercise 5-3

1. Ping 127.0.0.1 or *localhost* at the command prompt of your computer. If *C:>ping 127.0.0.1* or *localhost* returns responses as below, this means that the TCP/IP protocol stack (transport and internet layer standards) and NIC (data link and physical layer standards) are adequately coupled and ready for networking. If there is an error message, it is an indication that the TCP/IP stack is not properly installed.

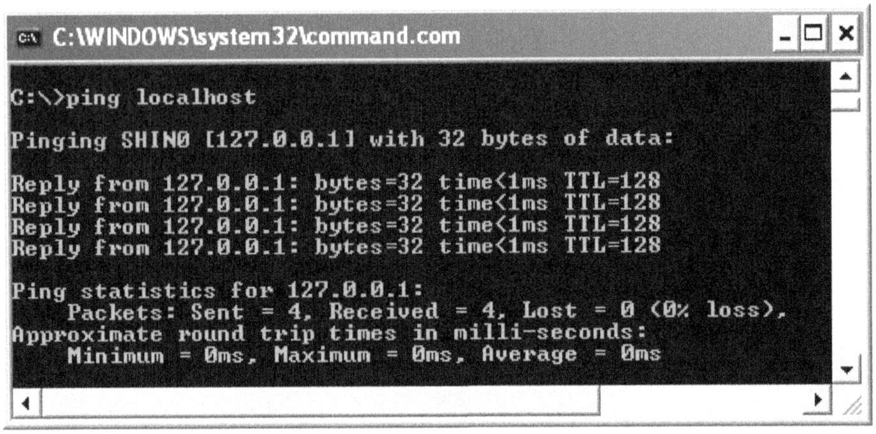

```
C:\WINDOWS\system32\command.com                        _ □ ×

C:\>ping localhost

Pinging SHIN0 [127.0.0.1] with 32 bytes of data:

Reply from 127.0.0.1: bytes=32 time<1ms TTL=128
Reply from 127.0.0.1: bytes=32 time<1ms TTL=128
Reply from 127.0.0.1: bytes=32 time<1ms TTL=128
Reply from 127.0.0.1: bytes=32 time<1ms TTL=128

Ping statistics for 127.0.0.1:
    Packets: Sent = 4, Received = 4, Lost = 0 (0% loss),
Approximate round trip times in milli-seconds:
    Minimum = 0ms, Maximum = 0ms, Average = 0ms
```

Figure 5.3 Successful pinging of localhost

2. Ping 127.123.123.123. Does it have the same effect as 127.0.0.1? Why or why not?

Offline Testing of an Application

Loopback is also useful in testing a network application in offline mode. For example, you can install a web server program (e.g., Apache) in your local machine and then test-drive web server pages you created using the loopback function. With both the client (web browser) and server programs on the same local machine, *http://127.0.0.1* or *http://localhost* is issued at the browser's (client) URL. Then, the browser generates a HTTP request message intended for the web server and dispatches it (see Section 1.2.6 for the sample HTTP syntax).

With the loopback address, the browser's request will be directed back to the web server after going through the lower layers. Remember that because HTTP is designed for correspondence between the web browser and web server programs, *http://127.0.0.1* from a browser is delivered to the web server in the same machine. This request triggers a server response (i.e., web page provision) to the browser, subsequently enabling browser request and server response cycles within the same machine, a convenient way to test server pages before putting them into production (see Figure 5.4).

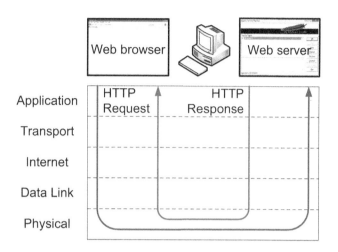

Figure 5.4 Internal client-server communications with a loopback IP

5.6.2   Broadcasting

Broadcasting results in the flooding of a packet from a node to all the other nodes of a subnetwork. There are protocols such as DHCP (to request a dynamic IP address) and ARP (to obtain a station's MAC address from its IP address) (see Section 3.8) that rely on broadcasting to perform intended functions. The router is generally configured not to relay broadcasted packets for such reasons as network security and the prevention of triggering *broadcast storms*. In other words, the effect of broadcasting is confined to the broadcast domain separated by a router port (revisit Section 3.10.2). There are two different types of packet broadcasting: *limited broadcasting* and *directed broadcasting*.

Limited Broadcasting

Limited broadcasting is when a node sends a packet to all other nodes within the same subnetwork. For example, when a computer broadcasts an IP packet with the destination address of 255.255.255.255 (all 32 1s in binary), it is flooded to all nodes within the local network. However, the connecting router does not relay the broadcasting to other subnetworks. A packet's broadcasting IP address 255.255.255.255 is translated into the frame's MAC address of 48 1s (FFFF.FFFF.FFFF) at the data link layer (see Figure 5.5).

Exercise 5-4

1. Think logically on what will happen if the PC (192.168.1.1) in Figure 5.5 issues *C:\>ping*

153

255.255.255.255?

2. What will be the effect if the PC (192.168.1.1) in Figure 5.5 sends a packet with the destination IP address of 192.168.1.255 instead of 255.255.255.255?

3. The 'broadcast domain' concept was introduced in Chapter 3. Discuss the relationship between the broadcast domain and limited broadcasting.

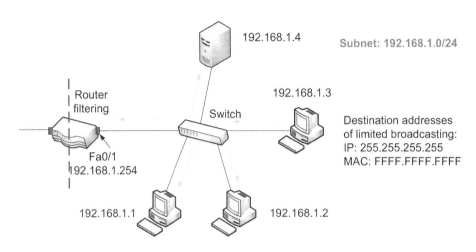

Figure 5.5 Limited broadcasting

Directed Broadcasting

With directed broadcasting, a packet is disseminated to all hosts of a subnetwork away from the sender's local subnetwork. For directed broadcasting, again all 1s are used for the host ID part to flood a packet to a target subnetwork. Routers can be configured for directed broadcasting although their default setup is not to forward broadcasting. When directed broadcasting is programmed in a router, it relays broadcasting packets to a target network just like unicasting packets. The directed broadcasting works in various conditions such as within a LAN or over the Internet.

Figure 5.6 demonstrates directed broadcasting in which a host from 192.168.100.0 broadcasts an IP packet to 192.168.200.0 (a server farm subnetwork) for its concurrent delivery to all three servers. To that end, the sending host creates an IP packet with the destination address of 192.168.200.255/24 in which 255 (= 11111111) means packet broadcasting to the target subnetwork of 192.168.200.0 (/24 represents a subnet identifier in prefix).

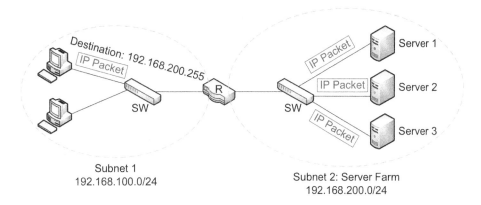

Subnet 1
192.168.100.0/24

Subnet 2: Server Farm
192.168.200.0/24

Figure 5.6 Directed broadcasting

5.6.3 Multicasting (224.0.0.0 – 239.255.255.255)

Multicasting results in packet delivery to a selected group of target nodes locally or remotely located. For multicasting, the IP range of 224.0.0.0 – 239.255.255.255 has been reserved. There are many existing and future applications for which multicasting makes much sense. The technology is effective in supporting communications through video on demand, audio streaming, and multi-party distributed videoconferencing or conference calls. It is also used widely for other applications such as stock trading, security surveillance, and online video gaming. It is not difficult to see the growing importance of the multicasting function.

One major benefit of multicasting is that it can significantly reduce network traffic in providing such business applications and communication services. For instance, for the video on demand (VOD) service, the video streaming server sends just one packet to a number of clients. Without the multicasting technology, the server has to generate a unicast packet to each client and send it to possibly thousands of client computers one by one.

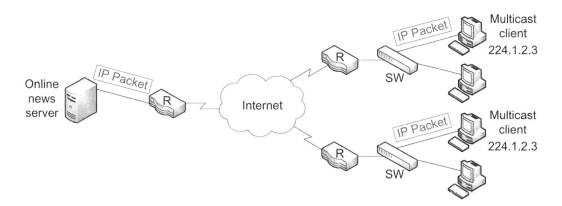

Figure 5.7 IP multicasting

To become a multicast client, the host uses software such as Windows Media Player or Real Player.

155

To listen to the MP3 music or watch videos online, for instance, the client host dynamically associates or disassociates with a so-called *multicast group*. When client hosts join a multicast group to subscribe an online service, they are assigned the same multicast IP address (e.g., 224.1.2.3) for connectivity with the multicast server. At this point, the client hosts retain both the multicast IP and a regular unicast IP, and accept packets destined to the two different IP addresses. IP multicasting primarily relies on UDP rather than TCP at the transport layer as UDP is faster (refer to Section 2.7). *Internet Group Management Protocol* (IGMP) is a well-known internet layer protocol designed to manage multicasting of packets. Multicasting over the Internet is possible when routers are multicasting enabled.

5.6.4 Private IP and NAT

Private IP addresses are intended for usage only within the boundary of a public/private organization or home network, and thus border routers do not route packets with private IPs to the Internet. Three private IP address ranges (one for each class under the classful scheme) are in use:

- 10.0.0.0 ~ 10.255.255.255
- 172.16.0.0 ~ 172.31.255.255
- 192.168.0.0 ~ 192.168.255.255

These days, companies take advantage of private IPs for internal hosts and they are translated to one or more public IP addresses by the border router or firewall when packets are routed beyond the firm boundaries. The address conversion is called *network address translation* (NAT), *network masquerading,* or *IP-masquerading*. There are two different approaches for NAT: *one-to-one IP mapping* and *many-to-one IP mapping*. NAT shields internal computers and intermediary devices from casual snooping by outsiders. NAT is applied to the sender's address (source) but not the receiver's address (destination) of an outgoing packet.

NAT: One-to-One IP Mapping

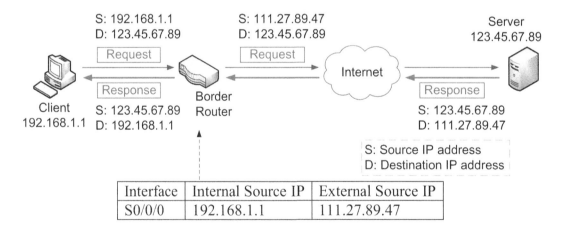

Figure 5.8 Router's one-to-one IP mapping and address conversion table

With the one-to-one mapping, one private IP address is converted to one public IP address either statically or dynamically. With the static approach, one public IP is pre-assigned to a particular private IP and the pairing is pre-programmed in a node (e.g., border router) that does the translation. With the dynamic approach, a range of public IP is retained for NAT. On receiving a packet with a private source IP, the NAT node (e.g., border router) chooses a public IP from the address pool and pairs it with the private IP. Then, the private IP is replaced by the public IP before the packet is dispatched toward the destination, and the mapping record is updated to the address conversion table. This dynamic choice of a public IP is more effective when there are many internal hosts. Figure 5.8 demonstrates the flow of packets through a corporate boundary when the one-to-one mapping (either static or dynamic) is in use.

NAT: Many-to-One IP Mapping

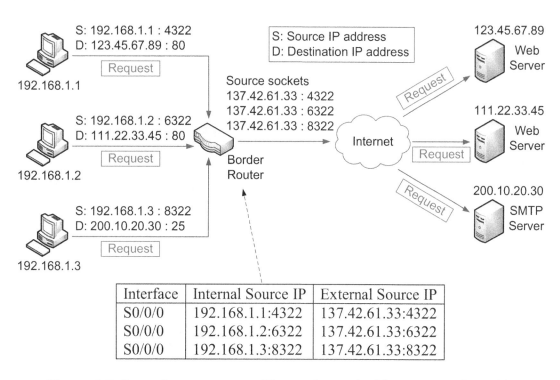

Figure 5.9 Router's many-to-one IP mapping and address conversion table

The many-to-one mapping is when several internal hosts with different private IPs share a single public IP. To make this possible, the NAT node identifies each host computer by its *socket*, the combination of a private IP and a source port found in the transport layer's PDU (either segment or datagram) (see Section 2.7.3). With the port number's inclusion in the mapping process, multiple private IPs can share one public IP. As a result, the source socket before and after the conversion becomes:

Source socket before conversion	Source socket after conversion
Source private IP + source port	Source public IP + source port

Generally, the mapping uses the same source port number for the conversion (e.g., from 192.168.1.1:4000 to 123.45.67.89:4000). When two source hosts are transmitting IP packets with the same source port, the NAT node (e.g., router, firewall) assigns two different port numbers from the available port pool to differentiate packets. The NAT approach that relies on sockets is known as *network address port translation* (NAPT) or *port address translation* (PAT). Figure 5.9 demonstrates a scenario in which three packets are sharing one public IP address (137.42.61.33) for NAPT.

Exercise 5-5: Based on the scenario in Figure 5.9, describe the reverse NAT process the router performs on receiving response packets issued by the three different external servers.

Pros and Cons of NAT

Besides the improved security, NAT provides other benefits:

- **Flexibility in internal IP allocation**: By utilizing private IP addresses for internal nodes, more address space becomes available than when relying on public IPs. Recall that an organization can freely use any of the three private IP ranges to accommodate its needs. This makes network design, management, and expansion quite flexible at least in IP addressing. As a very simple example, several hosts with private IPs at a home network can share one public IP (instead of having 3 different public IPs) to access the Internet concurrently.

- **Consistency in internal IP allocation**: If internal network nodes rely on public IPs, an organization may face situations that require renumbering of node addresses (This is not a trivial task!). If the internal network is on private IPs, existing IP assignment is less affected by such circumstantial changes. For example, the change of an ISP by a business client does not affect the IP configuration of its internal nodes. Also, with the large address space available, IP allocation to each subnetwork can be more generous expecting future business growth and other changes.

NAT has its share of drawbacks:

- **Potential performance degradation**: The border router or firewall has to conduct address translation for each inbound and outbound packet and this can affect packet forwarding performance. As a result, deploying such time-sensitive applications as IP telephony and video streaming could be affected when they are implemented along with NAT. In order to better serve these packets, the NAT node can implement such measure as priority based routing.

- **Possible conflicts with some network applications**: Some network functions that rely on public IP address information such as packet filtering, tunneling for *virtual private network* (VPN) (more in Chapter 10), TCP connections originated from outside, and communications based on the connection-less protocol (e.g., UDP) may be affected if

158

NAT is not adequately set up.

5.7 SUBNETTING

This section explains assignment of subnet addresses within an organization. An enterprise network may contain one or more subnets, reflecting unique needs and structures of the enterprise.

5.7.1 Defining Subnet Boundary (Review)

By definition, the segment of an enterprise network connected to a router port becomes a subnetwork (or subnet). As explained in previous chapters (i.e., Chapter 1 through Chapter 3), a subnetwork generally contains layer 1 or 2 devices (e.g., switches, wireless access points) and client/server hosts. As an example, the enterprise network in Figure 5.10 is composed of five subnetworks separated by 2 routers, R1 and R2. You can assume that R1 is a border router of the branch LAN in New York and R2 is a border router of the main office LAN in London. The main office LAN is composed of three subnetworks (subnet 3, 4, and 5) that connect to R2's Fast Ethernet ports (i.e., Fa0/0, Fa0/1, and Fa0/2). Subnetwork 2 is a leased WAN link that interconnects the serial ports (S0/0) of R1 and R2.

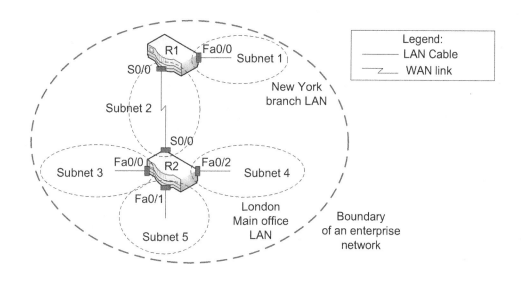

Figure 5.10 Subnets defined by router ports

There are good reasons to divide a LAN into smaller subnets. Some of the main benefits are:

1. *Security management*: Subnets allow customized planning and implementation of network security at different levels. For example, at a university's campus network, core academic systems such as student records, human resources, and financials should be securely protected with additional layers of defense. By placing them in a tightly protected subnet, it is separated from the remaining campus network including WiFi sections that are more vulnerable to security attacks.

2. ***Customization of network segments***: Each subnet can be better customized in its design (e.g., choice of layer 2 devices and their physical connectivity) to serve the needs of information systems and systems users. For example, the subnetwork with a firm's server farm is highly service-oriented and should enable fast and stable access. This performance requires that design and implementation of the segment emphasize enhanced network accessibility, reliability, redundancy, and security.

3. ***Limit broadcasting effect***: The negative effects of broadcasted messages (e.g., those of DHCP and ARP) are contained at the subnet level. Unlike switches that relay broadcasted packets, routers block them by default and prevent a network from becoming a victim of excessive traffic.

Exercise 5-6: How many subnets do you see in the hypothetical enterprise network in Figure 5.11? Do not count the Internet connection. Assume that the WAN links are leased lines.

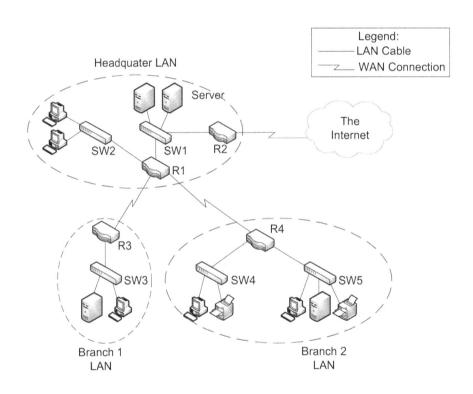

Figure 5.11 A hypothetical enterprise network

5.7.2 IP Assignment of a Subnetwork

Creating subnetworks in an enterprise results in IP addresses that contain three identifiers of network, subnet, and host (see Figure 5.2). For instance, the network in Figure 5.10 has one network ID that represents the enterprise and five subnet IDs. Zooming in one subnet, Figure 5.12 demonstrates that the network ID can be 192.168.0.0 and the subnet ID is 192.168.1.0. Recall that a router's LAN port, with its own MAC and IP addresses, shares the same subnet ID as other hosts stations directly or indirectly attached to it.

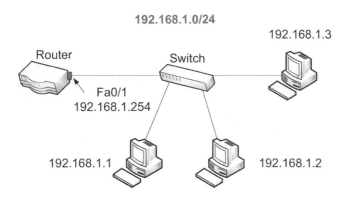

192.168.1.0/24

Figure 5.12 A subnet attached to a router's LAN port (Fa0/1)

As another example, Figure 5.13 demonstrates a LAN with network address of 192.168.0.0. The network is divided into three subnets (i.e., 192.168.1.0, 192.168.2.0, and 192.168.3.0), the third octet uniquely identifying a subnet within the LAN. You can observe that each LAN port of the router is also configured with an IP of a particular subnet.

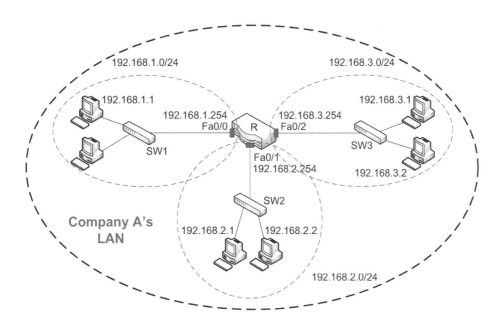

Figure 5.13 A firm's LAN with three subnetworks

An enterprise network comprised of multiple subnets may be just a LAN with one or more routers that join the subnets (see Figure 5.13). Or, an enterprise network may be a combination of LANs and WAN links as in Figure 5.10 and Figure 5.11. As explained, each WAN link between two border routers is a subnet and is given a unique subnet ID. There are several WAN link options including leased lines and packet switched data network (PSDN) from common carriers such as AT&T and British Telecom (Details of PSDN are in Chapter 9). Figure 5.14 illustrates assignment of subnet IDs when two LANs and a WAN connection form an enterprise network.

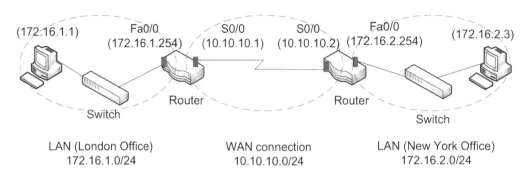

Figure 5.14 An organization's network with three subnets

5.8   SUBNET MASK

5.8.1   Subnet Mask

The *subnet mask* is a 32 bit number used by a network node (e.g., computer, router) to determine the subnet address of a particular IP address. More specifically, the *subnet mask* indicates the subnet address bits (network ID + subnet ID) of an IP address by 'masking' the host ID. Many industry practitioners use two terms *network mask* and *subnet mask* interchangeably. This can cause much confusion to students, although becomes less of an issue with practical experience.

The *subnet mask* uses either a *prefix* or a *combination of continuous 1s and 0s* in order to indicate the *network and subnet* combined portion of an IP address. Continuous 1s represent the 'network ID + subnet ID' part and continuous 0s indicate the host ID part of an IP address.

As a simple example, for the host address: 172.16.10.101
    with network address: 172.0.0.0 (10101100.00000000.00000000.00000000)
    with subnet address: 172.16.0.0 (10101100.00010000.00000000.00000000),
the subnet mask becomes 255.255.0.0 (11111111.11111111.00000000.00000000) or */16*. The prefix value (/16) represents the number of continuous 1s in the subnet mask.

The *subnet mask* is a critical piece of information because it is constantly referenced by routers and computers to determine the forwarding path of IP packets. For example, Figure 5.15 demonstrates a subnet mask included in a host computer's IP configuration. The computer can determine its own subnet address based on the IP and subnet mask. The usage of subnet masks by routers is explained in Chapter 6.

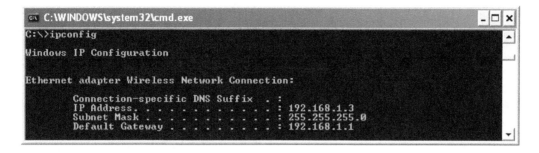

Figure 5.15 IP configuration of a host station

Let's take a look at more examples. It is always a good idea to work with binary first and then translate the outcome into decimal to figure out the subnet mask and subnet address.

Example 1:   Host address: 176.20.38.4
Network ID: 176.20
Subnet ID: 38
Host ID: 4

Items	Decimal	Binary
Host address	176.20.38.4	10110000.00010100.00100110.00000100
Network address	176.20.0.0	10110000.00010100.00000000.00000000
Subnet address	176.20.38.0	10110000.00010100.00100110.00000000
Subnet mask (network ID + subnet ID)	255.255.255.0 or "/24" (prefix)	11111111.11111111.11111111.00000000
Host address with subnet mask	176.20.38.4/24	
Subnet address with subnet mask	176.20.38.0/24	

Example 2:   Host address: 192.168.1.51
Network ID: 192
Subnet ID: 168
Host ID: 1.51

Items	Decimal	Binary
Host address	192.168.1.51	11000000.10101000.00000001.00110011
Network address	192.0.0.0	11000000.00000000.00000000.00000000
Subnet address	192.168.0.0	11000000.10101000.00000000.00000000
Subnet mask (network ID + subnet ID part)	255.255.0.0 or "/16" (prefix)	11111111.11111111.00000000.00000000
Host address with subnet mask	192.168.1.51/16	
Subnet address with subnet mask	192.168.0.0/16	

Example 3 (Challenge)
In this example, the subnet bits are not divided into the 8 bit block.

      Host address: 192.168.1.51

      Network ID: 192

      Subnet ID: 160

      Host ID: 8.1.51

Items	Decimal	Binary
Host address	192.168.1.51	11000000.10101000.00000001.00110011
Network address	192.0.0.0	11000000.00000000.00000000.00000000
Subnet address	192.160.0.0	11000000.10100000.00000000.00000000
Subnet mask (network ID + subnet ID)	255.224.0.0 or "/11" (prefix)	11111111.11100000.00000000.00000000
Host address with subnet mask	192.168.1.51/11	
Subnet address with subnet mask	192.160.0.0/11	

Exercise 5-7

1. For the host address, 195.112.36.59, where

        Network ID: 195   Subnet ID: 112.36   Host ID: 59

    Decide the subnet address and subnet mask in both decimal and binary.

2. For the host address, 207.34.15.187, where

        Network ID: 207.34   Subnet ID: 15   Host ID: 187

    Decide the subnet address and subnet mask in both decimal and binary.

3. For the following IP addresses, determine their subnet addresses and subnet masks in both decimal and binary.

    o   195.205.36.5/13

    o   192.168.36.5/21

    o   10.11.46.51/15

4. For the following IP addresses, determine their subnet addresses and subnet masks in decimal.

IP Address of a host	Subnet address	Subnet masks
10.15.123.50/8 17.100.222.15/13 128.100.54.11/24 141.131.75.162/13 115.125.129.227/16 162.15.115.2/21 173.102.75.224/18 192.168.124.31/20 172.31.200.201/22		

164

5.8.2 Subnetting Address Space

An organization can create as many subnets as needed internally by borrowing bits from the host ID part (see Figure 5.2). For instance, let's think of a scenario in which an enterprise's network address is 130.191.0.0 and subnets are created by borrowing 2 bits from the host ID part. If 2 bits are borrowed, the subnet mask becomes 11111111.11111111.11000000.00000000 that is equivalent to 255.255.192.0 (or /18 in prefix). With 2 bits, four different subnets can be created within the enterprise network. They are listed next (2 bits in the 17th and 18th positions uniquely identify a subnet. Yes, all 0s and all 1s are available to represent two different subnets).

#	Subnet address (binary)	Subnet address (decimal)	Subnet mask
1	10000010.10111111.00000000.00000000	130.191.0.0	255.255.192.0
2	10000010.10111111.01000000.00000000	130.191.64.0	255.255.192.0
3	10000010.10111111.10000000.00000000	130.191.128.0	255.255.192.0
4	10000010.10111111.11000000.00000000	130.191.192.0	255.255.192.0

Then, 14 bits become available to create host IDs. The number of hosts that can own an IP address within each subnet becomes $2^{14} - 2 = 16382$. Two (all 0s = 000000.00000000 and all 1s = 111111.11111111) are excluded from the counting because they are reserved for special functions (i.e., broadcasting and default route – more details in Chapter 6). So, the counting of possible subnets (2^n) and that of possible hosts ($2^n - 2$) based on available bits slightly differ. In above example, the first subnet (130.191.0.0) has a usable host address range of:

10000010.10111111.00000000.00000001 ~ 10000010.10111111.00111111.11111110
= 130.191.0.1 ~ 130.191.63.254 (Remember to exclude all 0s and all 1s in the host range.)

Exercise 5-8: Determine usable host address ranges of subnet 2, subnet 3 and subnet 4 above.

Each of the four subnets created above by borrowing 2 bits from the host ID portion may be assigned to a well-defined functional (e.g., business department, workgroup) or geographical location (e.g., branch office).

Exercise 5-9

1. For the network address, 130.190.0.0, 4 bits are borrowed from the host bits.
   a) How many total subnets can be created?
   b) What is the subnet mask?
   c) List available subnet addresses.

2. Given the network address of 172.191.183.0 (first 24 bits), the firm decided to use 4 bits to create subnets.
    a) What is the subnet mask?
    b) List all possible subnet addresses.
    c) List usable host IPs of the first subnet (remember to exclude all 0s and all 1s).

3. Given the network address of 230.195.10.0 (first 24 bits), the firm's network administrator figures that 6 subnets are necessary.
    a) What is the minimum number of bits to be borrowed from the host ID part?
    b) Assuming that the minimum number of bits has been borrowed, what is the resulting subnet mask?
    c) List all possible subnet addresses.
    d) List usable host IPs of the last subnet.

5.8.3   Broadcasting within a Subnet

Previously, the broadcasting concept was explained in terms of limited - and directed broadcasting (see Section 5.6.2). This section is an extension of the coverage. It was stated that, with all 1s for the host ID field of a packet, the packet is broadcasted to all nodes of a subnetwork.

Example 1: The host IP, 172.16.100.141, with the subnet mask, 255.255.0.0 (/16 in prefix), is translated into:

Host IP address: 10101100.00010000.01100100.10001101   (= 172.16.100.141)
Subnet mask: 11111111.11111111.00000000.00000000   (= 255.255.0.0)
Subnet address: 10101100.00010000.00000000.00000000   (= 172.16.0.0)

As the subnet is identified by the first 16 bits, broadcasting of a packet within a subnet uses all 1s for the remaining 16 host bits. The broadcast address, therefore, becomes

Broadcast address: 10101100.00010000.11111111.11111111   (= 172.16.255.255)

Example 2: The host IP, 192.168.10.141, with the subnet mask, 255.255.255.192 (/26 in prefix), is translated into:

Host IP address: 11000000.10101000.00001010.10001101   (= 192.168.10.141)
Subnet mask: 11111111.11111111.11111111.11000000   (= 255.255.255.192)
Subnet address: 11000000.10101000.00001010.10000000   (= 192.168.10.128)

With 26 bits of the subnet address, broadcasting of a packet within a subnet uses all 1s for the remaining 6 host bits. The broadcast address, therefore, becomes

Broadcast address: 11000000.10101000.00001010.10111111   (= 192.168.10.191).

Exercise 5-10

1. Determine the broadcast address of each subnet. Remember that working with binary is always easier. Assume directed (not limited) broadcasting.

Subnet address	Subnet mask	Broadcast address
130.191.0.0	255.255.192.0 (or /18)	
130.191.64.0	255.255.192.0	
130.191.128.0	255.255.192.0	
130.191.192.0	255.255.192.0	

2. Determine the broadcast address of each host assuming directed (not limited) broadcasting.

Host address	Subnet mask	Broadcast address
192.168.150.121	255.255.128.0 (or /17)	
172.57.237.200	255.248.0.0 (or /13)	

3. Given the following information:
   - Host IP address: 130.191.31.21
   - Network address: 130.191.31.0 (first 24 bits)
   - Subnet mask: 255.255.255.240 (/28)

   Determine:
   a) Total number of subnets possible
   b) Number of host bits in each subnet
   c) Number of host addresses possible in each subnet
   d) Subnet address of the host, 130.191.31.21
   e) Broadcast address of the host, 130.191.31.21
   f) The first host address of the subnet, 130.191.31.16
   g) The last host address of the subnet, 130.191.31.16

4. A company has 192.10.10.0 (first 24 bits) as its network address. It needs to have 14 subnets. Answer the following questions.
   a) Minimum number of bits to borrow from the host ID part
   b) Subnet mask
   c) Total number of subnets possible
   d) List all subnet addresses
   e) Number of usable host addresses per subnet
   f) List the host IP range of the subnet, 192.10.10.16
   g) Broadcast address of the subnet, 192.10.10.16

5. A company has 192.168.3.0 (first 24 bits) as its network address. It needs to have 6 subnets. Answer the following questions.
   a) Minimum number of bits to borrow from the host ID part
   b) Subnet mask

c) Total number of subnets possible
d) List all subnet addresses
e) Number of usable host addresses per subnet
f) List the host IP range of the subnet, 192.168.3.32
g) Broadcast address of the subnet, 192.168.3.32

5.9 SUPERNETTING

Supernetting of IP addresses, also known as *classless inter-domain routing* (CIDR), is a concept opposite from *subnetting*. With supernetting, multiple subnet IDs are combined (or summarized) into a larger subnet ID. Summarizing multiple subnets into a larger subnet is an effective way of maintaining a network (e.g., router configuration) and boosting network performance (e.g., faster routing decision).

As an example, imagine a hypothetical situation (Figure 5.16) in which two routers R1 and R2 exchange packets and R1 is connected to three subnets each with a subnet address and subnet mask. Assume that 192.168.0.0/16 is the supernet address and mask that summarizes three subnets. The supernet is a higher abstraction that embraces the three subnets. One main benefit of the summarization is that the R2's router table adds only one entry instead of 3 subnet entries, making the overall list of the R2's routing table smaller and subsequently enabling faster routing decisions by R2.

Replacing 3 entries with one summarized entry in R2's routing table may not be that significant. However, if one supernet can substitute 200 subnets, then R2's routing table becomes substantially smaller as it will have only one entry in place of 200 entries. With the smaller routing table, R2 takes less time in determining the optimal routing path of a packet and improves packet forwarding performance (More on this are explained in Chapter 6).

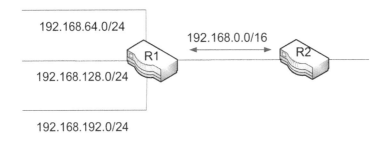

Figure 5.16 A supernet that summarizes 3 subnets

Now, let's take a look at how to do IP supernetting (or IP summarization) using the same example in Figure 5.16. Router 1 is connected to three subnets:

Subnet address & mask (decimal)	Subnet address (binary)
192.168.64.0/24	11000000. 10101000.01000000.00000000
192.168.128.0/24	11000000. 10101000.10000000.00000000
192.168.192.0/24	11000000. 10101000.11000000.00000000

The highlighted parts represent the subnet address. Their subnet mask therefore becomes 11111111.11111111.11111111.00000000 (or 255.255.255.0).

For the supernetting of three subnets above, we need to come up with the longest common denominator of the subnet addresses. You can observe that the first 16 digits 11000000. 10101000 are shared by all three subnets, making them the longest common denominator. As a result, 11000000.10101000 becomes the supernet address that embraces all three subnets. The new subnet address and subnet mask of the supernet becomes:

Supernet address: 11000000. 10101000.00000000.00000000 = 192.168.0.0
Supernet's subnet mask: 11111111. 11111111.00000000.00000000 = 255.255.0.0 (= /16)

Exercise 5-11: A network administrator configured R2 in Figure 5.16 to summarize the following subnets connected to R1. Determine the supernet address and its subnet mask that are entered into the R2's routing table.

1) 192.168.1.0/24   192.168.2.0/24   192.168.4.0/24

2) 192.168.129.0/24   192.168.130.0/24   192.168.132.0/24   192.168.145.0/24

The example in Figure 5.16 is a relatively simple one because each subnetwork has a subnet mask that is a multiple of an 8-bit block. In fact, even when subnet masks are not a multiple of 8-bits, the same mechanism applies to the summarization of subnets into a supernet. The key in figuring out the supernet is to work on binary, not decimal. Let's use the following example in which 3 subnets need to be summarized (The subnet addresses are highlighted).

Subnet address & mask	Subnet address in binary	Subnet masks in decimal
172.16.35.0/24	10101100.00010000.00100011.00000000	255.255.255.0
172.16.39.0/24	10101100.00010000.00100111.00000000	255.255.255.0
172.16.31.0/24	10101100.00010000.00011111.00000000	255.255.255.0

To come up with the summarization, we need to decide the longest bit stream common to all three subnet addresses. It can be seen that the first 18 bits *10101100.00010000.00* become the longest common denominator. Therefore, the new summarized network in binary will be (The highlighted represents the supernet address):

$$10101100.00010000.00000000.00000000 \text{ (or } 172.16.0.0/18)$$

The subnet mask of the supernet "/18" (or 11111111.11111111.11000000.00000000) is equivalent to 255.255.192.0 in decimal.

~~~~~~

Exercise 5-12

1. Summarize the following three subnet addresses into a supernet. Also, show its new subnet mask.
    172.16.163.0/20   172.16.167.0/22   172.16.159.0/23
2. Summarize the following four subnet addresses into a supernet. Also, show its new subnet mask.
    10.20.30.41/17   10.20.65.52/18   10.20.95.34/20   10.20.160.78/21

~~~~~~

5.10 MANAGING IP ADDRESS SPACE

Allocating IP addresses to network nodes should be the result of a well-planned process. IP planning could be a complicated process, especially at a large enterprise with multiple functional departments/business units and distributed geographical locations, because it has implications on network performance, access control of network resources, and security. Once IP addresses are allocated and configured in intermediary devices and host computers and devices, reconfiguring them due to circumstantial changes such as organizational growth and restructuring can be painful. Accordingly, the assignment of IPs requires well thought-out planning anticipating such changes and also the details of IP deployment should be thoroughly documented for future network planning, management, and updates.

There are several key elements in planning IP allocation at an organization.
    1. Determining the number of nodes that need an IP address
    2. Determining subnetworks including the DMZ (De-militarized zone) subnet
    3. Having an IP assignment policy
They are explained next.

5.10.1 Determining Number of Nodes

Given that there are many different node types that need an IP to be network-enabled (see Table 5.3), the total number of nodes that need an IP address on a temporary (or dynamic) or permanent (or static) basis should be determined. Also necessary is to project the future growth of network nodes. Depending on the nature of intermediary devices and hosts, decisions can be made on the usage of static versus dynamic IP addresses. Categorically, user stations including desktop and laptop computers, and other personal productivity tools such as mobile devices are assigned temporary IPs as they don't have to be up and running all the time.

Configuring user stations with permanent IPs pose several problems.
• This can waste available IP space because an IP address permanently assigned to a user station

170

cannot be reclaimed for reuse unless the computer is retired from production.

- The management (e.g., configuration/reconfiguration of each user station and necessary documentation) of IPs becomes an administrative burden, especially when the network gets larger. Dynamic IP assignment by DHCP (see Chapter 2 and 10) curtails the management overhead considerably and also eliminates the chance of mistakes (e.g., repeat assignment of an IP) during manual configuration.

Network nodes other than end-user stations are generally given permanent IPs to perform intended functions such as providing various types of resources (e.g., web pages, storing files, printing, executing database transactions), enabling communications (e.g., emails, fax), and handling packet deliveries. Table 5.3 categorizes major devices with permanent IPs into (a) those offering various resources and services to user stations and (b) those enabling link connectivity as intermediary devices. Recall that, unlike the managed switch that needs an IP address only for its remote setup and management over the network, the router needs a permanent IP for each port (or interface) to perform packet routing.

Node Categorization	Nodes	"Preferred" IP addressing
Resource consumers	End user stations (e.g., workstations, smartphones, personal productivity tools)	Temporary (or Dynamic) IPs
Resource or service providers	• Dedicated servers • Peripherals including printers, fax, and backup devices • Specialty devices including surveillance cameras, AC sensors, and alarms	Permanent (or Static) IPs
Intermediary devices	• Router LAN and WAN ports (interfaces) • Firewall • Managed switch (An IP address is assigned to remotely access its OS over the network) • Managed wireless access point (An IP address is assigned to remotely access it over the network)	Permanent (or Static) IPs

Table 5.3 Classification of network nodes

Assigning a static IP to a host computer requires the input of four information items (see Figure 5.17 for the case of Microsoft Windows):
1. IP address
2. Subnet mask
3. Default gateway: the router port address that forwards IP packets beyond the subnet boundary (more in Chapter 6)
4. DNS server(s) that maps a domain name (e.g., www.facebook.com) to its corresponding IP address

5.10.2 Determining Subnets

A decision should be made on the number of subnetworks within a corporate network. The decision can be based on several technical and non-technical factors such as:

- Physical layout including building locations, occupied floors of a building, and geographical distribution of offices.
- Importance of limiting the scope of a broadcast domain so that possible broadcast storms do not impede network performance.
- Importance of defining functional boundaries of the corporate network to better serve business requirements. The logical boundaries of business functions include academic units (e.g., departments, colleges), business departments and units (e.g., marketing, accounting), and project workgroups.
- Importance of having different levels of security control for subnetworks.

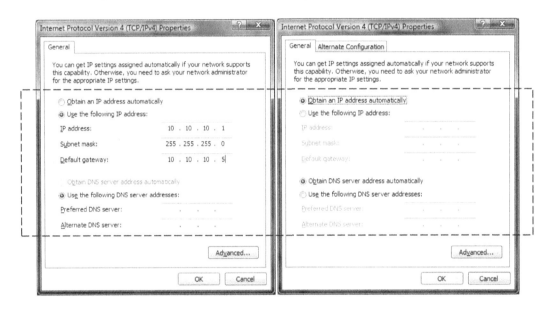

Figure 5.17 Static (left) versus Dynamic (right) IP assignment in MS Windows

5.10.3 Managing Security with DMZ Subnet

As explained, many organizations rely on private IPs for internal nodes because they can better protect internal resources from probing and attack attempts, and also offer more flexibility in address management (e.g., more room for future growth). Some server hosts, especially web and email servers, are more exposed to the Internet by nature because they provide communication and information access service. To better safeguard an enterprise from external threats, these servers are generally separated from the main production network by placing them in the *demilitarized zone* (or DMZ) subnet. Servers in a DMZ can be configured with private or public IP addresses. When DMZ servers are equipped with private IPs, *network address translation* (NAT) is performed by the border router or firewall for necessary address translations (see Figure 5.18).

5.10.4 Developing IP Assignment Policy

An organization maintains an inventory of many network nodes whose subnets and IP addresses should be planned, assigned, and maintained systematically. In particular, if the assignment of IP addresses to network nodes is not performed in a structured manner according to a formal policy, IT staff can face much confusion and inefficiency in managing them later on. Moreover, the lack of consistency in IP assignment driven by the advanced planning can have negative consequences on the integrity of network security and access control.

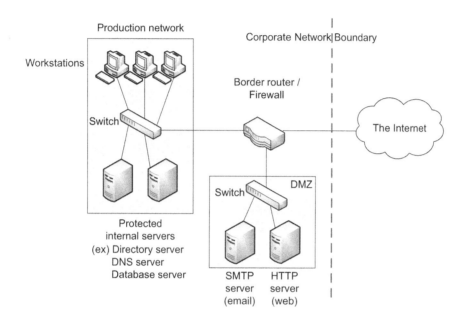

Figure 5.18 General setup of DMZ as a subnet

Because of unique functions performed by various network nodes, it is a good idea to group them into categories in order to define a consistent policy on IP allocation. This consistency in IP assignment makes the management (e.g., initial IP setup, troubleshooting, configuration changes) of network nodes much less troublesome. For example, imagine that an IT specialist needs to troubleshoot the source of network malfunctioning and should quickly locate the IP of a particular router port on a subnet. If the IP assignment policy requires that the router port be given the last available IP address of a subnet, the person can easily guess the router port's IP without resorting to the IP database.

For demonstration purpose, a hypothetical IP policy is developed in Table 5.4 for a university network comprised of various functional units and network nodes. The policy becomes a high level guideline in planning subnets and node addressing in a consistent manner. Table 5.4 is rather a simplified view and the real IP management policy can be more complicated for reasonably sized organizations. Besides, although most business firms rely on private IPs for internal nodes, public institutes especially colleges and universities whose infrastructures operate in a more open environment may depend more on public IPs for network nodes.

IP Range	Assignment
• Network address: 192.168.0.0 • Subnet mask: 255.255.255.0 (/24)	
• Subnet range (third octet)	
192.168.1.0	DMZ (accessible from the Internet)
192.168.2.0 ~ 192.168.7.0	University administration
192.168.8.0 ~ 192.168.40.0	Academics (colleges & departments)
192.168.41.0 ~ 192.168.43.0	Library
192.168.44.0 ~ 192.168.50.0	Student labs
192.168.51.0	Campus storage area network
192.168.52.0	Campus operation and maintenance
192.168.53.0	Campus safety and security
192.168.54.0 ~ 192.168.55.0	Athletics
192.168.56.0 ~ 192.168.60.0	WAN links
192.168.61.0 ~ 192.168.62.0	Internet links
• Host range within a subnet (fourth octet)	
x.x.x.1 ~ x.x.x.2:	Router (gateway) & firewall interface(s)
x.x.x.3 ~ x.x.x.10:	Managed switches (core & workgroup switches)
x.x.x.11 ~ x.x.x.15:	Managed wireless devices (e.g., access points)
x.x.x.16 ~ x.x.x.25:	Servers
x.x.x.26 ~ x.x.x.40:	Peripherals (e.g., printers, fax, back-up devices)
x.x.x.41 ~ x.x.x.250:	General user stations
x.x.x.251 ~ x.x.x.254:	Network technician/administrator stations

Table 5.4 A hypothetical policy for IP allocation

Exercise 5-13: Based on the information in Table 5.4, describe the nature of the following IP addresses.

1. 192.168.44.16
2. 192.168.54.50
3. 192.168.4.4
4. 192.168.53.11

The focus of this chapter has been IPv4. With the prevalent usage of 32 bit-based IPs, the IPv4 address space available from *Internet Assigned Numbers Authority* (IANA) has been drained. Several approaches have been taken to utilize available IPv4 space more effectively and to extend its life. These include:

• Dynamic provision of temporary IPs (rather than permanent IPs) to client hosts using such protocol as DHCP

- Reliance on private IPs (rather than public IPs) for internal nodes and the deployment of network address translation (NAT) for conversion between private and public IPs
- Adoption of the classless (instead of classful) IP addressing scheme

Despite these measures, the shortage of IPv4 address space only gets worse as more devices, especially mobile devices including smart phones, are joining the Internet. The shortage will undoubtedly expedite migration from IPv4 to IPv6 that relies on lengthy 128 bits (or 32 hexadecimal numbers). Ultimately, we will witness a world where the Internet will interconnect computers, mobile devices, sensors, electronic appliances (e.g., refrigerators), electronics (e.g., HDTVs), and other gadgets running on IPv6 addresses.

KEY TERMS

1-to-1 IP address mapping
broadcast storm
broadcasting IP address
class A network
class B network
class C network
classful IP address
classless inter-domain routing (CIDR)
classless IP address
default route
de-militarized zone (DMZ)
directed broadcasting

Host identification
Internet Assigned Numbers Authority (IANA)
Internet Group Management Protocol (IGMP)
IP assignment policy
IP masquerading
limited broadcasting
localhost
loopback
m-to-1 IP address mapping
multicast group
multicasting IP address

network address port translation (NAPT)
network address translation (NAT)
network identification
network masquerading
port address translation (PAT)
private IP address
Regional Internet Registry (RIR)
subnet mask
subnetting
supernetting

CHAPTER REVIEW QUESTIONS

1. Which organization allocates IP address blocks to large ISPs?
A) Internet Assigned Numbers Authority
B) Regional Internet Registry
C) International Standard Organization
D) Internet Engineering Task Force
E) VeriSign

2. What is the largest decimal value of the 8 bit octet?
A) 100
B) 32
C) 255
D) 128

E) 256

3. The IP address should have AT LEAST_____ part(s).
A) network ID
B) host ID
C) network ID and subnet ID
D) network ID and host ID
E) network ID, subnet ID, and host ID

4. A Class C network that uses 4 bits for the subnet ID can have up to _____ hosts in each subnet.
A) 14

B) 12
C) 16
D) 65,000
E) 4

5.   When a packet is broadcasted to a target subnet that is different from the source host's subnet, it becomes ____ broadcasting.
A) focused
B) subset
C) targeted
D) directed
E) limited

6.   Which term represents IPs used only internally at an organization?
A) private IPs
B) campus IPs
C) internal IPs
D) encoded IPs
E) reserved IPs

7.   When the destination address of a packet is 255.255.255.255:
A) The packet is delivered to all hosts on the Internet.
B) The packet is delivered to all hosts of an enterprise network to which the source host belongs.
C) The packet is delivered to all hosts of a multicasting network on the Internet.
D) The packet is self-addressed and thus does not leave the source host.
E) The packet is delivered to all hosts that are in the same subnet as the source host.

8.   For a packet outgoing to the Internet, *network address port translation* generally changes its:
A) source port number only.
B) destination IP address only.
C) destination and source IP addresses.
D) source IP address and maybe source port number.
E) destination IP address and maybe source port number.

9.   Imagine a network (175.140.x.x) that uses 8 bits for the subnet ID. If a computer releases a packet with 175.140.115.255 as the destination IP, what should happen?
A)   The packet is delivered to the host, 175.140.115.255.
B)   The packet is delivered to the host, 175.140.115.0.
C)   The packet is delivered to all hosts within the subnet, 175.140.115.0.
D)   The packet is delivered to all hosts within the network, 175.140.0.0.
E)   The packet is delivered to the host, 175.140.0.255.

10. The network ID of an IP address, 10.7.12.6, is 10.7.0.0. The network plus subnet parts are ____.
A)   10
B)   10.7
C)   10.7.12
D)   10.7.12.6
E)   cannot say

11. When a firm uses 8 bits for its network identification (or ID), what does the subnet mask 255.255.255.0 tell you?
A)   Eight bits are assigned to the subnet identification.
B)   Sixteen bits are available to uniquely identify a host station.
C)   Four bits are assigned to the subnet identification.
D)   Eight bits are used to indicate the host identification.
E)   No bits are available to create subnets.

12. A firm has the network ID of 65.10.0.0 and the subnet mask of 255.255.0.0. What is the destination address of a packet to be broadcasted to all nodes in a subnet?
A)   65.10.255.255
B)   65.0.255.255
C)   65.0.0.255
D)   65.10.255.0

E) 65.255.0.0

Questions 13 - 17:
Think of a network, 192.168.125.x, with the following requirements:
--- Number of necessary subnets: 14
--- Number of usable hosts per subnet: 14
Assuming that the minimum number of bits is borrowed from the host ID part.

13. What is the subnet mask of all subnets?
A) 255.255.255.255
B) 255.255.255.64
C) 255.255.255.240
D) 255.255.255.192
E) 255.255.255.224

14. For the subnet 192.168.125.16, what is the first usable host IP?
A) 192.168.125.16
B) 192.168.125.17
C) 192.168.125.32
D) 192.168.125.20
E) 192.168.125.64

15. For the subnet 192.168.125.32, what is the last usable host IP?
A) 192.168.125.33
B) 192.168.125.46
C) 192.168.125.32
D) 192.168.125.47
E) 192.168.125.64

16. For the subnet 192.168.125.128, what is the broadcast IP?
A) 192.168.125.129
B) 192.168.125.240
C) 192.168.125.255
D) 192.168.125.15
E) 192.168.125.143

17. How many (usable) IP addresses are available for a subnet?
A) 6
B) 10
C) 14

D) 15
E) 16

18. Which represents a host IP address at the home network that shares a public IP?
A) 123.7.86.215
B) 127.0.0.1
C) 192.168.0.1
D) 255.255.255.255
E) 127.127.127.1

19. In the screenshot below, I just
A) temporarily assigned an IP to a host.
B) contacted a server with the IP address of 127.0.0.1.
C) broadcasted a packet to the subnet of 127.0.0.x.
D) obtained the MAC address of 127.0.0.1.
E) tested my computer's TCP/IP protocol stack.

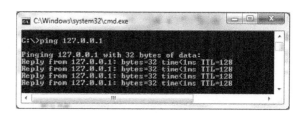

20. Which statement is INCORRECT regarding *network address translation*?
A) It is implemented in layer 2 switches.
B) It converts a private IP to a public IP.
C) Routers or firewalls are used for its implementation.
D) It can better protect the enterprise network.
E) The port address translation allows several hosts to share a public IP.

21. An IPv4 address with the first octet of 127 can be used for
A) classless IP assignment to a host.
B) private IP assignment to a host.
C) multicasting to a subnet
D) testing connectivity to a router
E) offline testing of web server pages

22. Under the classful IP allocation scheme, Class B networks can use maximum _____ bits to indicate the host identification.
A) 4
B) 8
C) 16
D) 24
E) 32

23. The subnet mask of a class B network is 255.255.255.0 at a firm. How many subnets can be created in that firm?
A) 128
B) 256
C) 64
D) 255
E) 254

24. The following measures help in extending IPv4's life expectancy EXCEPT:
A) Use of dynamic IPs assigned by the DHCP server
B) Utilization of private IP addresses
C) Reliance on switches than routers for corporate networking
D) Use of network address translation (NAT)
E) Switching from classful IPs to classless IPs

25. Which is the general delegation process of IP space to ISPs?
A) IEEE => Regional Registry => ISPs
B) InterNIC => Regional Registry => ISPs
C) IANA => Regional Registry => ISPs
D) Regional Registry => ICANN => ISPs
E) Regional Registry => InterNIC => ISP

HANDS-ON EXERCISE: Enterprise IP Management at Atlas Co.

The figure below represents a planned enterprise network of Atlas Co. that is headquartered in Houston, TX and has two branch offices in Los Angeles and New York. The network will be composed of multiple LANs and leased line-based WAN connections for which 3 routers (R1~R3) and 5 switches (SW1~SW5) are used. Atlas Co. will be using AT&T's WAN service to interconnect the three distributed locations. The company already has a T-1 Internet connection from R1 whose subnet is 160.96.4.0/24. You are the company's chief network administer and are responsible for planning subnet IDs and assigning permanent IPs to all network nodes (servers, printers, copiers, backup devices, managed switches, wireless access points, and selected workstations).

The company decided to use private address 192.168.20.0/24 for its internal network ID. This means that all packets going out to the Internet have to rely on NAT configured in R1. As the result of network planning, it was decided that:

- The HQ LAN's switch 1 will connect 20 hosts with permanent IPs.
- The HQ LAN's switch 2 will connect 10 hosts (3 of them are servers) with permanent IPs.
- The LA Branch LAN requires 15 permanent IPs.
- The NY Branch LAN's switch 4 will connect 15 hosts with permanent IPs.
- The NY Branch LAN's switch 5 will connect 10 hosts with permanent IPs.
- The WAN link between R1 and R2 requires a permanent IP for each router interface.
- The WAN link between R1 and R3 requires a permanent IP for each router interface.

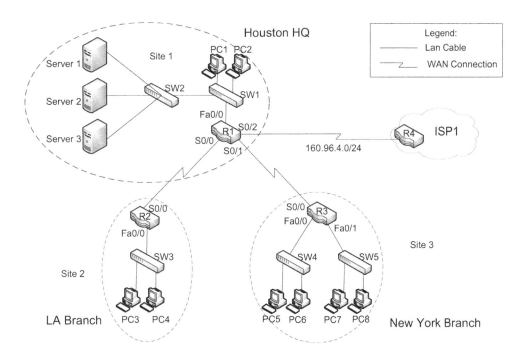

Figure: Planned enterprise network of Atlas Co.

Answer the following questions:

a) How many subnets are shown in the network?
b) At least, how many bits have to be borrowed from the host ID to create the subnets?
c) How many different subnets can be created after borrowing the bits (remember to include all 0s and all 1s as legitimate subnet IDs)?
d) Up to how many hosts can have a permanent IP within each subnet?
e) What is the subnet mask in decimal?
f) What is the subnet mask in binary (or bit mask)?
g) Complete the following table regarding all available subnets and host IP ranges within a subnet. Begin with the lowest valued subnet address.

#	Subnet address	First available Host IP address	Last available Host IP address	Broadcast IP address
1				
2				
3				
4				
5				
6				
7				
8				

h) Assign above subnet addresses to hosts based on the following directions and complete the table below.
   1. Subnet #1 is assigned to the HQ LAN.
       Assign the first available host IP to the Fa0/0 router port (interface).
       Assign next three available host IPs to servers 1,2, and 3 connected to switch 2.
       Assign the last two available host IPs to PC1 and PC2 connected to switch 1.

   2. Subnet #2 is assigned to the LA Branch LAN.
       Assign the first available host IP to the Fa0/0 router port.
       Assign the last two available host IPs to PC3 and PC4 connected to switch 3.

   3. Subnet #3 is assigned to the NY Branch LAN.
       Assign the first available host IP to the Fa0/0 router port.
       Assign the last two available host IPs to PC5 and PC6 connected to switch 4.

   4. Subnet #4 is assigned to the NY Branch LAN.
       Assign the first available host IP to the Fa0/1 router port.
       Assign the last two available host IPs to station PC7 and PC8 connected to switch 5.

   5. Subnet #5 is assigned to the WAN link between R1 and R2.
       Assign the first available host IP to the R1's S0/0 port.
       Assign the last available host IP to the R2's S0/0 port.

6. Subnet #6 is assigned to the WAN link between R1 and R3.
   Assign the first available host IP to the R1's S0/1 port.
   Assign the last available host IP to the R3's S0/0 port.

Nodes	Port (Interface)	Subnet Address	IP Address	Subnet Mask	Default Gateway
R1	Fa0/0				N/A
	S0/0				N/A
	S0/1				N/A
R2	Fa0/0				N/A
	S0/0				N/A
R3	Fa0/0				N/A
	Fa0/1				N/A
	S0/0				N/A
Server 1	NIC				
Server 2	NIC				
Server 3	NIC				
PC1	NIC				
PC2	NIC				
PC3	NIC				
PC4	NIC				
PC5	NIC				
PC6	NIC				
PC7	NIC				
PC8	NIC				

CHAPTER 6 FUNDAMENTALS OF PACKET ROUTING

6.1 INTRODUCTION

This chapter explains issues relevant to the routing decision process of IP packets. Forwarding IP packets requires that the router develop and periodically update its routing table as a reference table. The table is placed in the router's main memory to allow a quick look-up whenever an IP packet arrives. The router searches routing table entries when it receives an IP packet and determines the packet's best forwarding path. So, there is a resemblance in the roles of the switch table and the routing table as two different reference sources: the one for *frame switching* decisions for intra-networking (layer 2) and the other for *packet routing* decisions for internetworking (layer 3). The summary of their procedural equivalence is:

A frame arrives at a switch port	A packet arrives at a router port
→ The switch refers to its *switch table*	→ The router refers to its *routing table*
→ Decide the frame's exit port	→ Decide the packet's exit port

The router constructs and maintains a routing table that enables decision-making regarding the delivery path of IP packets across an internet or across the Internet. To update the routing table, routers periodically advertise and exchange information regarding network 'conditions' using the so-called *dynamic routing protocol*. The dynamic routing protocol performs functions necessary to maintain and update the routing table and, thus, fundamentally differs from the IP protocol whose responsibility is packet development and delivery. This chapter explains structural details of the routing table and demonstrates how the dynamic routing protocol updates the routing table.

An enterprise such as a business firm, or ISP can have multiple internal routers to couple its subnetworks and this makes the enterprise network an internet as a whole. Routers are divided into two types: internal and border routers. Internal routers provide connectivity of network segments within an enterprise (i.e., internal or intra-domain routing) and border routers are responsible for dispatching packets to destinations beyond the enterprise network boundary (i.e., external or inter-domain routing). Internal and border routers rely on different types of dynamic routing protocols to exchange (or advertise) information necessary to update their routing tables. The focus of this chapter is the internal (or intra-domain) routing decision. The external (or inter-domain) routing is briefly covered at the end this chapter, but much of its technical detail is beyond the scope of this textbook.

The key learning objectives of this chapter are to understand:
- Fundamentals of the routing mechanism
- Internal structure of the routing table
- The process of IP packet forwarding decision
- Types of routing table entries: directly connected, static, and dynamic routes
- The dynamic routing protocol
    - Protocol types: interior vs. exterior gateway protocols
    - General understanding of its working mechanism
- Basics of external (or inter-domain) routing

6.2 ROUTING MECHANISM

In Chapter 2, it was explained that routing moves packets across multiple subnetworks based on their destination IP addresses. Then, Section 3.7 further explained the differences between switching and routing and how they work together to transport an IP packet between two hosts across subnetworks. On a related note, the important role of *address resolution protocol* (ARP) was explained as well. In this section, the focus is on explaining how the router uses its routing table entries to make forwarding (or routing) decisions of IP packets.

Let me begin with a hypothetical corporate network (Figure 6.1) where two subnets are joined by the router R1. Imagine a situation in which PC1 (172.20.1.1) exchanges IP packets with Server (172.20.2.1) via the router. The packet delivery between the two hosts needs *routing* and, to make it possible, R1 should maintain a routing table as the reference source. R1's two ports (interfaces) are configured with an IP address pertaining to each attached subnetwork (recall that the IPs are manually set up). They are:

172.20.1.254 (Fa0/0) attached to the 172.20.1.0/24 subnet,
172.20.2.254 (Fa0/1) attached to the 172.20.2.0/24 subnet.

On sending a packet to the Server, PC1 learns from the Server's IP address (172.20.2.1) that the destination is in a different subnet and therefore dispatches the packet (encapsulated within a frame) directly to Fa0/0 of R1 for routing. Once the packet arrives at Fa0/0, R1 refers to its routing table as in Figure 6.1, finds that the routing table's entry 172.20.2.0/24 matches the Server IP's first three numbers (172.20.2.1) and uses the corresponding Fa0/1 as the exit port of the packet.

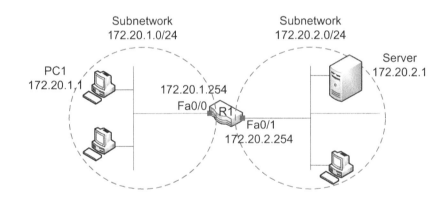

Destination Subnetwork/Mask	Exit Port/ Interface	Next hop IP	Metric
172.20.1.0/24	FastEthernet0/0	N/A	0
172.20.2.0/24	FastEthernet0/1	N/A	0

(Note: Hosts including PCs and Servers are generally connected to the router through one or more switches, which are not shown in the diagram for visual brevity.)

Figure 6.1 A case of two subnets and a router

184

To enable the packet routing, you can observe that subnet addresses (not host IP addresses) and their subnet masks are listed in the routing table. Among the columns of the routing table, you don't have to worry about *Next hop IP* and *Metric* at the moment. Given that there are only two subnets in Figure 6.1, the R1's routing table only needs two entries to enable packet routing.

Building on the very simple demonstration in Figure 6.1, let us take a look at a little more expanded internet in Figure 6.2. It illustrates a small enterprise network made up of three subnets (172.20.1.0/24, 172.20.2.0/24, and 172.20.3.0/24) conjoined by two routers, R1 and R2. The table in Figure 6.2 illustrates the R1's routing table. For all hosts stations to be able to exchange IP packets, the routing tables of both R1 and R2 have to contain entries of all three subnets.

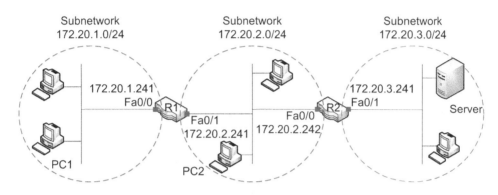

Destination Subnetwork/Mask	Exit Port/ Interface	Next hop IP	Metric
172.20.1.0/24	FastEthernet0/0	N/A	0
172.20.2.0/24	FastEthernet0/1	N/A	0
172.20.3.0/24	FastEthernet0/1	172.20.2.242	1

(Note: Presume that, in the subnet 172.20.2.0/24, R1 and R2 are *indirectly* connected through one or more switches. The other subnets also have switches for intra-networking.)

Figure 6.2 A case of three subnets and R1's routing table

~~~~~~

Exercise 6-1

1. Construct R2's routing table in Figure 6.2. The routing table should include columns of *destination subnet addresses*, *subnet masks*, and *exit ports* (Do not worry about additional details including *next-hop IP* and *metric*).

2. Imagine a corporate LAN composed of six subnetworks interconnected by three routers.
   a) Draw a network topology in which three routers interconnect six subnetworks (There can be several solutions).

b) Choose a network address of the company.

c) Create six subnet addresses and subnet masks, and assign them to the network. Clearly indicate which router port (e.g., Fa0/0) connects to which subnet.

d) Construct routing tables of the three routers to enable internetworking among host stations. The routing table should include columns of *destination subnets*, *subnet masks*, and *exit ports* only.

~~~~~~

6.3   ROUTING TABLE

6.3.1   Background

One key function performed by the router is to develop its own routing table as in Figure 6.2, a reference table necessary to decide forwarding paths of IP packets. The routing table, stored in the router's memory, can have entries that are manually added or automatically created. When there are a small number of routers within a network and/or when there is little need for updating the routing table, the manual addition of its entries makes sense. However, when a network has a number of routers in it, the manual construction and maintenance of each routing table becomes costly and also prone to mistakes. For these reasons, a majority of routing table entries are dynamically created by the router itself based on information obtained from other routers.

To enable the automated creation of the routing table and dynamic updates of its entries, routers advertise information based on a (or sometimes more) standard protocol, termed *dynamic routing protocol*. Several dynamic routing protocols (e.g., RIP, OSPF, IS-IS and BGP) have been introduced to specify what *information* is shared and how to do the sharing between routers. By now, you should be able see the difference between the routing protocol (e.g., RIP, OSPF, IS-IS and BGP) and the IP protocol (oftentimes called a *routed protocol*) in their functional orientations:

- The routing protocol is intended to advertise information necessary to construct and update the routing table.
- IP as a routed protocol is responsible for packet transportation for which the routing table becomes a reference source.

The internet layer's essential and fundamental responsibility is the forwarding of IP packets according to the routing table information. As for routing protocols including RIP, OSPF, IS-IS and BGP, they are not necessarily defined at the internet layer. In fact, confusing enough to readers, several of them belong to the application layer, yes application layer. This means that constructing the routing table by a router is not necessarily the work of the internet layer. Even if it conducts non-internet layer functions, the router becomes a layer 3 device because its primary function is moving packets based on the IP protocol and other functions are rather supplementary to it.

6.3.2   Routing Table Elements

In this section, information elements stored in the routing table are explained. As explained, its entries can be manually inserted (i.e., static entries that stay unchanged) or dynamically added/updated based on information regularly advertised by other routers. The frequent routing table updates reflect changes in network conditions and topology. In Figure 6.2, the routing table is shown to contain such information fields as *destination network*, *subnet masks*, *exit ports*, *next-hop IPs*, and *metric* values. Among them, *destination network*, *subnet masks*, and *exit ports* are most fundamental to enable packet routing. The role of the remaining columns (i.e., *next-hop IPs* and *metric*) is supplementary or informational. They are explained below.

a) **Destination subnetwork addresses and their subnet masks**: Remember that the column contains subnet addresses, not host addresses.

b) **Exit ports (interfaces)**: The router port used to forward an IP packet to ultimately reach the destination subnetwork or less frequently the destination host (e.g., server).

c) **Next-hop IP**: The port address of the next router to which a packet is forwarded to reach the destination host eventually. The *next-hop* may be cabled directly (e.g., router-to-router over a WAN link) or indirectly via one or more switches. The switches between two routers are not included in the hop count (Remember that switches are layer 2 devices that do not understand IP).

Figure 6.3 demonstrates the *exit port* and *next-hop IP* address. According to the figure, two routers R1 and R2 interconnect two LANs (i.e., 10.10.1.0/24 and 172.16.1.0/24) via the WAN link (192.168.10.0/24). If the PC (10.10.1.1) sends an IP packet to the server (172.16.1.20), R1 will route the packet to R2 after referring to its routing table entries. In this situation, 192.168.10.2 of R2 becomes the next-hop IP address for R1 and R1's S0/0/1 becomes the exit port. You can observe that the exit port and next-hop are two ends of a subnetwork. In the case of Figure 6.1, there are no other routers except R1 and thus the R1's routing table has exit ports but not next-hops.

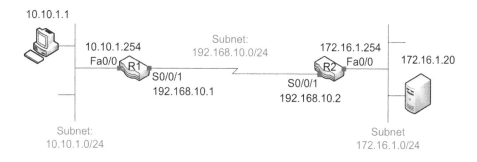

Figure 6.3 Exit port (interface) and next-hop IP address

d) **Metric**: The metric represents a value obtained from such cost factors as *hop count*, *bandwidth, network load,* and *delay*. Some of the cost items such as *bandwidth* can be manually configured in the router (e.g., S0/0/1 is linked to T-1 at 1.54Mbps) and others such as *network load* are dynamically computed by the router based on sampled data (e.g., the amount of data arrived at S0/0/1 during a measured time period). *The metric value is used to break a tie when a router finds more than one optimal routing path to a particular* *destination in its routing table.* The process of the packet forwarding decision is explained in the next section.

A dynamic routing protocol can use one or more factors to compute overall 'cost' of a particular route. For example, RIP relies on *hop count*; OSPF's choice is *bandwidth*; and EIGRP (Cisco's proprietary protocol) uses *bandwidth* and *delay* as the default cost factors. Among cost variables frequently used to compute the metric value are:

- **Hop count**: The number of routers an IP packet has to pass through before reaching the destination network. The lower the hop count, the better (i.e., lower cost) the route path becomes. For instance, in Figure 6.3, if a packet is in R1, delivering it to the server (172.16.1.20) via R2 takes one hop.

- **Bandwidth**: It represents the connection speed of a route and generally a static value that is pre-assigned. For this, the lowest speed of all links of a delivery path can become the path's bandwidth value. For instance, if a particular end-to-end route takes four LAN and WAN links of 100Mbps (Fast Ethernet), 1.5Mbps (T-1), 155Mbps (OC-3), and 2.0Mbps (DSL), its bandwidth is 1.5Mbps. Alternatively, the combined bandwidth of all links of a delivery path can be used to decide the metric value. In both approaches, the higher the bandwidth value the better (i.e., lower cost) the route path becomes. In the previous example, the combined bandwidth of four links is 258.5Mbps.

- **Delay**: The estimated delay of a particular path is decided by the type of link to a router port. The estimated delay is therefore primarily static rather than dynamic. For example, the delay of 100Mbps Fast Ethernet is 100 microseconds and that of 1.5Mbps T-1 line is 20,000 microseconds. With this metric, the lower the delay value, the better a route path becomes.

- **Reliability**: This metric is an indication of a network link's dependability in which the lower the probability of link-failure, the higher the link reliability. It can be computed dynamically by a router based on average network performance during a certain time duration (e.g., 5 minutes) and presented as a percentage out of 100 (e.g., 80% reliable out of 100%). The higher the reliability, the better a route path becomes.

- **Load**: This metric reflects the rate of link utilization as a percentage out of 100 (completely utilized). It can be examined dynamically during a certain time interval (e.g., 5 minutes). For instance, the load value of 80% of a link means 80 percent of the link capacity was used during the measurement period. The lower the load, the better a route path becomes.

~~~~~~

Exercise 6-2

1. Answer questions based on Figure 6.2.
   a) On the R2's routing table constructed in the previous exercise, add columns of *next-hop IP,* and *hop count* as the metric.

b) If R1 routes a packet from PC1 to Server, what is R1's next-hop address?
c) If R2 routes a packet from PC2 to Server, what is R2's next-hop address?
d) If R1 routes a packet from PC1 to Server, what is R1's exit port?
e) If R2 routes a packet from Server to PC1, what is R2's exit port?
f) If R2 routes a packet from Server to PC2, what is R2's next-hop address?
g) If R2 routes a packet from Server to PC1, what is R2's next-hop address?

2. Based on Figure 6.3, construct a routing table of R1 and R2. The routing table should include columns of *destination network*, *subnet mask*, *exit port*, *next-hop IP,* and *hop count* as the metric.

3. Figure 6.4 is a hypothetical enterprise network in which three routers are interconnected by a high-speed switch. Answer questions.
    a) How many subnetworks do you see in the enterprise network and what are subnet addresses?
    b) If R1 routes a packet from PC1 to Server1, what is R1's next-hop address?
    c) If R2 routes a packet from PC2 to Server1, what is R2's next-hop address?
    d) If R1 routes a packet from PC1 to PC2, what is R1's exit port?
    e) If R3 routes a packet from Server1 to PC2, what is R3's exit port?
    f) Construct routing tables of R1, R2, and R3. The routing tables should include columns of *destination network*, *subnet mask*, *exit port*, *next-hop IP,* and *hop count* as the metric.
    Hint: The routing table has to list all subnets of the enterprise network to enable packet routing between hosts. Below is a sample routing table of R1.

Destination Network/Subnet Mask	Exit Port/ Interface	Next hop IP	Metric
192.168.10.0/24	FastEthernet0/1	…….	0
172.20.1.0/24	FastEthernet0/0	……	0
10.10.1.0/24	FastEthernet0/1	192.168.10.252	1
192.168.1.0/24	FastEthernet0/1	192.168.10.253	1

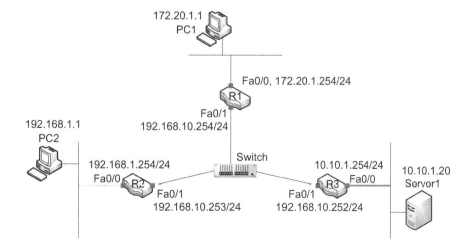

Figure 6.4 A hypothetical enterprise network

189

4. The Green Tech Co's enterprise network in Figure 6.5 interconnects LANs in four business locations through several leased line WAN links.
   a) What topology is used to interconnect the four routers?
   b) How many subnets do you see in the enterprise network?
   c) Assign adequate names to all router ports in use.
   d) Assuming that there are 100 hosts that need an IP address in each business location, assign a subnet address and subnet mask to all subnetworks. Then allocate an IP address to each router port being connected (Using the drawing of Figure 6.5 will be easier to work with.). Use a private IP range for the subnetworks.
   e) Once all subnetworks have their own subnet addresses, then each router should have a router table to route IP packets. Develop the routing table of each router that contains columns of *destination network, subnet mask, exit port, next- hop IP,* and *hop count* as the metric.

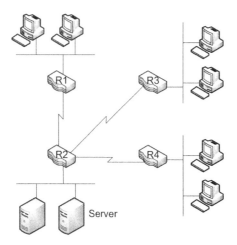

Figure 6.5 Enterprise network of Green Tech Co.

6.4 PACKET FORWARDING DECISION

This section explains the general mechanism used by routers to determine the forwarding paths of IP packets. Before doing so, the *default route* concept is briefly introduced. A routing table can include the *default route* indicated by 0.0.0.0/0 (subnet IP address: 0.0.0.0, subnet mask 0.0.0.0). When the router cannot find the destination network of an incoming IP packet among the entries of its routing table, it releases the packet through the port assigned to the default route. The default route of a router is generally tied to the port that eventually leads to the border router for a WAN or Internet connection.

When a packet arrives at a router port, the router searches its routing table going through all entries from top to bottom to locate all subnetwork addresses that match the packet's destination address. Here, *a match is found when the destination address of the IP packet contains a bit stream identical to a particular subnet address of the routing table.* The router performs this matching process for every IP packet it receives.

The router table search can result in a single match, multiple matches, or no match. Given the three different scenarios in matching, the following rules are applied for packet forwarding decisions:

1. When there is a single match between routing table entries and a packet's destination address, the packet is dispatched through the corresponding exit interface. For example, if the routing table includes ANY one of the following entries, the packet with the destination address of 100.50.30.10 has a match (pay a close attention to the subnet mask):
   100.50.30.0/24
   100.50.0.0/16
   100.0.0.0/8.

2. When multiple matches are found in the routing table, the router chooses the network path that has the most EXPLICIT or the LONGEST match with the destination IP address. If there is more than one best path, the metric value is used to break the tie.

   For example, assume that an IP packet with the destination address of 100.50.30.10 arrives at a router port and the router table contains the following subnet address/mask entries:
   [1] 100.50.30.0/24
   [2] 100.50.0.0/16
   [3] 100.0.0.0/8
   [4] 0.0.0.0/0 (default route)
   Of course, the router only understands binary values of 0s and 1s, and finding the longest match is always based on the string of 0s and 1s. The destination address 100.50.30.10 is equivalent to:
   01100100.00110010.00011110.00001010.

   Meanwhile, the above routing table entries in binary are (with subnet ID bits highlighted):
   [1] 01100100.00110010.00011110.00000000
   [2] 01100100.00110010.00000000.00000000
   [3] 01100100.00000000.00000000.00000000
   [4] 00000000.00000000.00000000.00000000

   Among the four entries, the subnet address of [1] has the longest (thus most explicit) match with the destination address, followed by [2] and then [3]. Therefore, the IP packet is dispatched to the 100.50.30.0 network. It is important to remember that the longest match does not have to be a multiple of 8-bits.

3. If there is no matching entry in the table, the router forwards the packet through the exit port assigned to the *default route* (0.0.0.0/0). When there is neither a matching entry nor a *default route* in the routing table, the router has no choice but to abandon the IP packet. As said, if any of the subnet ID bits differs from the arriving packet's destination address, there is no match. For instance, there is no match between the destination address of

100.50.30.10 (01100100.00110010.00011110.00001010) and the following routing table entries:

01100100.00100000.00000000.00000000/16
01100100.00110010.00010101.00000000/24.

Let us extend the example further. If the routing table only includes the entries below, the packet with the destination address of 100.50.30.10 has no match because of a discrepancy between their subnet ID bits and the packet's destination address. Then, the router releases the packet through the exit port of 0.0.0.0/0:

100.50.20.0/24
100.40.40.0/24
100.40.0.0/16
90.0.0.0/8
0.0.0.0/0

~~~~~~

Exercise 6-3

1. Decide matching between the destination address, 100.50.30.10, of a packet and the following routing table entries.

100.50.30.0/16	100.40.30.0/16	100.50.30.0/8	100.50.30.0/25
100.50.15.0/16	100.50.30.0/24	100.50.10.0/24	100.50.0.0/24
100.0.0.0/16	100.50.0.0/18	100.48.30.0/21	100.27.0.0/15

2. A router receives packets. What should be the exit port (interface) of each packet?

a) Packet destination: 172.164.32.25

Subnet/mask	Exit port
172.164.30.0/21	S0/0/0
172.154.24.0/20	S0/0/1
173.140.21.0/7	Fa0/0
173.120.21.0/15	Fa0/1
0.0.0.0/0	S0/0/1

b) Packet destination: 142.66.39.125

Subnet/mask	Exit port
142.64.130.0/16	S0/0/0
142.62.39.0/24	S0/0/1
142.140.21.0/7	Fa0/0
142.66.39.64/25	Fa0/1
0.0.0.0/0	S0/0/1

c) Packet destination: 11.87.234.111

Subnet/mask	Exit port
11.87.234.60/27	S0/0/0

11.87.200.60/22	S0/0/1
11.85.234.60/15	Fa0/0
11.87.234.160/25	Fa0/1
0.0.0.0/0	S0/0/1

6.5 ENTRY TYPES OF ROUTING TABLE

The routing table entries can be one of three types: *Directly Connected Routes*, *Static Routes*, and *Dynamic Routes*. Understanding their differences helps you to better comprehend what mechanisms are utilized to develop and update the routing table.

6.5.1 Directly Connected Routes

With the *directly connected route*, the destination subnetwork of an IP packet is directly linked to a router port. In other words, all subnets physically connected to the ports of a router are entered into its routing table as directly connected routes. For example, in Figure 6.1, two subnets 172.20.1.0/24 and 172.20.2.0/24 are routes directly connected to R1 through Fa0/0 and Fa0/1. *A directly connected route is added to the routing table whenever an IP address and a subnet mask are manually assigned to a router port.* This means that a router has as many directly connected routes in its routing table as the number of ports that are physically cabled and activated.

Example: Adding a directly connected route to the Cisco router's routing table

This example demonstrates how the directly connected route is added to the routing table of Cisco routers by issuing several relatively simple commands. Using Figure 6.1 as an example, three commands assign an IP address/subnet mask to *Fastethernet0/0* and activate the port. On their completion in succession, the router enters the directly connected subnet (172.20.1.0/24) into its routing table.

(1) R1(config)# *interface Fastethernet0/0* ⤳
   Comment: This command points to a particular port of R1 to be configured.
(2) R1(config-if)# *ip address 172.20.1.254 255.255.255.0* ⤳
   Comment: This command assigns an IP address and a subnet mask to *Fastethernet0/0*. With this, R1 automatically learns that the subnet 172.20.1.0 is physically connected to its *Fastethernet0/0* port.
(3) R1(config-if)# *no shutdown* ⤳
   Comment: This command activates the *Fastethernet0/0* port. The router port is not operational unless it is manually activated.

Exercise 6-4: Assume that you are configuring a Cisco router.

1. In Figure 6.1, what 3 commands are necessary to create the directly connected route (172.20.2.0/24) in the R1's routing table?
2. In Figure 6.3, how many directly connected routes should be entered into the R1's routing

table?

3. In Figure 6.3, what 3 commands are issued to create the directly connected route (192.168.10.0/24) in the R1's routing table?

6.5.2 Static Routes

Static Routes of a Router

With the static route, the routing path to a destination network is manually added to the routing table and it remains there unless manually changed. Although this definition bears a close resemblance to the directly connected routes above, the key difference is that the destination network of a static route is not directly cabled to the router port. As another difference, configuring and activating each cabled router port (that will add a directly connected route to the routing table) are necessary for it to be operational but adding certain static routes (e.g., default route) is not a requirement. There are situations where such manual addition of static routes makes much sense:

- Adding a default route to the routing table
- There is little need for changing an entry (or entries)
- Configuring a small network with limited number of routers

As an extension of the R1's routing table in Figure 6.1, for example, Table 6.1 demonstrates two directly connected routes and one static entry of the default route (IP address = 0.0.0.0 and subnet mask = 0.0.0.0). As explained, if there is no matching between an incoming IP packet's destination address and the routing table entries, then the router will forward the packet to the *default route* via the FastEthernet0/0 port.

Destination Network/Subnet Mask	Exit Port/ Interface	Next hop IP	Metric
172.20.1.0/24	FastEthernet0/0	N/A	0
172.20.2.0/24	FastEthernet0/1	N/A	0
0.0.0.0/0	FastEthernet0/0	N/A	1

Table 6.1 Default route as a static route

Example: Adding a default route to the Cisco router

Adding the static, default route in Table 6.1 to the routing table is done by a simple statement as below. It basically tells the router that the default route path (destination IP: 0.0.0.0 with subnet mask: 0.0.0.0) is through the exit port, *FastEthenet0/0* (or shortly *Fa0/0*).

R1(config)# *ip route 0.0.0.0 0.0.0.0 Fa0/0* ✍

194

Static Routes of a Host

So far, the explanation of static entries has focused on the router's routing table. Host computers also have their own routing table whose entries generally stay unchanged. As an example, Figure 6.6 demonstrates the routing table of a PC running Windows OS. To display it, issue "*C:\>route print*" or "*C:\>netstat –r*" at the command prompt. Recent OS version including Windows 7 provides two routing tables (one for IPv4 and another for IPv6), but we focus on IPv4. Although there are a number of entries in the table, the first line is the most important one that enables the computer to route IP packets to the Internet. Basically, the first line says that the default routing path (subnet address 0.0.0.0 with subnet mask 0.0.0.0) of IP packets from the host station (192.168.1.2) is through the *gateway* (router port) of 192.168.1.1. The gateway is also known as a *default gateway*. The interface, 192.168.1.2, is the host's IP address.

```
C:\WINDOWS\system32\cmd.exe                                        _ □ x
===========================================================================
Active Routes:
Network Destination        Netmask          Gateway       Interface  Metric
          0.0.0.0          0.0.0.0      192.168.1.1      192.168.1.2      10
        127.0.0.0        255.0.0.0        127.0.0.1        127.0.0.1       1
      192.168.1.0    255.255.255.0      192.168.1.2      192.168.1.2      10
      192.168.1.2  255.255.255.255        127.0.0.1        127.0.0.1      10
    192.168.1.255  255.255.255.255      192.168.1.2      192.168.1.2      10
        224.0.0.0        240.0.0.0      192.168.1.2      192.168.1.2      10
  255.255.255.255  255.255.255.255      192.168.1.2                3       1
  255.255.255.255  255.255.255.255      192.168.1.2      192.168.1.2       1
Default Gateway:        192.168.1.1
```

Figure 6.6 A sample routing table of a host station

Exercise 6-5: Modification of PC routing table

The static routing table entries in Figure 6.6 can be modified using commands including *route print*, *route add* and *route delete* as shown below. Keywords are in upper characters.

      C:\>route **PRINT** ⮐
      C:\>route **DELETE** *network* ⮐
      C:\>route **ADD** *network* **MASK** *mask gateway-IP address* ⮐

For example, you can erase the default gateway in Figure 6.6 by issuing *C:\>route DELETE 0.0.0.0*. Then, the first entry "*0.0.0.0 0.0.0.0 192.168.1.1 192.168.1.2*" will be removed from the routing table. Also, you can add the default route back with *C:\>route ADD 0.0.0.0 MASK 0.0.0.0 192.168.1.1*.

Now, you are repeating the process with your own computer.

1. At the command prompt, issue a ping request to a well-known portal site such as *www.yahoo.com* and see if there are responses. If there is no response, then try other sites until you come up with one that responds.

2. Bring up the routing table of your computer.
3. Delete the default route from the routing table (make sure to write down the original statement before its deletion). Use the *route print* command to confirm the removal of the default route.
4. After removing the default route, ping again the web server identified in Step 1 and describe what happens. Explain why.
5. Now add the deleted default route back to the routing table. Use the *route print* command to confirm the addition.
6. After the addition, ping the web server again and describe what happens.
7. Explain what you have learned from this.
8. Explain how the host station knows its gateway IP address even when the information is not manually configured? Hint: DHCP

Note: If you are using recent Windows versions, you may be alerted that "*The required operation requires elevation.*" This means that you can run the command with an administrator privilege. To do this, go to: *All Programs > Accessories > right click Command Prompt* and click *Run as administrator!*

You should now know that *default gateway* (or just *gateway* as in Figure 6.6) is the IP address of the router port to which a host station sends IP packets when their destination addresses are not in the same subnet. Packets arriving at the default gateway are relayed to the outside of the subnet and a majority of them reach the Internet. The default gateway can be viewed with '*C:>ipconfig*' as well as '*C:\>route print*' or '*C:\>netstat –r*'. As seen in Figure 6.7, the default gateway, therefore, should share the same subnet address as host stations.

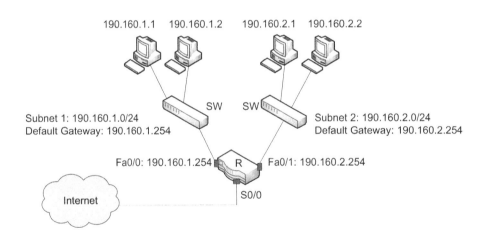

Figure 6.7 Demonstration of default gateway

Exercise 6-6

1. Answer questions based on Figure 6.4.
   a) Determine the default gateway of PC1, PC2, and Server1.

196

b) Suppose that the network administrator forgot to configure the default gateway address of Server1, providing only the permanent IP address and its subnet mask. PC1 and PC2 are given IP addresses, subnet masks, and default gateways by the DHCP server. If PC1 pings Server1, will PC1 receive Server1's response? Why or why not?

c) Suppose that the network administrator forgot to configure the default gateway address of PC1, configuring only its permanent IP address and subnet mask (assume that DHCP is not used). Server1 is configured with an IP address, subnet mask, and default gateway. If PC1 pings Server1, will PC1 receive Server1's response? Why or why not?

2. Answer questions based on Figure 6.7.
   a) Can the serial port S0/0's IP address be the default gateway for host stations in subnet 1 or subnet 2? If not, why?
   b) Which cannot be a default gateway for host stations in Subnet 1?

190.160.1.0	190.160.2.0	190.160.1.3
190.160.2.3	190.160.1.255	190.160.2.255

3. Refer to Figure 6.8 and answer questions.

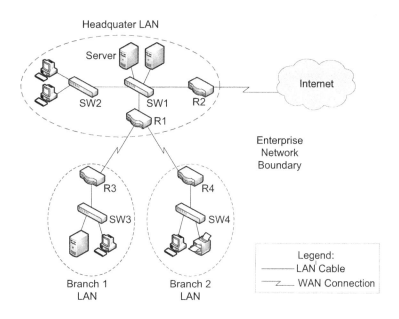

Figure 6.8 A hypothetical enterprise network

a) The list of permanent IP addresses and subnet masks available is given below. Assign them to all user stations, servers, the printer, and router ports of the enterprise network.

Available IP ranges	Subnet masks
192.168.5.251 ~ 192.168.5.252	255.255.255.0
192.168.10.253 ~ 192.168.10.254	255.255.255.0
192.168.20.1 ~ 192.168.20.6	255.255.255.0
172.18.10.1 ~ 172.18.10.3	255.255.255.0

| 172.19.110.1 ~ 172.19.110.3 | 255.255.255.0 |

b) Once IP addresses and subnet masks are assigned, then identify default gateways of all hosts including workstations, servers, and the printer.

6.5.3 Dynamic Routes

The router adds dynamic entries to its routing table using information obtained through communications with other routers. Adding and updating dynamic entries into the routing table requires that routers advertise such information using the dynamic routing protocol. The advertising takes place according to certain periodic/scheduled time intervals or is triggered when there is a change in the network such as router crash/rebooting or unexpected corrections in network topology. On receiving advertisements from other routers, a router uses a built-in algorithm to compute the best delivery path and its metric value to each destination subnet and updates them to its routing table.

Depending on the dynamic routing protocol activated, advertised information items vary. Several routing protocols have been in use including RIP, OSPF, IS-IS and EIGRP. They are not compatible and, generally, one routing protocol is activated within an enterprise network although routers can rely on more than one routing protocol to gather information. When there are two or more protocols activated in a router, each routing protocol comes up with its own best path to a subnetwork, resulting in as many best paths as the number of routing protocols in action. The routing table, however, includes only one path chosen according to the preference order.

Example: Preference of routing protocols in Cisco routers

Cisco routers have the following order of preference when two or more dynamic routing protocols are concurrently used:
1. EIGRP-determined routes
2. OSPF-determined routes
3. RIP-determined routes

The entries of a routing table represent the combination of directly connected route(s), static route(s), and/or dynamic route(s) depending on how it is constructed. Some routing tables may have only directly connected routes and static routes; some only directly connected routes and dynamic routes; and others with all three types.

In addition, although not shown previously for brevity (e.g., Figure 6.1, 6.2, 6.4 and Table 6.1), the routing table can contain an 'information' column that tells how each entry was created. As an example, the routing table in Table 6.2 has the 'Type' column in which the first two entries (C) are directly connected routes; the next two entries (O) are added by the OSPF dynamic routing protocol; and the last (S) is a static default route manually added.

Exercise 6-7: Based on the results associated with Figure 6.8 in Exercise 6-6, develop a routing table of R1, R2, R3, and R4. Each table should contain columns of *destination subnet*, *subnet mask*, *exit port* and *next-hop IP*. Also, add a default route to each routing table so that it enables forwarding of IP packets from the local network to the Internet.

Type	Destination Subnetwork/Mask	Exit Port/ Interface	Next hop IP	Metric
C	192.168.10.0/24	FastEthernet0/1	N/A	0
C	172.20.1.0/24	FastEthernet0/0	N/A	0
O	10.10.1.0/24	FastEthernet0/1	192.168.10.254	120
O	192.168.1.0/24	Serial0/1	172.16.10.254	120
S	0.0.0.0/0	Serial0/1	172.16.10.254	1

Table 6.2 Routing table with entry *Type* information

6.6 DYNAMIC ROUTING PROTOCOLS

6.6.1 Protocol Categories

Dynamic routing protocols that enable the dynamic and automated additions and updates of routing table entries are divided into *interior gateway protocols* (IGP) and *exterior gateway* protocols (EGP).

Interior Gateway Protocols

The *Interior Gateway Protocol* (IGP) is activated on routers placed within the network boundary of a so-called *autonomous system* for intra-domain (or internal) routing. By definition, an autonomous system represents the scope of a network within which a consistent routing policy (e.g., choice of protocol) can be applied internally. A large organization (e.g. enterprise, university, ISP) forms its own *autonomous system* by obtaining a globally unique *autonomous system number* as well as a network IP address from a Regional Internet Registry (see Section 10.2.3 for more details).

The internal routers of an *autonomous system* depend on the IGP to exchange information necessary to develop their routing tables. Among the popular IGPs are RIP (Routing Information Protocol), EIGRP (Enhanced Interior Gateway Routing Protocol), OSPF (Open Shortest Path First), and IS-IS (Intermediate System to Intermediate System).

- RIP was originally developed by Xerox and later adopted as an industry standard. It has evolved with the Internet from RIPv1 for classful IPv4 networks to RIPv2 for classless IPv4 networks. RIPng (or RIP next generation) for IPv6 has been released as well. RIP is a good choice for relatively small networks.

- OSPF, as a popular IGP, was developed for the TCP/IP protocol suite by *Internet Engineering Tasks Force* (IETF) and currently two versions are available OSPFv2 for IPv4 and OSPFv3 for IPv6.
- IS-IS was introduced by *International Organization for Standardization* (ISO) for the OSI protocol suite and is used widely by large network service providers including ISPs and telcos.
- EIGRP is a proprietary protocol from Cisco.

Exterior Gateway Protocols

The Exterior Gateway Protocol (EGP) is utilized for dynamic and automated updates of the routing table of border routers for inter-domain (or external) routing between *autonomous systems*. In other words, border routers use EGPs to exchange routing information with other border routers placed at the network boundaries of ISPs, companies and universities (as *autonomous systems*). *Border Gateway Protocol* (BGP) is the most well-known EGP.

6.6.2 Delivery of Advertisement

The advertisements by dynamic routing protocols are conveyed in IP packets. For example, the RIP's advertising message is encapsulated within the UDP datagram at the transport layer, which then becomes an IP packet at the internet layer and subsequently a frame at the data link layer. Meanwhile, the encapsulation process of OSPF messages slightly differs from that of RIP in that the IP packet encapsulates OSPF advertisement in its data field (therefore no UDP header). Despite the relatively minor differences, dynamic routing protocols share a resemblance as their advertisements are delivered to other routers in IP packets.

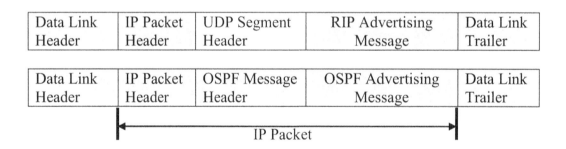

Data Link Header	IP Packet Header	UDP Segment Header	RIP Advertising Message	Data Link Trailer

Data Link Header	IP Packet Header	OSPF Message Header	OSPF Advertising Message	Data Link Trailer

IP Packet

Figure 6.9 Encapsulation of dynamic routing protocol advertisement

6.6.3 Determination of Dynamic Routes

Once a router receives advertisements from other routers, what mechanism is used by the active routing protocol to determine the best path from the router to all subnetworks in a domain? Routing protocols use different algorithms. Among them, the approach utilized by OSPF, a popular so-called *link-state* protocol, is demonstrated in a simplified manner. The process takes the following steps:

200

a) **Learn directly connected links**: A router learns about subnets directly connected to its ports (or interfaces). This includes: the IP address and subnet mask of a port; subnet type (e.g., Ethernet, WAN link); and the cost of a link (e.g., bandwidth). The router learns the information when a network administrator manually configures its ports (refer back to Section 6.5.1).

For example, from the manual input, R1 in Figure 6.10 learns that its Fa0/0 port has the IP address and subnet mask of 172.17.20.1/24 (therefore 172.17.20.0 is the subnet address), and connects to Fast Ethernet at 100 Mbps. R2 and R3 also obtain such information through the same process.

b) **Form adjacency**: Each router sends out *hello* messages through its connected ports to learn if any directly connected router runs the same dynamic routing protocol of OSPF. Neighbor routers running the same OSPF protocol respond with *hello* messages, thus forming adjacency.

c) **Build link-state information**: Each router builds an advertisement message with link-state information gathered and also calculated, which includes:
   - IP address and subnet mask of a port
   - Link type (e.g., Ethernet, WAN serial)
   - Neighboring router (if exists)
   - Cost metric of a link (e.g., bandwidth)

As a demonstration, Figure 6.10 shows hypothetical link-state information of R1's three links that are directly associated with its Fa0/0, S0/0/0, and S0/0/1 ports.

d) **Advertise link-state information**: The *link-state* information is advertised to all routers running OSPF. For example, in Figure 6.10, R1 floods the link-state information to adjacent R2 and R3. R2 and R3 store the received information in their *databases* and then flood the R1's link-state information to other adjacent routers (if there are). This flooding repeats until all routers in the internal domain (e.g., a campus) receive the R1's link-state information. R2 and R3 also flood their own link-state information to other routers. With the periodic link-state advertisements by all routers, each router possesses link-state data of all the other routers in a database.

e) **Construct a map**: Once a router (e.g., R1) receives link-state information from all the other routers (e.g., R2 and R3) in the same internal domain, it uses the database to develop a complete map (or graph) of router/subnet interconnectivity and also uses the map to determine the best packet routing path to each subnet based on the *shortest path first* principle (thus called OSPF – Open Shortest Path First).

For instance, Figure 6.11 demonstrates a map developed by R1 with transmission cost of each link (Note that the transmission cost such as link bandwidth is also included in the advertisement). When bandwidth is used as the cost metric, for example, the higher the bandwidth of a link, the lower the transmission cost becomes. Given the principle of *shortest path first*, the optimal routing path between any two routers should have the lowest cumulative cost. For example, the best route from PC1 to the Server becomes "PC1-R1-R2-R5-R4-Server" with the total cost of 24.

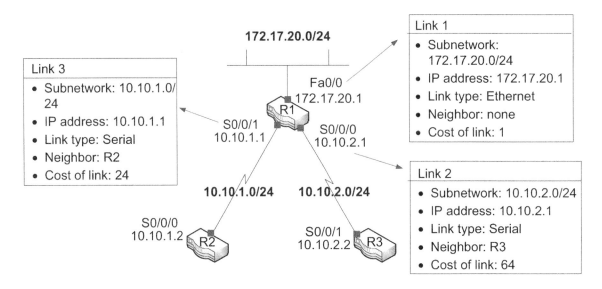

Figure 6.10 Link-state information of R1

f) **Update routing table**: Once the best route from R1 to each subnet is calculated based on the shortest path first principle, it is entered into the R1's routing table to assist the router's packet forwarding decision. For example, if the Server in Figure 6.11 is in the subnet address and subnet mask of 192.168.20.0/24, R1 will add an entry "192.168.20.0 (subnet), /24 (subnet mask), and Fa0/1 (R1's exit port)" to its routing table. The entry means that, to reach 192.168.20.0/24 in the shortest path, packets should be released through its Fa0/1 port.

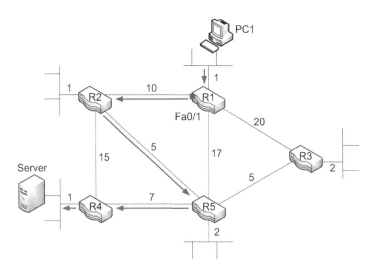

Figure 6.11 A sample router map

6.6.4 Security Management

There is potentially a security risk in developing the routing table relying on information advertised by other routers. For example, imagine the situation in which a malicious attacker can advertise falsified link-state information. Also, a misconfigured router can be mistakenly added to a network by someone other than the authorized person. The router can advertise flawed link-state or other related information and subsequently corrupt other routers' routing tables. This will disrupt the integrity of packet routing, negatively affecting network performance (e.g., more lost packets).

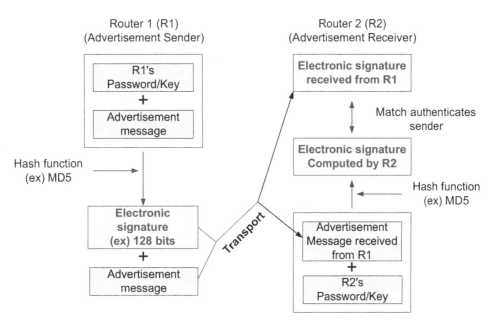

Figure 6.12 Authentication of advertisement

To reduce potential security risks, routers can be configured to authenticate and encrypt advertisements. For this, all routers can be set up with the same authentication information including the password (or key). Then, using the password (key), a router with an advertisement message (e.g., R1 in Figure 6.12) can produce an *electronic signature* unique to the message. To generate the electronic signature, the password and the advertisement message in combination can be fed into a hash function such as MD5 that produces a one-way, unique value of a certain size (e.g., MD5 produces 128 bit hash values). The hash value as an electronic signature and the advertisement message are, then, sent to neighboring routers (e.g., R2 in Figure 6.12). The router (e.g., R2), on receiving them, repeats the same process of producing an electronic signature using its own password that is identical to the sender's. If the locally computed hash value (i.e., signature) is identical to that from the sender, then this completes sender authentication. The authentication process is summarized in Figure 6.12.

~~~~~~

Example: Activating RIP on a Cisco router.

In this example, to demonstrate how a dynamic routing protocol is activated, the necessary commands to run RIP on a Cisco router are introduced (see Figure 6.13). Dynamic routing protocols (e.g., RIP, OSPF) share a similarity in that their activation on a router requires listing of all subnets *directly connected* to it. For example, in Figure 6.13, each router should be given all *directly connected* subnets. The activation of RIP on R1, thus, takes the following commands:

R1(config) #***router rip***   : Enter the RIP configuration mode
R1(config-router) #***network 172.20.1.0*** : Add 172.20.1.0 as a directly connected network
R1(config-router) #***network 172.20.2.0*** : Add 172.20.2.0 as a directly connected network
R1(config-router) #***end***   : Exit the RIP configuration mode

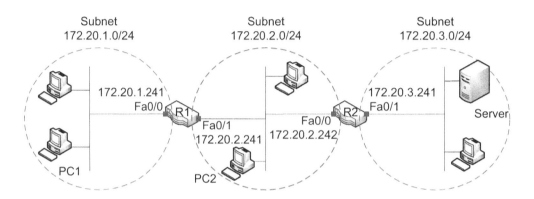

Figure 6.13 A hypothetical network

Exercise 6-8

1. What are commands you need to issue on R2, another Cisco router, so that the two routers (R1 and R2) begin exchange of advertisements based on RIP? Don't worry about the difference in prompt (e.g., R1(config) vs. R1(config-router)).

2. Refer to Figure 6.4. What commands are used on R1, R2, and R3 so that the three routers begin to advertise information based on RIP?

6.6.5 Static Routing vs. Dynamic Routing

As shown previously (see Table 6.2), a router's routing table can have a combination of directly connected, static and dynamic entries. Dynamic entries are continuously updated by the dynamic routing protocol to reflect situational changes (e.g., changes in traffic volume or network topology). This dynamic update is important for effective forwarding of IP packets to their ultimate destinations. Dependence on advertisements of the dynamic routing protocol, however, results in a considerable overhead to the network (e.g., increased network traffic due to periodic advertisements) and to routers (e.g., processing of received advertisements to update the routing table). On the other hand, although the static configuration of the routing table does not burden the network and routers, it results in higher administrative costs and a greater chance of making

204

configuration mistakes, especially as the number of routers grows. The pros and cons of static (manual) versus dynamic (automated) addition and update of routing table entries are summarized in Table 6.3.

Compared aspects	Comparison	
	Static approach	Dynamic approach
Difficulty in configuration	More difficult	
Chance of configuration errors	Higher chance	
Security of routing table entries	More secure	
Responsiveness to changes in network topology		More responsive
Burden (overhead) on network		Higher burden
Burden on router (e.g., CPU, memory)		Higher burden

Table 6.3 Static vs. dynamic updates of routing table

6.7 INTER-DOMAIN ROUTING

As inter-domain routing is an advanced concept even in the networking field, it is briefly explained here hiding the complex technical details in order to provide readers with general understanding of how it enables global routing of IP packets. Border Gateway Protocol (BGP) is the most widely used Exterior Gateway Protocol (EGP) developed for inter-domain (i.e., between autonomous systems) routing of IP packets.

Each autonomous system has a network address and an ASN (AS number). Each border router of an AS contains, in its routing table, network addresses of the entire autonomous systems in the world (It is a long list!) for IP packet routing. Relying on BGP, the border router of each autonomous system develops a routing table that contains such a long list of entries.

A simplified example is presented here to demonstrate how border routers learn the existence of other networks and their autonomous systems. For the sake of explanations, let's assume that the entire Internet is composed of only five autonomous systems (see Figure 6.14), although there are more than 50,000 autonomous systems in reality.

The following describes the learning process in a nutshell:
1) Each ASN is given a network address. For example, assume that AS10 is 100.0.0.0/8.
2) AS10's border router advertises its "AS10 and 100.0.0.0/8" to its neighboring AS20 and AS30.
3) AS20 and AS30 relay "AS10 and 100.0.0.0/8" to their neighbors. Also included in the relay is the information regarding the AS chain to AS10. For example, AS40 gets the chain information of "AS20-AS10" from AS20, and AS50 gets "AS40-AS20-AS10" from AS40 and "AS30-AS10" from AS30.
4) Now, AS50 (its border router) knows that there are two paths to AS10: one through AS40

and the other through AS30, and its routing table entries include AS10's 100.0.0.0/8 and the AS chain information.

5) When an IP packet originating from AS50 is destined to AS10, the AS50's border router delivers it through the path that involves the smallest number of AS (i.e., AS50-AS30-AS10) on the way.

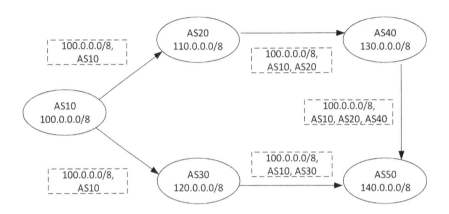

Figure 6.14 A demonstration of BGP mechanism

6.8   PERSPECTIVES ON PACKET ROUTING

Packet forwarding is highly process intensive because the router needs to look up its routing table to find the best delivery path whenever a packet arrives at one of its ports (interfaces). When the routing table has a large number of entries, searching through them from top to bottom for each arriving IP packet causes latency affecting the router's packet forwarding performance. When the end-to-end transportation of an IP packet needs to go through several routers, the aggregate delay can be substantial and may become intolerable to certain applications, especially when they are time-sensitive in nature (e.g., VoIP, online gaming, video conferencing, online movies).

As a measure to alleviate shortcomings of the conventional *routing* technology, especially to enhance delivery speed of IP packets, the industry has heavily embraced MPLS (Multiprotocol Label Switching). As the name implies, MPLS takes advantage of *switching* as a substitute for *routing* to transport IP packets. To refresh the *switching* concept, recall that LAN standards (e.g., Ethernet) rely on the layer 2 switching technology to transport frames. For this, the LAN switch table contains layer 2 MAC address and exit port pairs, which enable rapid relay of an incoming frame to its destination host or next switch. The switch table lookup process is significantly simpler and faster than that of the routing table (see Section 3.7 that compares switching and routing). MPLS is explained in Chapter 9 as a popular WAN standard.

KEY TERMS

advertisement
autonomous system (AS)
AS number (ASN)
bandwidth
Border Gateway Protocol
(BGP)
default gateway
delay
directly connected route
dynamic route
dynamic routing protocol
Enhanced Interior Gateway
Routing Protocol (EIGRP)
exit port/interface

exterior gateway protocol
(EGP)
gateway
hard boundary
hop count
interior gateway protocol
(IGP)
Intermediate System to
Intermediate System (IS-IS)
intra-domain routing
inter-domain routing
link-state information
load
metric

next hop IP
Open Shortest Path First
(OSPF)
packet routing
reliability
route print
router map
routing
routing information protocol
(RIP)
routing table
soft boundary
static route

CHAPTER REVIEW QUESTIONS

1. The router's packet forwarding decision is based on an IP packet's _____.
A) source IP address
B) destination IP address
C) source MAC address
D) destination MAC address
E) source and destination ports

2. To determine metric values of the routing table, a protocol gathers information on the *failure rate of router links*. Then, the protocol is using the ____ factor to determine the metric values.
A) load
B) reliability
C) delay
D) bandwidth
E) throughput

3. If multiple entries in the routing table match a packet's destination IP address, the router _____
A) forwards the packet to the default gateway.
B) forwards the packet to the path with the longest match.

C) discards the packet.
D) forwards the packet to the first-matched path.
E) forwards the packet to the last-matched path.

4. Entries (routes) of the routing table are divided into _____
A) directly connected routes, indirectly connected routes, and remotely connected routes.
B) directly connected routes, static routes, and remotely connected routes.
C) directly connected routes, static routes, and dynamic routes.
D) directly connected routes, dynamic routes, and remotely connected routes.
E) directly connected routes, indirectly connected routes, and dynamic routes.

5. The _____ is a router port that relays IP packets of a host beyond the subnet boundary.
A) default path
B) direct route
C) static route

D) default gateway
E) dynamic route

6. Border routers use _____ to exchange (or advertise) information needed to develop their routing tables.
A) exterior gateway protocol (EGP)
B) routing information protocol (RIP)
C) open shortest path first (OSPF)
D) intermediate system to intermediate system (IS –IS)
E) transmission control protocol (TCP)

7. Which routing table entry may NOT be a dynamic route?

Destination Subnetwork /Subnet Mask	Exit Port/ Interface
A) 192.168.0.0/16	FastEthernet0/1
B) 130.0.0.0/8	FastEthernet0/0
C) 10.10.1.0/24	FastEthernet0/1
D) 192.192.0.0/10	Serial0/1
E) 0.0.0.0/0	Serial0/1

8. Which is a popular exterior gateway protocol?
A) intermediate system to intermediate system (IS –IS)
B) open shortest path first (OSPF)
C) border gateway protocol (BGP)
D) routing information protocol (RIP)
E) enhanced interior gateway routing protocol (EIGRP)

9. How often does the router make the packet forwarding decision?
A) Once for each packet that it receives
B) Once for a group of packets that it receives with the same source and destination addresses
C) Once for a group of packets it receives with the same source address
D) Once for a group of packets it receives with the same destination address
E) Once for a group of packets it receives with the same source port number

10. Which dynamic routing protocol is a good choice for a relatively small network?
A) RIP
B) BGP
C) OSPF
D) EIGRP
E) IS-IS

11. Routers use the _____ to share information necessary to update their routing table.
A) IP protocol
B) dynamic routing protocol
C) address resolution protocol
D) advertising protocol
E) domain name protocol

12. Choose a CORRECT statement on the routing protocol technology.
A) The *default gateway* of a subnet is equivalent to the border router of the organization.
B) The Border Gateway Protocol is an interior dynamic routing protocol.
C) Routers rely on unicasting to advertise information necessary to update routing table entries.
D) A university can have several internal routers that run the same interior gateway routing protocol.
E) RIP, OSPF, and EIGRP are designed to help manual updates of the routing table.

13. When a router receives a packet with the following IP addresses, what should be the exit interface?
    Source IP address: 171.56.73.25
    Destination IP address: 183.69.53.151

Network address	Mask	Exit interface
183.69.48.0	/20	S0/0/0
183.69.32.0	/19	S0/0/1
183.69.0.0	/18	Fa0/0

(Routing Table)

| 183.69.52.0 | /22 | Fa0/1 |
| 0.0.0.0 | /0 | S0/0/2 |

A) S0/0/0
B) S0/0/1
C) Fa0/0
D) Fa0/1
E) S0/0/2

14. When a router receives a packet with the following IP addresses, what should be the exit interface?

Source IP address: 141.56.73.25
Destination IP address: 200.100.150.140

(Routing Table)

Network address	Subnet mask	Exit port
200.100.150.0	255.255.0.0.	S0/0/0
200.100.150.0	255.255.224.0	S0/0/1
200.100.150.0	255.255.128.0	Fa0/0
200.100.150.64	255.255.240.0	Fa0/1
0.0.0.0	0.0.0.0	S0/0/2

A) S0/0/0
B) S0/0/1
C) Fa0/0
D) Fa0/1
E) S0/0/2

15. When using the metric value to break a tie between entries in a routing table, the router _____
A) selects the matching row with the highest metric value.
B) selects the matching row with the lowest metric value.
C) selects the matching row with the latest update value.
D) selects the matching row with the oldest update value.
E) selects the matching row with the highest or the lowest value depending on the metric.

16. What information is LEAST used to compute the metric value of a routing table?

A) hop count to the destination
B) bandwidth of a link
C) network load of a link
D) estimated delay of a link
E) physical distance to the next router

17-18. Answer questions based on the hypothetical network in the figure.

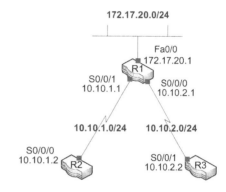

17. Link-state protocols such as OSPF advertise link information of a router to other routers. When R1 advertises link-state, information of how many links should be included?
A) 1
B) 2
C) 3
D) 4
E) 5

18. Which may NOT be link information related to S0/0/0 (Link 1) of R1?
A) Subnet address of the link
B) Subnet mask of the link
C) Type of the link (e.g., Ethernet)
D) Transmission cost (metric) of the link
E) Operating system of the router

19-25. Answer questions based on the hypothetical enterprise network in the figure.

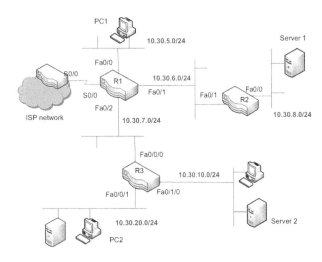

19. How many subnets do you see in the enterprise network? (Exclude the connection between R1 and the ISP router)
A) 4
B) 5
C) 6
D) 7
E) 8

20. Assume that there are 3 subnets in the enterprise network: 10.30.165.0/24, 10.30.145.0/24, and 10.30.185.0/24. The firm's network administrator decided to configure the border router R1 using a supernet that represents all three subnets. Which can be a supernet address and its subnet mask?
A) 10.30.0.0/16
B) 10.30.128.0/20
C) 10.30.128.0/21
D) 10.30.192.0/17
E) 10.30.192.0/18

21. Which address can become the default gateway of PC2?
A) 10.30.20.255
B) 10.30.7.1
C) IP address of R1's S0/0
D) IP address of S0/0 of the ISP router
E) 10.30.20.254

22. The following is Server 1's IP configuration:
• IP address: 10.30.8.254
• Subnet mask: 255.255.255.0
• Default gateway: 10.30.6.254

If PC2 pings Server 1, what should happen? Assume that all routing tables and IP addresses of router ports are correctly configured.
A) The ping request is blocked by R3 and PC2 will not receive the ping response.
B) The ping request is blocked by R2 and PC2 will not receive the ping response.
C) The ping request is blocked by R1 and PC2 will not receive the ping response.
D) The ping request is delivered to Server 1, but PC2 will not receive the ping response.
E) The ping request is delivered to Server 1 and PC2 will receive the ping response.

23. The following is Server 2's IP configuration:
• IP address: 10.30.10.254
• Subnet mask: 255.255.255.0
• Default gateway is not entered.

If PC1 pings Server 2, what should happen? Assume that all routing tables and IP addresses of router ports are correctly configured.
A) The ping request is blocked by R1 and PC1 will not receive the ping response.
B) The ping request is blocked by R3 and PC1 will not receive the ping response.
C) The ping request is delivered to Server 2, but PC1 will not receive the ping response.
D) The ping request is delivered to Server 2 and PC1 will receive the ping response.
E) PC1 does nothing.

24. If the following command is entered on a router's command prompt, what type of entry this statement creates in the routing

table? (Assume that the command is issued to a Cisco router.)

"#ip route 0.0.0.0 0.0.0.0 Serial0/0"

A) Directly connected route
B) Static route
C) Dynamic route based on RIP
D) Dynamic route based on OSPF
E) It can create any of directly connected, static, or dynamic route.

25. Which information is NOT included in the OSPF advertisement from R3? (Think logically)

A) Fa0/0/0's network address and subnet mask
B) Fa0/0/0's IP address
C) Fa0/0/0's neighbor is R1
D) Fa0/0/0's link is Ethernet
E) Fa0/0/0's MAC address is 1A.B4.56.8A.36.9C

CHAPTER 7   ETHERNET LAN

7.1   INTRODUCTION

Ethernet has been the dominant land-based (or wired) LAN and its technological specs have been continuously evolving to provide higher network speeds. Although there have been newer and technologically more advanced challengers such as Token Ring and Fiber Distributed Data Interface (FDDI), Ethernet has prevailed, demonstrating its enormous popularity and staying power. Since its introduction by Xerox in 1975 by the name of Ethernet, it has become the IEEE's 802.3 LAN standard. IEEE (Institute of Electrical and Electronics Engineers) is a non-profit and probably one of the largest professional associations in the world, working toward the advancement of information technology.

Along with Ethernet, IEEE 802.11(WiFi or Wireless LAN) is another dominant LAN standard. Ethernet and WiFi coexist supplementing each other. Although the official name of Ethernet is IEEE 802.3, more people are accustomed to Ethernet than the somewhat cryptic IEEE 802.3. With the extensive usage of switches in Ethernet LANs, the emphasis of this chapter is various issues associated with the *switched Ethernet* (i.e., Ethernet LAN running on switches). In fact, key technical elements of Ethernet were already explained in Chapter 3 (see Section 3.5 for switch and Section 3.10.1 for collision domain) and Chapter 4 (see Section 4.3.4 for Cabling). This chapter extends the coverage by focusing on:
- Standard layers covered by Ethernet
- Structure of the Ethernet frame
- Design approach of the Ethernet LAN: flat vs. hierarchical designs
- Spanning Tree Protocol (STP)
- Link aggregation (or bonding) technology
- Main issues of Virtual LANs (VLANs) including
  - Why VLANs?
  - VLAN Tagging and Trunking
  - VLAN Types
- Inter-VLAN routing

7.2   ETHERNET LAYERS

Just as with many other LAN and WAN standards, Ethernet's technical specifications are defined at the data link and physical layers. In fact, the data link layer is divided into two sub-layers of *logical link control* (LLC) and *media access control* (MAC) for LAN standards (see Figure 7.1). Technological details of Ethernet and WiFi are defined at the MAC sub-layer. The LLC sub-layer (as the IEEE 802.2 standard) provides an interface between the internet layer and the MAC sub-layer. A key function of LLC is to identify the upper (i.e., internet) layer protocol such as IP included in the frame. The technical specifications of Ethernet are, therefore, covered by the MAC sub-layer and the physical layer.

The Ethernet's MAC sub-layer is primarily responsible for:

- Creation of the Ethernet frame encapsulating a packet in the data field
- Controlling access to shared media such as the hub-based Ethernet (not switched Ethernet) in which only a single station may be allowed to transmit data at a time. Concurrent transmissions of data by two or more stations result in collisions. The media access control (or MAC) protocol used by Ethernet to avoid frame collisions is CSMA/CD (revisit Section 3.10.1).

The physical layer standards of Ethernet are summarized in Chapter 4 (Section 4.3.4). Building on the coverage in previous chapters, this chapter focuses on the data link layer functions of the switched Ethernet that relies on layer 2 switches (not layer 1 hubs) to connect host stations.

Internet Layer		TCP/IP standards (ex. IP)		
Data Link Layer	Logical Link Control Sub-Layer	802.2 standard		
	Media Access Control Sub-Layer	Ethernet (802.3) MAC Standard		Other Standards (ex. 802.11, 802.15)
Physical Layer		Interface standards (ex. RJ-45)		Other Physical Layer Standards
		100BASE-TX	1000BASE-T	...

Figure 7.1 Layers of Ethernet (IEEE802.3) standard

7.3 ETHERNET FRAME

7.3.1 Frame Structure

Ethernet has its own frame structure. The Ethernet frame carries the internet layer packet (primarily IP packet) in its data field. The frame contains a header and a trailer added before and after the data field (see Figure 7.2). The responsibility of each field in the header and trailer is summarized below.

- The *Preamble* is used for synchronization of clock rates between communicating nodes. The nodes should be exactly aligned in their process timing and the preamble bits (repetition of 1010...1010) are used to achieve that for synchronous transmissions (see Section 4.2.5).

- The bit combination (10101011) in the *Start Frame Delimiter* field indicates the starting point of a frame.

- The *Source/Destination MAC Address* field contains 48 bit MAC addresses of the source and destination nodes.

- The *Length/Type* field includes information on either the length of the data field in hexadecimal (the value is less than *0x0600*) or the type of the upper layer protocol (e.g., IP).

- The *Data* field includes the payload (or data) of varying sizes (ranging 46 through 1500 Octets). The field contains the internet layer's protocol data unit, primarily an IP packet. As the data field is limited in size, an IP packet can be fragmented to fit into the data field. However, such fragmentation of an IP packet can be problematic (e.g., additional process overhead to routers) and is generally avoided. To prevent the packet fragmentation, two communicating hosts pre-negotiate the maximum segment size.

- The *PAD* field is added if the data field is too small to meet the required size of at least 46 bytes.

- The *Frame Check Sequence* field contains an error detection code used by the destination host to discover any transmission error (e.g., bit change) in the frame. If the host's NIC detects an error, the frame is discarded. As explained in Chapter 2, the dropped frame is subsequently identified and retransmitted by the transport layer (TCP) of the source host.

Below is the error detection process.
Source host:
1. Frame value (bit stream) = X
2. Cyclic Redundancy Check (CRC) code = Y (a standardized value)
3. Division = Frame value/CRC code = X/Y
4. Remainder value of X/Y = R1
5. The frame with R1 in the FCS field is released.
Destination host:
6. On receiving the frame, the host repeats the steps 1 through 4 above and computes its own remainder value, R2.
7. If R1 = R2, then there is no error in the delivered frame.

Exercise 7-1: Go over the relationship between Figure 7.2 and Figure 2.22 from Chapter 2 to clarify what items are included in the data (or payload) field of a frame.

7.3.2 Addressing Modes

Ethernet frames are in three different addressing modes: unicasting, multicasting, and broadcasting. In broadcasting, the frame's destination address field carries FF-FF-FF-FF-FF-FF (1 bit repeating 48 times). This is similar to IP broadcasting for which the destination address field of an IP packet is filled with all 1s (i.e., 255.255.255.255).

The multicasting address in hexadecimal ranges between 01-00-5E-00-00-00 and 01-00-5E-7F-FF-FF. Multicasting is used for different applications such as exchanges of routing table information, video streaming, and multimedia conference calls. Just as unicasting relies on the mapping between the IP and MAC addresses in order to deliver an IP packet within a frame (revisit ARP in Section 3.8), multicasting and broadcasting also need the mapping between the two addressing schemes. For example, 255.255.255.255 (IP) results in FF-FF-FF-FF-FF-FF (MAC).

Preamble	7 bytes
Start-of-Frame Delimiter	1 byte
Destination Address	6 bytes
Source Address	6 bytes
Length (46~1500 bytes) or Type of Payload	2 bytes
Payload (Data)	variable
Pad (if necessary)	
Frame Check Sequence	4 bytes

Figure 7.2 Ethernet frame

7.4 ETHERNET LAN DESIGN

Switched Ethernet dominates wired LANs. When switches are used to create an Ethernet LAN, there is no limit to the number of switches that can be attached to it and therefore no limit to its maximum span at least in theory. The Ethernet standard (IEEE802.3) recommends that the maximum segment length between any two switches directly joined by the twisted pair be up to 100 meters in order to maintain the integrity of data transmissions. When optical fibers (primarily multi-modes) are utilized, their maximum segment distance increase considerably (e.g., 300 meters) because they are simply more reliable (e.g., lower signal attenuation and higher resistance to noise) than twisted pairs in signal transportation. With single mode fibers, the maximum segment length gets further extended.

7.4.1 Flat vs. Hierarchical Design

In creating a switched LAN, it can take a flat or hierarchical structure in terms of the relationship between switches. As illustrated in Figure 7.3, the flat design is mainly for a small LAN in which one or more switches are directly cabled with no apparent layered or tiered relationship between them. This approach is easy to implement and manage when the LAN size stays relatively small.

Figure 7.3 Ethernet with flat structure (logical view)

However, when the number of attached switches grows, the flat design approach becomes more difficult in managing (e.g., troubleshooting), maintaining performance, and ensuring network reliability. For example, the campus network as an oversized LAN is formed by a number of smaller LANs and thus poses special challenges in its management and operation. Imagine a university campus LAN that provides connectivity to thousands of servers, PCs, laptops and mobile devices scattered in 20 smaller building LANs through 400 switches of various speeds, 700 wireless access points, and 10 routers (including layer 3 switches). The campus LAN is simply too big to adopt the flat design.

If a large LAN consists of a number of smaller LANs, each with a number of network nodes, the three-tier hierarchical design (or topology) can be adopted to assign intermediary devices (e.g., layer 2 or 3 switches, routers) to the *access, distribution,* or *core* layers. As an example, imagine that the campus LAN above is comprised of 20 building LANs, each akin to Figure 4.25. Then, in each building, the distribution switch of the equipment room connects to access (or workgroup) switches in wiring closets forming the two-tier relationship (see Figure 4.28). Then, the distribution switches of 20 different buildings can be interlinked by the third-tier, core layer switches to complete the campus LAN.

Alternatively, when the LAN of a company is not large enough (e.g., covers a building of modest size) to justify the three-layer structure, the firm may opt for the two-tier architecture in which the core and distribution layers are combined to become one layer. In the two-tier approach, therefore, the core layer switch provides interconnectivity of access layer devices.

Figure 7.4 demonstrates a logical view of the two-tier versus three-tier structures of a LAN. The figures are labeled as 'logical' to highlight the association relationship of switches placed in different layers. In fact, their corresponding physical layout is quite different from the logical view because switches from different tiers may be co-located. For instance, imagine the situation where a distribution layer and a core layer switches are co-located in the main equipment room of a building. The physical layout of intermediary devices (see Figure 4.25 and 4.29 in Chapter 4) does not clearly show their hierarchical relationship.

7.4.2   Access Layer

In the access layer, computers, network printers, IP phones, and other end nodes are connected to the LAN via various intermediary devices including access (or workgroup) switches and wireless access points. Generally, layer 2 switches are popular choices to link user stations and servers to the network. Switches at the access layer are primarily equipped with Fast Ethernet or Gigabit Ethernet ports.

Access layer switches support many management functions. For example, switches can be configured for controlled access (e.g., restriction of a switch port to one or more pre-assigned MAC addresses) to prevent unauthorized computers from joining the network. Also, they allow the formation of *Virtual LANs* (or VLANs) so that hosts attached to a network can be logically divided into groups. More on VLANs in terms of their implementation and ensuing benefits are explained shortly. Besides, many access switches are *Power over Ethernet* (PoE) enabled so that the Ethernet cable can supply electrical power along with data to connecting nodes such as wireless access points, IP phones, and security cameras. With the PoE support, these devices can be flexibly placed in convenient or strategic locations not constrained by the availability of power sources (refer to Section 3.5.4).

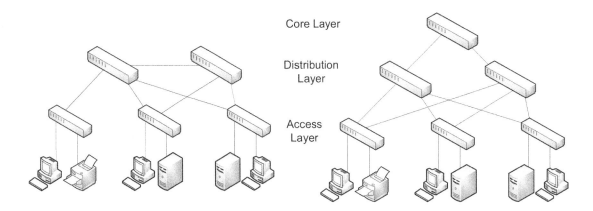

Figure 7.4 Two-tier vs. three-tier design of Ethernet LANs (logical view)

7.4.3 Distribution and Core Layers

The distribution layer mediates traffic between the access and core layers. The core layer's intermediary devices tie network segments of the access layer. Because of the hierarchical relationship among network nodes, much traffic is handled by the top two tiers and the planning of these layers should be concerned with rapid packet forwarding to prevent congestions. To ensure this, switches (or routers) in these layers have speeds (e.g., Gigabit, 10 Gigabit) faster than access layer switches.

Whether a hierarchical network is two-tiered or three-tiered, its designer has choices of interconnecting intermediary devices of the core and distribution layers in either *full mesh* or *partial mesh*. Having redundant paths in the two layers through full or partial mesh is critical to prevent the formation of a single point of failure and to minimize the risk of LAN downtime due to device or link failure(s).

The core and distribution layer devices may be layer 2 switches, layer 3 switches, or routers. Unlike layer 3 switches and routers, layer 2 switches cannot *route* IP packets but offer faster and more cost effective network services. In today's campus LAN, layer 3 switches are used widely in the distribution and core layers because they can also carry out IP packet routing faster than ordinary routers (see Section 3.5.4). Although they may not be as intelligent as routers in performing packet routing, layer 3 switches can handle relatively simple routing necessary within a LAN.

Lastly, the core and distribution layers are primarily responsible for interconnecting *virtual LANs* (VLANs) configured in access layer switches. The process of coupling VLANs is called inter-VLAN routing (to be explained).

7.4.4 Benefits of Hierarchical Design

The hierarchical network offers several benefits to an organization including its flexibility in adding a large number of hosts, managing the network, sustaining network performance, and ensuring network reliability.

- The network becomes more modular and the modularity makes it easy to manage, maintain (e.g., troubleshoot), and grow (i.e., scalability or expandability) the network as needed.

- With the layer approach, the access-level local traffic and the enterprise-level traffic at the distribution and core layers are separated and the separation contributes to better usage of network capacity.

- Optimizing network performance through such measures as *link aggregation* (see Section 7.6) becomes less complicated.

- It is easy to add link redundancy between intermediary nodes to improve network availability. During normal operations, however, only a single path (or data link) is activated between any two switch nodes and redundant paths are disabled to avoid loops (revisit Section 3.7). The function of maintaining only a single active delivery path between any two switches is performed by the *Spanning Tree Protocol* running on switches (to be explained).

Exercise 7-2: In this exercise, you are converting the logical design of an Ethernet LAN to its corresponding physical design as in Figure 4.25.

1. Assume that the two-tier LAN in Figure 7.4 is to be installed within a four story building that has a main equipment room on the 1st floor and a wiring closet on each of the 2nd, 3rd, and 4th floors.
2. Assign an identification number to each switch and link of the two-tier LAN in Figure 7.4.
3. On a blank sheet of paper, draw the building in which each floor has a wiring closet (or a main equipment room) and a large office space.
4. Place the network nodes (i.e., switches and hosts) so that each wiring closet houses an access (or workgroup) switch. Note: There is not a single solution in choosing the location of core layer switches.
5. Map all logical design access and trunk links onto physical design ones (i.e., horizontal and vertical cabling) to interconnect workgroup and core layer switches. Use the identification numbers to track the correspondence of network nodes and links between the logical and physical designs.
6. Discuss what security measures can be introduced to protect the Ethernet LAN and the switches.

7.5   SPANNING TREE PROTOCOL (STP)

7.5.1   Link Redundancy

In the previous section, it was explained that, when multiple switches are joined, redundant physical links are added to prevent a single point of device or cabling failure from crippling the network. Take Figure 7.5 as an example, the three access layer switches (D, E, and F) can be directly interlinked without additional switches (A, B, and C). However, with such flat design in which the switches D, E, and F are directly cabled, disruption of any trunk link affects integrity of the entire network, and thus it becomes a single point of failure. Meanwhile, Figure 7.5 shows that with the addition of A, B, and C switches, redundant paths are created between nodes. For example, the packet delivery from switch D to switch F can take the path: (1) D -> C -> F; (2) D -> B -> F; or (3) D -> B -> A -> C -> F. This redundancy is important to have improved accessibility and availability of a switched LAN even when a part of it goes down.

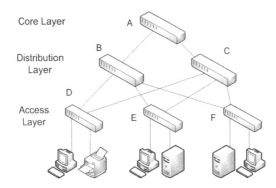

Figure 7.5 Availability of redundant paths (logical view)

Although link redundancy is intentionally introduced to increase network availability and survivability through backup paths, there are also situations in which such redundancy is formed unexpectedly. For example, because of the complexity of a large switched network, its network administrator may make mistakes in connecting and configuring switch ports, which results in link redundancy. The chance of making such configuration mistakes gets higher when an IT person deals with switches distributed in several wiring closets (e.g., Figure 4.25). In this situation, many cables coming from different rooms and floors can confuse him/her in cabling.

Additionally, unintended redundancy can be introduced by non-IT staff (e.g., computer end-users) when they add their own intermediary devices such as hubs to their workplace in order to attach additional end nodes. As a scenario, Figure 7.6 demonstrates a network in which two hubs are locally installed by office workers to connect more computers. When the two hubs are directly linked, this results in link redundancy.

Then, what is wrong with having additional links on a switched Ethernet, allowing multiple paths between nodes? As explained previously (e.g., Section 3.7), switches are data link devices relying on the switch table to forward frames. With layer 2 switching, there should be only a single active path (or data link) between any two hosts, making it different from the layer 3 routing that allows multiple delivery paths at one point. When there exists more than one active path to traverse between any two points in a switched network, this forms a loop. One or more loops in a switched Ethernet can be highly detrimental to its normal operation because the loop allows perpetual wandering of certain frames (e.g., broadcasted frames) in the network.

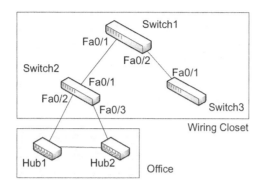

Figure 7.6 Network redundancy created at a work area

In layer 3 packet routing, the gradual decrement of the *time to live* (TTL) field value of an IP packet fundamentally prevents it from wandering the Internet endlessly (refer to Section 2.6.1). The Ethernet frame, however, does not contain such TTL value that automatically disqualifies it. For instance, assume that the redundant links in Figure 7.5 are all active and that a station broadcasts an ARP (address resolution protocol) packet to switch D. This triggers a continuous reproduction of ARP packets flooding the network. This risk becomes one important reason (besides the security concern) that the unauthorized installation of intermediary devices by end users should be banned.

To summarize, the Ethernet LAN may have redundant links between any two switch nodes to restore connectivity when there is a link or switch failure. However, only a single path should be active at a time to prevent the formation of a loop that can trigger broadcast storms and deteriorate network performance. The reproduction of broadcasting also results in repeated arrival of the same frame at a host computer (frame duplication).

Exercise 7-3: Using Figure 7.5, simulate how a frame broadcasted by a host station is propagated and reproduced by switches in an endless fashion when there are active redundant links.

7.5.2   Protocols and Mechanism

Ethernet switches are equipped with a protocol that can automatically recognize a loop between any two switch nodes and selectively block switch ports to sever the loop. For this, the protocol elects a switch as the *root switch*, and then redundant paths to the root switch are identified and blocked. The process itself is somewhat complicated and beyond the scope of this book. Here, the affected switch ports are not physically shut down but just blocked (similar to the sleep mode) so that they can be awakened if necessary (e.g., changes in network topology).

The IEEE standard protocol that identifies redundant paths and performs their de-activation and re-activation is *Spanning Tree Protocol* (STP). The newer version, *Rapid Spanning Tree Protocol*

(RSTP), performs much faster convergence than STP in identifying and removing loops or reactivating blocked switch ports to restore connectivity. As an improvement of STP, RSTP has become a preferred protocol to disable data link layer loops. RSTP is backwards compatible and thus rolled back to STP if any switch in the network does not support RSTP.

Figure 7.7 demonstrates two different scenarios in a simplified manner. During the normal mode of operations as in Figure 7.7a, STP/RSTP exchanges frames called *Bridge Protocol Data Units* (BPDUs) that contain information used by switches to ultimately locate redundant paths based on the built-in algorithm. Let's assume that after exchanging BPDUs and executing the STP/RSTP algorithm, it is determined that the direct link between switches B and C should be disabled to cut the loop. To do this, Switch B and Switch C exchange BPDUs for necessary coordination. Then, one port (either Fa0/2 of Switch B or Fa0/2 of Switch C) turns into the *blocking state* that does not accept regular frames.

Meanwhile, when there is a change in the network topology such as Switch A's failure as in Figure 7.7b, Switch B and Switch C exchange BPDUs and the blocked port is rolled back from the *blocking* to *forwarding* mode to reinstate the link. To make that happen, the switch port processes BPDUs even when it is in the blocking (or sleep) mode. STP/RSTP of a switch is automatically activated when the device is put into production.

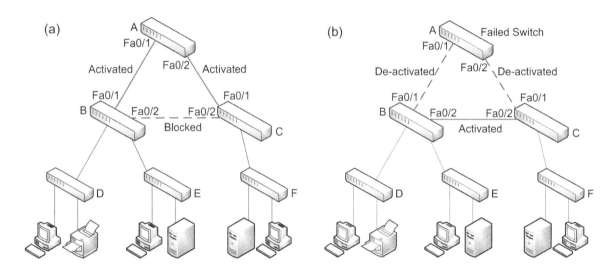

Figure 7.7 Demonstration of STP/RSTP (logical view)

7.6   LINK AGGREGATION

This section explains the *link aggregation* (also known as *port trunking* or *bonding*) technology used by Ethernet. With this technology, two or more physical links between any two network nodes (e.g., a server and a switch) are combined to become one logical link with a bigger capacity. With link aggregation, therefore, bandwidth between two devices is multiplied by the number of concurrent links.

Figure 7.8 demonstrates two different scenarios of link aggregation. In Figure 7.8a, the bonding of two Fast Ethernet ports (Fa0/0 and Fa0/1) between two switches increases bandwidth to 200 Mbps in both directions (full-duplex) when each link has a speed of 100 Mbps. This allows the two workstations connected to a switch to transmit at their full speed (100 Mbps) without delay. Also, with the bonding, there is no need for upgrading to a switch with a faster port speed (e.g., gigabit Ethernet). In Figure 7.8b, two Fast Ethernet ports (Fa0/1 and Fa0/2) are linked to two NICs (or a multiport NIC) of a server, effectively augmenting throughput to 200 Mbps in full-duplex.

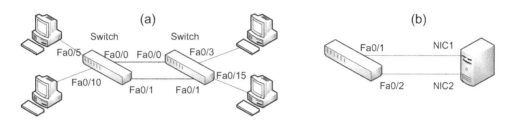

Figure 7.8 Usage of link aggregation

Think of another more complicated scenario in Figure 7.9. There are three core/distribution Gigabit Ethernet switches connecting three workgroup (or access) switches. All core/distribution switches have Gigabit Ethernet ports and workgroup switches have both Gigabit and Fast Ethernet ports. Access switches attach a number of hosts including servers via their Fast Ethernet ports. Servers use link aggregation to cut their response time. In this situation, if each of the trunk lines between A and B, and between A and C relies on a single Gigabit link, it can become a bottleneck when the aggregated traffic to switch A surpasses its link capacity. In that situation, aggregation of two or more links between A and B, and between A and C mitigates the bottleneck risk.

Link aggregation can be set up by issuing relatively simple commands to managed switches. The technology is standardized by IEEE as *Link Aggregation Control Protocol* (LACP). LACP-based link aggregation on a switch is implemented by issuing commands similar to (somewhat different depending on the device manufacturer):

```
----------------------------------------------------------------------
#lacp                    (Comment: activate LACP protocol)
#add port=1,3            (Comment: port 1 and 3 are bonded)
----------------------------------------------------------------------
```

In summary, using link aggregation offers several benefits:
- It multiplies the bandwidth of a network path, contributing to better network performance through load balancing.
- It is a cost effective way of augmenting link capacity without upgrading current hardware (e.g., intermediary device, cabling).
- Bundling of switch ports has an effect of maintaining a backup link between two nodes and thus enhances availability and accessibility of a network.

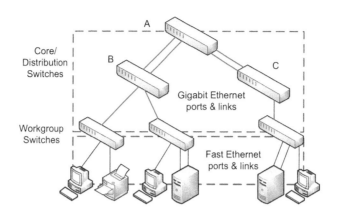

Figure 7.9 A link aggregation scenario

~~~~~~

Mini-Case: EQUIP Co.'s Ethernet LAN

This case is constructed from the actual network of a manufacturing firm. With about 100 employees, it is a mid-sized company and occupies a 3 story building. The *Main Equipment Room* is located on the building's first floor and houses main intermediary devices (e.g., core switches and router) and all servers. The wiring closets on the second and third floors house access (or workgroup) switches to connect end devices, mainly user stations and IP surveillance cameras.

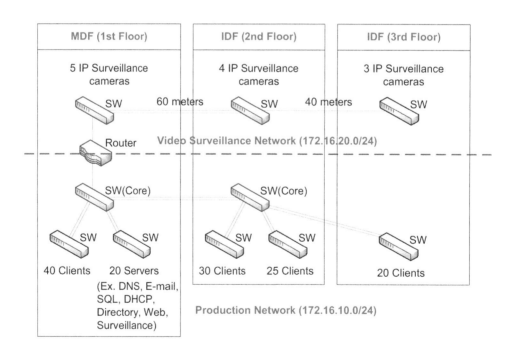

Figure 7.10 EQUIP Co.'s Ethernet LAN (logical view)

The enterprise LAN is divided into two subnets: the production network (172.16.10.0/24) that includes user stations and various servers, and the surveillance network (172.16.20.0/24) of video cameras installed to monitor the company facility. The surveillance camera has an IP address and connects to an access switch. The router separates the surveillance network from the production network. All switches are given an IP address just for remote configuration and management. The cabling and transmission speeds of network links are summarized below:

- Trunk links between intermediary devices (switches and router): 1 Gbps CAT6, All trunk links of the production network are running link aggregation effectively achieving 2Gbps bandwidth.
- Access links for user stations and surveillance cameras: 100 Mbps CAT5
- Access links for servers: 1 Gbps CAT6

Review Questions:
1. What cable is used for the trunk and access lines?
2. What is the connection speed of each trunk and access link?
3. What are connection speeds of internal servers and client stations to switches?
4. What measure is taken to double the link capacity?
5. Why do layer 2 switches have an IP address?
6. How many subnetworks are there and what can be the reason for dividing them?
7. How many broadcast domains exist in the network?
8. Assign IP address ranges to clients and servers.
9. Assign IP addresses to video surveillance cameras.
10. What approach is taken in the design of the surveillance network: flat or hierarchical design? How many layers (tiers) do you see?
11. What approach is taken in the design of the production network: flat or hierarchical design? How many layers (tiers) do you see?
12. Where would you place the router (wiring closet vs. equipment room) and why?
13. Design question: If the company adds a DMZ (de-militarized zone) subnet to the current enterprise LAN to place an email and web servers that are exposed to the Internet, what design approach can be taken? There can be several solutions and come up with one (refer to Figure 5.18 of Chapter 5).
14. Based on the logical design in Figure 7.10 above, draw its corresponding physical design similar to Figure 4.25 in Chapter 4.

7.7 VIRTUAL LANS (VLANS)

7.7.1 Background: Without VLANs

Imagine a firm's hypothetical LAN with several switches that attach many user stations and servers as in Figure 7.11. It shows that the computers belong to three different departments/groups: *IT, Marketing*, and *Accounting*. To be more realistic, you can assume that each computer represents a collection of hosts.

Assume that these computers are located in three different floors of a building interconnected by workgroup and core switches. This is the same network design approach EQUIP Co adopted. As the company is relatively small, the two-tier hierarchical solution with one subnet of the production network makes it easy to set up, maintain, and operate the LAN. However, when the company's network gets larger with many more user stations and servers belong to different departments/business units, the single subnet approach is not effective anymore because all nodes are in one large broadcast domain (revisit Section 3.10.2). Network nodes including switches, workstations, and servers routinely broadcast (or multicast) packets to conduct various network functions and the broadcasting reaches all of the nodes on the LAN.

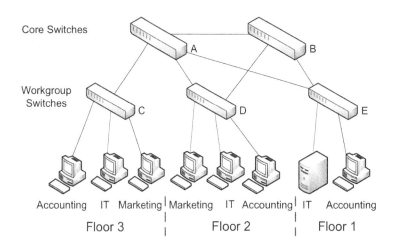

Figure 7.11 Logical layout of a LAN

For instance, the *Spanning Tree Protocol* (STP) installed in switches periodically releases multicasting messages to find redundant paths between any two network nodes. Also, the *Address Resolution Protocol* (ARP) triggers broadcasting frequently in order to obtain the MAC address of a node based on its IP address. As another example, the *Dynamic Host Configuration Protocol* (DHCP) request is broadcasted by host stations (e.g., laptops, tablets, smartphones) to obtain a dynamic IP address.

More often than not, such broadcasting should be limited to a sub-area (e.g., business department, project group) of the entire broadcast domain. In this situation, packets unnecessarily crossing functional boundaries (e.g., across business units) not only negatively affect overall network performance but also have security implications. The side effects become more evident and serious when the network gets larger by adding more hosts and covers functionally divided business units/groups. A clear solution for such a problem is *modularization* for which a network is segmented and managed as a collection of modules (or segments).

Then what solutions exist to divide the network into smaller segments? One approach is to place routers to create smaller subnetworks because the routers filter broadcasting (revisit Section 3.10.2). This solution makes sense when all hosts attached to a particular switch belong to the same functional group (e.g., accounting) as in Figure 7.12. In this case, a router port (interface) can be dedicated to the hosts of a functional group. This works neatly because the subnetwork boundary defined by a router port and the boundary of a business unit coincide.

However, using routers poses practical challenges when the ports of a switch are assigned to multiple functional or business groups that may share offices on the same building floor as in Figure 7.11 and this arrangement rather reflects the reality of many firms these days. This reality makes it difficult to utilize routers to limit traffic flows (especially broadcasting) to a business function. Then, is there a way that a switched LAN can be conveniently divided into logical segments as needed without relying on the router(s) while allowing the flexible addition of hosts from different departments/groups to switches regardless of their physical locations? This is where the VLAN technology comes in.

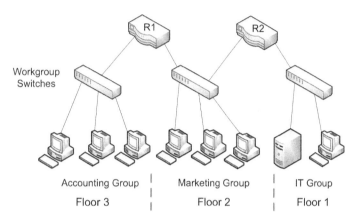

Figure 7.12 Router-based segmentation of a LAN

7.7.2 VLAN Concept

With the definition of VLANs in switches, a switched LAN normally as one broadcast domain can be further segmented into multiple broadcast domains according to certain logical boundaries such as workgroups, project teams, departments, or business units. Figure 7.13 demonstrates what happens when there is broadcasting over the switched LAN with two VLANs (1 and 2). You can observe that the broadcasting reaches only to stations and servers belonging to the same VLAN.

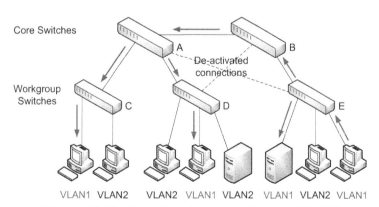

Figure 7.13 Broadcasting to nodes of a VLAN

227

7.8 VLAN SCENARIOS

7.8.1 Without VLANs

For a more in-depth demonstration of VLAN and its relationship with IP configuration, let me use a simple switched Ethernet in which all 6 computers from 3 business departments (*IT*, *marketing*, and *accounting*) and 3 switches belong to the same subnet of 192.168.10.0/24 (see Figure 7.14). As all end nodes belong to the same subnet, broadcasting by a station will reach all connected switch ports, except the broadcasting source port. Again, to be more realistic, you can assume that each computer represents a group of hosts.

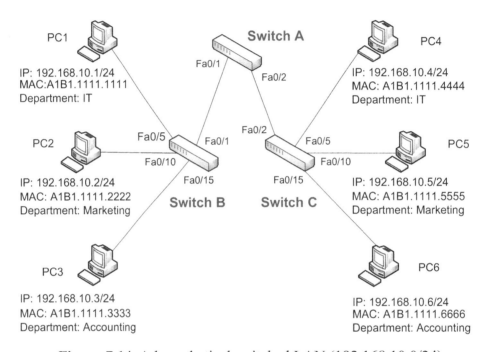

PC1
IP: 192.168.10.1/24
MAC:A1B1.1111.1111
Department: IT

PC2
IP: 192.168.10.2/24
MAC: A1B1.1111.2222
Department: Marketing

PC3
IP: 192.168.10.3/24
MAC: A1B1.1111.3333
Department: Accounting

PC4
IP: 192.168.10.4/24
MAC: A1B1.1111.4444
Department: IT

PC5
IP: 192.168.10.5/24
MAC: A1B1.1111.5555
Department: Marketing

PC6
IP: 192.168.10.6/24
MAC: A1B1.1111.6666
Department: Accounting

Figure 7.14 A hypothetical switched LAN (192.168.10.0/24)

In Figure 7.14, all hosts attached to the switches belong to the *default VLAN* (VLAN ID =1) when there are no specific VLANs configured in the switches. In other words, all hosts in Figure 7.14 belong to the same VLAN of VLAN ID=1 and this means that any host can send data link frames to any other host without restrictions. With no particular VLANs defined, the switch table for Switch B reads like Table 7.1. The table allows direct mapping between the destination MAC address and the exit port, and all exit ports belong to the same default VLAN of VLAN ID=1. It is a traditional switch table explained in Chapter 3 (see Table 3.4). The VLAN column is omitted in the Figure 3.8's switch tables assuming that all hosts belong to the default VLAN.

MAC Address	Exit Port	VLAN ID
A1B1.1111.1111	FastEthernet 0/5	1
A1B1.1111.2222	FastEthernet 0/10	1
A1B1.1111.3333	FastEthernet 0/15	1
A1B1.1111.4444	FastEthernet 0/1	1
A1B1.1111.5555	FastEthernet 0/1	1
A1B1.1111.6666	FastEthernet 0/1	1

Table 7.1 Switch B's switch table with default VLAN

Exercise 7-4: Based on Figure 7.14 and Table 7.1, answer the following questions presuming that creating additional VLANs is not an option.

1. What is the VLAN ID assigned to hosts at the IT, Marketing, and Accounting departments?

2. How many subnet IPs do you see in the network?

3. If the computer (192.168.10.1) broadcasts a frame to Switch B, which ports will relay the frame?

4. If the computer (192.168.10.1) broadcasts a frame to Switch B, which computers will receive the frame?

5. If the computer (192.168.10.1) broadcasts a frame to Switch B, what will be the destination IP (for packet) and MAC (for frame) addresses?

6. Construct the switch table of Switch A and Switch C (include VLAN ID).

7. What problems do you see with this switched Ethernet setup?

8. Without changing the switch and host configurations, can Switch A be replaced by a router to create network segments corresponding to the three business functions? Why or why not?

9. If the answer of question 8 is no, what change (e.g., network cabling, computer relocation) can be made to use a router(s) to create network segments pertaining to the three business functions? (Assume that all three switches are re-used.)

10. Let's consider question 9 in the context of a building. Assume that the network is implemented within a three story building and the location of each switch is as below:

> Switch A (core switch): Main equipment room, 1st floor
> Switch B (workgroup switch): wiring closet, 2nd floor
> Switch C (workgroup switch): wiring closet, 3rd floor

Assume that each of the 2nd and 3rd floors has several rooms occupied by the three different business units and all computers on a floor are connected to the same switch located in the wiring closet (revisit Section 4.4.2). In this situation, what can to be done to create three network segments corresponding to the three business functions if routers have to be used? Is it an effective solution?

7.8.2 With VLANs

Is there a way to divide a switched network into segments (i.e., broadcast domains) without relying on routers? Creating separate VLANs is the answer. VLANs are formed by adequately configuring switch ports. VLANs can be created in a static or dynamic manner. With the dynamic approach, switch ports are dynamically assigned to VLANs by a dedicated server based on such information as the MAC address of a computer attached to a switch port. This dynamic allocation, however, is not a widely accepted practice. In the rest of this chapter, therefore, the explanation focuses on setting up static VLANs. Once VLANs are in place as Figure 7.13, computers belonging to different VLANs cannot exchange frames directly through the switches and also frames broadcasted by a computer only reach other computers within the same VLAN. To establish static VLANs, a network specialist conducts the following tasks through the switch's command-line or web-based interface.

(1) Define VLANs in switches
(2) Plan the range of trunk and access ports
(3) Assign access ports to VLANs

(1) Define VLANs in Switches

In this stage, VLANs (VLAN IDs and VLAN names) are created in switches. Let's assume that there are 24 Fast Ethernet ports on each of the three switches in Figure 7.14 and it is decided to develop one VLAN for each business unit (i.e., IT, marketing, and accounting). For demonstration, a simple example is presented below where three VLANs with VLAN IDs of 10, 20, and 30 are assigned to the IT, Marketing, and Accounting departments respectively (It is unnecessary to memorize the commands.).

Example: Defining 3 VLANs in a Cisco switch
   # *vlan* 10
   # *name* IT
   # *vlan* 20
   # *name* Marketing
   # *vlan* 30
   # *name* Accounting

---

(2) Plan the range of trunk and access ports

A switch port becomes either an *access port* or a *trunk port* (Recall the definition of the access and trunks links in Section 1.2.3). In this stage, the ranges of trunk and access switch ports are pre-planned for subsequent configuration in the third stage. For instance, given 24-ports in each switch, we may decide that the first 3 (Fa0/1 ~ Fa0/3) are for trunk ports and the remaining 21 (Fa0/4 ~ Fa0/21) are for access ports.

Access port

The switch port that directly links a host (e.g., workstation, server) is set up as an *access* port and, therefore, the access port provides the host with physical connectivity to the network. In Figure 7.15, as an example, Switch B uses three access ports (Fa0/5, Fa0/10, and Fa0/15) for PC1, PC2, and PC3 respectively. Each *access link* connects a computer's NIC port (mostly RJ-45 port) to an access port of Switch B.

An access port belongs to a particular VLAN and it forwards frames only when the source and destinations computers are in the same VLAN. That is, computers attached to the access ports of VLAN 10 cannot communicate directly with computers attached to the access ports of VLAN 20 or VLAN 30, despite that the host computers are all hardwired to the same switch.

Trunk port

The switch port designated to connect another switch is configured as a *trunk* port and the cabling itself becomes a *trunk* link. Unlike the access port that belongs to a single VLAN, the *trunk port* transports Ethernet frames coming from different VLANs. The trunk link, therefore, is a point-to-point link that interconnects trunk ports of two different switches and transports Ethernet frames of different VLANs.

In Figure 7.15, as an example, Switch B's Fa0/1 is a trunk port that forwards frames from three different VLANs (VLAN10, VLAN20, and VLAN30) to Switch A's trunk port Fa0/1 over the trunk link. You can also observe another trunk link between Switch A's trunk port Fa0/2 and Switch C's trunk port Fa0/2.

(3) Assign access ports to VLANs

In this stage, each 'access' port is assigned to one VLAN in a non-overlapping manner (Although multiple VLANs can be assigned to a switch port, it is beyond the scope of this book). For example, let's assume that, in the planning stage, it was decided that the first 3 (Fa0/1 ~ Fa0/3) are for trunk ports and the remaining 21 (Fa0/4 ~ Fa0/21) are for access ports. Then, in one scenario, the 21 access ports can be assigned to VLANs as in Table 7.2. According to the allocation plan, ports Fa0/4 though Fa0/8 are for VLAN 10 in each switch. With that allocation, a computer connected to any switch port between Fa0/4 and Fa0/8 belongs to the IT department. The same applies to VLAN 20 and VLAN 30. Meanwhile, three switch ports (i.e., Fa0/1, Fa0/2, and Fa0/3) have been dedicated as trunk ports, and therefore cannot be assigned to a particular VLAN.

Port Type	Port Ranges	VLAN IDs	VLAN Names
Trunk ports	Fa0/1 ~ Fa0/3		
Access ports	Fa0/4 ~ Fa0/8	VLAN 10	IT
	Fa0/9 ~ Fa0/14	VLAN 20	Marketing
	Fa0/15 ~ Fa0/24	VLAN 30	Accounting

Table 7.2 Sample assignment of switch ports to VLANs

Demonstration of configuration

The definition of port types (access port vs. trunk port) and the VLAN assignment of an access port are manually performed on Switch B. Also, the same configuration should be done on Switch A and Switch C. In practice, 'manual' configuration of VLANs on each switch is unnecessary because a switch comes with a standard protocol used to replicate its VLAN configuration to all the other switches in the network. Using such a protocol saves much work and also prevents 'human' mistakes in setting up VLANs when many switches are attached to a network.

Once the necessary VLANs are programmed, the switch forwards Ethernet frames only when the source and destination hosts belong to the same VLAN. To visualize how a switch port becomes an access or a trunk port (see Table 7.2), the necessary commands are shown below based on the Cisco product.

Example: Cisco switch
Assigning an access port (Fa0/5) to VLAN 10 takes three commands entered successively into its operating system.

# *interface* Fa0/5	Note: Fa0/5 is to be configured
# *switchport mode* access	Note: Fa0/5 is an access port
# *switchport* access vlan 10	Note: assign Fa0/5 to VLAN 10

Setting up a switch port (Fa0/1) as a trunk port takes three commands entered in succession into its operating system.

# *interface* Fa0/1	Note: Fa0/1 is to be configured
# *switchport trunk encapsulation dot1q*	Note: Use 802.1Q (tagging protocol)
# *switchport mode* trunk	Note: Fa0/1 is a trunk port

- Comment: 802.1Q is to be explained as VLAN tagging (see Section 7.9)

7.8.3 How VLANs Work

Once VLANs are defined in the switches, only computers attached to the same VLAN ports (e.g., PC1 and PC4) can directly exchange frames through switches. Also, each VLAN becomes a broadcast domain, meaning that when a switch port receives a frame to be broadcasted, it is relayed only to 'other access ports sharing the same VLAN ID' and 'trunk port(s)'. The VLAN, therefore, restricts broadcasting to a much smaller segment. For example, once three VLANs are created in Figure 7.15, the single broadcast domain in Figure 7.14 is broken up into three broadcast domains, each pertaining to a business function.

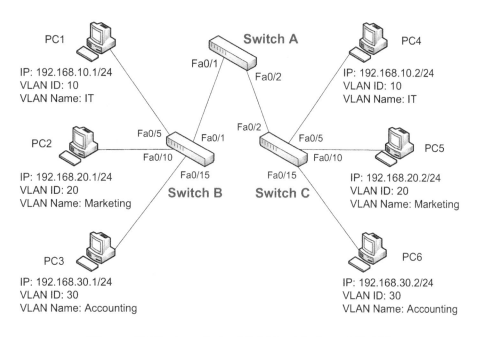

Figure 7.15 A switched LAN with three VLANs

Once the VLANs are assigned to switch ports and when enough frames are exchanged over the network (refer to switch learning in Section 3.5.3), each switch will complete its own switch table. The completed switch table of Switch B is shown in Table 7.3.

MAC Address	Exit Port	VLAN ID
A1B1.1111.1111	FastEthernet 0/5	10
A1B1.1111.2222	FastEthernet 0/10	20
A1B1.1111.3333	FastEthernet 0/15	30
A1B1.1111.4444	FastEthernet 0/1	10
A1B1.1111.5555	FastEthernet 0/1	20
A1B1.1111.6666	FastEthernet 0/1	30

Table 7.3 Switch B's switch table with three VLANs

Exercise 7-5: Refer to Figure 7.15 to answer the following questions.

1. Based on the Table 7.3 entries, determine MAC addresses of all PCs.
2. Once each PC's MAC address is identified, construct the switch table of Switch A and Switch C. For this:
   a) First, develop the table with MAC addresses and corresponding exit ports.
   b) Then, add the VLAN ID column to the table.

7.8.4   VLAN ID vs. Subnet IP Assignment

There is a question on what should be the relationship between the VLAN and the subnet address. Generally, one-to-one mapping between the VLAN ID and the subnet IP address (see Figure 7.15) is a popular practice, although one VLAN can include multiple subnets and multiple VLANs belong to one subnet. The one-to-one pairing between the VLAN and the subnet address simplifies network administration. This also means that the VLAN and subnetwork boundaries are identical on a switched Ethernet (without a router!). Convenience of this approach in network management is further explained in Section 7.11 while explaining inter-VLAN routing.

At the moment, however, tying a VLAN to a subnet can be confusing because it conflicts with early explanations that the subnet is defined by a router port. With deployment of VLANs, you can observe that the traditional subnet boundary is further divided into multiple subnets on a *switched network* without relying on the router. The one-to-one mapping relationship in Figure 7.15 is summarized as:

VLAN name	VLAN ID	Subnet IP
IT	10	192.168.10.0/24
Marketing	20	192.168.20.0/24
Accounting	30	192.168.30.0/24

~~~~~~

Exercise 7-6: Refer to Figure 7.15 and answer the following questions.

1. What are the access ports currently used by Switch A?

2. What are the access ports currently used by Switch C?

3. How many trunk ports are used on Switch A and Switch C and what are they?

4. Can Switch A's Fa0/1 and/or Fa0/2 be configured as access ports?

5. If Switch B's Fa0/1 is configured as an access port, what will be the effect?

6. Given the port range of each VLAN in Table 7.2, how many hosts can be attached to VLAN10, VLAN20, and VLAN30 respectively?

7. If PC1 broadcasts a frame, which switch(es) and which PC(s) should receive the frame?

8. If PC1 pings PC2 (C:\ping 192.168.20.1), would it reach PC2? If not, what is the reason? Hint: The switch is a layer 2 device and cannot perform packet routing.

9. If PC1 pings PC4, would the ping request reach PC4? Why or why not?

10. Now, let's assume that VLANs are removed from all three switches. However, IP addresses and subnet masks of 6 PCs remain the same.

    a) If PC1 pings PC4, would the message reach PC4? Why or why not?
    b) If PC1 pings PC5, would the message reach PC5? Why or why not?
    c) If PC1 pings PC2, would the message reach PC2? Why or why not?

~~~~~~

7.9   VLAN TAGGING/TRUNKING (IEEE 802.1Q)

7.9.1   Background

Going back to Figure 7.15, assume that PC1 and PC3 are on the same VLAN, let's say VLAN10. In this situation, if PC1 sends a frame to PC3, switch B will directly forward the Ethernet frame to PC3 after referring to its own switch table and confirming that both PCs are on the same VLAN 10.

When two PCs in the same VLAN are not directly connected to the same switch, delivering an Ethernet frame between them becomes a little bit tricky. For example, assume that an Ethernet frame needs to be delivered from PC1 to PC4 in Figure 7.15. The two PCs are attached to two different switches, Switch B and Switch C. This means that the Ethernet frame needs to travel through the two trunk links (i.e., the first one between Switch B and Switch A, and the second one between Switch A and Switch C).

As trunk links transport frames from different VLANs, there should be a mechanism that identifies the VLAN ID of a particular Ethernet frame. The delivery process of Ethernet frames from different VLANs over the trunk link is termed *trunking* (see Figure 7.16). So, VLAN trunking takes place between switches, but not between hosts and switches. The mechanism for implementing VLAN trunking is standardized by the *IEEE802.1Q* standard.

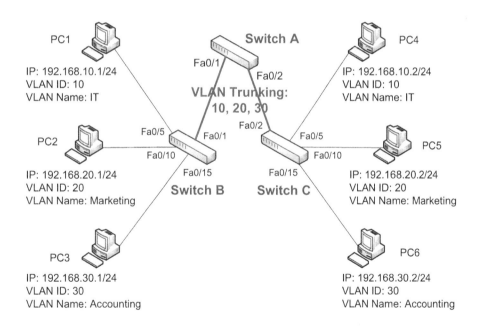

Figure 7.16 VLAN trunking

7.9.2   VLAN Tagging

To implement VLAN trunking, IEEE802.1Q uses *tagging* for which a switch inserts VLAN-related information into the regular Ethernet frame arriving from an attached host and then releases the tagged frame through a trunk port. In other words, regular frames are produced by hosts and they are transformed into VLAN tagged frames by switches. Figure 7.17 compares the regular frame with VLAN tagging-embedded frame. The tagged frame has two additional fields intended to convey VLAN information: *Tag Protocol Identifier* (TPID) and *Tag Control Information* (TCI).

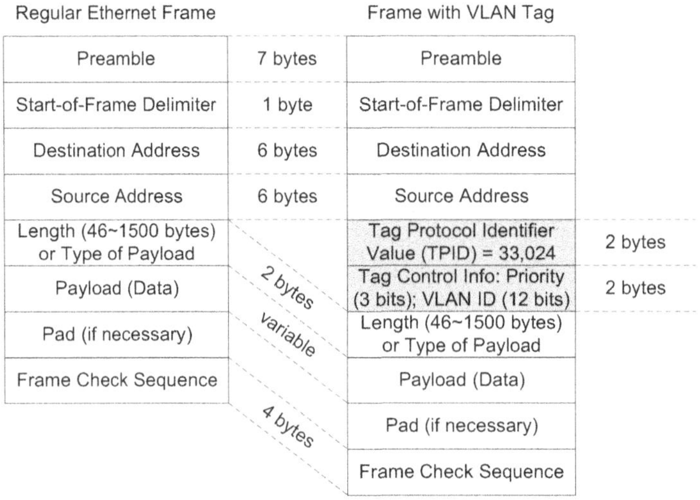

Figure 7.17 Ethernet frames: regular vs. VLAN tagged

The TPID field has a decimal value of 33024, which signals VLAN presence within an Ethernet frame. The length field of a regular frame can have only up to 1500 in decimal and, thus, a switch can tell the tagged frame. The TCI field is composed of *Priority* (3) and *VLAN ID* (12) bits. With the priority bits, an Ethernet frame is able to indicate its urgency in delivery. The priority bits are important because frames of certain VLANs (e.g., Voice over IP) cannot afford delays. The VLAN ID bits identify the VLAN of an Ethernet frame.

7.9.3 VLAN Tagging/Untagging Process

To demonstrate how the VLAN tagging works, let's assume that an Ethernet frame should be delivered from PC3 to PC6 in Figure 7.16. It is also assumed that VLANs have already been set up in the switches according to the Table 7.2's allocation plan. Also, presume that all three switches have their completed switch tables as with Table 7.3 for Switch B.

The delivery of a frame from PC3 to PC6 takes the following steps:

a. Initially, the PC3's NIC constructs a regular Ethernet frame (Figure 7.17) and dispatches it to Switch B's Fa0/15.

b. On receiving the frame, Switch B recognizes a VLAN configuration of the Fa0/15 port and adds a VLAN tag of TPID and TCI (see Figure 7.17) to the regular frame. Here, the VLAN ID field becomes 30.

c. Once the VLAN tag is added by Switch B, it refers to the switch table to identify the exit port for the PC6's MAC address and confirms that PC6 belongs to the same VLAN 30. Switch B releases the tagged frame through the trunk port, Fa0/1.

d. Switch A receives the tagged frame. It checks its switch table to determine the exit port for the PC6's MAC address, confirms that PC6 belongs to the same VLAN 30, and forwards the tagged frame to Switch C through its trunk port, Fa0/2.

e. Switch C, on receiving the tagged frame, checks its own switch table to determine the exit port for the PC6's MAC address and confirms that PC6 belongs to the same VLAN 30. It then removes the VLAN tag from the frame and dispatches the original regular frame to PC6 via its access port Fa0/15.

The tagging and untagging procedure between PC3 and PC6 is summarized in Figure 7.18.

Exercise 7-7: Referring to Figure 7.18, describe step-by-step what happens when below Ping packets are issued (Assume that the construction of all switch tables has been completed).

1. PC1 pings PC4.
2. PC1 pings PC6.
3. PC1 pings 255.255.255.255
4. PC1 pings 192.168.20.255

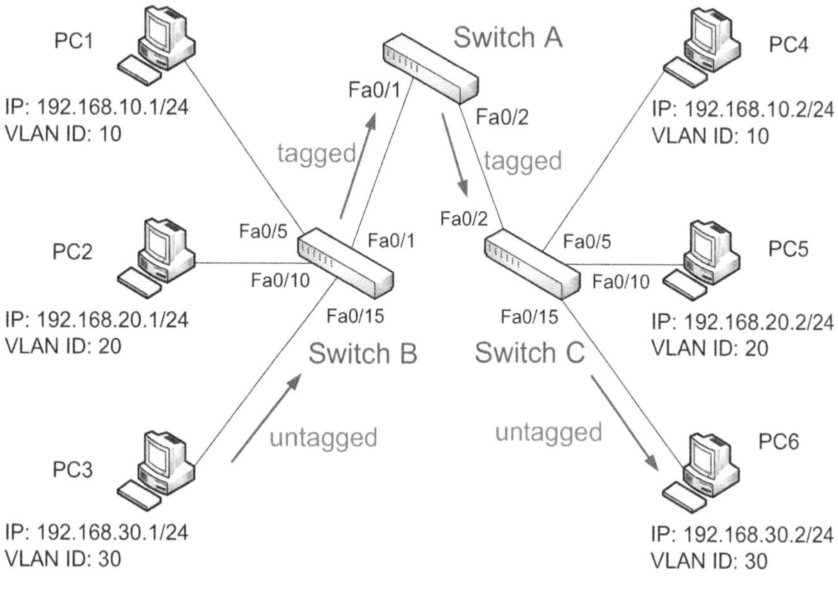

Figure 7.18 VLAN tagging and untagging

7.10 VLAN TYPES

Various VLAN types can be defined on a switched LAN, and *Default VLAN, Data VLAN,* and *Voice VLAN* are explained as popular VLAN types.

7.10.1 Default VLAN

All switch ports automatically belong to the *Default VLAN* when a switch is in the out-of-the-box condition and not configured with any other specific VLAN(s). In other words, all host stations attached to the switch belong to one broadcast domain of the default VLAN (see Table 7.1). As an example, all computers in Figure 7.14 are not segmented by additional VLANs and therefore they all belong to the default VLAN. In this mode, the regular frames (see Figure 7.2) produced by a source station are relayed by switches without VLAN tagging.

Example: Default VLAN in a Cisco switch.

The Cisco switch stores its VLAN information in the *vlan.data* file kept in its flash memory and it can be displayed by issuing '*show vlan*' at the command prompt. Figure 7.19 indicates that the switch has 24 Fast Ethernet (100Mbps) ports and all belong to the default VLAN. In other words, all 24 ports belong to the same broadcast domain with no restriction in communications between any two computers attached to the switch.

```
SwitchB#show vlan

VLAN    Name            Status          Ports
-----   --------------  -------------   -------------------------------------------
1       default         active          Fa0/1, Fa0/2, Fa0/3, Fa0/4, Fa0/5
                                         Fa0/6, Fa0/7, Fa0/8, Fa0/9, Fa0/10
                                         Fa0/11, Fa0/12, Fa0/13, Fa0/14, Fa0/15
                                         Fa0/16, Fa0/17, Fa0/18, Fa0/19, Fa0/20
                                         Fa0/21, Fa0/22, Fa0/23, Fa0/24
```

Figure 7.19 Default VLAN

7.10.2 Data VLAN

Data VLANs are designed to transport computer-generated data traffic and the majority of VLANs belong to this type. As an example, Figure 7.18 demonstrates three different data VLANs assigned to IT (VLAN 10), Marketing (VLAN 20), and Accounting (VLAN 30) units to segment the *switched* Ethernet into three logical boundaries (and three broadcast domains).

238

Example: Data VLANs in a Cisco switch

Figure 7.20 displays switch ports assigned to the three different data VLANs (VLAN 10, 20, and 30) according to the allocation plan in Table 7.2. In that plan, the ports ranging Fa0/4 through Fa0/24 are access ports. Meanwhile, the first three ports (Fa0/1, Fa0/2, and Fa0/3) were set up as trunk ports and therefore not assigned to any particular VLAN. As a result, the three ports are not listed in the VLAN summary.

```
SwitchB#show vlan

VLAN   Name           Status         Ports
-----  -------------  -------------  --------------------------------------------------
10     IT             active         Fa0/4, Fa0/5, Fa0/6, Fa0/7, Fa0/8
20     Marketing      active         Fa0/9, Fa0/10, Fa0/11, Fa0/12, Fa0/13, Fa0/14
30     Accounting     active         Fa0/15, Fa0/16, Fa0/17, Fa0/18, Fa0/19,
                                     Fa0/20, Fa0/21, Fa0/22, Fa0/23, Fa0/24
```

Figure 7.20 Data VLANs

Besides, data VLANs with more specific objectives can be created to serve organizational needs. For example, imagine the following scenarios in which VLANS aim to enhance network and data security.

- A firm's conference room is frequently occupied by guests and/or business clients. The room does not provide an access to the corporate network for security reasons, but may offer Internet connectivity through a WiFi access point (AP). Then, the AP may be assigned to a dedicated VLAN so that WiFi traffic is separated from other internal traffic in order to guard the corporate network from potential threats.

- A firm's data center (or datacenter) holds a number of networked servers that store and process large amounts of corporate data. Imagine that the servers are not logically or physically detached from the rest of the corporate network, thus belong to a larger broadcast domain. Then, attackers can find the servers (i.e., their IP addresses) easily by broadcasting address resolution protocol (ARP) requests. When the data center belongs to a particular VLAN (thus having its own broadcast domain), such IP probe is prevented.

7.10.3 Voice VLAN

Voice VLAN is the one dedicated for voice traffic. The computer network has emerged as a cost effective alternative to the traditional telephone system. Traditional voice communications require that an organization maintain voice network infrastructure separately from the data network. This incurs substantial maintenance and operational costs to the organization.

When the voice and data services are merged on the same network platform (see Figure 7.21), this convergence results in considerable cost savings in equipment purchase, operations, and management. For example, with the consolidation of voice and data, there is no need for additional purchase of telephone equipment, for hiring telephone network specialists, and for separate maintenance of voice and data networks.

In order to merge voice and data services without sacrificing call quality (e.g., call delay, call dropping), a VLAN can be dedicated for voice traffic. The voice VLAN transports digitized voice calls and also necessary signaling information (e.g., call setup, dial tones, caller ids). Given the time-sensitivity of voice traffic, calls should experience little transmission delays. To that end, the voice VLAN should be given a higher priority than the data VLAN in transporting frames over the trunk link (recall the priority bits of Tag Control Information in Figure 7.17).

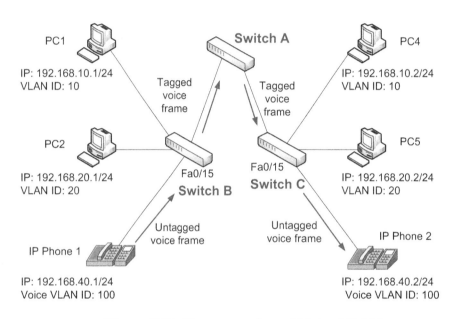

Figure 7.21 Demonstration of Voice VLAN

Figure 7.21 demonstrates two Data VLANs (VLAN 10 and VLAN 20) and one Voice VLAN (VLAN100). To implement the differentiated priority scheme, both Switch B and Switch C are instructed to give a higher priority bit to frames arriving at the switch port (Fa0/15) that processes voice-related frames.

In fact, the reality of Voice VLAN setup is more complicated than the simplified view in Figure 7.21. In that setup, the port Fa0/15 of Switch B and Switch C can be given two VLAN IDs: one for Data VLAN and one for Voice VLAN. By doing that, one cable is shared by the two VLANs connecting both a VoIP phone and a computer to the Fa0/15 switch port. This makes sense because a worker's desk needs both a phone and a computer, and having separate cabling for each device is simply not an attractive solution (The technical details are beyond the scope of this textbook).

7.11   INTER-VLAN ROUTING

This section explains solutions available to exchange frames between VLANs, commonly known as inter-VLAN routing. Remember that when a LAN has only Ethernet switches such as Figure 7.18, frames cannot cross different VLANs directly. For instance, PC1 and PC5 in Figure 7.18 cannot directly exchange frames as they belong to VLAN10 and VLAN20 respectively. Then, what solutions are available to forward a frame from one VLAN to another? When each VLAN is given a subnet address, then the inter-VLAN communication can rely on a layer 3 device, generally a router. Two different approaches of inter-VLAN routing based on the router are explained:

1. Assign a physical router port (interface) per subnet (thus per VLAN)
2. Assign *sub-interfaces* to a physical router port to bridge multiple subnets (thus multiple VLANs)

Another solution to pass frames between VLANs is to utilize the layer-3 capable switch, frequently called a *multi-layer switch* instead of the router. Previously in Chapter 3, it was stated that layer 3 switches can perform basic router functions and thus replace many routers in an enterprise LAN. The details of utilizing the layer-3 switch are beyond the scope of this book.

7.11.1 A Router Interface per VLAN

In this solution, a router's physical port is dedicated to a VLAN (i.e., a subnet); thus, interconnecting several VLANs by a router needs as many designated physical ports. This is consistent with the principle that a router comes with LAN (e.g., FastEthernet0/1 or Fa0/1) and WAN (e.g., Serial0/0) ports and the network segment linked to a particular router port becomes a subnet. For example, in Figure 7.22, the subnet 192.168.10.0/24 is linked to Fa0/0 of the router and the port has the IP address of 192.168.10.250. Recall that Fa0/0's IP address (192.168.10.250) becomes the default gateway of the two computers. Based on the review of the router port and subnet, let me explain the inter-VLAN concept in two different scenarios.

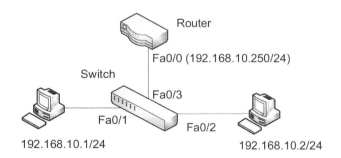

Figure 7.22 Router port connecting one subnet

Scenario 1

Figure 7.23 demonstrates a simple network with the inter-VLAN routing implemented based on *one physical port per VLAN* (thus, per subnet). There are two VLANs (VLAN 10 and VLAN 20) with corresponding two subnets. For IP packets to cross the VLANs, the router connects the switch via two separate ports (Fa0/0 and Fa0/1), each port designated for a subnet (thus a VLAN). VLAN 10 has a subnet address of 192.168.10.0/24 and the router's Fa0/0 with an IP address of 192.168.10.250 belongs to VLAN 10. Meanwhile, VLAN 20's subnet address is 192.168.20.0/24 and the router port Fa0/1 with 192.168.20.250 belongs to VLAN 20.

In this setup, although the switch cannot directly relay frames (thus IP packets) between VLAN 10 and VLAN 20, the router is able to bridge them with its routing capability. For the router to enable the inter-VLAN crossing, the router port's IP of a subnet is configured as the default gateway of computers in the subnet (see Figure 7.22). Therefore:

> PC1 and PC2 (VLAN10) have the default gateway of 192.168.10.250
> PC3 and PC4 (VLAN20) have the default gateway of 192.168.20.250

Furthermore, each switch port (Fa0/4 for VLAN 10 and Fa0/11 for VLAN20) that links to a router port becomes an access port (see Figure 7.23), not as a trunk port, because each link transports frames of a single VLAN (or single subnet). This is in conflict with the definition in Figure 1.5 of Chapter 1 in which any link between intermediary nodes is considered a trunk link. This is where the general definition of trunk links does not hold up.

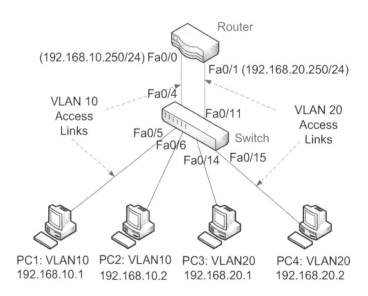

Figure 7.23 Assignment of a router port per VLAN

Once the router ports' IP addresses in Figure 7.23 are programmed, its routing table will be similar to Table 7.4 that enable packet forwarding between the two subnets (thus VLANs).

Subnet ID	Subnet Mask	Exit port(Interface)
192.168.10.0	255.255.255.0	FastEthernet0/0
192.168.20.0	255.255.255.0	FastEthernet0/1

Table 7.4 Routing table entries (a simplified view)

Exercise 7-8: Perform the following activities based on Figure 7.23.

1. Assign MAC addresses to four PCs and also the two router LAN ports (Fa0/0 and Fa0/1).

2. Assume that the switch has 24 ports. Develop a summary table similar to Table 7.2 by assigning its first 3 ports as trunk ports and the remaining ports as access ports to VLAN10 (Fa0/4 ~ Fa0/13) and VLAN20 (Fa0/14 ~ Fa0/24). Recall that, in practice, this port assignment should be implemented in the switch.

3. Now, configure the IP address, subnet mask, and default gateway on each PC consistent with Figure 7.23.

	PC1	PC2	PC3	PC4
IP address Subnet mask Default gateway	192.168.10.1			

4. The switch table is blank initially. The switch will, therefore, be forced to broadcast arriving frames whenever necessary. When enough frames are exchanged, the switch will be able to complete the switch table based on the information of frames it relayed and the VLAN information manually programmed in step 2. Develop the switch's switch table that contains columns of exit ports, MAC addresses and VLAN IDs.

5. Now, with the switch table (constructed in step 4) and the routing table (Table 7.4) available, explain step-by-step on what happens when the following commands are issued.
   a) PC1>ping 192.168.10.2
   b) PC1>ping 192.168.20.2
   c) PC1>ping 255.255.255.255

6. If the VLAN option is not available, what alternative design approach can be applied to create a network that is functionally identical to the one in Figure 7.23? What are the advantages and disadvantages of the alternative network design?

Scenario 2

Let us take a look at a little more complicated situation in which three switches connect two VLANs (Figure 7.24). Here, the ports linking Switch 1 (Fa0/1) and Switch 2 (Fa0/1), and Switch 1(Fa0/2) and Switch 3(Fa0/1) are configured as trunk ports because they have to carry both VLAN10 and VLAN20 frames. Meanwhile, all the other switch ports including those

(Fa0/3 and Fa0/24) between the Router and Switch 1 become access ports as they transport frames pertaining to only a particular VLAN (either VLAN10 or VLAN20). In other words, the router port Fa0/1 connects to 192.168.10.0/24 (VLAN10) while the router port Fa0/2 becomes a default gateway for the subnet 192.168.20.0/24 (VLAN20).

In this setup, the frames travelling between Switch 1 and Switch 2, and between Switch 1 and Switch 3, are tagged with VLAN information (i.e., TPID and TCI). However, Switch 1 untags the VLAN information when the frame is passed to the router for inter-VLAN routing. This approach of having one physical link to the router per subnet (thus VLAN) is relatively an easy solution when the VLAN structure is simple. However, if the number of VLANs increases, the solution becomes problematic because more router ports and switch ports should be dedicated for the inter-VLAN routing and it also results in more cabling.

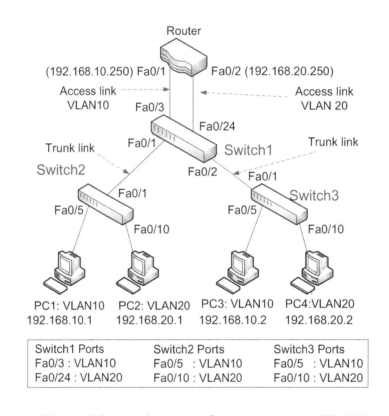

Figure 7.24 Assignment of a router port per VLAN

~~~~~~

Exercise 7-9: Perform the following activities based on Figure 7.24.

1. Assign MAC addresses to four PCs and also the two router LAN ports (Fa0/1 and Fa0/2).

2. Assume that each switch has 24 ports. Develop a summary table similar to Table 7.2 by assigning their first 2 ports as trunk ports and the remaining ports as access ports to VLAN10 and VLAN20. The port range assigned to each VLAN should reflect Figure 7.24.

3. Now, configure the IP address, subnet mask, and default gateway on each PC. Assume that

the first 24 bits represent the subnet address.

	PC1	PC2	PC3	PC4
IP address Subnet mask Default gateway	192.168.10.1			

4. Assuming that the router's ports including IP address and subnet mask are correctly configured, develop a simplified routing table that has the subnet address, subnet mask, and exit port columns (refer to Table 7.4).

5. Assume that enough frames have been exchanged over the network to complete the switch table. Develop the switch tables of all three switches. The table should contain the columns of MAC addresses, exit ports, and VLAN IDs (refer to Table 7.3).

6. Now, with the switch and routing tables completed, explain step-by-step on what happens to the internal structure of the frame (in terms of tagging and un-tagging) whenever it passes through a switch/router port as a result of the following commands.
   - PC1>ping 192.168:10.2
   - PC1>ping 192.168.20.2
   - PC1>ping 255.255.255.255

7. If the VLAN option is not available, what alternative design approach can be taken to create a network that is functionally identical to the one in Figure 7.24? What can be the advantages and disadvantages of the alternative network design?

7.11.2 Sub-Interfaces/Ports (Advanced)

A more advanced solution of inter-VLAN routing is to create multiple *virtual interfaces* (called sub-interfaces) tied to one *physical interface* (e.g., Fa0/1) and then assign a sub-interface to a VLAN. This means that the router can use just one physical interface to link multiple VLANs (thus, multiple subnets). With the use of virtual interfaces (or ports), the router does not need to have as many physical links as VLANs. This makes it fundamentally different from the *dedication of a physical interface (or port) per VLAN* as in Figure 7.23 and Figure 7.24, making the network topology simpler with reduced physical links.

For example, Figure 7.25 shows the same network topology as Figure 7.24 except that there is only one physical link between the Router and Switch 1. For this, the router's physical interface Fa0/0 can have two logical/virtual interfaces (let's say Fa0/0.10 for VLAN 10 and Fa0/0.20 for VLAN 20). The creation of logical/virtual interfaces is done through the router's operating system. As each VLAN has its own subnet IP address (192.168.10.0 and 192.168.20.0), the router's physical interface Fa0/0 ends up with corresponding two IP addresses (192.168.10.250 and 192.168.20.250 tied to two different virtual interfaces Fa0/0.10 and Fa0/0.20 respectively). The relationship is summarized in Table 7.5.

Physical interface	Virtual interfaces (Sub-interfaces)	VLAN ID	IP Address
Fa0/0	Fa0/0.10	10	192.168.10.250
	Fa0/0.20	20	192.168.20.250

Table 7.5 Relationships between physical interface, virtual interfaces, VLAN IDs, and IP addresses (This is not a routing table.)

With the use of virtual sub-interfaces, the mechanism of inter-VLAN routing by the router is identical to that of Figure 7.24, except that the router link now becomes a trunk link to transport two different VLAN traffic. In that setup, PC1 and PC3 should have 192.168.10.250 as their default gateway, and that of PC2 and PC 4 becomes 192.168.20.250.

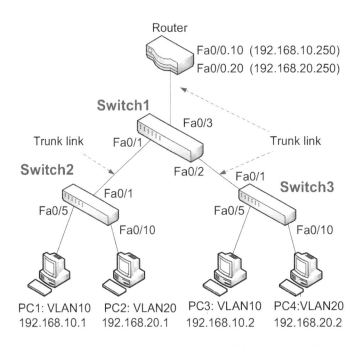

Figure 7.25 Inter-VLAN routing with sub-interfaces

Based on the topology of Figure 7.25, below Table 7.6 shows the Router's routing table that has two sub-interfaces (i.e., Fa0/0.10 for VLAN 10 and Fa0/0.20 for VLAN 20) created on one physical interface Fa0/0. The routing table shows that the subnet 192.168.10.0/24 for VLAN10 is tied to the Fa0/0.10 sub-interface and the subnet 192.168.20.0/24 for VLAN20 is coupled with the Fa0/0.20 sub-interface. Compare it with Table 7.4 and observe differences in the exit port field.

246

Subnet ID	Subnet Mask	Exit port (Sub-Interface)
192.168.10.0	255.255.255.0	Fast Ethernet0/0.10
192.168.20.0	255.255.255.0	Fast Ethernet0/0.20

Table 7.6 Routing table entries with sub-interfaces (a simplified view)

7.12 VLANS AND NETWORK MANAGEMENT

VLANs are prevalent in enterprise networks. There are several benefits of deploying VLANs and some of them were explained earlier. The main benefits are highlighted once again before concluding the chapter.

1. Above all, VLANs improve network performance by reducing traffic congestion. They protect a network from having broadcast storms because the broadcasting effect is confined to a VLAN and the inter-VLAN routing does not relay broadcasting. When there are hundreds or thousands of computers, the effect of controlled broadcasting on overall network performance is significant.

2. With VLANs, network management to dynamically reflect organizational changes (e.g., relocations of office space, job reassignments of employees) becomes more transparent and flexible. For example, imagine internal transfer of an employee from accounting to marketing in Figure 7.14. The employee's computer can be easily reassigned by hooking it up to a switch port pre-allocated to the marketing department's VLAN.

3. An employee's physical location (e.g., building floor) does not affect his/her association with a particular VLAN (and therefore subnet). In the early days, the creation of a network segment (e.g., subnet) was done according to the physical location of computers. This approach works fine when computers of a segment are co-located within an area such as the same floor of a building. However, when they have to be distributed over several floors or over different geographical locations due to certain reasons such as company growth, the location based network segmentation is not practical anymore. Naturally, logical (rather than physical) segmentation of a LAN into VLANs makes it easy to group and re-group computers as needed regardless of their physical locations.

4. VLANs improve network security. Computers belonging to a VLAN cannot directly reach those in other VLANs without relying on inter-VLAN routing, although they may be attached to the same switch. Also, broadcasting by a computer is confined to a VLAN protecting the data from eavesdropping by someone outside of the VLAN boundary. Besides, each VLAN can be customized with its own access and security policies.

KEY TERMS

access layer	blocking state	(BPDU)
access port	bridge protocol data unit	core layer

cyclic redundancy check (CRC)

data VLAN

default VLAN

distribution layer

forwarding state

frame check sequence

full mesh

IEEE802.1Q

inter-VLAN routing

link aggregation

Link Aggregation Control Protocol (LACP)

link redundancy

logical link control (LLC)

management VLAN

media access control (MAC)

pad

partial mesh

port bonding

port trunking

Power over Ethernet (PoE)

Preamble

Protocol (RSTP)

Rapid Spanning Tree Protocol (RSTP)

Spanning Tree Protocol (STP)

start frame delimiter

switched Ethernet

Tag Control Information (TCI)

Tag Protocol Identifier (TPID)

Tagging

trunk link (VLAN trunk)

trunk port

trunking

virtual interface

virtual LAN (VLAN)

voice VLAN

CHAPTER REVIEW QUESTIONS

1. When two or more lines are concurrently used between a pair of switches or between a host and a switch to increase throughput, it is termed as _____.
A) link aggregation
B) tunnel aggregation
C) virtual aggregation
D) trunk aggregation
E) bandwidth augmentation

2. The Spanning Tree Protocol (STP)
A) disables redundant paths in a switched Ethernet LAN, and re-activates them as needed.
B) is a protocol designed to exchange information necessary to develop the switch table.
C) is a protocol that automatically creates VLANs.
D) is a protocol that synchronizes the clock speed between switches.
E) is a protocol that allows bonding of two or more links to multiply throughput.

3. The Ethernet VLAN _____.
A) enables better recovery of transmission errors
B) creates smaller segments of a network
C) prevents frame broadcasting

D) generates redundant delivery paths between two hosts
E) widens available bandwidth between two network nodes

4. Ethernet standards are defined at the _____.
A) physical layer only
B) data link layer only
C) internet layer only
D) physical and data link layers
E) physical, data link, and internet layers

5. Ethernet synchronizes the transmission speed between network nodes using the _____ field of a frame.
A) preamble
B) frame check sequence
C) trailer
D) PAD
E) flow control

6. On the switched Ethernet, the priority (or urgency) level of a frame in delivery can be indicated using _____ information when VLANs are used.
A) Rapid Spanning Tree Protocol
B) Tag Control Information
C) Link Aggregation Control Protocol

D) Cyclic Redundancy Check
E) Tag Protocol Identifier (TPID)

7. One of the benefits of having VLANs is
_____.
A) higher network survivability
B) reduced network congestions
C) prevention of network loops
D) lower transmission errors
E) reduced errors in network cabling

8. VLANs in Ethernet are configured in
_____.
A) hubs
B) switches
C) routers
D) wireless access points
E) user hosts

9. When particular VLANs are not created
on a switched Ethernet LAN, all host
computers belong to the _____ VLAN.
A) data
B) management
C) voice
D) default
E) supervisory

10. Sub-interfaces can be assigned to the
_____ to enable inter-VLAN routing.
A) hub port
B) switch port
C) router port
D) repeater port
E) wireless access point

11. Corporations may introduce VLANs:
A) to make it easier to manage internal
changes (e.g., reassignment of a worker).
B) to avoid network maintenance.
C) to better interconnect wireless and wired
LAN segments.
D) to extend the scope of a LAN without
compromising network performance.
E) to effectively link wide area networks.

12. Which is NOT true regarding the
VLAN?
A) Switches are manually configured to
create VLANs.
B) Management of changes (e.g., relocation
of a business department) becomes
easier.
C) VLANs can improve network security.
D) Users of a VLAN can share the same IP
subnet, regardless of their physical
locations.
E) Developing VLANs requires that the
network be hierarchical with the access
and core layers.

13. Choose an INCORRECT statement
regarding VLANs.
A) VLANs can divide a network into
logical segments such as work groups.
B) VLANs are configured in switches but
not in host computers.
C) The layer 2 switch can be used to
exchange frames between two different
VLANs.
D) The VLAN scope can be identical to the
broadcast domain.
E) Oftentimes, an IP subnet and a VLAN
are paired.

14. The Ethernet switch determines the
VLAN ID of a frame coming from a
neighboring switch based on the _____.
A) destination address
B) source address
C) tag control information (TCI)
D) tag protocol identifier (TPID)
E) frame check sequence

15. Which statement is CORRECT?
A) The data link layer is divided into the
LLC (logical link control) and MAC
(media access control) sub-layers.
B) Ethernet has one physical layer standard.
C) The LLC layer is responsible for frame
organization and switch operation.
D) The Ethernet frame's Frame Check

Sequence ensures synchronization of data transmission speeds between two nodes.
E) Ethernet frames without the VLAN tagging can carry information on frame priority.

16. Sub-interfaces of a router port (interface) can be used in order to
A) relay packets between VLANs.
B) make Ethernet switches obsolete.
C) enable link aggregation.
D) remove packets going through the router port.
E) fragment a VLAN into smaller VLANs.

17. Choose a CORRECT statement on VLANs.
A) Layer 2 switches can forward frames across different VLANs.
B) With VLANs, cut-through switching should be used to minimize transmission delays.
C) VLAN tagging information is added to the Ethernet frame by host computers.
D) A host can be attached to a trunk port of a switch for data transmissions.
E) A switch port may be either an access or a trunk port, but not both at the same time.

18. The CRC (Cyclic Redundancy Check) code of the Ethernet frame is used to
A) detect data redundancy.
B) detect transmission errors.
C) perform flow control.
D) synchronize the clock cycle between two computers.
E) indicate the beginning of a frame.

19. Choose an ACCURATE statement on Ethernet.
A) A loop between two hosts is allowed.
B) In general, switches are interconnected in full mesh topology.
C) The RSTP is faster than the STP in

forwarding VLAN frames.
D) The STP was developed to detect overloaded links.
E) The layer 2 or 3 switch can be used at the core layer.

20. Choose a CORRECT statement on the Ethernet technology.
A) Switches do not regenerate arrived signals in their shapes and strengths.
B) The LLC sub-layer header describes the type of packet contained in the frame's data field.
C) Ethernet switches utilize CSMA/CD to control network access.
D) It is generally OK for office workers to install hubs or switches in their office because this does not affect overall network performance.
E) Most switches rely on the half-duplex mode of data transmissions.

21. The Ethernet frame's length field represents length information of the
_____.
A) data field
B) entire frame
C) address field
D) frame minus data field
E) frame check sequence field

22. When multiple Ethernet switches (core and workgroup switches) are interconnected, they are typically organized in a _____.
A) bus
B) ring
C) hierarchy
D) mesh
E) star

23. Refer to the figure below. On switch B, four ports are currently physically linked to other nodes. How many of them are configured as access ports if there are VLANs?
A) 0

B) 1
C) 2
D) 3
E) 4

24. Refer to the figure below. If the computer H sends a document to the printer G, which link(s) should be transporting the VLAN tagged frame?
A) H → F, F → C, and C → A
B) H → F and D → G
C) F → C, C → A, A → B, B → D
D) C → A and A → B
E) all links from H through G

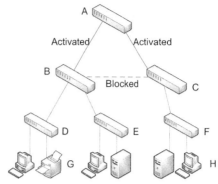

25. The Bridge Protocol Data Unit (BPDU) contains information relevant to _____.
A) link aggregation
B) VLAN configuration
C) VLAN tagging
D) inter-VLAN routing
E) redundant path identification

CHAPTER 8   WIRELESS LAN (WIFI)

8.1   INTRODUCTION

Various wireless technologies have been introduced and are currently in use. They can be classified into PAN, LAN, MAN and WAN technologies in terms of the general scope of coverage. IEEE is mainly responsible, except the cellular and satellite networks, for developing the standards. Among the well-known are:

1. Personal area network (PAN): IEEE802.15 - The standard was designed to cover a relatively small area, typically less than 10 meters in diameter. Because of the historical background, IEEE802.15 is better known as Bluetooth. Its connection speed is generally less than 2 Mbps, substantially slower than popular WiFi standards. For data transmissions, it relies on the 2.45GHz radio frequency band, available license-free to software and hardware manufacturers. IEEE802.15 is not suitable for high-speed networking.

2. Local area network (LAN): IEEE802.11 (or WiFi) represents a collection of wireless LAN standards including 802.11a, 802.11b, 802.11g, 802.11n, and 802.11ac. Designed to cover local areas such as a campus and a building, IEEE802.11 is not ideal for many IEEE802.15 applications because hardware components (e.g., WiFi chipset) have been bulkier and more costly. Accordingly, IEEE802.15 and IEEE802.11 standards have coexisted complementing each other's weaknesses. This complementary relationship, however, may change with the introduction of *WiFi Direct*. It enables direct communications between WiFi devices without the wireless access point (shortly AP or hotspot), and thus can pose a threat to IEEE802.15 (Bluetooth).

3. Metropolitan area network (MAN): IEEE802.16 (WiMax or WirelessMAN) is designed to cover a longer distance (e.g., the last mile link between an ISP and client houses) than IEEE802.11 standards. IEEE802.16 is primarily intended to offer wireless broadband service comparable to DSL or Cable. There are also MAN standards intended for network access in fast moving vehicles. Besides, IEEE802.11 (WiFi) is being adopted for MAN service as well. For example, several cities have deployed or started to implement a city-wide network based on the WiFi-mesh (IEEE802.11s) standard.

4. Wide area network (WAN): As the most popular wireless WAN platform, cellular networks are everywhere providing subscribers with voice and high-speed data transmission service. Although cellular networks operated by telecommunications carriers (or telcos) were originally introduced mainly for voice, they are now widely utilized to access the Internet with smart phones, tablet computers, and other mobile devices. As another wireless WAN, the satellite network has been in use for TV/radio broadcasting and long-distance voice/data service.

With the prevalence of WiFi, today's computer operating systems including Windows, Mac, and Linux family all support the technology. This chapter focuses on explaining WiFi (IEEE802.11) standards in their technical details and implementation issues.

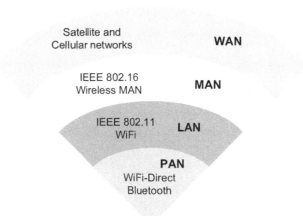

Figure 8.1 Select wireless networking technologies

The key learning objectives include:

- Standard layers of WiFi
- WiFi setup modes (Ad hoc vs. Infrastructure Modes)
- Service set (Basic Service Set vs. Extended Service Set)
- Service Set Identifier (SSID)
- Various WiFi standards currently available
- Methods of media access control
- Types of WiFi frames
- Radio frequency and channel usage by WiFi
- Authentication and association in WiFi network
- WiFi mesh network (IEEE802.11s)
- WiFi-based home networking

8.2 WIFI FUNDMENTALS

8.2.1 Layers of WiFi Technology

As is the case with Ethernet, technical elements of WiFi are defined in the data link and physical layers, and implemented in the wireless network interface card (or WNIC). Its data link layer performs the following functions:

- Creation of WiFi frames
- Implementation of measures for reliable data transmissions
- Authentication and association between nodes (e.g., laptop and wireless access point)
- Protection of transmitted data with encryption technologies
- Media access control based on the *Carrier Sense Multiple Access/Collision Avoidance* (CSMA/CA) and *Request to Send/Clear to Send* (RTS/CTS) protocols.

In the physical layer, WiFi uses radio waves for signal transmissions. For this, the layer specifies technical details of signaling including frequency bands and modulation methods. Just as with other wireless communication systems (e.g., Bluetooth and cellular phone networks), WiFi uses advanced spread spectrum technologies (e.g., OFDM - Orthogonal Frequency Division Multiplexing and SDMA - Space Division Multiple Access) to encode digital data in an effective manner to reduce signal propagation problems (e.g., interference between nearby stations) and to utilize available bandwidth more efficiently.

8.2.2 Setup Modes and Access Points

Ad Hoc Mode

Two different approaches are used to set up the WiFi network: *ad hoc mode* and *infrastructure mode*. With the *ad hoc mode* (or peer-to-peer mode), two or more wireless stations can directly exchange frames without relying on an AP. This mode is easier to set up and dismantle, and thus adequate to arrange a relatively small temporary network.

Figure 8.2 WiFi in ad-hoc mode

Infrastructure Mode

With the *infrastructure mode*, WiFi and the wired network (mostly Ethernet) coexist and APs provide connectivity between them. In Figure 8.3, for example, two APs are deployed within the corporate boundary. Most corporate and campus WiFi networks are in the infrastructure mode because key resources including servers and network printers are attached to high-speed Ethernet, and WiFi enables workstations and mobile devices to access the resources.

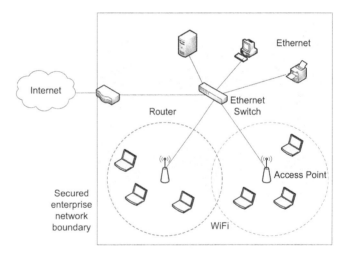

Figure 8.3 WiFi in infrastructure mode

Access Point (Hotspot)

The AP can be a dedicated device (see Figure 8.4) or software running on a computer or any other device. For instance, smartphones running recent Android or other operating systems have built-in capability to turn themselves into APs after simple setup. The AP device used in a corporate network (not the smartphone-enabled AP intended for personal usage) is designed to associate a number of clients, usually 15-50 host stations including laptops and mobile

255

devices. It is equipped with its own wireless NIC (or WNIC) and *bridging* capability to enable data flows between two different LAN standards. In fact, its primary role is to provide interconnectivity between Ethernet and WiFi through the translation of their frames (refer to Section 3.4 for the bridge function). This translation is necessary because Ethernet (see Figure 7.2) and WiFi (see Figure 8.11) have their own frame structures.

Figure 8.4 Wireless access point (Source: linksys.com)

The AP is therefore a layer 2 device, and thus a switch and all host stations attached to the AP belong to the same subnet. Although a layer 2 device, the AP may be configured with an IP address for remote access and management, but not for frame deliveries. Besides bridging, the AP in the infrastructure mode conducts other functions crucial to the WiFi network as summarized in Table 8.1. More details on them are explained throughout the chapter.

AP Functions	Description
Bridging	Conducts bridging in the form of frame conversion between WiFi (IEEE802.11) and Ethernet (IEEE802.3).
Authentication	Authenticates host stations attempting to join a WiFi network and allows association (a form of binding) once they are authenticated.
Media access control	Conducts media access control so that, regardless of the number of hosts associated with an AP, only a single host is allowed to transmit frames to the AP at a time to prevent frame collisions.
Data security	Utilizes data encryption for secure communications with host stations.
Frame routing	Advanced APs can relay frames to the destination host primarily on the WiFi infrastructure (see Section 8.8).

Table 8.1 Key functions of wireless access point (AP)

Each AP is able to cover certain limited space in offering WiFi connectivity, and the invisible boundary around an AP becomes a cell or basic service set (BSS). The size of each cell is limited because the distance between the AP and associated stations adversely affects effective *throughput* due to signal attenuation (or weakening). For example, it is said that the effective indoor range of APs is less than 50 meters. With the distance limit, a corporate LAN of reasonable size needs to deploy multiple APs. A university campus network may need hundreds or thousands of APs for effective coverage. Also, there should be overlapping between neighboring cells in order to allow handoffs when a mobile host moves from one cell to another. In general, neighboring cells are required to have 10-15 % overlap to enable roaming by WiFi clients.

A station should associate (or bind) itself to an AP before exchanging frames. The AP maintains an association table that lists associated/authenticated stations. The association table includes host information such as hostnames, IP addresses and MAC addresses (see Figure 8.5 for a sample table). As host stations continuously associate and de-associate with an AP, its association table is updated dynamically.

Host name	IP address	MAC address	State
Shin09	172.26.10.1	0203.23AB.D051	Associated
Jmon	172.26.10.12	0203.23A3.D591	Authenticated
Glan7	172.26.10.14	0203.236B.A031	Associated

Figure 8.5 Sample association table

With the growing complexity of the WiFi network in the infrastructure mode, APs have evolved into two types of *thick* and *thin* APs. The thick AP is a traditional AP that conducts key functions listed in Table 8.1. Meanwhile, the thin AP acts as a communication post, delegating the traditional AP functions to a master AP controller. For instance, in Figure 8.3, the Ethernet switch can become an AP controller that can reconfigure parameters of multiple thin APs remotely. By deploying thin APs, therefore, their management becomes less labor-intensive and thus can lower maintenance and operational costs.

8.2.3   Service Set Identifier (SSID)

The SSID is a WiFi LAN's unique identifier (e.g., SUSU_Wireless for a campus network) and is configured in APs. The screenshot in Figure 8.6 demonstrates a partial list of WiFi networks and their SSIDs detected at the author's residence. The AP periodically broadcasts beacon frames containing its SSID so that nearby client hosts can associate with it after authentication. Clients are required to include the case-sensitive SSID in the association-requesting frame. In public WiFi zones (e.g., airports and coffee shops), APs are set up with guest SSIDs to invite mobile clients without their authentication.

Alternately, an AP can be configured not to broadcast its SSID. In this case, the beacon cannot be completely turned off because it has other functions such as indicating the presence of an AP and, instead, it includes a null value in the SSID field. In this non-broadcast mode, SSID can be used to authenticate client stations that attempt to associate with the AP. Of course, this requires that clients be pre-programmed with the same SSID. When an SSID is used for authentication, it may be exchanged with or without encryption. Using the non-encrypted SSID to authenticate host stations is not safe at all because WiFi frames containing the plain-text SSID can be easily intercepted.

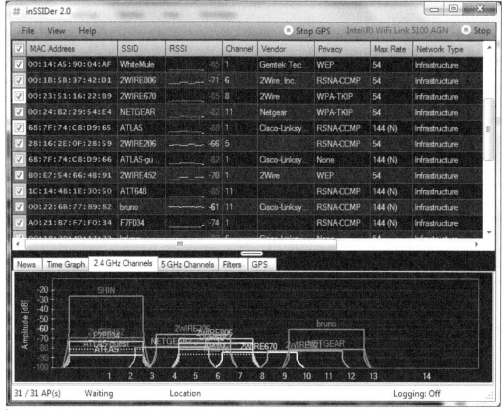

Notes:

- RSSI (Received Signal Strength Indication) is a negative value, and thus the lower the better.
- "RSNA-CCMP" is Latin for WPA2 with AES encryption.
- WiFi security gets stronger in the sequence of "None (or Open) => WEP => WPA-TKIP => WPA2-AES (or RSNA-CCMP)." To be detailed in Chapter 12.

Figure 8.6 SSIDs in my neighborhood (Demo: inSSIDer2.0)

8.2.4 Service Set (BSS vs. ESS)

The WiFi network is divided into two levels in its coverage scope: *basic service set* (BSS) and *extended service set* (ESS).

Basic Service Set (BSS)

The BSS is the smallest WiFi building block in ad hoc and infrastructure modes. In the ad hoc mode, the BSS is composed of at least two hosts. In the infrastructure mode, the BSS needs at least one host station and one AP. In general, it contains an AP and multiple user stations associated with it. Each BSS has a 48 bit *Basic Service Set Identifier* (BSSID) used to uniquely distinguish one from the other BSS. This means that a particular WiFi network can have as many BSSIDs as the number of basic service sets. In a BSS, the BSSID is the AP's MAC address. For example, you can observe a MAC address (as BSSID) associated with each SSID in Figure 8.6. It is important not to confuse BSSID and SSID. One SSID can have one or more *basic service sets* (BSS) and therefore one or more BSSIDs. At home networks, generally one AP (thus one BSS) is enough to cover the entire area and thus only one BSSID is shown.

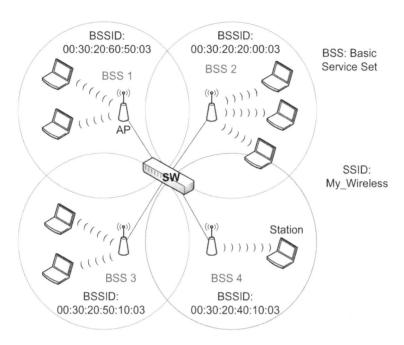

Extended Service Set (ESS) = BSS1 + BSS2 + BSS3 + BSS4

Figure 8.7 Basic service set vs. extended service set

Extended Service Set (ESS)

When multiple *basic service sets* are formed to cover a larger area and more stations, they as a whole become an *extended service set* (ESS). The ESS, therefore, contains multiple cells each with an AP and one or more stations. A host station's WNIC is associated with a single AP and deploying multiple APs (thus multiple *basic service sets*) to form an ESS increases the scope of a WiFi network. Neighboring basic service sets overlap to allow handoffs. Roaming between two *basic service sets* requires that a user station associates, de-associates, and re-associates with different APs.

For example, imagine a company's WiFi LAN (SSID = My_Wireless) that covers four large rooms in which each room, as a BSS, has an AP and multiple stations associated with it (see Figure 8.7). If the four *basic service sets* are interconnected by an Ethernet switch located in a wiring closet, the entire WiFi network results in an ESS. In terms of IP address allocation, all nodes including APs and user stations within the ESS belong to the same subnet and, therefore, only a single frame delivery path (as a data link) becomes active between any two user stations.

8.2.5 AP vs. Repeater Mode

Some APs can switch between the AP mode (Figure 8.7) and the repeater mode (Figure 8.8). The AP, in the repeater mode, relays (or rebroadcasts) radio signals in order to extend the range of a WiFi network or to overcome signal blockage. The AP in the repeater mode, therefore, does not need to be physically linked to Ethernet. A drawback of the repeater mode is that the relay of frames between two neighboring APs can result in considerable loss of throughput or actual transmission speed.

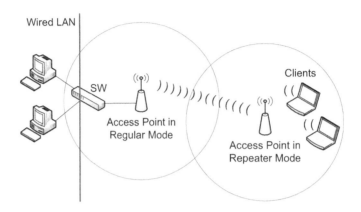

Figure 8.8 Access point in repeater mode

8.3   MEDIA ACCESS CONTROL

Due to data broadcasting, WiFi should enforce a mechanism to control network access and to avoid frame collisions *within the BSS*. This means that each BSS becomes a collision domain (refer to Section 3.10) in which only a single station is allowed to release data at a time to avoid collisions. The transmission collisions and subsequent process to restore normalcy degrade network throughput.

The process of granting network access only to a single station is handled by the *media access control* (MAC) protocol. The MAC protocol defines rules that hosts (more specifically their WNICs) comply with to ensure that only one station releases data at a time within the BSS. Two different MAC standards have been in use: *Carrier Sense Multiple Access - Collision Avoidance* (CSMA/CA) and *Request to Send/Clear to Send* (RTS/CTS). In the regular mode, CSMA/CA is activated and RTS/CTS becomes available as an option.

8.3.1   CSMA/CA

CSMA/CA shares similarities with CSMA/CD (Carrier Sense Multiple Access - Collision Detection), the Ethernet's MAC standard (see Chapter 3). The key difference is that WiFi adopts *collision avoidance* (CA) intended to 'prevent' collisions before frames are broadcasted. Meanwhile, Ethernet's *collision detection* (CD) accepts the possibility of transmission collisions and uses a procedure to restore normalcy should they take place. CSMA/CA's mechanism for preventing collisions beforehand and for maintaining communication reliability through the *acknowledgement* is summarized below:

CSMA/CA:

1. A host station's WNIC listens to WiFi activities.

2. When the channel of a BSS is clear (meaning no ongoing traffic), the station may send frames to the AP. This first-come-first-served principle represents the *Carrier Sense Multiple Access* (CSMA) part of the CSMA/CA protocol.

3. Before releasing frames, however, it must wait for a random amount of time (or random back-off time). This is what the *collision avoidance* (CA) part of CSMA/CA does. The station, however, may transmit frames without waiting if there has been no network traffic beyond a certain time period.

4. After the random waiting, the host begins frame transmissions to the AP if the network is still clear.

ACK (Acknowledgment):

5. The AP immediately returns back an acknowledgment (ACK) for each frame it receives from the client station. If there is no ACK from the AP within a predetermined time limit, the source node retransmits the frame.

The WiFi's CSMA/CA has its share of limitations. Above all, if several hosts within a cell try to transmit frames concurrently, collisions still can occur due to such reason as blind spots. Also, with CSMA/CA, all nodes within a BSS have an equal chance (i.e., first-come-first-served) of accessing the network. That is, no priority scheme is applied to frames so that urgent or real time ones (e.g., Voice over IP) can be delivered ahead of the others. Lastly, one transmitting station may occupy the channel capacity as long as it needs. As a result, the potential lack of equity in network access and capacity sharing can result.

8.3.2 RTS/CTS

As a form of handshaking between the AP and the host station, RTS/CTS is designed to provide additional assurance in collision avoidance through the fine-tuning of the WiFi operation. The protocol has been introduced mainly to resolve the 'hidden node' problem in which two stations associated with an AP are at opposite sites (Figure 8.9a) or are located at each other's blind spots (Figure 8.9b). When stations are unable to sense each other, they may release data simultaneously resulting in collisions. The RTS/CTS protocol is utilized as an optional measure to keep such incidents from happening.

The process of RTS/CTS is depicted in Figure 8.10. When RTS/CTS is activated on a host's wireless network card (WNIC), the station sends RTS to its associated AP. Then, the AP broadcasts the CTS frame to grant the requesting client the right to transmit data and also to alert others to hold off their transmissions. Once this handshaking based on RTS/CTS is complete, the host station starts sending data frames. The activation of RTS/CTS, however, increases network overhead because of additional RTS/CTS frames exchanged and thus can negatively affect WiFi performance. This is especially so when the activation of RTS/CTS is not necessary (e.g., little chance of collisions).

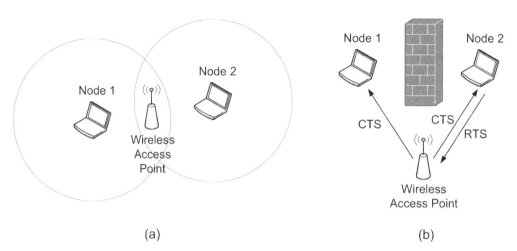

(a)   (b)

Figure 8.9 Hidden node problems

When a WiFi network with CSMA/CA experiences many collisions, RTP/CTS built into the host's WNIC may be activated. APs are configured to automatically broadcast CTS in response to a client's RTS message. As an optional feature, the RTS/CTS function is generally offered in more costly, high-end WNICs. Therefore, chances are that inexpensive home or SOHO (small office home office) products do not come with the capability.

The access control mechanism based on CSMA/CA or RTS/CTS has one drawback -- frames are permitted to enter the network on the first-come-first-served basis. Under the access scheme, emails are given the same priority as voice calls, a clear problem. The *IEEE802.11e* standard complements the MAC protocols by offering Quality of Service (QoS) for the WiFi network so that frames are processed according to their urgency level. This QoS affords much better throughput for time-sensitive applications such as Voice over IP, audio/video streaming, and video conferencing. The IEEE802.11n standard supports IEEE802.11e for the QoS-based frame prioritization.

In closing this section, it is necessary to add that the technical details of CSMA/CA and RTC/CTS have been further extended, especially with the arrival of MIMO (multi-input, multi-output) for IEEE802.11n and IEEE802.11ac (see Sections 8.7.1 and 8.7.2). Although their technical details are beyond the scope of this book, the extensions are still in accordance with the general principles of media access control mechanisms explained here.

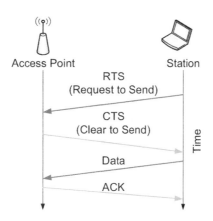

Figure 8.10 4-Way handshake with RTS/CTS

8.4 WIFI FRAMES

When frames are broadcasted through the unguided medium (air), things are more complicated than when they are propagated through a guided (wired) medium such as the twisted pair and fiber optic cable. For instance, wireless links are subject to disruptions caused by such conditions as interference, data stream collision, signal attenuation, and hand off. Also, with the frame broadcasting, WiFi nodes become much more vulnerable to security threats. This hostile circumstance demands that more coordination and control functions be in place for wireless networking. Facing such challenges, WiFi uses three different frame types in order to exchange user-produced data and conduct supervisory functions: *data frame, management frame,* and *control frame.*

Data Frame

Data frames carry actual user data (e.g., emails). Figure 8.11 demonstrates the data frame's structure -- composed of the header, data, and trailer fields. As can be seen, the header is more complicated than the Ethernet frame's. When, an AP is linked to an Ethernet switch, WiFi frames have to be converted into Ethernet frames (or vice versa) by the AP for their transportation across the two different platforms. Figure 8.11 is for demonstration only and thus the details are not explained.

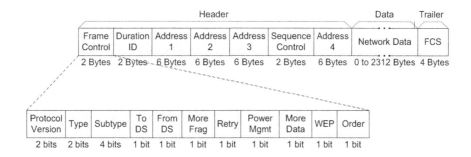

Figure 8.11 WiFi data frame structure (for information only)

Management Frame

The management frame's primary role is to establish/handshake and maintain connections between nodes (e.g., AP and client stations) through the *authentication* and *association* procedure. For this, management frames include authentication frames, association/de-association frames, and beacon frames.

Above all, only qualified stations should be allowed to join an AP. For this, a host station authenticates itself to a target AP by sending the authentication frame. Also, they exchange the association and de-association frames to establish an association (or binding) and to terminate it. Additionally, beacon frames are periodically broadcasted by an AP to announce its presence. The beacon frame includes an AP's MAC address and SSID. The WNIC of a host station continually scans all WiFi frequency channels and listens to beacons to choose the best AP to associate with.

Control Frame

Control frames are used to aid the delivery of data frames. For example, the *acknowledgment* (ACK) frame that confirms the receipt of a client frame is an example of the control frame. Frames carrying *Request-to-Send* (RTS) and *Clear-to-Send* (CTS) are also this type.

8.5 WIFI AND RADIO FREQUENCY

8.5.1 Radio Spectrum

In this section, the *radio wave* (shortly radio) used for the delivery of WiFi frames is explained. Radio is a type of *electromagnetic radiation* wave that also includes *light*, *X-rays*, and *Ultraviolet*. Among them, radio is most heavily utilized to offer various traditional (e.g., AM and FM radio) and advanced (e.g., WiFi and cellular network) services in which network nodes can be either fixed or mobile.

As in Table 8.2, the radio spectrum is divided into a number of frequency ranges starting from *very low frequencies* all the way to *extremely-high frequencies*. Radio waves that cover the *ultra-high (UHF), super high (SHF),* and *extremely high (EHF)* frequency ranges of the radio spectrum are called *microwaves*. Recent development of advanced communication technologies including WiFi, Bluetooth, WiMax, satellite broadcasting, GPS (global positioning system), and cellular phone systems all take advantage of microwave.

Low vs. High Radio Frequency

What are the implications of relying on low versus high radio frequencies in wireless networking? Most notably, high frequency channels use more power (therefore higher signal strength) than low frequency ones, and this results in better quality of data (e.g., songs) delivered. The trade-off is that radio signals in higher frequency ranges lack flexibility in transmissions, making them more susceptible to interferences and subsequently limiting their effective distance. That is, a lower frequency signal is more flexible in getting around barriers (e.g., mountains) and thus can propagate farther than a higher frequency one. Referring to Table 8.2, you should be able to see why AM signals travel much farther than FM signals but FM delivers better sound quality than AM does.

Radiowave Frequency Ranges	
Name	**Frequency ranges**
Extremely Low Frequencies (ELF)	30 – 300 Hz
Voice Frequencies (VF)	0.3 – 3 kHz
Very Low Frequencies (VLF)	3 – 30 kHz
Low Frequencies (LF)	30 – 300 kHz
Medium Frequencies (MF)	0.3 – 3 MHz
High Frequencies (HF)	3 – 30 MHz
Very High Frequencies (VHF)	30 – 300 MHz
Ultra High Frequencies (UHF)	0.3 – 3 GHz
Super High Frequencies (SHF)	3 – 30 GHz
Extremely High Frequencies (EHF)	30 – 300 GHz

MF → AM Radio

VHF → FM Radio

UHF, SHF, EHF → TV, GPS, Wi-Fi, 3G, 4G, Satellite

Table 8.2 Radio frequency spectrum and microwave ranges

Governance

Usage of the radio frequency spectrum in a country is generally regulated by the government. In the United States, for example, *Federal Communications Commission* (FCC) oversees the non-Federal Government usage of radio (e.g., cellular phone service by Verizon) and *National Telecommunication and Information Administration* (NTIA) is responsible for the management of radio ranges utilized by the government for national defense, law enforcement & security, transportation, emergencies, and others. FCC and NTIA coordinate through an advisory committee.

Licensed vs. Unlicensed Radio

ISM Bands	Frequency range
900 MHz	902 - 928 MHz
2.4 GHz	2.4 - 2.4835 GHz
5.0 GHz	5.180 - 5.825 GHz

Table 8.3 ISM bands (North America)

The radio spectrum includes both licensed (license required) and unlicensed (license-free) frequency bands. At present, a large share of the radio spectrum is regulated, thus licensing is required for its exclusive usage. There are also unlicensed bands frequently known as *Industry, scientific, and medical* (ISM) bands. Vendors use ISM bands to develop software and hardware products ranging from traditional home appliances and electronics (e.g., microwave oven, cordless phones) to networking devices for WiFi and Bluetooth. The license-free ISM bands include 900MHz, 2.4GHz and 5.0GHz bands whose frequency ranges in North America are summarized in Table 8.3.

Exercise 8-1

1. What is the bandwidth of each ISM band in North America? Refer to Table 8.3 and compute it in terms of megahertz.
2. When the bandwidths of three ISM bands are compared, what can you say in terms of their relative capacity?

8.5.2 WiFi Channels

This section explains how the frequency range of the 2.4GHz ISM band is further divided into WiFi channels used by 802.11 standards. In North America including US and Canada, there are 11 frequency channels in the 2.4GHz band with channel capacity (or bandwidth) of 22MHz. Other regions define different number of frequency channels. In fact, many countries in the world have 13 channels in the 2.4GHz band.

In North America, the frequency ranges of 11 neighboring channels are overlapped (see Figure 8.12). For example, Channel 1's frequency range (2.401~2.423 GHz) overlaps with those of Channel 2, 3, 4, and 5. This makes only 3 channels (1, 6, and 11) out of 11 2.4GHz channels *non-overlapping* from each other. Even if the bandwidth of each channel is 22MHz, 20MHz are available for data transmissions and the remaining 2MHz is used as a 'guard' band to prevent signal interference.

Channel	Lower Frequency	Upper Frequency
1	2.401	2.423
2	2.406	2.428
3	2.411	2.433
4	2.416	2.438
5	2.421	2.443
6	2.426	2.448
7	2.431	2.453
8	2.436	2.458
9	2.441	2.463
10	2.446	2.468
11	2.451	2.473

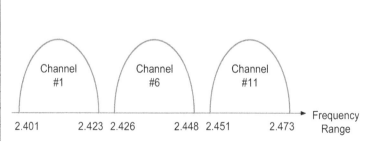

Figure 8.12 2.4GHz non-overlapping channels (in the US and Canada)

Things are a little bit more complicated with the 5.0GHz band. In the US, for example, there are

25 non-overlapping channels (e.g., 36, 40, 44, 100, 132, and 165), each with 20MHz bandwidth. These channels are not necessarily contiguous for technical reasons (e.g., to avoid conflicts with other existing wireless services). Just as with the 2.4GHz band case, countries differ in allocating channels for the 5.0GHz band. *Remember that each 20MHz channel of 2.4GHz and 5.0GHz bands becomes a building-block of WiFi link capacity.*

Exercise 8-2: The bandwidth necessary for voice communication is about 4 kHz for one direction. How many voice calls can be accommodated within the 2.4GHz band and within each channel?

8.5.3 Planning Basic Service Sets (BSS)

Why are frequency channels overlapped as explained in the previous section? The short answer is to capitalize the available bandwidth more effectively through channel reuse. Let us see how it works. When neighboring APs operate in non-overlapping channels, this reduces signal interferences and improves transmission speed. That is, when multiple APs are deployed to cover an area, their locations should be chosen in a manner that the three non-overlapping channels are assigned to neighbors.

Figure 8.13 demonstrates a case in which APs of neighboring cells are instructed to use non-overlapping channels in order to minimize signal interferences. Figure 8.13 also shows that the same frequency channels are reused when they are separated. The five APs represent five different cells or Basic Service Sets (BSS), and all five of them as a whole become one Extended Service Set (ESS). Remember that no matter how many host stations are associated with an AP *on a single channel*, CSMA/CA -- the WiFi's *media access control* protocol -- allows only one station to exchange data with the AP at a time.

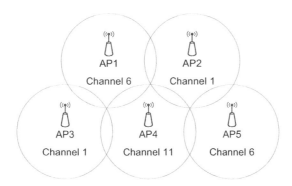

Figure 8.13 WiFi channel selection in an area

When there is only one AP in an area (e.g., home), you can choose any of 11 channels as you don't have to worry about channel reuse by adjacent cells. However, if your and your neighbors' APs are configured to use the same channel, your WiFi LAN's performance may be affected by the potential interference. As shown in Table 8.3, the 5.0GHz band has a much larger capacity than the 2.4GHz band supporting more transmission channels (e.g., 3 versus 25 non-overlapping channels). This allows creation of more basic service sets, making the 5.0GHz band much more flexible than the 2.4GHz band in channel allocation.

Lastly, the relationship of the three terms (*spectrum, bands*, and *channels*) that have been introduced thus far is further clarified.

- The radio wave *spectrum,* the entire frequency range of radio (see Table 8.2), is divided into a number of *service bands* for various communication/broadcasting services. For instance, the service band of AM radio is 500-1500 kHz in the US (see Table 8.3 for another service band example).

- A particular service band is, then, further divided into multiple *service channels* For example, the service band of AM radio can be divided into many 10 kHz channels for AM radio stations (see Figure 8.12 for another example of service channels).

Exercise 8-3: Figure 8.14 is a hypothetical corporate network with several APs. It indicates that at least one laptop computer is associated with each AP. Answer below questions based on the figure.

1. What is the smallest number of SSID(s) the network can have?
2. How many basic service sets do you see in the network?
3. How many BSSIDs the network should have?
4. How many extended service sets do you see in the network?
5. Which AP is in the repeater mode?
6. Can AP4 and AP5 use 802.11g and 802.11n concurrently? Why or why not?
7. How many subnets do you see in the enterprise network?
8. The company decides to use private IPs with 172.16.0.0/16 as the network ID. Assuming that it uses the third octet to create subnets, assign subnet addresses and allocate the last available IP address of each subnet to the router port. What are IP addresses of router ports Fa0/0, Fa0/1, and Fa0/2?
9. Assign an IP address to H4 through H7 based on the subnet address. What are they?
10. Assign a MAC address to H4 through H7, and also to the router's LAN port Fa0/1. What are they?
11. Based on the results so far, develop a correct switch table for S2, S3, and S4. Include columns of MAC address, exit port, and VLAN in the switch table.
12. Assuming that the switch table for S2, S3, and S4 are completed, what happens if H4 broadcasts an IP packet?
13. Assume that the subnet attached to the router's Fa0/1 will be divided into two data VLANs for better traffic management. It is a logical decision because SW3 and SW4 belong to two different business departments. Then, which switch ports of S2 and S3 should be configured as trunk ports (refer back to Section 7.8).
14. After creating the VLANs, how many extended service sets do you see in the corporate network

if there is pairing of a subnet address and a VLAN ID?

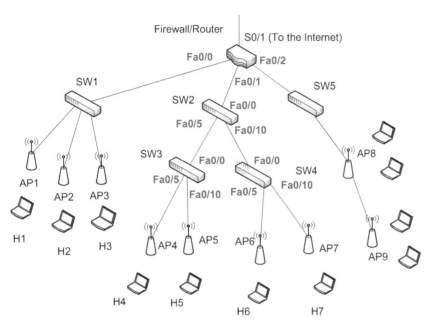

Figure 8.14 A hypothetical corporate network

8.6 AUTHENTICATION AND ASSOCIATION

Stage	State	Description
1	Unauthenticated/ Unassociated	No relationship between a client station and an AP
2	Authenticated/ Unassociated	o The client is authenticated by the AP. o For this, the client submits an authentication frame to the AP. o At an enterprise, there is generally a designated authentication server. This centralized control of WiFi access improves network security.
3	Authenticated/ Associated	o Upon successful authentication, the client sends an association request frame to the AP. o The AP's association response completes the binding. o At this stage, other options including security and data transmission rate are finalized.

Table 8.4 Three stages of authentication and association

Prior to the exchange of data between an AP and a host station, the two nodes should complete the *authentication* and *association* process. This is intended for access control that prevents unauthorized hosts or people from entering a WiFi LAN.

269

8.6.1 Three Stage Process

The relationship between a user station and an AP can be in one of three states: (1) unauthenticated/unassociated, (2) authenticated/unassociated, and (3) authenticated/associated (see Table 8.4). For the eventual binding, therefore, the two nodes should undergo the three-step sequence for which several management frames are exchanged.

8.6.2 Authentication Methods of a Station

There are different options available to authenticate a client station, each with its own pros and cons. Among them, *open authentication, pre-shared key authentication,* and *authentication server* solutions are explained. *Open authentication* and *Pre-shared key authentication* of client stations are performed by the AP. With the *authentication server* approach, the authentication is handled by a designated server and the AP's role is reduced to the relay of authentication frames between the server and host stations.

Open Authentication

Open authentication uses SSID for authentication. In this mode, a client station furnishes such basic information as its MAC address and SSID to a target AP to request authentication. The AP responds with either success or failure, making the authentication a two-step process. For this mode of authentication, communicating nodes can be pre-configured with an SSID so that the AP's periodic broadcasting of the SSID is turned off.

Open authentication uses clear text making it easy to intercept with a software tool and thus it is not a serious form of authentication. With open authentication, both parties (i.e., client and AP) may be pre-programmed with a *pre-shared* secret key to encrypt data exchanged after authentication, but the encryption function is not utilized for initial authentication (see Figure 8.15).

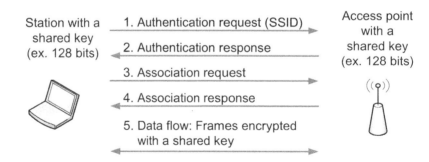

Figure 8.15 Two-way open authentication (step 1 and 2)

Pre-Shared Key Authentication

To authenticate user stations, a pre-shared secret key of a certain length (e.g., 128 bits) is used. The pre-shared key may be derived from a user provided password/passphrase, which is stored in the client nodes and AP to avoid re-entries. With the direct derivation of the pre-shared key, choosing a strong password/passphrase is important to make it difficult to break the pre-shared key.

The pre-shared key-based authentication requires 4-way communications, unlike the *open authentication*'s two-way *request* and *response* cycle. First, when a client station initiates an association request to an AP, the AP sends a random challenge text back to the requesting station. Then, the client station encrypts the challenge text with the pre-shared secret key and returns the encrypted challenge text back to the AP. On receiving it, the AP validates the encrypted text and determines the client's eligibility to grant an association. This seemingly secure authentication method has a weakness because hackers can recover the shared secret key by monitoring the traffic. To make it much more difficult to recover the pre-shared key, current WiFi standards use technology where, once a client is authenticated, the pre-shared key does not stay the same but is dynamically changed (more details in Chapter 12).

The general procedure of the pre-shared key authentication is shown in Figure 8.16. The four-step procedure replaces the two-step open authentication (step 1 and 2) in Figure 8.15.

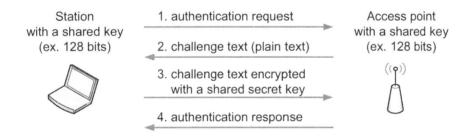

Figure 8.16 Four-way shared-key authentication

Authentication Server

Many organizations deploy a central authentication server to manage the authentication process. Such protocols as *RADIUS (Remote Authentication Dial in User Service)* and *TACACS+ (Terminal Access Controller Access-Control System Plus)* are used to manage communications between an authentication server and an AP that forwards authentication requests coming from client stations. Besides the authentication of WiFi clients, the server can handle other security-related functions such as the authorization of remote access through dial-in or through the virtual private network (VPN) link over the Internet (see Figure 8.17).

Additional Notes on Security

In addition to authentication, an AP may come with another layer of security that filters client devices or device users based on such additional information as the destination IP address, protocol in the data field, TCP/UDP port, and MAC address. Also, an AP may be configured to turn off application services deemed unnecessary. For example, if a corporation does not allow such application services as Telnet (for remote access) or FTP (for remote file transfer), they should be disabled by APs. As a final note, using data encryptions in WiFi should be mandatory unless it is for public usage (e.g., store visitors). In addition, any WiFi open for guest access should be completely disengaged from the production network of a corporation.

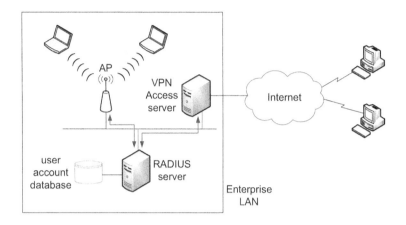

Figure 8.17 Authentication of WiFi stations with RADIUS

Exercise 8-4: There are various tools that can find WiFi LANs around your place. In this exercise, we take advantage of two programs: inSSIDer2.0 and the command mode utility program, *netsh*.

1. Download a recent version of the open source-based WiFi scanning program, inSSIDer (as shown in Figure 8.6), and activate it.
   a) Search SSIDs around your place.
   b) What is the channel most heavily used by APs?
   c) How many BSSIDs do you see?
   d) What security (or privacy) standards are the most or least used?
   e) What are different speeds of WiFi networks?
   f) Does any WiFi network running 802.11n take advantage of more than one frequency channel? What are the channels?
   g) Is any WiFi network running on the *ad hoc* mode?
   h) How many of the networks are using 2.4GHz vs. 5.0 GHz channels?
   i) What is the highest amplitude, shown as decibel, among WiFi signals?
2. (Optional) This time, you are to use the command mode utility program, *netsh*, in Windows. Among its available commands are:
   C:\netsh
   C:\netsh>wlan
   C:\netsh wlan>show interfaces
   C:\netsh wlan>show networks
   C:\netsh wlan>show networks mode=bssid.
   Using the commands, answer the inSSIDer questions above to the extent possible.

8.7 WIFI STANDARDS

Several WiFi standards have been introduced by IEEE and they, including legacy ones (i.e., 802.11a and 802.11b), are summarized in Table 8.5. Currently, the 802.11n and 802.11ac standards dominate the marketplace. 802.11n and 802.11ac are much different from the legacy WiFi standards and, thus, their distinctive features are explained here.

WiFi standards have different *rated speeds,* maximum speeds that can be theoretically achieved under ideal conditions. There is, however, a considerable gap between *rated speeds* and actual *throughputs* that we experience. For example, although 802.11n's rated speed is more than 100Mbps, its actual throughput is typically less than 50Mbps, varying greatly depending on the setup.

There are various factors that contribute to the significant gap between rated speeds and actual throughputs of WiFi standards:
- Sharing of channel capacity by multiple hosts within a BSS
- Distance between an AP and associated hosts
- Number of client hosts associated with an AP
- Signal attenuation (or weakening)
- Waiting time necessary to prevent transmission collisions (see MAC in Section 8.3)
- Required acknowledgments of delivered frames

Status	IEEE WiFi Standards	Rated speeds
Legacy	802.11b	11 Mbps
	802.11a	54 Mbps
On the path to legacy	802.11g	54 Mbps
Current	802.11n	100-600 Mbps
	802.11ac	Up to 1.3 Gbps

Table 8.5 WiFi standards

8.7.1 IEEE802.11n

802.11n is intended to offer wired LAN-like performance as high data rates are critical for transporting multimedia data such as high-quality videos. 802.11n builds on the legacy 802.11 standards and this backwards compatibility allows their co-existence. Some of the key features that differentiate 802.11n from the legacy standards are summarized here.

Throughput Modes

Unlike the legacy standards in which each link between an AP and a client gets 20MHz channel bandwidth, 802.11n supports two throughput modes: 20MHz and 40MHz. Designed to further enhance WiFi speeds, the 40MHz mode uses *channel bonding* for which two neighboring 20MHz channels are combined to create a bigger pipe. In developing hardware/software for 802.11n, the vendor support for the 20MHz throughput mode is mandatory, but that for 40MHz remains optional.

2.4/5.0 GHz Bands

While the legacy standards utilize one frequency band (e.g., 2.4GHz band for 802.11g), 802.11n can take advantage of both 2.4GHz and 5.0GHz bands either concurrently or non-concurrently. Assuming that there are two antennas on a device, the dual band technology allows that one antenna transmits data on a 2.4GHz frequency channel and the other on a 5.0GHz channel.

If two 2.4GHz and 5.0GHz frequency channels can be used concurrently, it is *concurrent dual-band transmissions*. If two antennas alternate 2.4GHz and 5.0GHz channel usage, then it becomes *non-concurrent dual-band transmissions*. The 5.0GHz band is much less crowded than the 2.4GHz band and thus less subject to signal interferences.

Single-User MIMO

The traditional standards (i.e., 802.11a, 802.11b, and 802.11g) rely on "*single input, single output*" (or SISO) technology in which one data stream flows between two nodes (e.g., client host and AP) through a 20MHz channel of either 2.4GHz or 5.0GHz band.

On the other hand, 802.11n supports both traditional SISO and "*multiple inputs, multiple outputs*" (or MIMO) transmissions. As a radical shift from the SISO paradigm, 802.11n's MIMO supports up to four simultaneous data streams between two devices (e.g., AP and laptop client). As multiple data streams (also called spatial streams) are established between two nodes, it is also known as *single-user MIMO*. The multi-path propagation of data streams considerably increases overall bandwidth.

To achieve *single-user MIMO*, 802.11n-enabled client WNICs and APs come with multiple antennas (Figure 8.18). Each antenna transmits and receives an independent data stream between two communicating nodes. That is, concurrent flows of four data streams require 4 antennas.

Currently, the majority of 802.11n-ready APs and computers sold in the marketplace have 2 or 3 antennas, supporting fewer data streams and lower speeds than the maximum capacity possible. *Remember that 802.11n only supports single-user MIMO. That is, within a Basic Service Set, only one client is allowed to exchange data (through multiple data streams) with the AP at a time.*

QoS Support

802.11n supports the Quality of Service (QoS) standard (IEEE 802.11e) so that client stations with time-sensitive data are given a higher priority in network access to prevent transmission delays.

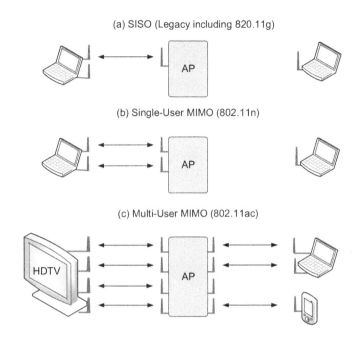

Figure 8.18   SISO, single-user MIMO, and multi-user MIMO

8.7.2 IEEE802.11ac

802.11ac is the latest WiFi standard and has notable technical advancements. The enhanced features enable 802.11ac to achieve throughputs considerably higher than that of 802.11n, theoretically as high as 8Gbps. In practice, however, vendor products are expected to support rated speeds anywhere from 500 Mbps up to 1.3 Gbps. To achieve the very fast data rates, standards in both physical layer (e.g., new modulation and encoding techniques) and media access control of the data link layer have been updated from those of 802.11n. Some of the changes are summarized here.

5.0 GHz Band

802.11ac utilizes only the 5.0GHz band, which is less crowed and thus risks less interferences than the 2.4GHz band. The 5.0GHz band also supports more non-overlapping 20MHz channels (e.g., 25 in the US) than 2.4GHz (e.g., 3 in the US, see Figure 8.12) enabling greater flexibility in WiFi network design and improved performance. 802.11ac is backwards compatible and thus can co-exist with other 802.11 devices running on the 5.0GHz unlicensed band.

Throughput Modes

802.11ac supports various channel speeds including 20MHz and 40MHz for backwards compatibility, and 80MHz and 160MHz for faster throughputs. 802.11ac-compliant hardware/software devices are required to support 20MHz, 40MHz, and 80MHz throughput modes, but support for 160MHz remains optional.

Remember that, in 802.11n, the 40MHz throughput mode is created by bonding two neighboring 20MHz frequency channels. 802.11ac, therefore, extends 802.11n further by allowing the formation of the larger 80MHz pipe through the aggregation of four 20MHz basic channels (and thus achieving much faster speeds).

Capitalizing on the several channel options, 802.11ac-enabled APs can switch the channel size dynamically on a frame-by-frame basis in order to utilize available network capacity more efficiently. For example, an AP initially exchanging frames with a client node based on a 20MHz channel can add an idle 20MHz channel next to it to grow the overall bandwidth to 40MHz, thus forming a 40MHz channel. This way, 40MHz channel bandwidth can dynamically grow to 80MHz through the bonding with the next channel of 40MHz if it is not in use. The channel bonding introduced by 802.11n simply becomes more flexible under 802.11ac.

Multi-User MIMO (MU-MIMO)

802.11ac introduces *multi-user MIMO* for the first time. In MU-MIMO, multiple nodes transmit and receive data streams concurrently (see Figure 8.18c). Whereas 802.11n (single-user MIMO) supports up to 4 data streams within a BSS, 802.11ac can have up to 8 simultaneous data streams in either single-user or multi-user environment.

With 8 spatial streams, an AP can exchange frames with up to 4 different client hosts concurrently. To make this possible, 802.11ac (and 802.11n as well) uses *beamforming* technology, which concentrates data signals on each of the targeted device instead of radiating them out into the atmosphere as legacy 802.11 standards do.

The bandwidth available on a WiFi network is proportional to the number of spatial streams utilized. For example, the AP supporting 8 spatial streams, each with 20MHz bandwidth, attains the transmission speed 8 times faster than the AP relying on a single data stream of 20MHz (e.g., 802.11g). That is, 802.11ac (with up to 8 data streams) effectively doubles the throughput of 802.11n (with up to 4 data streams).

In the single-user environment, however, establishing 8 spatial streams between two nodes (e.g., AP and laptop client) requires 8 antennas in each node, which is somewhat costly and thus less practical. So, practically most APs are expected to use multi-user MIMO for simultaneous data exchanges with several client hosts (see Figure 8.18c).

In concluding the section, a question remains as to "Does the traditional media access control of CSMA/CA and RTS/CTS apply to standards that support MIMO?" The answer is yes but details of CSMA/CA and RTC/CTS have been further extended to accommodate the technology advancement. Basically, MAC works at the 20MHz channel level. That is, when 802.11ac dynamically grows its transmission capacity by fusing next idle channels (e.g.,

20MHz to 40MHz), the MAC mechanism applies to each 20MHz channel to detect its availability.

Features	802.11g	802.11n	802.11ac
Frequency bands (unlicensed)	2.4 GHz	2.4 and 5.0 GHz	5.0 GHz
Channel bandwidth options (in MHz)	20	20 (mandatory) 40 (optional)	20, 40, and 80 (mandatory) 160(optional)
No. of concurrent data (or spatial) streams supported	1	up to 4	up to 8
MIMO-support	N/A (SISO)	Single-user MIMO	Multi-user MIMO
No. of clients concurrently supported by an AP	1	1	up to 4

Table 8.6 Comparison of WiFi standards

8.8 WIFI MESH NETWORK (IEEE802.11S)

The WiFi mesh (shortly Wi-Mesh) network runs on WiFi standards, but it covers a considerably larger territory (e.g., metropolitan area) using mesh networking of APs (frequently called *mesh points*). In traditional WiFi, APs are typically connected to a wired network through such devices as Ethernet switches because they lack routing capability.

The uniqueness of Wi-Mesh is that *mesh points* can route frames among themselves and thus they do not need to depend on the wired LAN for packet propagation. They use their own routing capacity -- a transportation mechanism similar to switching -- to relay frames to a particular *mesh point* attached to a wired network. Depending on the circumstance, *mesh points* intelligently figure out the best possible route to avoid slow or troubled *mesh points* in relaying frames. With the relay function between *mesh points*, only one or a few *mesh points* need to be cabled to a wired network.

The Wi-Mesh network is, thus, a good technology choice when a place (e.g., building, campus) lacks wired network infrastructure. As it does not require hardwire connectivity to every *mesh point*, Wi-Mesh can cover a much larger area (e.g., city) than the traditional WiFi can. With its late arrival, however, the biggest drawback of Wi-Mesh has been that the routing technology has not been standardized, forcing an adopting organization to be locked in to a particular vendor's products. Recognizing the increasing popularity of Wi-Mesh, IEEE issued a standard routing protocol, 802.11s, for Wi-Mesh networking.

Wi-Mesh is expected to compete with WiMax (or IEEE802.16), a fixed broadband wireless standard designed to cover metropolitan areas (up to 30-40 miles). The announced speed of WiMax is at around 70-100 Mbps, considerably faster than Wi-Mesh's 11- 54Mbps. WiMax can provide interconnectivity between WiFi networks. The WiMax standard, however, is not compatible with WiFi as Wi-Mesh is. Given the huge popularity of WiFi standards, this lack of compatibility is a main drawback of WiMax despite its notable strength in bandwidth. With both pros and cons of WiMax and Wi-Mesh, the jury is still out on which technology is going to ultimately prevail.

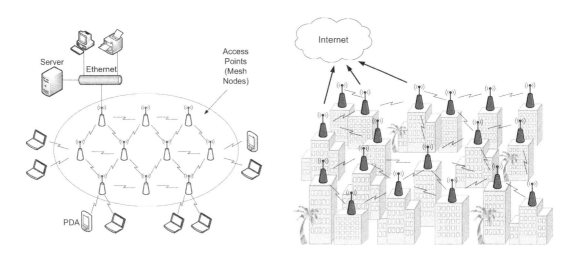

Figure 8.19 Wi-Mesh networks at an enterprise and in a city

8.9 WIFI HOME NETWORK

In this section, we take an in-depth look at the implementation details of WiFi at home (and SOHO – Small Office & Home Office) and its connectivity to the Internet. These days, most home networks are running on the WiFi standard as computers come with built-in wireless network cards (or WNICs). The WiFi home network is generally composed of a *broadband modem* (e.g., DSL or Cable Modem), a *wireless access router* as an intermediary device, and *end stations* such as laptops, tablet computers, and smart phones. Figure 8.20 demonstrates a general arrangement of the WiFi network and structural details of the wireless access router.

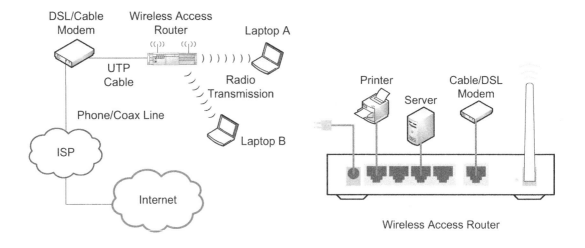

Figure 8.20 WiFi home networking and wireless access router

8.9.1 DSL/Cable Modem

The DSL/Cable modem, as a physical layer device, is similar to the traditional dial-up modem in its functionality. The modem provides conversion between digital and analog signals (refer to Section 4.2.3). More specifically, it translates computer/router-generated digital signals to analog signals for transmissions over the phone (for DSL) or coaxial (for Cable) line. The modem also converts incoming analog signals back into digital signals, and forwards them to a router/computer. Generally, the UTP cable is used for connectivity between the DSL/Cable modem and the wireless access router.

8.9.2 Wireless Access Router

The majority of wireless access routers combine switch, router, and AP functions altogether for home networking. The particular product - not an actual model - shown in Figure 8.20 has four Ethernet switch ports and a WAN port to link the Cable/DSL modem. Key functions commonly incorporated into the wireless access router are:

a) **Router function** to access the Internet through an ISP network. The router (as a border router) connects two different subnets: (1) a home network and (2) a WAN subnet that links the home router to an ISP's router. The ISP's DHCP server provides a dynamic, public IP address to the home network, thus becoming the IP address of the WAN router port.

b) **Ethernet switch function** to enable connectivity between wireless and wired hosts at the home network.

c) **Wireless access point (AP) function** for wireless/mobile stations (e.g., smart phones).

d) **Internal DHCP server function** to provide temporary, private IP addresses to the home network's internal nodes. As explained, private IP addresses are not routable over the Internet and its usage is limited to the residential LAN.

e) **Network address translation (NAT) function** for internal nodes (e.g., laptop, tablet, smart phone) to share a single public IP address offered by the ISP's DHCP server (see Section 5.6.4).

f) Other optional functions including firewall and DNS

Figure 8.21 demonstrates logical relationships among the technical components of the wireless access router. Implementing several intermediary device functions (i.e., AP, Ethernet switch, and router) in one physical unit makes sense because, unlike the corporation network that contains a large number of client and server hosts and handles much network traffic, the home network is much smaller in scale, generally composed of only a few hosts, and thus does not justify the separation of device functions.

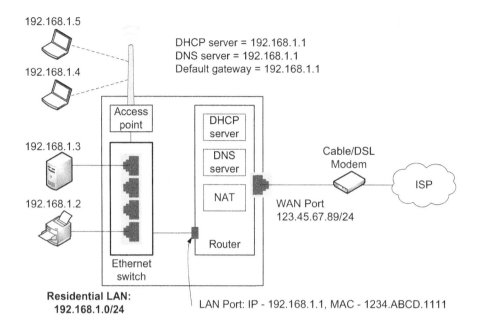

192.168.1.5

192.168.1.4

DHCP server = 192.168.1.1
DNS server = 192.168.1.1
Default gateway = 192.168.1.1

Access
point

DHCP
server

DNS
server

NAT

Cable/DSL
Modem

ISP

192.168.1.3

192.168.1.2

WAN Port
123.45.67.89/24

Router

Ethernet
switch

Residential LAN:
192.168.1.0/24

LAN Port: IP - 192.168.1.1, MAC - 1234.ABCD.1111

Figure 8.21 Wireless Access Router – Logical View

8.9.3 IP Configuration of Home Network

Figure 8.21 also demonstrates a scenario of IP address assignment to a home network:

- The home network is given a network address of 192.168.1.0/24. All node addresses on the 192.168.1.0/24 network are therefore private IPs that cannot be used for packet routing over the Internet.

- The WAN port is on a different subnet (123.45.67.0/24) and is given an IP address of 123.45.67.89.

- The wireless access router has an internal LAN port with an IP address of 192.168.1.1 and a MAC address of 1234.ABCD.1111. The LAN port is invisible to us, but it internally ties the router to the Ethernet switch. The router's LAN port (192.168.1.1) therefore becomes the default gateway of hosts at the home network.

- The router has a DHCP server that allocates private IPs to internal nodes. The IP address (123.45.67.89) that publicly represents the home network is provided by the ISP's DHCP server.

- The router has a DNS server that stores hostnames in the home network and their corresponding IP addresses.

- The router has Network address translation (NAT) function that translates non-routable private IPs to the public IP address (123.45.67.89).

The screenshot of the laptop (192.168.1.4) in Figure 8.22 summarizes the IP assignment in which the router's LAN port (192.168.1.1) becomes the default gateway and, at the same time, the same IP address is shared by the DHCP and DNS servers.

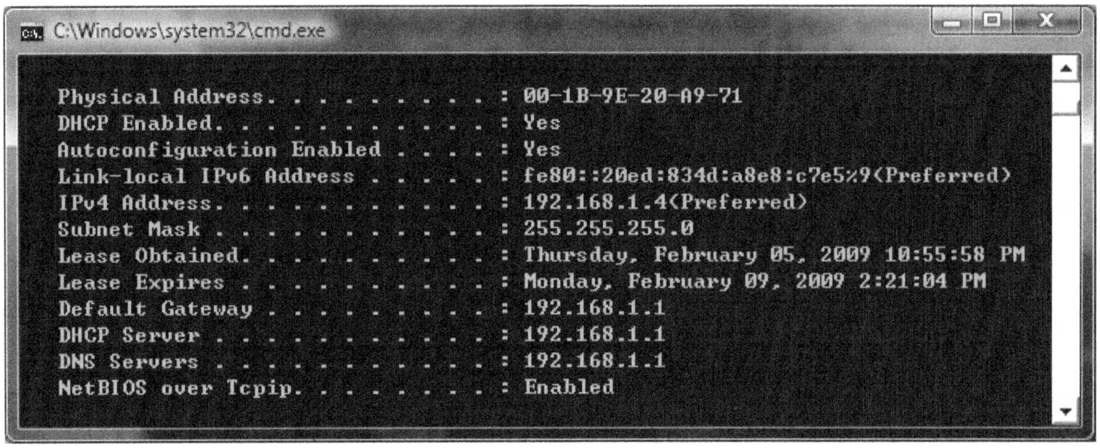

Figure 8.22 IP Configuration of home network

Exercise 8-5: Certain ISPs offer a router bundled with a DSL/Cable modem. Then, there are two intermediary nodes at a home network: (1) a router with a built-in DSL/Cable modem and (2) a wireless access point with the Ethernet switch function built-in. Under this scenario, redraw Figure 8.21 to reflect the changed setup and reassign IP addresses to the router's LAN and WAN ports.

8.9.4 Mini-Case: Wireless Access Router Configuration

This case based on an actual product demonstrates WiFi configuration options generally available on the wireless access router for home networks. The access router comes with a HTTP server -- in addition to the DHCP and DNS servers -- so that its OS can be accessed through a web browser for configuration. In this example, all servers including the HTTP server installed in the router share the IP of 192.168.1.1. The HTTP server is accessed with 'http://192.168.1.1:80' or simply 'http://192.168.1.1' from a client's web browser.

In the Wireless Settings screen (see Figure 8.23), it indicates that the SSID is SHIN and uses channel 1 of the 2.4GHz band. Then, we can choose a security option (e.g., disable, WEP, WPA-Personal, WPA2-Personal) to protect (or not to protect) the network. When WEP is chosen, the secret key value derived from *Shared Secret* (see Figure 8.23) remains static leaving it highly vulnerable to hacking and thus should be avoided. The identical *Shared Secret* is also configured in other WiFi clients so that the secret key values derived by all WiFi nodes match.

When a more advanced WPA2-Personal is chosen, you define the *Key Renewal* time (e.g., 600 seconds). In WPA2-Personal (and WPA-Personal as well), the secret key value derived from *Shared Secret* is dynamically changed according to the *Key Renewal* interval, making it much more resistant to hacking than WEP. A shorter *Key Renewal* interval makes a WiFi network more secure, but puts more work on the AP. *AES* is the encryption technology utilized by the WPA2-Personal standard. More on the security standards are explained in Chapter 12. Lastly, as an additional security measure, the wireless router offers *Connection Control List* in which MAC

281

addresses allowed to associate with the AP are specified.

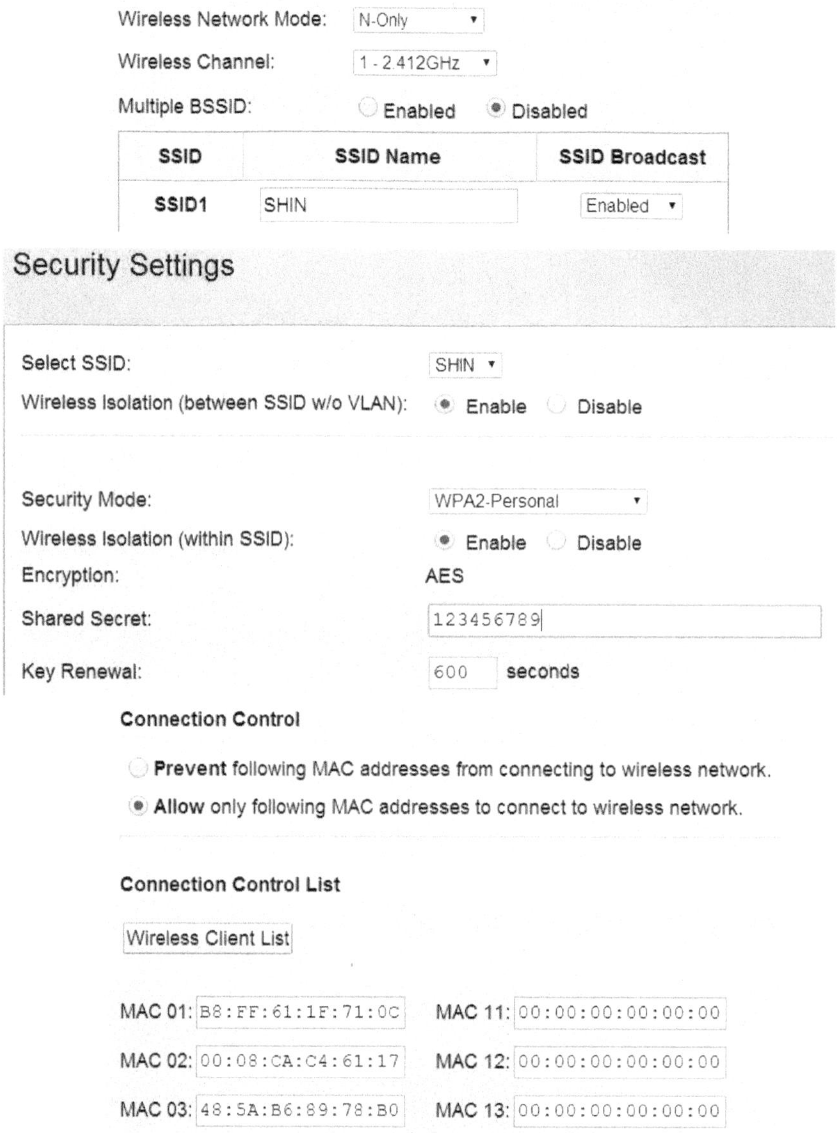

Figure 8.23 Configuration of wireless access point

Exercise 8-6: The screenshot in Figure 8.24 summarizes 'router settings' of a wireless access router. Answer following questions referring to the sections 8.9.2 and 8.9.3. Hint: The *Internet port* is the router's WAN port.
1. What is the router's public IP address that represents the home network to the Internet?
2. Who provides the public IP address of the WAN port?
3. What is the subnet address of the public IP address?
4. Can you find out the address of the ISP's DHCP server(s)?

5. What are the addresses of the ISP's DNS servers that provide mapping between IPs and host names?
6. What is the subnet address of the home network?
7. What should be the default gateway address of home computers?
8. Given the subnet address of the home network, how many hosts can be assigned an IP address?
9. Does the access router rely on network address translation (NAT)? Why or why not?
10. Does the access router have an internal DHCP server?

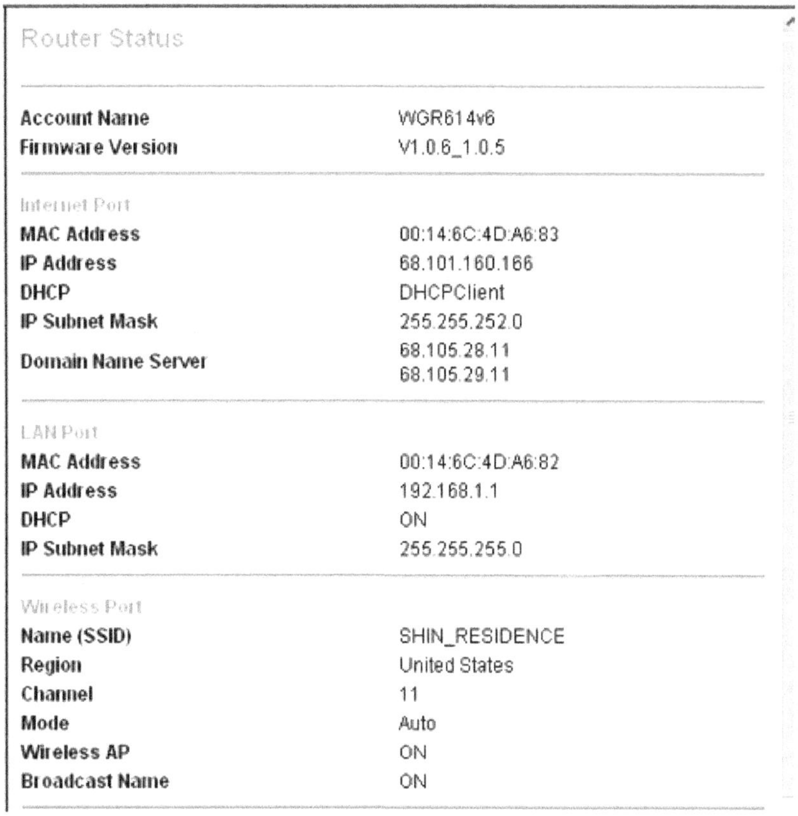

```
Router Status

Account Name                    WGR614v6
Firmware Version                V1.0.6_1.0.5

Internet Port
MAC Address                     00:14:6C:4D:A6:83
IP Address                      68.101.160.166
DHCP                            DHCPClient
IP Subnet Mask                  255.255.252.0
Domain Name Server              68.105.28.11
                                68.105.29.11

LAN Port
MAC Address                     00:14:6C:4D:A6:82
IP Address                      192.168.1.1
DHCP                            ON
IP Subnet Mask                  255.255.255.0

Wireless Port
Name (SSID)                     SHIN_RESIDENCE
Region                          United States
Channel                         11
Mode                            Auto
Wireless AP                     ON
Broadcast Name                  ON
```

Figure 8.24 Router configuration

KEY TERMS

ad hoc mode
association
authentication
authentication server
band
basic service set (BSS)
basic service set identifier
(BSSI)

broadband modem
Carrier Sense Multiple
Access/Collision Avoidance
(CSMA/CA)
cell
channel
channel bonding
clear to send (CTS)

concurrent dual-band
transmission
control frame
data frame
Direct Sequence Spread
Spectrum (DSSS)
extended service set (ESS)
Federal Communications

283

Commission (FCC)
Frequency Hopping Spread
Spectrum (FHSS)
IEEE802.11
IEEE802.11n
IEEE802.11ac
IEEE802.11e
IEEE802.15
IEEE802.16
"industry, scientific, and
medical (ISM) band"
infrastructure mode
management frame
master controller
mesh point
miscrowave
Multi-input-multi-output

(MIMO)
multi-user MIMO
non-overlapping channel
open authentication
peer-to-peer mode
pre-shared key (PSK)
authentication
radio spectrum
radio wave
Remote Authentication Dial in
User Service (RADIUS)
repeater mode
request to send (RTS)
service band
service channel
service set identifier (SSID)
single-input-single-output

(SISO)
single-user MIMO
spectrum
Terminal Access Controller
Access-Control System Plus
(TACACS+)
thick access point (AP)
thin access point (AP)
AP mode
WEP
WiFi direct
wireless access point (AP)
wireless access router
wireless mesh network
WPA-Personal
WPA2-Personal

CHAPTER REVIEW QUESTIONS

1. Which statement CORRECTLY describes
the IEEE802.11n standard?
A) Its rated speed is less than 10Mbps.
B) With channel bonding, a 2.4GHz
   channel and a 5.0GHz channel can be
   combined to create a larger channel.
C) It uses a single antenna to achieve the
   multiple inputs and multiple outputs
   (MIMO) mode.
D) It does NOT support quality of service
   (QoS) as all frames get the same priority.
E) The dual-band transmission can use both
   2.4GHz and 5.0GHz concurrently.

2. What is the key difference between the
basic service set (BSS) and the extended
service set (ESS)?
A) number of clients
B) number of servers
C) number of overlapping channels
   available
D) number of access points
E) number of wireless switches

3. An AP may be in the regular AP mode or

in the _____ mode.
A) firewall
B) modem
C) router
D) repeater
E) switch

4. With the _____ protocol activated, when
a user station wishes to transmit data, it has
to obtain AP's permission.
A) Carrier Sense Multiple Access/Collision
   Avoidance + Acknowledgement
B) Carrier Sense Multiple Access/Collision
   Avoidance
C) Carrier Sense Multiple Access/Collision
   Detection
D) Request to Send/Clear to Send
E) Carrier Sense Multiple Access/Collision
   Detection + Acknowledgement

5. When an AP issues an acknowledgement
of a frame it receives, the acknowledgement
is delivered in a _____ frame.
A) control
B) data

C) beacon
D) supervisory
E) management

6. Which function is generally NOT built into the wireless access router designed for home networking?
A) wireless access point
B) Ethernet switch
C) DHCP server
D) network address translation
E) CSU/DSU

7. The 2.4GHz band supports _____ non-overlapping channels in North America.
A) 1
B) 3
C) 7
D) 11
E) 2

8. Which is CORRECT regarding the IEEE 802.11 standard?
A) At an enterprise network, the router translates WiFi frames into Ethernet frames.
B) With 802.11n, multiple client stations can exchange data with an AP concurrently.
C) The pre-shared key authentication uses SSID for authentication.
D) At a home network, the pre-shared key is derived from the password/passphrase.
E) The AP acts as a router in the infrastructure mode.

9. IEEE802.11 supports at least two different solutions to authenticate user stations: open authentication and _____ authentication.
A) pre-shared key
B) closed key
C) public key
D) private key
E) dynamic key

10. Bluetooth is a popular wireless standard

for the _____.
A) MAN (Metropolitan Area Network)
B) PAN (Personal Area Network)
C) WAN (Wide Area Network)
D) LAN (Local Area Network)
E) Enterprise network

11. There are two unlicensed bands used for WiFi: 2.4GHz (ranging 2.4 -2.48 GHz) and 5.0GHz (ranging 5.20 – 5.85). Which statement is CORRECT?
A) The bandwidth of the 5.0GHz band is roughly 4 times larger than that of 2.4 GHz.
B) The bandwidth of the 2.4GHz band is roughly 8 times larger than that of 5.0 GHz.
C) The bandwidth of the 2.4GHz band is roughly 4 times larger than that of 5.0 GHz.
D) The bandwidth of the 5.0GHz band is roughly 8 times larger than that of 2.4 GHz.
E) The bandwidth of the 2.4GHz band is roughly equal to that of 5.0GHz.

12. How laptops associated with an AP can avoid transmission collisions?
A) Using electronic tokens
B) Using the spread spectrum technology
C) Using random back-off time even when the network is quiet
D) Using a collision detection mechanism
E) Using the first-come-last-served approach

13. Key functions of the AP do NOT include:
A) Frame conversion primarily between WiFi and Ethernet
B) Authentication of host stations attempting to join a WiFi network
C) Dynamic selections of a radio transmission channel to avoid interference between basic service sets

D) Media access control to prevent collisions
E) Data encryptions for secure communications with clients

14. Which is ACCURATE?
A) authentication request – control frame
B) association request – management frame
C) acknowledgement – data frame
D) RTS/CTS – management frame
E) beacons – data frame

15. Which is a CORRECT statement on the WiFi technology?
A) The Wi-mesh network uses routers for frame routing.
B) The wavelength of radio waves as the WiFi medium is primarily measured in GHz.
C) Radio waves used for WiFi are in the frequency range of microwaves.
D) WiFi uses the ring topology to deploy APs.
E) WiFi uses licensed frequency ranges of the radio spectrum.

16. Which is NOT true regarding the IEEE 802.11 standard?
A) In North America, 11 channels are defined within the 2.4GHz frequency band.
B) In North America, channel 1, 6, and 11 are non-overlapping channels of the 2.4GHz frequency band.
C) An AP may periodically broadcast the beacon frame to announce its presence and it may include SSID.
D) The ad hoc mode is more popular than the infrastructure mode in implementing WiFi at a university campus.
E) Binding between a user station and an AP is called association.

17. Sometimes, the _____ is all it takes for a host station to join a WiFi network.
A) digital certificate
B) public key
C) digital signature
D) service set identifier
E) beacon

18. The media access control layer of IEEE802.11 conducts the following functions EXCEPT
A) Maintains communication reliability using acknowledgements.
B) Controls access (transmission) to the shared radio channel.
C) Protects frames with encryption.
D) Authenticates client stations.
E) Chooses a transmission channel randomly.

19. Select a CORRECT statement of the IEEE802.11n standard.
A) It uses CSMA/CD to control data transmissions by host stations.
B) It supports only single-input-single-output between an AP and a client.
C) It works only in the 2.4GHz band.
D) It mandates RTS/CTS for media access control.
E) It supports quality of service (QoS) to deliver time sensitive frames without delays.

20. The technical details of WiFi are defined at the_____.
A) physical layer only
B) physical and data link layers only
C) physical, data link, and internet layers only
D) physical, data link, internet, and transport layers only
E) physical, data link, internet, transport, and application layers

CHAPTER 9   WIDE AREA NETWORK

9.1   INTRODUCTION

The WAN link spans a state, a nation, or across nations, covering geographically much larger areas than LAN does. Unlike the LAN installed by a business, university, or government organization, the WAN infrastructure is owned and maintained by carriers (or common carriers) in order to provide WAN service to the general public. Traditional telephone companies (or telcos) and Internet Service Providers (ISPs) offer various voice/data services to individuals and businesses.

WAN services offered by carriers are generally regulated by the government. In the US, for example, the *Federal Communications Commission* (FCC) as an independent agency of the US government regulates carriers that offer interstate and international WAN services. These carriers have the right-of-way to install networks necessary to offer WAN services to clients. Remotely dispersed branch locations and mobile workers (e.g., telecommuters and traveling salesmen) of an organization can reach each other through the carrier's WAN service. As a result, many enterprise networks are comprised of both local LANs and WAN connections.

With more carriers offering both voice and data network services, there is increasing convergence between them and the traditional distinction among telephone companies, ISPs, and cable companies is becoming less meaningful as they are competing with each other to grow businesses. The WAN service is fee-based in which service costs are decided by various factors including the standard technology utilized, connection speed, quality of service, and link distance. This chapter is to explain popular WAN services offered on the infrastructure wholly owned by the carrier.

Aside from the 'private' WAN infrastructure of the carrier, the Internet, to which no single service provider has an exclusive ownership, is also a wildly popular platform for low cost WAN connections. The Internet's general architecture and the *virtual private network* technology heavily used to form secure WAN connections through the Internet are separately explained in Chapter 10.

The primary learning objectives of this chapter are to understand:
- Scenarios of WAN link usage
- Principal elements of the WAN infrastructure
- Key WAN topologies and design considerations
- Layers of WAN technologies: Physical and Data Link layers
- IP addressing for WAN links
- WAN access link services: leased lines and broadband services
- WAN layer 2 standards:
  - Leased line standard focusing on PPP
  - Packet switched data network (PSDN) standards including Frame Relay, Asynchronous Transfer Mode (ATM), Carrier Ethernet, and Multiprotocol Label Switching (MPLS)
- Wireless WAN technologies focusing on the cellular network

9.2 WAN AND ENTERPRISE NETWORKS

9.2.1 WAN Connection Scenarios

As structural entities of an organization are becoming more distributed (e.g., from local to national and global) and the business relationship (e.g., inter-firm partnership, supply chain, and business outsourcing) gets more complicated, the demand for WAN connection service is keep growing to better manage intra- and inter-business communications and operations. Let's take a look at some of the prevalent situations where WAN service becomes instrumental:

- A company has its main office and several branch offices across the nation or world. The company's distributed business locations and their local networks (LANs) are interconnected by WAN links available through a carrier's 'private' WAN infrastructure and the Internet.

- Firms of partnership (e.g., part suppliers, manufacturers, and wholesalers) may tie their networks over the WAN link so that they can electronically conduct business transactions. For instance, inter-firm database access and updates, inventory monitoring, product ordering, and invoicing over the WAN link can transform business processes cheaper, faster (e.g., real-time), and more accurate because of reduced manual engagement. They are important activities of supply chain management between partnership firms and, not surprisingly, the WAN link has become an artery of the practice.

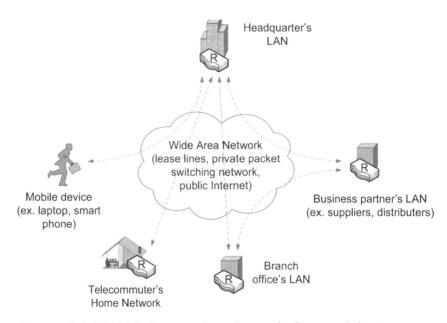

Figure 9.1 WAN links over the private platform and the Internet

- Telecommuters working at home can access their corporate systems to conduct job-related functions such as file uploading and downloading, updating databases, and business communications. Their computers remotely connect to corporate systems over various broadband WAN technologies including DSL, Cable, and cellular.

- Mobile workers including traveling salesmen and onsite customer service agents can access corporate systems to perform business tasks over WAN connections. Mobile workers may be in one location today, but in another location tomorrow. Unlike those that stay unchanged (e.g., inter-LAN connections), WAN links for mobile workers are dynamically established and terminated as needed.

9.2.2 Service Level Agreement

In offering the WAN connection service, a carrier and a client organization exchange a formal Service Level Agreement (SLA) that specifies its terms and conditions. Detailing the SLA is important to both parties because their expectations (e.g., service quality) do not necessarily coincide and disputes can occur regarding the details of the service provision. Among the agreed terms and conditions of WAN service are:

- Data rate (speed)
- Latency (e.g., round-trip transmission delay) and how it is measured (e.g., Average latency should be less than 90 milliseconds based on sample measurement.)
- Acceptable error rate and how it is measured (e.g., Average percentage of packets dropped by the carrier network based on sample measurement.)
- Availability of network service and its calculation method (e.g., Uptime of network should be at least 99.95%)
- Penalty provisions for service failures (e.g., compensation of service credits to clients)
- Details of scheduled/unscheduled maintenance
- Customer support options and service call procedure
- Service cancellation terms

9.2.3 CPE vs. SPF

Category	Equipment/facility
Customer premises equipment (CPE)	• Modem (e.g., dial-up, DSL, and Cable modem) • CSU/DSU (Channel service unit/Data service unit) • Router
Service provider facility (SPF)	• Central Office (CO) • Local access link • WAN backbone network

Table 9.1 Building blocks of the WAN connection

The WAN link is formed by the *Customer Premises Equipment* (CPE) that resides at a client site and the *Service Provider Facility* (SPF) that enables WAN connectivity between the remote client sites. The CPE contains such well-known networking elements as modem, CSU/DSU, and router. The SPF includes: (1) Central Offices that are local ending points of a carrier's WAN backbone network; (2) local access lines that link CPEs to Central Offices; and (3) the WAN backbone that transports customers' data between Central Offices. These days, *Central Offices* and *Point of Presence* (POP), an access point to the Internet, are used interchangeably although they have distinct historical roots: the former for voice- and the latter for data communications.

Demarcation Point

The *demarcation point* represents the point where *CPE* meets *SPF*. It is generally a cabling junction box (or system) located at the customer premises (both business and individual clients) and becomes a dividing point of network maintenance responsibility. At a business-occupied building, the *building entrance facility* (refer to Section 4.4) becomes the demarcation point. At a house, the junction box is also called a *Network Interface Device* (NID) and is generally attached to its outside wall so that a service technician can access it as needed (see Figure 9.2). The WAN provider is responsible for all maintenance and repairs of cabling and equipment up to the demarcation point, and the owner of a house is liable for maintaining the integrity of wiring inside the house leading to the demarcation point.

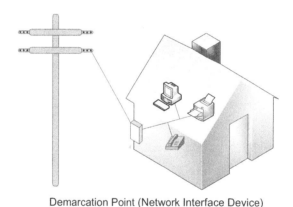

Demarcation Point (Network Interface Device)

Figure 9.2 Demarcation point of a house

9.2.4 WAN Design Considerations

Any business organization experiences continuous changes (e.g., firm growth or downsizing, restructuring and reengineering, forming business partnerships, and merger or acquisition). This poses challenges as the enterprise network including WAN links needs to be adapted to changing business requirements. The enterprise network of a company is thus a result of continuous planning, deployments, and adjustments over the time period. Firms may take different approaches in designing their WANs given that each topology has its own strengths and weaknesses (refer to Chapter 1 for network topologies). The WAN design of an enterprise, therefore, should be contingent on a number of internal and external factors including:

- Available resources (e.g., budget, internal IT staff)
- Cost assessment (e.g., total cost of ownership)
- Required data rate of applications (e.g., emails, voice over IP, and large-scale data backup)
- Necessary service quality (e.g., best effort service vs. guaranteed Quality of Service for real-time and mission-critical applications)
- Necessary reliability of WAN links
- Scalability (e.g., future growth and expandability) of WAN links
- Importance of protecting data (e.g., data security and privacy)

9.3 LAYERS OF WAN STANDARDS

Similar to LAN standards (e.g., Ethernet and WiFi), a carrier's WAN infrastructure primarily utilizes physical and data link layer technologies. For example, the T1 circuit is a popular physical layer technology (and service) that transports data link layer frames of WAN standards (e.g., Frame Relay and PPP).

9.3.1 Physical Layer

The physical layer defines technical details relevant to data transmissions over the WAN link including standard ports, transmission speeds, signal strengths and bit encoding mechanisms. WAN connection speeds subscribed to by business and individual customers are considerably slower than those of a LAN. As an example, the T1 (1.54Mbps) that has been a popular WAN link choice at the physical layer is much slower than prevalent LAN standards such as Fast Ethernet (100Mbps) and Gigabit Ethernet (1Gbps). However, with WAN increasingly transporting more time-sensitive and bandwidth-consuming traffic (e.g., multimedia and voice over IP), the demand for higher throughput and quality of service (QoS) is growing. There are several physical layer standards developed for WANs including *T-carrier & E-carrier*, *Synchronous Optical Network* (SONET), *Digital Subscriber Line* (DSL), and wireless WANs including cellular and satellite *networks*.

9.3.2 Data Link Layer

The layer is responsible for such functions as addressing and packet encapsulation within the frame (refer to Chapter 2). WAN standards at the data link layer are designed to support either *circuit switching* or *packet switching*.

Circuit Switching

With circuit switching, an end-to-end circuit is created beforehand between the source and destination nodes (or local sites) with certain *bandwidth reserved* for the circuit. For example, imagine the situation in which a car is given a highway lane exclusively reserved for it between Boston and New York. The end-to-end circuit is established via multiple high-speed WAN switches and the circuit capacity is exclusively used only by the two communicating parties during the engagement period (e.g., a conference call).

The leased line service relies on circuit switching and *Point-to-Point* (PPP) is a popular data link layer standard for dedicated leased lines.

Packet Switching

With packet switching, data are packaged as discrete units and physically transported "independently" from other units. With this approach, two communicating parties (or sites) do not need reserved capacity as in circuit switching. Signals carrying packets just take advantage of available network space in a more dynamic fashion. For that reason, packets traveling between two end nodes (or between two sites) do not need to take the same delivery path along the way. Packets from the same source are reassembled once they have arrived at the destination. This technology was initially developed for the Internet to physically transport IP packets and was subsequently adopted by WAN carriers.

Packet switching has several advantages. Most notably, it utilizes network capacity much more effectively than circuit switching. With the on-demand use of network capacity, the carrier's WAN infrastructure can be dynamically shared by more customers. It resembles the situation in which a highway lane between Boston and New York is shared by many automobiles, using the lane capacity much more effectively. *The packet switched data network* (PSDN) *is a carrier's WAN platform that moves clients' voice/data traffic using the packet switching technology.* The PSDN is frequently shown to clients as a "cloud" as they are not responsible for its operation and maintenance.

These days, most PSDNs take advantage of *virtual circuits* for data transmissions. The *virtual circuit* represents a *logical* end-to-end path pre-determined between two remote client sites. It therefore does not dedicate physical capacity between two distant locations as circuit switching does, but only pre-determines the delivery path formed through high-speed WAN switches. That is, the virtual circuit is technically analogous to LAN switching, for which the delivery path of frames between any two hosts is determined in advance (see Chapter 3).

Frame-Relay, Carrier Ethernet and Multi-Protocol Label Switching (MPLS) have been well received data link layer standards for PSDN service. *Asynchronous Transfer Mode* (ATM) is another PSDN standard although its acceptance has been dwindling. Table 9.2 summarizes primary WAN technologies at layer 1 and layer 2.

Layer	Leased lines	Packet Switched Data Network (PSDN)
Data Link (Layer 2)	• Point-to-Point (PPP)	• Frame-Relay • Carrier Ethernet • Multi-Protocol Label Switching • Asynchronous Transfer Mode
Physical (Layer 1)	• T-carrier and E-carrier (e.g., T-1/E-1, T-3/E-3) • Synchronous Optical Network (SONET) • Digital Subscriber Line (DSL) • Broadband wireless (e.g., WiMax, Cellular)	

Table 9.2 Popular WAN standards

9.3.3 Comparison: WAN vs. LAN

It is worthwhile to highlight differences between LAN and WAN standards. Each LAN technology such as Ethernet defines both data link (e.g., media access methods, frame construction) and physical layer (e.g., speeds, signaling, cabling) standards. For instance, Fast Ethernet specifies the transmission speed (e.g., 100Mbps), available cables (e.g., twisted pairs, optical fibers), each cable's required physical specs (e.g., maximum segment distance, number of twists per foot), and transmission technologies (e.g., digital signaling methods). Meanwhile, WAN standards generally do not require that a particular data link standard be tied to one or more physical layer standards. For example, T-carrier/E-carrier circuits at the physical layer are used to carry various data link layer frames including those of Frame Relay, ATM, and PPP.

Additionally, to optimize network performance and reduce operational costs, carriers utilize WAN data link standards in a flexible manner (e.g., encapsulation of one data link frame into another data link frame), which can be quite confusing to readers. For example, border routers at customer sites can be configured to transport Frame-Relay frames over T1, but the carrier's backbone network may be running on ATM as another data link standard. Transporting Frame-Relay frames between two remote client sites through the ATM backbone requires encapsulation of Frame-Relay frames within ATM frames. Putting one frame within another frame in order to capitalize on the strengths of two different WAN standards does not happen in the LAN environment.

Figure 9.3 demonstrates connectivity of Ethernet LANs and Frame Relay WAN, which allows IP packet exchanges between two end stations. In that scenario, the border router should support both Ethernet and Frame Relay data link standards for necessary frame translation. In other words, the border router converts Ethernet frames arriving at its LAN port into Frame Relay frames and releases them through the WAN (or serial) port. Of course, both the Ethernet and Frame Relay frames contain the same IP packets produced by the source host computer. On arrival at the destination LAN, the Frame Relay frames are translated back to the Ethernet frames for their delivery to the destination host. Remember that physical layer technologies utilized to transport WAN and LAN frames differ as well.

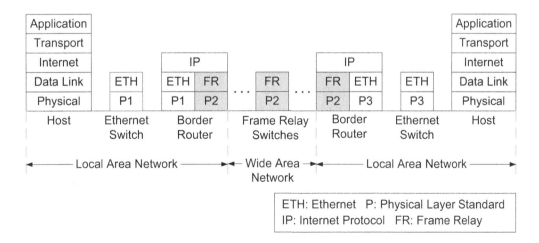

Figure 9.3 LAN vs. WAN standard layers

9.4   IP ADDRESSING FOR WAN LINKS

The WAN links of an enterprise network interconnect dispersed LANs, each with one or more subnetworks. Imagine an enterprise network with offices in three different locations and the border routers from three sites exchange IP packets through a carrier's WAN links that are either leased lines or PSDN (Not the Internet). Then, each WAN link between two remote border routers becomes a subnet with its own subnet address and the routers' WAN ports are configured with IP addresses pertaining to the subnet. This means that, in Figure 9.4, there are three subnets created by the three WAN links and each subnet has two permanent IP addresses assigned to the connecting routers' WAN ports.

As for the IP addressing of leased line or PSDN-based WAN links, the company can choose either public IPs or private IPs to the subnets because the links, although subscribed from a carrier, are an integral part of its enterprise network. Many firms opt for private IPs when the WAN link runs on a common carrier's network to enjoy the benefits of private IP assignment such as:
- Improved security (e.g., invisible internal nodes)
- Flexibility in internal IP allocations (e.g., large IP space becomes available)
- Consistency in internal IP allocations (e.g., IP addresses of internal hosts are not affected when the firm changes its WAN carrier) (see Section 5.6.4 for more details)

9.4.1   Leased Lines

If the border router connects to multiple leased lines, a router port (interface) with an IP address is assigned to each leased line. For example, Figure 9.4 shows that R1 of the main office is using two different ports S0/0/0 (10.10.10.1/24) and S0/0/1 (172.16.10.1/24) for two separate leased lines. In this setup, each leased line connection becomes a subnet. Figure 9.4 displays three subnets with subnet addresses of 10.10.10.0/24, 172.16.10.0/24, and 192.168.10.0/24. Note that all three subnets are on private IP ranges.

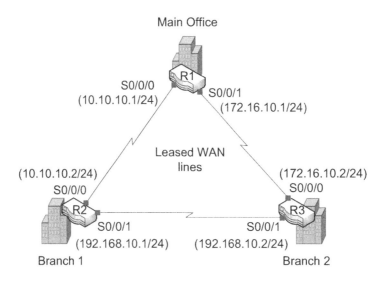

Figure 9.4 IP addressing on leased lines

294

9.4.2   Packet Switched Data Network (PSDN)

When WAN links are through the PSDN cloud, the border router at a client site just needs one physical link to the carrier network to connect several remote locations through as many virtual circuits. For example, Figure 9.5 shows that R1 just needs one WAN link (e.g., generally a leased line) to the PSDN cloud to exchange packets with R2 and R3 rather than two separate WAN links as in Figure 9.4. Instead, the R1's single physical link attached to the WAN interface S0/0/0 should carry packets to R2 and R3 through the use of virtual circuits. Two different IP addressing approaches are possible to enable this:

> (1) Each WAN link (e.g., R1-R2) between two locations becomes a single subnet
> (2) All WAN links (i.e., R1-R2, R1-R3, and R2-R3) are assigned to a single subnet.

The two different addressing approaches are explained next.

One subnet between two locations

This approach creates a dedicated subnet address between two locations (or two border routers). R1's S0/0/0, therefore, connects to two separate subnets, one to R2 and one to R3. It was explained that the router port is normally tied to a single subnet. Linking multiple subnets to one physical router port needs a non-orthodox measure known as a *sub-interface*. A router's interface (e.g., S0/0/0) can be coupled with multiple sub-interfaces, each with a unique IP address (revisit Section 7.11.2). Remember that, while the ordinary port/interface (e.g., S0/0/0) is a physical entity, the sub-interface does not physically exist but is *logically* defined by a router's operating system. Once defined, the sub-interface acts just like an ordinary router interface. For example, Figure 9.5 shows that R1 at the main office location defines two sub-interfaces (let's say S0/0/0.10 and S0/0/0.20) under the physical interface S0/0/0. Each sub-interface has its corresponding IP address, 10.10.10.1/24 and 172.16.10.1/24 belonging to two different subnets. Then, the two sub-interfaces are assigned to VC1 and VC3 respectively.

The result is the creation of such mapping table for R1 as Table 9.3. The table can be created either automatically or manually and stored in the R1's memory. Remember that the mapping table includes the IP addresses of *destination border routers*. Also, keep in mind that a virtual circuit is *unidirectional* and therefore VC1 and VC3 are used for delivering frames from R1 to R2 and from R1 to R3 respectively, but not reverse directions. This means that the packet delivery from R2 to R1 requires a separate virtual circuit (V2). The R1's table, therefore, keeps only VC1 and VC3 that R1 needs to know to dispatch packets over the WAN links, but does not need to know about VC2, VC4, VC5, and VC6.

IP address of Destination Routers	Virtual circuit identifier	Exit interface (or sub-interface)
10.10.10.2 (to Branch1)	VC1	S0/0/0.10
172.16.10.2 (to Branch2)	VC3	S0/0/0.20

Table 9.3 IP address-to-VC mapping table of R1

To transport an IP packet (e.g., from R1 to R2), R1 refers to the mapping table to find the corresponding virtual circuit (VC1) and encapsulates the IP packet within a data link frame that contains VC1 as the virtual circuit ID (For easier comprehension, imagine that the virtual circuit ID for a WAN is equivalent to the MAC address for a LAN). The data link frame is released through the exit port of S0/0/0.10, and therefore physically S0/0/0. On receiving the frame, the carrier's PSDN network delivers the WAN frame purely on the virtual circuit information (For example, Frame delivery on the virtual circuit is exemplified in Section 9.10). You should be able to see that what the mapping table in Table 9.3 does for WAN connections (i.e., mapping between VC identifiers and IP addresses) is identical to what the ARP table does for LANs (i.e., mapping between MAC and IP addresses).

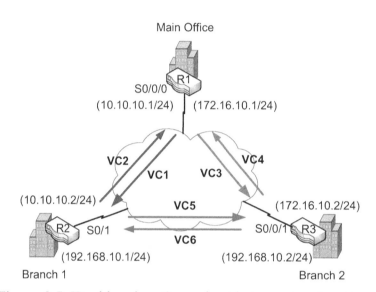

Figure 9.5 IP addressing: One subnet between two locations

Exercise 9-1: Refer to Figure 9.5 to answer questions.

1. Develop the IP address-to-VC mapping table of R2 and R3 referring to Table 9.3.
2. How many virtual circuits are needed to fully interconnect (full mesh) the three business locations?

One subnet for all locations

As another approach, all WAN links of an enterprise can belong to one subnet address. In this setup, each border router's WAN port just needs one IP address belonging to the same subnet. Figure 9.6 demonstrates a scenario in which all three router ports use IP addresses (172.16.10.1/24, 172.16.10.2/24, and 172.16.10.3/24) of one subnet (172.16.10.0/24). The packet delivery process is identical to the previous case. To transport an IP packet from a site (e.g., R1) to another site (e.g., R2), for example, R1 refers to its mapping table to find the

296

corresponding virtual circuit (VC1) and encapsulates the IP packet within a data link frame that contains VC1 as the virtual circuit ID. The data link frame is released via the exit port of S0/0/0.

Exercise 9-2: Refer to Figure 9.6 to answer questions.

1. Develop the IP address-to-VC mapping table of R1, R2, and R3 referring to Table 9.3.
2. How many virtual circuits are necessary to fully interconnect (full mesh) the three business locations?

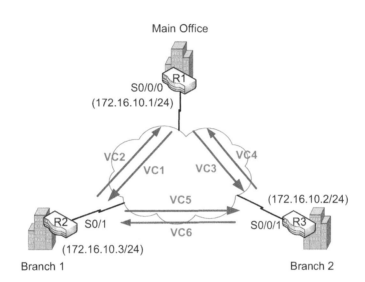

Figure 9.6 IP addressing: One subnet for all locations

With two different options available for IP addressing, the question remains which is a better choice? In a nutshell, the decision should be based on the assessment of the business context and planned WAN link usage. For example, the choice has implications on network security. By having separated subnets as in Figure 9.5, accessibility from one location to other locations can be better controlled. On the other hand, let's assume a situation where frequent broadcasting or multicasting of IP packets between remote locations is necessary. Then, having one subnet for all remote connections makes the job easier.

9.5   PHYSICAL LAYER OPTIONS: LEASED LINES

This section explains technology options available to access WAN service at the physical layer. They include several *leased lines* and other WAN links that offer high-speed connectivity to the carrier's network and to the Internet, which include *Digital Subscriber Lines*, *cable*, and *broadband wireless*. Among the various options, popular leased line technologies are explained here.

The leased line service available from a carrier results in a point-to-point link with dedicated link capacity. There are two main usages of the dedicated leased line.

(1) The end-to-end leased line connection between two distant client sites through a carrier network (see Figure 9.4): This end-to-end connection is through the *local loops* that link client sites to the carrier's Central Office (CO) and the carrier's *trunk links* that provide the client with guaranteed channel capacity (Although not shown in Figure 9.4, the leased lines go through Central Offices).

(2) The local link between a client site and a carrier's Central Office (see Figure 9.5 and 9.6): The local leased line is intended to provide a client with an access to the carrier's PSDN platform whose capacity is shared by many customers.

Subscribers of the leased line pay for the link capacity committed by the WAN provider regardless of its usage level. With the dedicated capacity, leased lines pose no such quality problems as packet losses, packet delays, and call dropping (for voice communications). There are many situations where the end-to-end leased line is well justified despite the relatively high cost, especially when packets are highly time-sensitive and mission critical, demanding guaranteed performance in delivery. For instance, imagine a financial network that relays real-time financial transaction data (e.g., stock day trading). The company simply cannot afford the risks of non-dedicated WAN link capacity. T-carrier/E-carrier and SONET/SDH are two popular leased line technologies.

9.5.1   T-Carrier/E-Carrier

As the first digital transmission system, the T-Carrier service is offered according to the *digital signal* (DS) speed hierarchy (see Section 4.2.7). Although introduced to support digitized voice communications initially, it is widely used for both voice and data these days. There are two different leased line standards: (1) T-carrier based on the North American digital speed hierarchy and (2) E-carrier based on the International digital speed hierarchy from ITU-T (*International Telecommunication Union – Telecommunication Standardization Sector*). Their channel speeds are summarized in Table 9.4 for information purpose.

T1 and T3 Circuits

As one of the most popular leased line services, T1 is designed to transport data at the DS1 (1.54Mbps) speed, which represents 24 DS0 digital voice channels (64kbps x 24 channels = 1.54 Mbps) (refer to Section 4.2.7). Voice and data traffic from the 24 channels are combined (or multiplexed) using *Time Division Multiplexing* (TDM) for transmission (see Figure 4.16). With full-duplex capacity, one T1 circuit sends and receives data at 1.54Mbps in both directions. Channel usage may be voice only, data only, or in hybrid (combination of voice and data). T1 is available on both UTP and optical fiber, although UTP tends to be a preferred choice. Service providers also offer *Fractional T1* in increments of 64kbps such as 256 kbps and 384 kbps for customers who need lower throughput at a reduced price.

As another popular leased line option, the T3 circuit delivers the DS3 speed of 44.7 Mbps (28

T1 channels combined) generally on the fiber optic cable because of its high bandwidth. Instead of the T-carrier, most international countries adopted the E-carrier for the leased line service. The E1 channel at the bottom of the E-carrier hierarchy is designed to transport 2.0 Mbps in each direction, equating to the multiplexing of 30 DS0 channels.

North American Hierarchy	Digital Data Rate	International (ITU) Hierarchy	Digital Data Rate
T1	1.5 Mbps	E1	2.0 Mbps
T1C	3.1 Mbps	E2	8.4 Mbps
T2	6.3 Mbps	E3	34.3 Mbps
T3	44.7 Mbps	E4	139.2 Mbps
T4	274.1 Mbps	E5	465.1 Mbps

Table 9.4 Leased line speed hierarchies

9.5.2 SONET/SDH

SONET/SDH is intended for high speed leased line services on optical fiber. The SONET standard is used in North America and its sibling adopted as the international standard is SDH. The SONET service is offered according to the *optical carrier* (OC) data rate hierarchy (see Section 4.2.7) with the base speed of 51.84 Mbps for OC1.

SDH's data rate is based on the *Synchronous Transport Module* (STM) speed hierarchy. The base data rate for STM1 is 156Mbps (equivalent to OC3). Just as with T-carrier/E-carrier, the SONET/SDH technologies are defined at the physical layer. SONET/SDH uses so-called *Dense Wave Division Multiplexing*, a type of Frequency Division Multiplexing technology, to produce a bigger pipe by multiplexing lower speed channels.

Although available as a leased line service for business clients, SONET/SDH is widely adopted by carriers to define the bandwidth of their backbone networks to which business customers connect via such lines as T1/E1. The SONET infrastructure generally relies on the dual-ring architecture to improve fault-tolerance so that the network can quickly restore even if the primary ring fails. The *Add-Drop Multiplexer* (ADM) is a device that inserts and removes traffic to/from the SONET ring. Figure 9.7 demonstrates a SONET architecture that has two SONET rings coupled at the carrier's Central Office: the backbone ring that interconnects access rings and the access ring that provides entry to the backbone ring from customer sites. The figure displays that, while the access ring's speed runs at 155 Mbps, the backbone ring has a substantially higher bandwidth such as OC12 (622 Mbps).

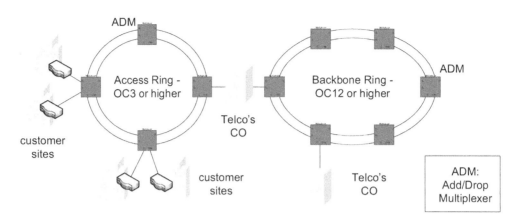

Figure 9.7 A demonstration of SONET's ring architecture

Popular circuit speeds of the leased line and prevalent cabling are summarized in Table 9.5.

Standards	Channel speed (bandwidth)	Popular cabling
T1/E1	1.54 Mbps/2.04 Mbps	UTP
Fractional T1	Varies (e.g., 256 kbps, 384 kbps)	UTP
Bonded T1	Multiple T1 lines combined	UTP
T3/E3	44.7 Mbps/34 Mbps	Optical fiber
SONET/SDH	Varies (e.g., 51.8 Mbps, 156Mbps)	Optical fiber

Table 9.5 Popular leased line options

9.6   DATA LINK STANDARD: LEASED LINES

Several data link layer protocols have been in use to transport IP packets over the leased line and *Point-to-Point Protocol* (PPP) has been a popular choice. As explained, the leased line standard at the physical layer (e.g., T1) is generally not tied to any particular data link protocol. In other words, the PPP frame with an IP packet inside can be transported by various physical layer technologies including T-Carrier/E-Carrier and DSL.

9.6.1   PPP Frame Structure

The general structure of the PPP frame is shown in Figure 9.8.

Flag	Address	Control	Protocol	Information	FCS
8 bits	8 bits	8 bits	16 bits	Variable	16/32 bits

Figure 9.8 PPP frame structure

The function of each information field is summarized below:

- *Flag* bits, 01111110, mark the beginning of a PPP frame.
- The *Address* field becomes meaningless on the point-to-point link (as there is only one possible destination) and communicating devices fill it with all 1s.
- The *Control* field plays little role and is filled with the value of 00000011.
- The *Protocol* field identifies the protocol (e.g., IP) included in the *Information* field.
- The *Information* field contains an IP packet from the Internet layer. Its size varies and generally up to 1500 bytes.
- The *FCS (Frame Check Sequence)* field carries an error detection code.

9.6.2 Router Authentication

PPP has several features designed to maintain performance and reliability of a WAN link. These include monitoring of link quality, data compression for effective use of available bandwidth, and peer router authentication. Among them, *router authentication* as a measure to maintain network security is briefly explained.

Assuming that border routers at two remotely dispersed customer sites are already configured with the same username and password, they can authenticate each other prior to exchanging data frames. This is an important function as more networks are exposed to security risks today. For router authentication, two protocols are available for PPP: *Password Authentication Protocol* (PAP) and more advanced *Challenge Handshake Authentication Protocol* (CHAP).

PAP vs. CHAP

As shown in Figure 9.9, PAP defines two-way router authentication but CHAP takes three steps for the process. While PAP exchanges the username and password in plaintext making it vulnerable to interceptions, CHAP does not. Instead, on receiving a challenge text from a remote router, the local router produces a hash value based on the combination of the pre-configured password and the challenge text. *Message Digest 5* (MD5) is a one-way hash function used widely to produce the hash value (see Section 11.3.1 for more details of hashing). The hash value thus produced is sent back to the challenger. On receiving the hash value, the remote router computes its own hash value using the challenge text and its own pre-configured password. If they match, then the local router is authenticated and allowed for WAN connectivity.

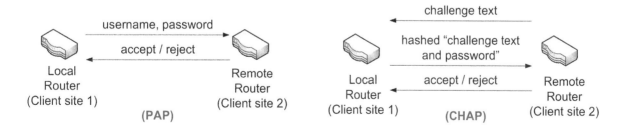

Figure 9.9 Authentication with PAP and CHAP

Example: Configuring Cisco router to enable PPP

Figure 9.10 displays two routers (R1 and R2) connecting through the T-1 lease line. Assuming that each router is already set up with the same access password, the point-to-point protocol (PPP) is activated on *Serial0/0/1* by issuing the following commands to R1's and R2's operating system.

```
---------------------------------------------------------------------------------------
R1(config)#interface serial 0/0/1
     Comment: At R1, choose the Serial0/0/1 interface.
R1(config-if)#encapsulation ppp
     Comment: Instruct R1 to use the PPP frame to encapsulate an IP packet.
R1(config-if)#ppp authentication CHAP
     Comment: Enable router authentication based on the CHAP protocol.
---------------------------------------------------------------------------------------
```

The three commands above are repeated on R2. Once complete on both R1 and R2, all IP packets exchanged between them are encapsulated within PPP frames. Also, router authentication based on CHAP (see Figure 9.9) is performed prior to data exchange.

Figure 9.10 T-1 leased line connection with PPP

9.7   DATA LINK STANDARDS: PSDN

The leased line service is highly reliable in data transmissions because of the dedicated circuit capacity between two locations. However, when the number of remote sites to be interconnected grows and the network topology of an organization becomes more complicated, creating WAN links of an enterprise network relying exclusively on the leased line becomes costly. Besides the leased line, carriers also offer WAN services using their own PSDN infrastructure that takes advantage of the packet switching technology. The service paradigm of PSDN is fundamentally different from that of the leased line because, in PSDN, available capacity of the carrier's WAN platform is dynamically shared (rather than dedicated) by business clients.

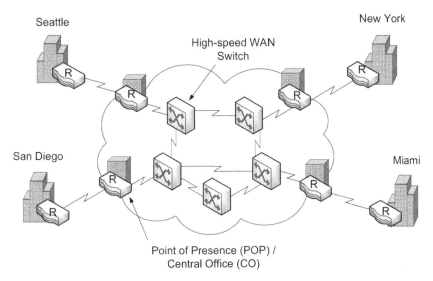

Seattle

New York

High-speed WAN
Switch

San Diego

Miami

Point of Presence (POP) /
Central Office (CO)

Figure 9.11 PSDN: general architecture of the cloud

The PSDN-based WAN link that connects two distant customer sites is composed of two network segments: (1) local access links and (2) PSDN backbone cloud. The PSDN backbone is presented as a cloud because the carrier fully controls its operation and maintenance making it virtually transparent to business customers. PSDN customers generally use leased lines to reach the carrier's Central Office (CO), an entry point to the PSDN cloud. The cloud's network capacity is, therefore, shared by WAN service subscribers. Figure 9.11 offers a general view of the 'inside cloud' in which many high speed WAN switches (or routers) are interconnected to become the backbone network and a customer site connects to the backbone by linking its border router to a router of a Central Office.

9.7.1 General Attributes of PSDN Service

Shared Capacity

With capacity sharing, more clients can be served using the same network capacity. As an example, think of the following scenario in which 1.54 Mbps, equivalent to T1 capacity, can serve 24 dedicated data sources concurrently with each source transmitting at 64 kbps. When the same 24 channels are dynamically allocated, more than 40 different data sources can be served because chances are that not all connected user systems transmit data simultaneously (Refer to *Statistical Time Division Multiplexing* in Section 4.2.6 as a related concept). The shared usage of available capacity lowers the cost of WAN service as well.

Customization of Speeds

PSDN is more flexible than leased lines in meeting customer demands. With the leased line service, bandwidth available to clients is generally in the increment of 64kbps (one voice call capacity). However, with PSDN, the increment can be much smaller than 64kbps offering better customization of client needs. For example, a business client may want a WAN link of

303

30kbps between its two branch locations. With leased line, however, Fractional T1 at 64kbps or 128kbps may be the closest speed available from a carrier. When PSDN running *Frame Relay* is chosen instead, a carrier can offer a much smaller increment such as 4 kbps, which results in significant cost savings for clients.

Data and Voice

With non-dedicated capacity for WAN links, PSDN was originally designed for data rather than voice that cannot afford transmission delays. However, because of technology maturation and lower cost, more businesses are choosing PSDN for voice communications.

Frame Multiplexing

The PSDN cloud of a carrier consists of high speed WAN switches that interconnect trunk lines. These switches are arranged in a mesh to have redundant paths between user locations. WAN frames, each containing an IP packet, are *multiplexed* at Central Offices and transported over the cloud's trunk links.

Unreliable Transmission

PSDN generally depends on the *unreliable* transmission in data link. That is, there is no error control during packet delivery and the correction of transmission errors is left to the WAN subscriber's host stations (TCP at the transport layer). Delivering IP packets in an unreliable manner results in cost savings of WAN services. Besides, the PSDN service is generally full-duplex (simultaneous flow of packets in both directions) and symmetric (identical transmission speeds in both directions).

9.7.2   Virtual Circuits

PSDN relies on the virtual circuit, a logically defined delivery path, to transport frames between remote locations. The virtual circuit is therefore different from the leased line's physical circuit, a dedicated channel capacity between two ending points. To identify the virtual circuit and decide frame forwarding path, the virtual circuit table is constructed and maintained in each WAN switch of PSDN and used as the reference source.

WAN Switch Table

Information items stored in the LAN and WAN switch tables differ. The LAN switch table is composed of MAC addresses and their corresponding exit ports (see Chapter 3). Meanwhile, the WAN switch table contains virtual circuit (VC) identifiers and their corresponding exit ports. The LAN switch table can be constructed in an automated fashion (through switch learning), but the WAN switch table is manually programmed. For this, the carrier adds a business client's VC identifier to its WAN switches and the client programs the same VC identifier to its own border router that connects to the PSDN cloud. Then, all frames originating from the client's premise carry the pre-configured VC identifier in the header. WAN switches (or routers) in the cloud forward the frames based on the VC identifier.

PVC vs. SVC

There are two different virtual circuit types: *permanent virtual circuit* (PVC) and *switched virtual circuit* (SVC). With the PVC, once a client's virtual circuit is set up in WAN switches by the carrier, it remains unchanged lasting months or years. Meanwhile, the SVC is transient as it is dynamically decided in the beginning of a communication session and lasts only until the session ends. For practical reasons (e.g., easy to maintain, less process burden on WAN switches), carriers use PVCs these days.

Access Link Speeds

As stated, the access links between customer premises and Central Offices are primarily leased lines such as T1/E1. In this situation, the router at the customer premise is configured to produce WAN frames (e.g., Frame Relay), each encapsulating an IP packet. The access link should be faster than the contracted WAN throughput in order to fully capitalize on the VC's bandwidth. Also, if a local client site sets up multiple PVCs with remote locations, its access link to the WAN cloud should have enough bandwidth to allow simultaneous flows of WAN frames through the PVCs.

Exercise 9-3: Figure 9.12 demonstrates a hypothetical enterprise network in which WAN links interconnect distributed LANs through the carrier's PSDN cloud. The client's border router at the Houston location has three PVCs (1 PVC to each branch office) on one physical link, with 3 different speeds. What is the minimum data rate of the physical link necessary to avoid transmission delays?

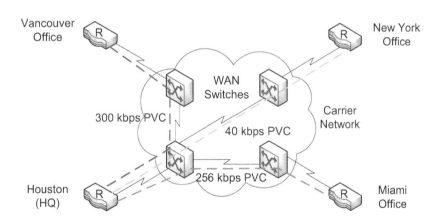

Figure 9.12 A physical link with 3 permanent virtual circuits

Next, major PSDN technologies including Frame Relay, ATM, Carrier Ethernet, and MPLS are explained with more focus on Frame Relay to demonstrate the mechanism of virtual circuits in their setup and operation.

9.8 FRAME RELAY

9.8.1 General Characteristics

Frame Relay has been the most popular PSDN service as it satisfies the speed range most enterprises demand at a competitive price. To link to the carrier's backbone network, a client firm generally uses: (1) a router capable of producing data link layer frames based on the Frame Relay protocol or (2) a Frame Relay Access Device (FRAD) supplied by the carrier.

Frame Relay is characterized by:
- The use of *permanent virtual circuits* between client sites
- *Low overhead* (simple header structure) and efficient frame delivery
- *Unreliability* (no acknowledgment from WAN switch nodes) during frame forwarding.

The carrier switches in the cloud can detect faulty frames using the *Frame Check Sequence* (FCS) error detection codes and drop them from the network. Recovery of the dropped frames is left to TCP of the destination host.

Although initially introduced for data service, Frame Relay is widely used for voice as well, in which telephone calls and faxed documents are digitized and packaged in frames for delivery. The *voice over Frame Relay* offers at least two significant benefits.

- It is a cost-effective solution compared to the traditional voice service offered on the carrier's *Public Switched Telephone Network* (PSTN) that adopts more expensive circuit switching technology. The PSTN circuit established between two communicating parties is given a dedicated capacity during the call session making it expensive to subscribers.

- An organization does not need to maintain two separate voice and data networks and equipment. Their convergence in corporate networking curtails costs associated with operation and maintenance, subscription of WAN connections, and hiring of specialized IT professionals.

9.8.2 Frame Structure

As a data link layer standard, Frame Relay accepts an IP packet from the internet layer, encapsulates the packet in its frame, and passes the frame down to the physical layer for delivery. As in Figure 9.13, the frame has a lean structure because Frame Relay is designed to minimize network overhead in exchange for low service cost to customers. Among the frame fields, Flags (01111110 bits), FCS (detection of transmission errors), and Data fields perform functions identical to other protocols. The address field contains the *data link connection identifier* (DLCI), virtual circuit information.

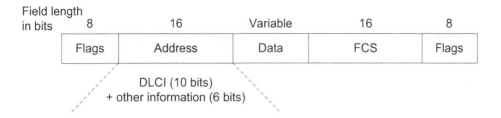

Figure 9.13 Frame structure of Frame Relay

9.8.3 Data Link Connection Identifier (DLCI)

The DLCI is a permanent virtual circuit identifier used to deliver Frame Relay frames to the destination router (not the host station) of a network. When a client company signs up for Frame Relay from a carrier, the carrier configures the client's DLCIs (10 bits) on its WAN switches in the cloud. Then, the carrier informs the client of the DLCI(s) that should be programmed in the client's border router.

A particular DLCI is used to transport Frame Relay frames 'over a single physical link' between two neighboring network nodes. In other words, although the virtual circuit between two remote client locations can pass through any number of WAN switches in the cloud, the DLCI is only *locally significant*, meaning that a unique DLCI is assigned to a direct connection between any two nodes. The DLCI of a frame is, therefore, changed whenever it passes through a carrier's WAN switch. As a result, an end-to-end *permanent virtual circuit* (PVC) is composed of several DLCIs. DLCIs are bi-directional in which the same DLCI can be used for both directions (that means two separate virtual circuits) between two locations.

How DLCI Works

To illustrate how DLCIs are used to form an end-to-end virtual circuit, an example is presented in Figure 9.14 in which a permanent virtual circuit is established between two remote routers of a company: Houston main office (*A*) and Toronto branch location (*E*). Assume that a frame is sent from *A* to *E*, and the pre-established virtual circuit enables frame forwarding through 3 WAN switches, *B*, *C*, and *D*. The router *A*'s and *E*'s S0/0/1 port is assigned DLCI 101 and 210 respectively, and four different DLCIs (i.e., 101, 203, 301, and 210) form the end-to-end virtual circuit. It can be seen that each physical link uses a unique DLCI (therefore, locally significant). For example, DLCI 101 is for the link between *A* and *B*, DLCI 203 for the link between *B* and *C*, and so on, and the DLCIs are entered into the cloud's WAN switches.

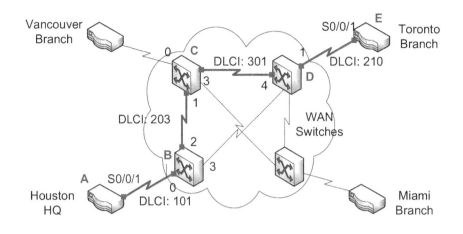

| Nodes | Arrival | | Departure | |
	DLCI	Port (Interface)	DLCI	Port (Interface)
A			101	S0/0/1
B	101	0	203	2
C	203	1	301	3
D	301	4	210	1
E	210	S0/1		

Summary of DLCI changes within the virtual circuit from A through E router

Source DLCI: 101

Destination DLCI: 210

Figure 9.14 Change of DLCIs from router A to router E

FR Switch Table

Each WAN switch in the cloud maintains a switch table just as the LAN switch has its own switch table. To enable frame forwarding based on the virtual circuit, the carrier adds DLCIs on WAN switches. The structure of the WAN switch table is explained based on Switch B in Figure 9.14. The switch table contains four different columns: incoming port#, incoming DLCI#, outgoing port#, and outgoing DLCI#. The switch table's general structure is demonstrated in Table 9.6. The first entry of Table 9.6 means that if a frame with DLCI 101 arrives at the port#0 of Switch B, the switch changes the frame's DLCI value to 203 and then sends it out through the port#2. The second entry enables frame forwarding in the reverse direction. The two entries in Switch B enable frame delivery following the bidirectional virtual circuit established between the Houston and Toronto offices.

Incoming port #	Incoming DLCI #		Outgoing port #	Outgoing DLCI #
0	101		2	203
2	203		0	101
...	...		...	...

Table 9.6 Switch table entries (Switch B of Figure 9.14)

Multiple VCs and DLCIs

The access line that connects a customer's local router to the Frame Relay network can carry multiple permanent virtual circuits (PVCs), each with a unique DLCI number. For instance, a company (headquartered in Houston) with three branch offices (Vancouver, Toronto, and Miami) can set up three PVCs from the main office to branch locations. In this case, Figure 9.15 shows three virtual circuit numbers (101, 112, and 120) assigned to the router port S0/0/1 at the Houston location. DLCI 101 is for the virtual circuit to Toronto; DLCI 112 to Vancouver; and DLCI 120 to Miami.

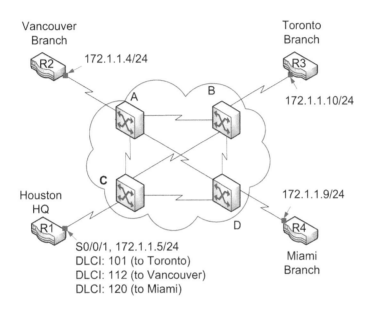

Figure 9.15 A physical circuit with three virtual circuits

9.8.4 Mapping IP Addresses

For the border router at a customer premise to construct a layer 2 WAN frame with DLCIs, it has to have an IP address-to-DLCI mapping table developed either manually or automatically. The mapping table is used by the router to identify a DLCI that goes into the frame's address field based on a destination router's IP address. For example, the mapping table of the local router (172.1.1.5/24) at Houston HQ (Figure 9.15) contains destination routers' IP addresses and their corresponding DLCIs (see Table 9.7). Table 9.7 is structurally identical to Table 9.3. Also, note that the mapping table in Table 9.7 resembles the ARP (address resolution protocol) table for LANs (see Figure 3.17b), except that the ARP table contains MAC addresses instead of DLCIs.

IP Addresses of destination routers	Local DLCI #	Router exit port
172.1.1.10/24 (to Toronto)	101	Serial 0/0/1
172.1.1.4/24 (to Vancouver)	112	Serial 0/0/1
172.1.1.9/24 (to Miami)	120	Serial 0/0/1

Table 9.7 IP address-to-DLCI mapping table of R1 (Houston HQ)

Example: Configuring IP address-to-DLCI mapping with Cisco router

Creating the IP-to-DLCI mapping table of R1 in Table 9.7 can be either manual or automatic. Below demonstrates manual programming of R1 to enable IP-to-DLCI mapping.

R1# **interface Serial0/0/1**
    Comment: Configure the router port, Serial0/0/1
R1# **ip address 172.1.1.5 255.255.255.0**
    Comment: Assign IP (172.1.1.5) and subnet mask (255.255.255.0) to Serial0/0/1
R1# **encapsulation frame-relay**
    Comment: Serial0/0/1 is to produce layer 2 frames of Frame Relay.
R1# **frame-relay map ip 172.1.1.10 101 broadcast**:
    Comment: Map between destination IP 172.1.1.10 and local DLCI 101
R1# **frame-relay map ip 172.1.1.4 112 broadcast**:
    Comment: Map between destination IP 172.1.1.4 and local DLCI 112
R1# **frame-relay map ip 172.1.1.9 120 broadcast**:
    Comment: Map between destination IP 172.1.1.9 and local DLCI 120

9.9   ASYNCHRONOUS TRANSFER MODE (ATM)

9.9.1   Background

ATM is another well-known data link layer standard for WAN services. ATM generally supports higher data rates than Frame Relay. The ATM network's bandwidth is specified in terms of the optical carrier (OC) hierarchy that has the base speed of about 52Mbps. With its high speed connectivity, the ATM technology has been largely adopted by the carrier's backbone network. Figure 9.16, for example, demonstrates that the ATM backbone provides Frame Relay links to business customers. In this case, the border routers or frame relay access devices (FRAD) at the customer premises produce FR frames. Arriving at the carrier's ATM backbone, however, the FR frames are moved through the cloud by the high speed ATM technology. For the 'Frame Relay over ATM', such methods as *header translation* can be used.

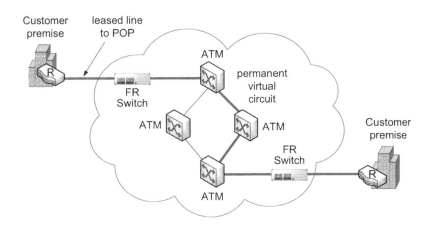

Figure 9.16 Transporting Frame Relay frames over ATM cloud

9.9.2 Cell Switching

Similar to Frame Relay, ATM also takes advantage of packet switching utilizing permanent virtual circuits (PVC). In ATM, the virtual circuit identifier is the combination of the *virtual path identifier* (VPI) and the *virtual channel identifier* (VCI) (see Figure 9.17). The ATM's virtual circuit identifier is, therefore, equivalent to the Frame Relay's DLCI. ATM uses fixed size frames called *cells* with 48 octets of payload (data) and 5 octets of header (there is no trailer), making each cell 53 octets or bytes. The fixed payload size is what makes ATM different from Frame Relay and other WAN standards that allow the data field of variable size. ATM's packet switching is called *cell switching*. With the fixed size cell, ATM switching becomes very effective, especially when switches handle real-time traffic that cannot afford delays. When the ending point of an arriving cell is anticipated in advance, switching becomes faster.

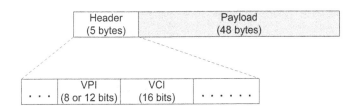

Figure 9.17 ATM cell and virtual circuit identifier in the header

9.9.3 Quality of Service (QoS)

The ATM technology is designed to handle both real-time voice/multimedia traffic and non-real time data traffic efficiently. For this, ATM defines several service classes and offers *quality of service* (QoS) that guarantees certain performance in network service (e.g., maximum latency for time-critical applications) (see Section 1.7.4). The four representative classes are CBR, VBR, ABR, and UBR, and each class defines a set of parameters regarding network connectivity. A brief description of each class is:

- *Constant bit rate* (CBR) for video and voice applications that demand fixed channel capacity
- *Variable bit rate* (VBR) for high-priority applications
- *Available bit rate* (ABR) for applications that need a minimum guaranteed data rate
- *Unspecified bit rate* (UBR) for applications that can use remaining (or unused) network capacity

Despite the technical sophistication and early anticipation of its ultimate supremacy as a WAN standard, it has been losing its market to other WAN technologies such as Carrier Ethernet and Multi-Protocol Label Switching (MPLS). Several factors have contributed to the slow adoption of ATM despite its technological advancement. Among them are ATM's technical complexity; expensive intermediary devices; and high overhead in which 5 bytes out of the 53 byte frame are taken up by the header to support cell switching. Finally, as the WAN carrier's backbone network (cloud) runs on optical fibers with literally unlimited bandwidth, effective management of network capacity through such advanced but complicated technology as ATM has become a less pressing matter.

9.10 CARRIER ETHERNET

WAN carriers have been heavily investing to bring the Ethernet technology to the world of WAN, thus called Carrier-Ethernet. Riding on the enormous popularity of Ethernet as a LAN standard, it was initially adopted by carriers to offer MAN service, called Metro Ethernet. Intended to cover a city or a suburban area, the Metro Ethernet's main usage has been:
- To interconnect distributed LANs within a particular metropolitan area
- To connect a business client's LAN to the Internet
- To bridge a business client's LAN to the carrier's WAN backbone

When it was first introduced in early 2000, Metro Ethernet had several relative shortcomings compared to other more established WAN counterparts (e.g., Frame Relay, ATM, SONET) in provisioning:
- Network reliability expected to run MAN services
- Network scalability that can handle growing traffic in a graceful manner
- Quality of Service (QoS) that guarantees network performance

This is not surprising because Ethernet was initially designed as a LAN technology while others were intended for WANs from the beginning.

WANs demand technical and service features much different from LANs. For example, a LAN may connect hundreds or thousands of network nodes, but a carrier's WAN infrastructure should scale it much bigger, say millions of nodes. Also, while service types available for LANs are limited (e.g., best effort delivery), WANs should be able to support several service options tailored to various needs (e.g., QoS provisions) of large enterprise clients, small/medium-size businesses, SOHO/residential customers, and even mobile workers.

With the rapid rise of Metro Ethernet in the past, carriers are upgrading the technology to offer a truly global WAN platform – Carrier Ethernet. Already, there are indications that Carrier Ethernet is going to become an extremely popular WAN service platform, largely driven by its capacity to provide customers with competitively priced, high performance connectivity.

9.10.1 Strengths

Among the notable strengths of Carrier Ethernet are:

- Ethernet already has a massive installation base and its advanced features such as Virtual LAN (see Chapter 7) enables handling of mission-critical applications better than before (e.g., VLAN's priority bits).

- Compared with other WAN platforms (e.g., SONET), service costs of Carrier Ethernet are very competitive. One main reason is that Carrier Ethernet uses intermediary devices (e.g., Ethernet switches) whose manufacturing costs already enjoy a significant economy of scale.

- Carrier Ethernet offers high bandwidth leading up to 100 Gbps between sites separated by several hundred miles apart. Supports for 400 Gbps and 1 Tbps are on the horizon. Corporate customers can purchase bandwidth incrementally to meet their needs.

- Carrier Ethernet provides flexible WAN design choices to business clients, which include simple point-to-point as well as multipoint-to-multipoint connections.

- The service provision is not limited by a single WAN provider's network span. That is, clients can build global scale, end-to-end WAN connections on multiple providers' Carrier Ethernet platforms.

- Corporate clients are already familiar with Ethernet and, thus, linking their Ethernet LANs to Carrier Ethernet is relatively easy. If the end-to-end WAN connectivity between two client LANs is purely through Carrier Ethernet, there is no need to make protocol translations (e.g., frame conversion) at the connecting points.

- Carrier Ethernet's technological compatibility with Ethernet LAN makes it highly cost effective for business clients to setup and operate WAN connections. For instance, network administrators of a client firm do not need costly training to manage Carrier Ethernet.

9.10.2 Service Transport

WAN carriers have been using different approaches in transporting the Metro- or Carrier Ethernet service.

- Relying on pure Ethernet in which the WAN platform is composed of layer 2 Ethernet switches. Just as the Ethernet LAN, frames are forwarded referring to the switch table that contains MAC addresses and exit ports. When the switch table is kept relatively small, the WAN should be able to perform well. When the table size gets larger, however, switching performance can suffer considerably, having ripple effects on service quality for corporate customers. As pure Ethernet is not dependable to support the large-scale WAN platform, its usage was limited to early Metro-Ethernet.

- These days, carriers transport Ethernet frames relying on other WAN standards primarily SDH/SONET (see Figure 9.7) and MPLS (see section 9.11). Unlike Ethernet, SDH/SONET and MPLS were developed as WAN standards and, thus, provide necessary reliability and scalability in transporting WAN data. This hybrid approach is especially attractive when a carrier already has SONET/SDH or MPLS infrastructure in the service area.

9.11 MULTI-PROTOCOL LABEL SWITCHING

Multi-Protocol Label Switching (MPLS) is another important WAN technology that has become extremely popular. MPLS has been adopted by carriers as a solution to "fast forward" IP packets using a mechanism similar to *layer 2 switching* rather than traditional *layer 3 routing*. With MPLS in place, therefore, the traditional IP-based routing is skipped in a network. This is what makes it different from other WAN technologies conceived as layer 2 standards from their inceptions. To make that possible, MPLS relies on the *label*, conceptually similar to the *virtual circuit* of Frame Relay and ATM, as a way to expedite forwarding of IP packets by MPLS-enabled *routers*. The router refers to its *MPLS table* with *labels* for quick IP packet forwarding decision, bypassing the traditional routing decision. Standardized by *Internet Engineering Task Force* (IETF), MPLS has been well received by carriers as a measure to improve WAN performance.

9.11.1 Labels and Label Information Base (LIB)

As stated, the *label* itself is similar to the virtual circuit identifier (e.g., DLCI of Frame Relay). The label is added between the IP packet header and the layer 2 frame header (see Figure 9.18) so that MPLS-enabled routers can forward IP packets relying on the label rather than the destination IP address. As MPLS-enabled 'routers' are used for packet forwarding, it is different from the layer 2 switching explained in Section 3.5 and 3.7. For this reason, MPLS is considered a 2.5 layer technology.

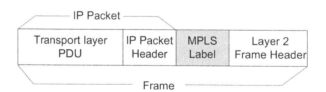

Figure 9.18 IP packet with a MPLS label

For label switching, each MPLS-enabled router called a *Label Switching Router* (LSR) maintains a *Label Information Base* (*LIB*) (Figure 9.19). The LIB keeps pairing information of label numbers and exit ports (interfaces). This pairing literally turns connectionless IP routing into connection-oriented *virtual* switching. The label is *locally significant* meaning that each link between two MPLS routers uses a unique label. For instance, the first entry of the LIB in Figure 9.19 indicates that when a packet containing 10 as its label arrives at S0/0/0, it will be re-labeled as 15 and released through S0/0/1. This re-labeling repeats until the packet completes its journey inside a WAN cloud or an ISP network. Can you observe that the working mechanism of the label based switching closely resembles that of the *virtual circuit*?

Edge LSRs are routers that insert or remove the label. Figure 9.19 demonstrates that when an MPLS-enabled router (as edge LSR) in the cloud receives an IP packet from a client network, it adds a label to the packet. Each intermediate LSR reads only the label information, instead of the IP header, to re-label and dispatch the packet to the next router. The last LSR (as edge LSR) in the cloud removes the label before passing the packet to the destination network.

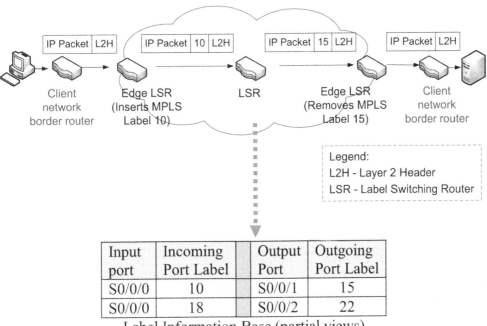

Input port	Incoming Port Label		Output Port	Outgoing Port Label
S0/0/0	10		S0/0/1	15
S0/0/0	18		S0/0/2	22

Label Information Base (partial views)

Figure 9.19 MPLS-enabled ISP network

9.11.2 Benefits of MPLS

MPLS offers several benefits. Above all, IP packet forwarding gets faster when routers rely on labels rather than IP addresses and this is the primary reason for the popularity of MPLS. MPLS has other benefits including:
     (1) traffic engineering (or traffic load balancing)
     (2) provision of *QoS* (Quality of Service)

With traffic engineering, the packet delivery path between two locations can be pre-planned for balanced use of network links and resources. This traffic engineering addresses a weakness of traditional IP packet routing in which the routing path is decided by such factors as *shortest delivery path* and network *throughput* (see Section 6.6). Using such criteria to prioritize the packet routing path can result in uneven utilization of routers and develop congestion in heavy traffic areas, negatively affecting the overall performance of a network infrastructure.

MPLS can offer better QoS for different data types by utilizing more than one label type between two locations so that the IP packet carrying time sensitive or mission critical information (e.g., Voice over IP and video streaming) gets a higher priority in delivery.

9.12 WIRELESS WAN: CELLULAR NETWORK

This section explains the cellular wireless WAN, arguably one of the most important developments in telecommunications. Broadly speaking, its technology fits into the layer architecture covered in Chapter 2, although the relationship is a little more nebulous than other landline-based WAN standards. Despite that much of the technical detail belongs to the physical and data link layers, there are elements crossing higher layers. Emphasis here, therefore, is on introducing the fundamentals without relating their technology elements to the layer architecture.

9.12.1 General Architecture

The cellular network's general architecture is demonstrated in Figure 9.20

Cell

> The cellular network is constructed by a carrier (e.g., Verizon, AT&T) to provide wireless WAN service for both voice and data through high radio frequency ranges (e.g., UHF, SHF, and EHF in Table 8.2). For this, the carrier divides operating areas into cells, conceptually similar to the WiFi's Basic Service Sets. Each cell, spanning around 100 meters within a city but larger in suburban and rural areas, is allocated a certain number of frequency channels, which limits the number of users that can be served at once. Although cells may be hexagonal, square, circular or other regular shapes, hexagonal remains a popular design choice. Adjacent cells use different frequency ranges to avoid interference or crosstalk and to allow frequency reuse by other, sufficiently separated cells.

Base Station

> The cell has a base station that communicates with mobile hosts, mostly cellphones, using high-frequency radio signals in an area. The base station comes with antenna, transmitter, receiver, and controller devices. The controller device handles call process. Generally, the base station is mounted on a cell tower and connected to a MTSO (see Figure 9.20) through a fixed line. Each MTSO serves multiple base stations.

Mobile Terminal Switching Office (MTSO)

> The MTSO, similar to Central Office (CO) of PSTN (Public Switched Telephone Network), performs fully automated functions essential for service provision including call setup and termination, call routing, handoffs, roaming, and monitoring calls for billing. A MTSO connects to other MTSOs for wireless communications and to the traditional telephone network, PSTN, for landline connectivity.

Call Channels

There are two types of communication channels between mobile devices and a base station: traffic and control channels. The traffic channel transports actual voice and data. In each cell, one channel is set aside as a control channel to exchange signaling information (e.g., host location, call setup, caller ID) and to perform such functions as domestic/international roaming and handoff/handover that allows a mobile host to move from cell to cell while communicating.

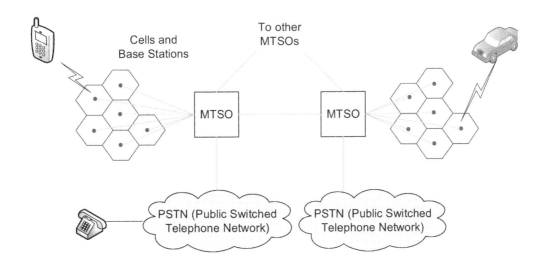

Figure 9.20 Cellular system architecture

9.12.2 Multiple Access Technologies

Cellular systems take advantage of *random access* technologies that can cram multiple phone calls and Internet connections into a limited frequency band. For this, different frequency separation- or so called "multiple access" techniques such as FDMA, TDMA, CDMA, and OFDMA have been introduced.

FDMA (Frequency Division Multiple Access)

- It divides an available frequency band into smaller frequency channels, each of which is allocated to an individual. This conceptually resembles to Frequency Division Multiplexing (see section 4.2.6).
- It was used by the analog-based AMPS (Advanced Mobile Phone Service) system

TDMA (Time Division Multiple Access)

- It further divides each frequency channel resulting from FDMA into several time slots (e.g., 3 slots) and each time slot is allocated to an individual, resulting in the usage of one channel for multiple concurrent connections. This process, therefore, resembles to Time Division

Multiplexing (see section 4.2.6).

- It was used by the GSM (Global System for Mobile communications) system

CDMA (Code Division Multiple Access)

- In CDMA, a frequency band available is not divided as in FDMA and TDMA; instead, radio signals carrying voice/data are scattered across the frequency range using the "spread spectrum" technology.
- Several methods (e.g., Frequency Hopping Spread Spectrum) that spread a signal over a large frequency band have been introduced. With spread spectrum, a unique key is appended to each digitized voice/data for identification by the receiver device. It is used by CDMA and CDMA2000 standard services.

OFDMA (Orthogonal Frequency Division Multiple Access)

- OFDMA is a multi-user version of OFDM (Orthogonal Frequency Division Multiplexing), which itself is an advanced form of FDM (Frequency Division Multiplexing). OFDM has been widely adopted by such single user (or single access)-oriented technology as WiFi including IEEE 802.11a, g, n, and ac. The 4G standard, LTE, depends on OFDMA.

9.12.3 Generations of Cellular Network

Cellular networks have evolved through four major generations, currently in the fourth generation (see Table 9.8). The first generation (1G) cellular network was purely analog and introduced primarily for voice communications. AMPS (Advanced Mobile Phone Service) was a well-known 1G technology.

Digital phones replaced analog phones from the second generation (2G) and more people started Internet access and email exchange over the digital network. The downstream speeds of digital data was approximately up to 200Kbps. The cellular system provided encryption to prevent eavesdropping. Also, to improve voice quality, the system had error detection and correction capability. GSM (Global System for Mobile Communications) and CDMA (Code Division Multiple Access) are best known 2G standards.

Generation	Period	Primary features	Popular Systems/Services	Multiple Access Technologies
1G	1980s	Voice centric analog networks	AMPS	FDMA
2G	1990s	Voice and slow data, circuit switching networks	GSM, CDMA	TDMA, CDMA
3G	2000s	Voice and faster data, circuit switching networks	UMTS, CDMA2000	
4G	present	IP-based packet switching networks	LTE	OFDMA

Table 9.8 Cellular generations

The arrival of 3G service improved access to the Internet significantly with downloading speeds up to 2 Mbps through such standard technologies as UMTS (Universal Mobile Telecommunications Systems) and CDMA2000. The worldwide roaming for travelers became available with 3G. 2G and 3G technologies rely on *circuit switching*, but the LTE's 4G network only uses *packet switching* to move voice and data.

9.12.4 LTE and Future

Long-Term Evolution (LTE)

Although there are several 4G technologies, LTE has received global acceptance, which include support from all US carriers. The following summarize some of the LTE's primary features.

- As a wireless broadband data service, it supports only IP-based packet switching. This is different from 2G/3G technologies (e.g., GSM, UMTS, CDMA2000) that rely on circuit switching.
- Its peak uplink and downlink speeds are 75 Mbps and 300 Mbps respectively, significantly faster than 2G/3G technologies.
- It supports fast-moving mobiles (e.g., automobiles), and multi-cast as well as broadcast streams.
- It handovers both voice and data to cell towers that rely on 2G/3G technologies.

In the US, carriers currently use both 4G LTE (for data transmissions based on packet switching) and 2G/3G GSM/CDMA (for voice calls relying on circuit switching) concurrently. For example, as the two largest carriers, AT&T uses GSM for voice and LTE for data, while Verizon's choice is CDMA for voice and LTE for data. This makes the two systems from AT&T and Verizon incompatible. In the near future, LTE will become a common platform for both data and voice.

What the Future Holds?

The next generation (or 5G) technology is in the discussion stage. Past experience indicates that, its introduction (if realized) could take about 10 years, sometime in 2020s (i.e., 5 years of technology standardization and 5 years of implementation). One of the 5G's greatest achievements will be its superfast data rate that, theoretically, could be about 1000 times faster than now and thus can download a high resolution movie in seconds. It is expected to take advantage of 20-60 GHz high frequency wavebands to achieve such data rates (Current 4G LTE generally depends on frequency bands below 2 GHz).

The 5G network will offer an ideal platform on which emerging technology marvels, such as Internet of Things (IoT), self-driving cars, augmented virtual reality, and three dimensional holograms, truly prosper. These technologies are expected to generate enormous amount of data that need be transferred over the network, oftentimes in near real time, between communicating parties. As a simple example, the 3D hologram will allow mobile-commerce customers to try on newly arrived clothes on their smart phones, consuming large network bandwidth.

KEY TERMS

add-drop multiplexer (ADM)
Asynchronous Transfer Mode (ATM)
available bit rate (ABR)
base station (BS)
Carrier Ethernet
cell
cell switching
cellular network
Central Office
Challenge Handshake Authentication Protocol (CHAP)
circuit switching
Code Division Multiple Access (CDMA)
common carrier
constant bit rate (CBR)
customer premise equipment (CPE)
data link connection identifier (DLCI)
demarcation point
E-Carrier
edge label switching router
fractional T1

Frame Relay
frame relay access device (FRAD)
Frequency Division Multiple Access (FDMA)
Global System for Mobile Communications (GSM)
label
label information base (LIB)
label switching router (LSR)
leased line
local loop
Long-Term Evolution (LTE)
Metro Ethernet
mobile terminal switching office (MTSO)
Multi-Protocol Label Switching (MPLS)
network interface device (NID)
optical carrier (OC)
Orthogonal Frequency Division Multiple Access (OFDMA)
packet switching
packet switched data network (PSDN)

Password Authentication Protocol (PAP)
permanent virtual circuit (PVC)
point of presence (POP)
Point-to-Point (PPP)
public switched telephone network (PSTN)
service level agreement (SLA)
service provider facility (SPE)
switched virtual circuit (SVC)
Synchronous Optical Network (SONET)
Synchronous Transport Module (STM)
T-Carrier
Time Division Multiple Access (TDMA)
traffic engineering
traffic load balancing
unspecified bit rate (UBR)
variable bit rate (VBR)
virtual channel identifier
virtual circuit
virtual path identifier

CHAPTER REVIEW QUESTIONS

1. Which item may be included in the service level agreement?
A) minimum latency
B) minimum number of hops in packet forwarding
C) maximum availability
D) minimum error rate
E) maximum delay in service response time

2. Chose a CORRECT statement regarding the WAN service.

A) Most firms use leased lines to create a full mesh network.
B) The WAN link is generally faster than the LAN link.
C) T-carrier/E-carrier and SONET/SDH are PSDN services.
D) T-carrier/E-carrier is faster in downstream than in upstream.
E) A carrier may offer Frame Relay service on its ATM backbone cloud.

3. Which is customer premise equipment of the WAN link?
A) central office
B) backbone network
C) local access link
D) point of presence
E) border router

4. One of the key differences between 4G and 2G/3G cellular systems is:
A) While 4G uses packet switching, 2G and 3G depend on circuit switching to deliver voice/data.
B) 4G supports handovers (or handoffs) and roaming that are not available from 2G and 3G.
C) 4G supports both voice and data, but 2G and 3G support only voice.
D) Whereas 2G and 3G rely on FDMA, 4G takes advantage of CDMA.
E) Unlike 2G and 3G that are analog, 4G is a pure digital system.

5. The demarcation point is a junction point where
A) the access link of a customer meets the carrier's Point-of-Presence (POP).
B) the local network of an ISP meets the Internet backbone.
C) the customer premise equipment meets the service provider facility.
D) the access link of a customer meets the Internet.
E) ISP networks are joined together.

6. Which of the following describes the cellular network's general architecture?
A) The base station is mainly responsible for handoff and roaming functions.
B) The cellular network takes advantage of high radio frequency ranges such as UHF and SHF.
C) Each cell has a MTSO that directly communicates with mobile hosts such as smartphones.
D) MTSO is mounted on a cell tower.

E) The base station is a connecting point to the traditional landline phone.

7. Choose an INCORRECT statement in regards to the WAN connection service.
A) The access link that connects a customer premise to a carrier's WAN platform is a service provider facility.
B) PPP (point-to-point) is a popular layer 2 standard for the leased line service.
C) The access line of a customer is connected to the carrier's WAN cloud through the POP.
D) The demarcation point of the WAN service is located at the POP.
E) The permanent virtual circuit is more popular than the switched virtual circuit in PSDN.

8. Which standard defines several classes of QoS (Quality of Service) to offer more customized WAN services?
A) ATM
B) Frame Relay
C) T-1
D) CDMA
E) Multi-Protocol Label Switching

9. Technical details of leased lines such as SONET and T-carrier are defined in the _____ layer.
A) application
B) transport
C) internet (or network)
D) data link
E) physical

10. The permanent virtual circuit is or becomes
A) available when a corporate customer enrolls for the leased line service.
B) less used than switched (or dynamic) virtual circuit due to its inflexibility.
C) established when communication starts between two hosts.
D) created between two communicating

hosts within a campus site.
E) set up by a carrier in its WAN cloud.

11. SONET/SDH generally adopts the _____ architecture in implementing the WAN service platform.
A) hierarchical
B) dual ring
C) mesh
D) point-to-point
E) star (hub-and-spoke)

12. Which statement is CORRECT about the Frame Relay service?
A) It uses the virtual circuit established at the beginning of each communication session.
B) The carrier provides virtual circuit identifiers to business customers for the customer site setup.
C) A popular connection choice between client sites and the Frame Relay cloud is WiMax.
D) Its technical details are defined at the Internet (or network) layer.
E) It is one of the most popular leased line standards.

13. The SONET leased line determines its bandwidth according to the _____ speed hierarchy.
A) DS (digital signal)
B) T-carrier
C) E-carrier
D) OC (optical carrier)
E) T-carrier or E-carrier

14. Refer to the figure. If a computer in Dallas sends an IP packet to a server in Toronto, how many different virtual circuit identifiers are used to reach the destination over Frame Relay?
A) 1
B) 0
C) 3
D) 4

E) cannot decide

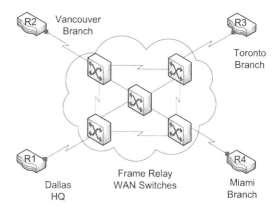

15. The DLCI (Data Link Connection Identifier) is a(n) the ___.
A) virtual circuit number
B) destination router address
C) sender's authentication code
D) router's layer 2 address
E) unique identification of an ISP

16. Which statement is ACCURATE in describing MPLS?
A) MPLS is designed to replace layer 2 switching by LAN switches.
B) The MPLS link is a physical layer link.
C) MPLS is used whenever a TCP session is established between two hosts.
D) MPLS treats all IP packets equally in their transportation priority.
E) MPLS supports load balancing that moves traffic from congested links to less-congested ones.

17. The following describe the cell of a cellular system EXCEPT:
A) The control channel of a cell transports signaling information necessary for call setup.
B) The cell is equally sized regardless of its location (e.g., city, suburban, rural).
C) Neighboring cells use the same frequency ranges as long as there is no interference.
D) The frequency band used in a cell is reused in other cells.
E) All cells are designed to have the

hexagonal shape.

18. Which does NOT represent the responsibility of carriers that provide WAN services?
A) day-to-day operation of the WAN cloud
B) QoS guarantees for all WAN services
C) service administration including client billing
D) programming intermediary nodes in the cloud
E) maintenance of access links

19. The service classes of Constant Bit Rate and Variable Bit Rate are available in

_____.
A) Carrier Ethernet
B) VPN (virtual private network)
C) ATM (asynchronous transfer mode)
D) Frame Relay
E) MPLS (multi-protocol label switching)

20. Which statement is CORRECT regarding the T-carrier service (e.g., T-1)?
A) Its technology details belong to the data link layer.
B) It can carry Frame Relay frames.
C) Its channel bandwidth is generally large enough to match that of Fast Ethernet.
D) It can carry multiple sources of data using frequency division multiplexing.
E) It is designed to support OC speeds.

21. Which of the following is NOT designed as a packet switching technology?
A) Frame Relay
B) Point-to-point (PPP)
C) Carrier Ethernet
D) Multi-Protocol Label Switching
E) Asynchronous Transfer Mode

22. Which is INCORRECT with regard to MPLS?
A) Traffic engineering blocks certain IP packets from entering the WAN network.

B) To transport IP packets with MPLS, routers should be MPLS-enabled.
C) The MPLS label of an IP packet is locally significant.
D) MPLS results in faster IP packet forwarding than conventional routing.
E) MPLS is a popular standard adopted by ISP networks.

23. When the leased line and PSDN services are compared:
A) Transmission capacity can be better tailored to client needs by the PSDN service.
B) Unlike the leased line that relies on digital transmissions, PSDN uses analog transmissions.
C) The leased line is more cost effective than PSDN.
D) The leased line generally offers faster data rates than PSDN.
E) Both offer reliability of data transmissions through the frame acknowledgement.

24. *CHAP* is a part of the _____ standard and is used for node (e.g., router) authentication.
A) Carrier Ethernet
B) PPP (Point-to-Point)
C) ATM (asynchronous transfer mode)
D) Frame Relay
E) MPLS (multi-protocol label switching)

25. A firm has three business sites. It decided that each site is going to have a permanent virtual circuit with two other sites through PSDN. What is the total number of PVCs the company will have?
A) one
B) two
C) three
D) six
E) cannot decide

CHAPTER 10 THE INTERNET AND CLIENT-SERVER SYSTEMS

10.1   INTRODUCTION

The core technologies of the Internet have been explained in previous chapters focusing on TCP/IP standards (Chapter 2 and Chapter 5) and routing mechanisms (Chapter 6) necessary move IP packets. This chapter focuses on key infrastructure and architectural aspects of the Internet. In addition, this chapter covers four technologies that dominate or will dominate the Internet space: (1) virtual private network (VPN); (2) IPv6 as the next generation IP standard intended to replace current IPv4; (3) client-server computing model; and (4) server virtualization, a form of client-server technology fundamental to realize cloud computing over the Internet.

As explained, the Internet as the single biggest network on the planet is different from an internet by definition. There are organizations that govern the policy and operational aspects of the Internet (e.g., IP addresses and domain names). Among them are *Internet Corporation for Assigned Names and Numbers* (ICANN), *Internet Assigned Numbers Authority* (IANA), and *Internet Engineering Task Force* (IETF). These organizations were introduced briefly in Chapter 2 and 5. Going over their roles, ICANN/IANA oversee the management of IP address space, top-level domains of Domain Name System (DNS), and autonomous system numbers (to be explained). IETF is responsible for the standardization of core TCP/IP protocols (refer to Chapter 2). In addition to the previous coverage of TCP/IP, the explanation of key architectural elements in this chapter should provide students with more complete understanding of how the Internet works.

The learning objectives of this chapter are to understand:
- Internet architecture:
  o Internet Service Providers
  o Internet Exchange Points
  o Autonomous Systems
  o Search Engines
- Virtual private network (VPN) technology
  o Benefits and risks
  o Implementation approaches of VPN
  o Popular VPN protocols: IPSec and SSL/TLS
- IPv6 as the next generation IP standard
- Client-server systems with in-depth look at HTTP, DNS, and DHCP
- Virtualization technology focusing on server virtualization

10.2   INTERNET ARCHITECTURE

The Internet is a truly global network that is joined by wired and wireless (e.g., satellite) networks of many ISPs (e.g., AT&T, British Telecom, Verizon). With its enormity and complexity, numerous routers on the Internet move IP packets between corporate networks and ISP networks, and between ISP networks. Depending on the location of communicating hosts, IP packets have to pass through several ISP networks to reach their destinations. For the packet delivery across networks, ISPs have to work together, although they also have to compete with each other to attract more individual and corporate clients to their Internet access service. This section covers the Internet's important architectural elements including *Internet Service Providers* (ISPs), *Internet Exchange Points* (IXPs), and *Autonomous Systems* (AS). Also explained are search engine systems that make the Internet an enormously popular space for everything.

10.2.1 Internet Service Provider (ISP)

National ISPs

ISPs use their own networks to offer Internet access to large and small businesses as well as to individual clients. In the US, ISPs are primarily fall into three categories: *National ISPs* (or Tier 1 ISPs) and *Regional/local ISPs* (Tier 2/Tier 3 ISPs). The network infrastructure operated by each *National ISP* constitutes the Internet *backbone*. The Internet is, therefore, a gigantic entity as a whole made up of many backbone networks owned and operated by *National ISPs*. *National ISPs* provide regional/local ISPs with access to the Internet in exchange for contracted service fees. *AT&T, Level 3 Communications, Nippon Telegraph and Telephone* (NTT), *British Telecomm, UUNet*, and *Sprint* are some of the largest backbone providers. The backbone network of a *National ISP* is comprised of trunk links of bundled optical fibers, transporting data at high speeds according to the optical carrier (OC) hierarchy. Figure 10.1 demonstrates a hypothetical backbone network of a National ISP in which trunk links between cities have data rates such as 9.95 Gbps (OC-192). ISPs are continuously adding network capacity to keep up with the rapid increase in Internet traffic.

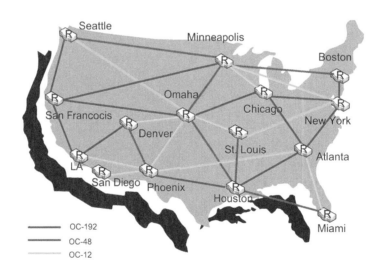

Figure 10.1 A hypothetical Internet backbone of a *National ISP* (US)

Regional/Local ISPs

The *Local* and *Regional ISPs* provide Internet access to individual and business clients in a relatively limited geographical area (e.g., Washington metropolitan area) by forwarding their

IP packets to *National ISPs'* backbone networks. In the US, many *Local ISPs* connect to *National ISPs* via *Regional ISPs*. With the local and regional ISPs' role to bridge customer LANs and the Internet backbone, their networks are frequently called *feeder networks*. The connectivity between local, regional, and national ISPs is based on contracted business relationships that include service fees. In other words, service fees local/regional ISPs pay to access the Internet become an important source of revenue for backbone providers. Individual and organizational customers, on the other hand, pay fees (e.g., monthly charge) to local/regional ISPs for Internet access. Many Tier-1 carriers offer Internet access to local/regional ISPs and also individual/corporate customers.

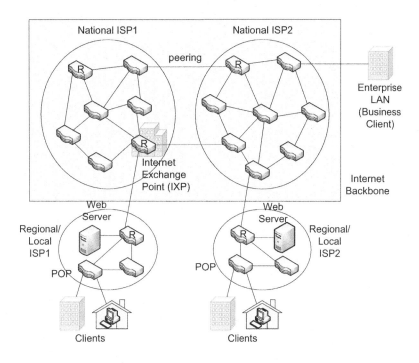

Figure 10.2 Internet architecture and ISPs

ISP Network Architecture

An ISP network is composed of one or more POPs (Point-of-Presence) as customer gateways to the Internet and trunk links that interconnect them. The large ISP owns a number of POPs, each of which is literally a large structure (e.g., building) with its own internal high speed LAN. Each POP houses different types of routers including:

- One or more access routers that connect to customer premises (individuals/organizations)
- Core routers that connect to other POPs of its own
- Border routers that connect to other ISP networks
- Hosting routers that link web servers stationed inside the POP. The webs servers provide Internet surfers with accelerated web access. You might have noticed that popular portal sites such as Google.com and Yahoo.com respond much faster than most

other sites. It is because portal servers are strategically placed at POPs right next to customer premises, making it unnecessary for user requests to cross the Internet backbone, cutting response time considerably.

POPs of an ISP are primarily interconnected by the SONET ring (see Figure 9.7) implemented on optical fibers at such high speeds as OC-192 (9.95 Gbps). Tier 1 ISPs generally use circuit speeds higher than those of Tier 2 and Tier 3 as the Tier 1's backbone should handle a large influx of IP packets from its Tier 2 and Tier 3 feeder networks.

10.2.2 Internet Exchange Point (IXP)

ISP networks are coupled together so that IP packets can travel across them to reach destinations. ISPs interconnect each other through designated access locations called *Internet Exchange Points* (IXPs) or through *peering* (see Figure 10.2). The IXP, also known as a *Network Access Point* (NAP) for a historical reason, is itself a high-speed LAN running on such high speed standard as 10 Gigabit Ethernet installed in a building and becomes a junction point of participating ISP networks.

There are many IXPs throughout the world (see Figure 10.3 for select locations of IXPs). ISP networks joined together through an IXP are bound by bi- or multi-lateral commercial contracts. In the case of the U.S, there were initially four *Network Access Points* in New York, Washington, D.C., Chicago, and San Francisco when the Internet was born. Now, there are a lot more IXPs across the country, the majority owned and operated by national-level carriers.

Figure 10.3 Select IXP locations on the planet (Go Green!)

With the continuous growth of Internet traffic, IXPs oftentimes become bottlenecks and relying solely on them as gateways to the Internet can be problematic. As a result, ISPs also use *private peering* in which ISPs directly interconnect their networks bypassing IXPs to improve Internet accessibility and to gain other benefits such as link redundancy and lower cost of Internet access. For the arrangement of private peering, ISPs agree on contract terms.

Exercise 10-1: As explained in Chapter 2 (see Figure 2.11), *traceroute* (Linux and Mac)/*tracert* (Windows) is a utility tool that uses ICMP (Internet control message protocol) to keep track of an IP packet's delivery path from the source to the destination.

1. Issue the tracert command targeting a website that is in the opposite side of the planet. Observe the difference between "*C:\>tracert*" and "*C:\tracert –d*".

2. What are the router names and their IP addresses the packets go through to reach the target website?

3. The router names may not clearly reveal the ISPs they belong to. However, an Internet registry site such as *www.arin.net* can be used to search the ISP ownership information of a router based on its name or IP address. Based on the obtained results in (2), identify ISPs the tracert packets went through to reach the target site.

4. Repeat steps 1, 2, and 3 for two other websites from different continents.

10.2.3 Autonomous System (AS)

The *autonomous system* (AS) represents a collection of interconnected subnets of a region or an organization that is under one 'administrative' control. An AS, therefore, adopts a consistent packet routing policy in which routers use the same routing protocol(s) internally and are programmed with a uniform set of packet routing rules. For this reason, the AS is also known as *routing domain*. A large enterprise or university is assigned an AS because there is a natural boundary within which it can decide its own routing policy. For example, MIT's campus network is an *autonomous system.* Relatively smaller campus networks or corporate networks belong to *autonomous systems* of their ISPs. As of 2014, there are about 66,000 autonomous systems in the world. Each AS is assigned an *autonomous system number* (ASN) by *Internet Assigned Numbers Authority* (IANA) to represent the network. In other words, the ASN uniquely identifies a network domain (NOT subnet) on the Internet. ASNs can be searched from a registry website such as *www.arin.net*.

Each autonomous system is comprised of a number of subnets held together by internal routers and autonomous systems are interconnected through border routers. Routers within an AS rely on an *Interior Gateway Protocol* such as OSPF (refer to Section 6.6) to develop their routing tables for the intra-domain (or local) routing of IP packets. Meanwhile, border routers of autonomous systems use the *Exterior Gateway Protocol* most notably BGP (Border Gateway Protocol) to develop their routing table entries necessary for the inter-domain routing of IP packets. Although the details are beyond the scope of this book, the AS number becomes a key information piece that enables inter-domain (or between autonomous systems) routing of packets. So, the delivery of an IP packet over the Internet between two remotely distanced hosts takes a combination of both intra-domain and inter-domain routing.

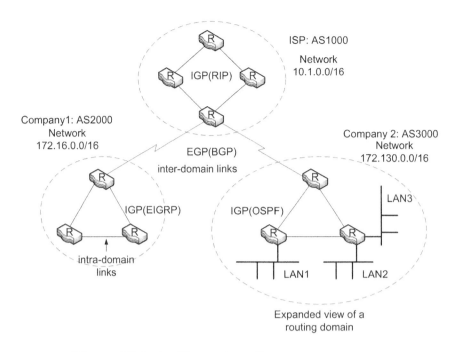

Figure 10.4 An illustration of autonomous systems

~~~~~~

Exercise 10-2

1. Identify the autonomous system number(s) of the following companies and universities from *www.arin.net* : Google, Facebook, MIT, and Stanford University
2. The vast majority of companies belong to the autonomous systems of their ISPs rather than having their own ones. Based on the provided AS numbers, search the ARIN database and decide the ISPs of the following companies.
   - Proctor and Gamble (AS3561)
   - Toyota (AS3549)
   - BusinessWeek (AS7843)
   - McDonald (AS3707)

~~~~~~

10.2.4 Search Engine

The Internet enables access to millions of web sites covering an amazing variety of subjects. According to a source, there are more than 650 million active sites in 2012. Naturally, search engines offered by such IT companies as Google, Yahoo and Microsoft are absolutely crucial for web surfers to locate a list of relevant web sites they are looking for. Powerful search engines respond to billions of user queries per day. To offer the service, search engines should find, obtain, organize, and store information on the web sites. This takes basic tasks common to all search engines and they are briefly explained here.

First, to find and document the numerous web sites and web pages, search engines use special software robots (or bots) called spiders. Web spiders crawl the Internet, gather information from each of visited sites and corresponding web pages, build lists of relevant words, and send them back to the master (e.g., Google). The spider generally begins the journey from a popular web site (e.g., web portal), obtains its web page data, and follows listed hyperlinks. For instance, Google is said to use multiple spiders, each of which crawls over 100 pages per second, gathers around 600 kilobytes of data each second, and passes them back to Google.

In gathering the data, spiders take different approaches in terms of how much data is gathered; how deeply it scours each web site with a number of web pages; and how often the same site is revisited to obtain updated data. For example, in terms of how much data is gathered, some spiders may be designed to capture every significant word of a webpage, but other spiders may be instructed to collect only the words appearing in the title, subtitles, meta-tags and particular positions of a webpage. There are also spiders programmed to copy the entire web pages of visited sites and send them back. For example, Google's search service has an option of viewing "cached" pages. This is possible as the entire web pages visited are copied and stored in Google's own server.

Second, information gathered and sent back by the spider is organized according to an indexing scheme that enables fast search and retrieval of relevant sites by web surfers. At this stage, web site ranking is also calculated based on various weighting criteria including word location, word frequency, distance between words, words included in META tags, and labels in referring links. Search sites use different formulas to assign weights to differing criteria. This results in differences among search engines in their listings and rankings even when the same keywords are issued by web surfers. When the indexing is complete, the resulting information is encoded and stored in a large-scale database to enable keyword searches of websites. This whole process including indexing is highly automated (see Figure 10.5).

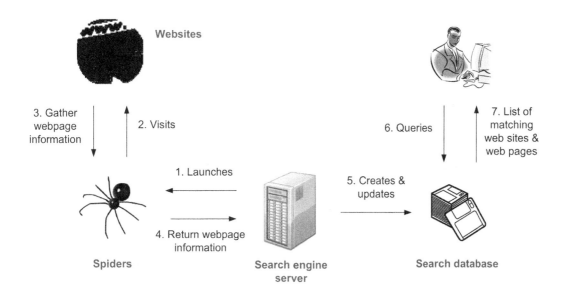

Figure 10.5 How search engine works.

10.3 VIRTUAL PRIVATE NETWORK (VPN)

10.3.1 Technology

Background

The Internet, with its global coverage, has become an ideal platform for creating WAN links through which corporate networks can be accessed by authorized people (e.g., travelling salesmen, business partners) from anywhere in the world. Despite the obvious benefits (e.g., low cost of connections) of the Internet as a WAN platform, many organizations have been reluctant to embrace it because of security concerns, uncertain network reliability (e.g., packet delays, packet delivery errors), and limited quality of service in packet transportation.

VPN Technology

Introduction of the *virtual private network* (VPN) technology has changed much of that negativity of the Internet as a WAN platform. VPN uses so-called *tunneling* to securely transport IP packets. Tunneling is the process of encapsulating an encrypted IP packet within another packet for secure delivery. It is like transmitting packets within a secured pipe over the Internet. The encapsulation includes encrypting the original packet and adding a new IP header. At the receiving end, a router/VPN gateway performs the packet de-encapsulation and forwards the decrypted, original packet to the destination host.

VPN, therefore, differs from the traditional WAN connection services such as leased lines and Frame Relay offered by carriers over their own private infrastructure (see Chapter 9). Although VPN runs through the public Internet, the resulting connection is considered *virtually private* because the technology protects IP packets in transition. With VPN, remote employees such as mobile workers, home-based workers (telecommuters), and branch offices become a part of the virtual enterprise network.

10.3.2 Benefits of VPN

Cost Effectiveness

The Internet is a very cost effective communication platform because most businesses already have Internet access and VPN does not incur additional cost of network services. Empirical data indicate that, compared to leased lines or carrier's PSDN-based services, VPN considerably curtails costs associated with network equipment, maintenance, administration, and communications. When a public or private organization maintains a large contingent of mobile workers, telecommuters, or branch offices, cost savings could be even more significant.

Accessibility and Scalability

The Internet with its global presence offers accessibility that no other private carrier networks can match. Organizations can add VPN-based WAN links anywhere, anytime, and any-to-any connectivity because of the Internet's ubiquity. Also, VPN has bandwidth scalability in which the data rate between a client site and an ISP can grow as needed taking advantage of various (e.g., DSL, cable, leased lines) services available for Internet access.

Flexibility

VPN increases flexibility in business operations as links can be formed dynamically as needed and torn down when no longer necessary. For example, suppliers or customers of a firm can be easily added to its enterprise network over the Internet. This will benefit the firm in various ways such as improved customer service and better management of business processes. As economic activities become more distributed and global, firms can take advantage of VPN for cost effective communications and networking with global partners. Imagine a salesman who travels much and access corporate databases over the Internet using his/her smart phone or tablet that can securely download or upload sales-related information and data. Whenever the salesman exercises remote access to the corporate network, it becomes a WAN link. And when (s)he severs the remote link, the connection is terminated. The traditional WAN link on the carrier's own platform takes lead time (e.g., order placement and processing) to setup and dismantle, thus unable to match the VPN's flexibility in dynamically forming and changing remote links.

10.3.3 Risks of VPN

Reliability

While a VPN can bring about significant benefits to adopting organizations, there are potentially high risks compared to the traditional services offered on the carrier's WAN platform. Above all, VPNs depend upon the speed, reliability, and performance of the Internet. The Internet is relatively more vulnerable to congestion and slowdown than carrier networks, and therefore more difficult in maintaining stability and dependability of data transmissions for mission-critical applications. Also, Internet-based connections can be less reliable than those on the carrier's WAN platform because the majority of IP packets have to cross multiple ISP networks to reach their destinations. The reliability problem can be mitigated if a client firm can rely on one ISP whose Internet backbone can cover all remote sites of the client and thus can offer QoS guarantee.

Security

Although security technologies (e.g., encryption) can safely protect data these days, VPN may still not be perceived as secure as the carrier's WAN platform because the Internet operates in open environment. In the early days, the security concern hampered the widespread industry adoption of VPN. With continued advancement of the VPN technology, more firms are jumping on the VPN bandwagon. It is also true that, despite the VPN's improved data protection capability, the rampant security breaches on the Internet can discourage many businesses from VPN adoption when they need bullet-proof security in protecting sensitive data.

10.3.4 Types of VPN

Different approaches are available in setting up VPN and they are largely divided into Remote-Access VPN and Site-to-Site VPN.

Remote-Access VPN

This mode enables remotely located employees of a firm to access corporate systems to transfer field data or to download necessary information (e.g., marketing materials). It implements a Person-to-LAN connection in which the person may be a telecommuter, mobile worker, or travelling salesman. Remote access VPN allows workers in remote locations take advantage of the worldwide Internet as a WAN channel to reach back to their corporate sites and conduct assigned tasks in a timely manner.

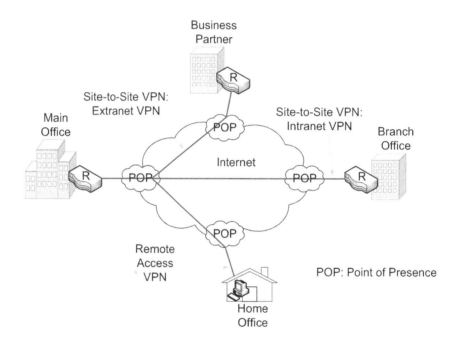

Figure 10.6 VPN Types

Site-to-Site VPN

With the site-to-site VPN, secure connections are established between two geographically separated LANs to protect IP packets in transition using encryptions. On arriving at the destination, the packets are decrypted and forwarded to destination hosts. In this mode, the border router (or VPN gateway/firewall) does the work of encrypting and decrypting the packets to protect their privacy. The site-to-site VPN comes in two modes: intranet-based and extranet-based.

The intranet-based VPN interconnects office LANs of a firm over the Internet. Normally both ends (e.g., branch offices) are considered safe and reliable; therefore, these LAN-to-LAN connections are assumed to have minimal security risks. The extranet-based VPN, also known as *business-to-business* VPN, connects LANs of two different business entities to streamline business processes such as supply chain management. While the intranet-based VPN involves trusted endpoints, the extranet-based VPN is intended to interconnect business partners, customers, suppliers, and/or consultants.

10.3.5 VPN Standards

Several protocols are available to implement VPN, and *SSL/TLS* (shortly SSL) and *IPSec* are among the well received. While IPSec is independent of applications, SSL is frequently embedded into applications most notably web browsers (e.g., HTTP + SSL => HTTPS). There are also other VPN standards such as *PPTP* and *L2TP* defined at the data link layer. IPSec and SSL are covered in more detail next.

Layer	Protocols
Transport	SSL (Secure Socket layer/Transport Layer Security)
Internet	IPSec (IP Security)
Data Link	PPTP (Point-to-Point Tunneling Protocol)
	L2TP (Layer 2 Tunneling Protocol)

Table 10.1 Popular VPN protocols

10.3.6 IPSec (IP Security)

Among the standards that have been introduced for VPN (see Table 10.1), IPSec is generally regarded as the most secure protocol. IPSec was developed by *Internet Engineering Task Force* (IETF) to offer key security functions including authentication, integrity, and confidentiality in exchanging data over the Internet.

- *Authentication* is for the validation of communicating parties in their true identities.
- *Data integrity* assures that packets in transition are not changed accidentally or manipulated by unauthorized parties. If the unintended moderation of a packet takes place, this should be detected.
- *Data confidentiality* (or *privacy*) means that packets in transition should be protected from eavesdropping.

To satisfy the security requirements, various technology components are utilized by the IPSec protocol. They include pre-shared keys and digital certificates, encryption technologies including DES and 3 DES, and hashing algorithms such as MD5 and SHA-1.

IPSec operates at the internet layer and, therefore, can protect all protocol data units (PDUs) coming down from the transport and application layers (see Figure 10.7). This protection is necessary because the IP protocol itself has no such capability. Using IPSec is optional for IPv4, but will ultimately become mandatory under IPv6. IPSec can encrypt data exchanged between network nodes (e.g., router-router, firewall-router, client-router, client-server) as long as the necessary software is installed in them. A dedicated, independent IPSec server may be set up at the corporate boundary or it may be installed on the firewall/border router. When the IPSec server and the firewall/border router are separated, the latter needs to be adequately configured for the IPSec traffic to pass through.

| Application layer (e.g. HTTP, SMTP) |
| Transport layer: TCP/UDP |
| Internet layer: IPSec Protocol |
| Internet layer: IP Protocol |

Figure 10.7 The IPSec layer

The IPSec standard is implemented in two different modes: *tunnel mode* and *transport mode* (see Figure 10.8).

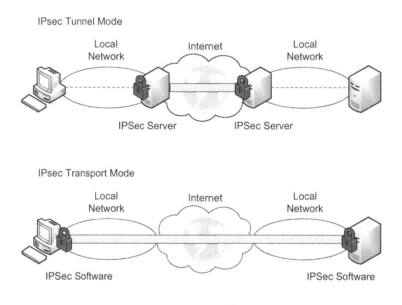

Figure 10.8 IPSec tunnel mode vs. transport mode

Tunnel mode

IPSec implemented in the tunnel mode has the following features:
- IPSec servers are placed at the boundary of local sites securing all inter-site transactions through data encryption (site-to-site security).
- Internal hosts are not aware of the IPSec server's existence, making it transparent to them.
- No security is provided for IP packets outstanding in a local network. In other words, packets inside of a corporate network remain unencrypted.
- The tunnel mode is popular in implementing both remote access and site-to-site VPNs.

In terms of packet encryption/decryption, the IPSec server encrypts an outgoing IP packet and encapsulates the encrypted packet within another IP packet (see Figure 10.9). In doing so, the IPSec server adds an IPSec header that contains required information on the encryption to the encrypted original IP packet. Then, a new IP header is added for packet routing over the Internet. In this mode, therefore, the original IP packet is entirely encrypted and protected from eavesdropping in transition. The new IP header is added only for packet routing between the two IPSec servers placed at the two different sites.

Transport mode

IPSec implemented in the transport mode provides end-to-end (or host-to-host) security. For this, IPSec software needs to be installed on each host station making its implementation considerably more costly and labor intensive than the tunnel mode. With the transport mode, a packet remains encrypted even while it traverses inside a LAN (see Figure 10.8). In this mode, only the original data field of a packet is protected by encryption, but not the IP header because information (e.g., destination IP address) in the original IP header is necessary to deliver the packet to the destination host.

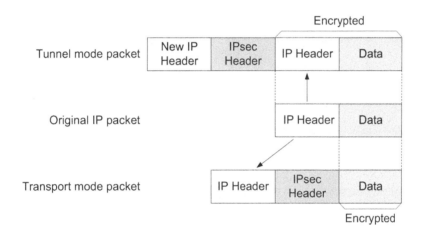

Figure 10.9 IP packet encapsulation: tunnel mode vs. transport mode

IPSec's tunnel mode and transport mode can be combined to offer double protections of IP packets. When the two IPSec modes are used together, hosts communicate in the end-to-end transport mode so that nobody else is able to read encrypted data. In addition, the site-to-site tunneling is established between LAN boundaries for further protection of the encrypted data. This, however, entails a considerable process overhead and is also costly.

10.3.7 SSL (Secure Socket Layer)

Broad Acceptance

SSL is a protocol that performs authentication, data encryption, and data integrity, offering a secure means to transport data over the Internet. SSL was initially developed by Netscape Co. for secure communications, information access, and e-commerce transactions (e.g., online banking, product purchasing with a credit card) between the web browser and the web server based on HTTP. When HTTP is combined with SSL to enhance transactional security, it becomes HTTPS (or HTTP over SSL). When a browser visits a sensitive web site (e.g., online banking), the web server enforces the browser to use HTTPS to protect exchanged data.

SSL became TLS *(Transport Layer Security)*, a standard from *Internet Engineering Task Force* (IETF). SSL rose quickly because the protocol is built into the web browser and thus there is no need to install the program separately to take advantage of its security functions. Besides HTTPS, SSL has been applied to turn other insecure protocols into secure ones. For instance, FTP (File Transfer Protocol) and SMTP (Simple Mail Transfer Protocol) exchange data and files in clear text, making them vulnerable to interceptions. With the addition of SSL, FTPS (FTP over SSL) and SMTPS (SMTP over SSL) protect FTP and SMTP data.

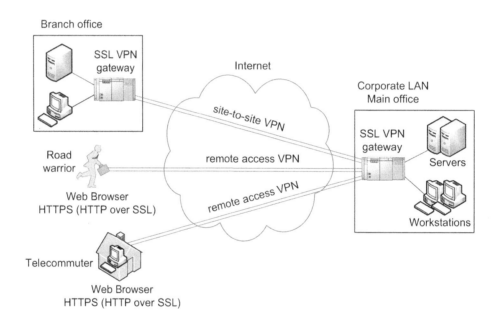

Figure 10.10 VPN implementations with SSL

VPN Implementation

SSL has also been a popular choice to implement VPN. As is the case with IPSec, SSL-based VPN can be flexibly implemented in both transport- and tunnel modes (see Figure 10.10). When SSL is used for VPN, both the browser (client) and the SSL server should authenticate each other by exchanging their credentials (e.g., digital certificate). This avoids such risk as *man-in-the-middle* in which a session is hijacked by an attacker (see Sections 11.9 and 11.12). Especially, prevalence of WiFi networks makes the mutual authentication in VPN important.

SSL and Internet Commerce

When SSL is used in e-commerce, it is difficult for the online store's HTTP server to enforce mutual authentication. The client (browser) authentication is generally skipped because most web browsers do not come with a digital certificate. The digital certificate is generally purchased from a Certificate Authority and installed in the computer, but most Internet surfers do not buy it. For that reason, only the server (e.g., Amazon.com server) authenticates itself to the browser (client) using its own digital certificate to protect online shoppers from fraudulent web sites (more on digital certificates in Section 12.6). The server authentication is based on the following steps and Figure 10.11 summarizes the procedure.

1. The web browser contacts the web server and there is a brief negotiation of security options for exchanging data.
2. The server authenticates itself to the client by sending its digital certificate that contains the server's public key.
3. The browser contacts the Certificate Authority sever and checks the *certificate revocation list* to confirm that the digital certificate is genuine and has not expired.
4. On validating the server's digital certificate, the browser generates a symmetric session key, encrypts it with the server's public key, and sends it to the server.
5. From thereon, data exchanged between the browser and the web server are encrypted with the session key until the session is terminated.

Figure 10.11 Server authentication with SSL in e-commerce

10.3.8 IPSec vs. SSL

IPSec and SSL as two most popular VPN standards have their own pros and cons, and the key differences are summarized in Table 10.2. In fact, IPSec and SSL can be used in combination to provide enhanced VPN security.

	IPSec (IP Security)	SSL (Secure Socket Layer)
Layer	Internet layer	Transport layer
Software	Should be installed and maintained for each user station.	Built into the web browser and No additional client-side software is necessary.
Setup and maintenance cost	High setup cost as software needs to be separately installed. Maintenance and updates become a substantial burden if there is a large installation base.	Low maintenance and update cost as it is pre-loaded in the web browser.
Ease of use	End-user training is necessary for its usage.	No need for end-user training as the software is built into the browser.
Overall security	Generally provides a higher level of security than SSL.	Considered less secure than IPSec.
VPN implementation	Complicated as security configuration in each station requires expertise.	On the client-side, it works more like plug-and-play as the software is built into the browser.

Table 10.2 Comparison: IPSec vs. SSL

10.4   IPv6 (IP NEXT GENERATION)

10.4.1 Background

One of the drawbacks of IPv4 has been its limited address space due to the 32 bit address structure. When it was first introduced, IETF (*Internet Engineering Task Force*) didn't anticipate such an explosive growth of IP demands. This has been especially fueled by the addition of mobile devices such as smart phones and tablets. Further, it is safe to say that sooner or later most (if not all) computing and communication devices, home appliances, game consoles, and other consumer electronics will join the Internet triggering enormous consumption of IP addresses.

Although measures including private IP addressing and network address translation have extended IPv4's lifespan, *Internet Assigned Numbers Authority* completed its allocation of available IPv4 address to *Registries* in 2011. The classful IP scheme adopted in the early stage of the Internet contributed to the ineffective distribution and usage of the IPv4 address space. Before long, we will have no choice but to move to IPv6. Already major operating systems including Windows support both IPv4 and IPv6 reflecting the slow but gradual migration to the new frontier. To find out if your computer supports IPv6, use the 'ipconfig' (Windows) or 'ifconfig' (Unix, Linux) command. The adoption of IPv6 is faster in Europe and Asia due to the shortage of IPv4 addresses in these regions. This section introduces IPv6 with a special focus on its addressing mechanism.

10.4.2 IP Packet Structure

Regular IPv6 packets contain a 40-byte header (see Figure 10.12), significantly longer than that (20 bytes in length) of IPv4. IPv6 also allows extended headers of various lengths, but the explanation here focuses on the regular 40-byte header structure. Although the header is longer than that of IPv4 (see Figure 2.8) largely because of the lengthy IP address bits, IPv6 has a simplified header structure with fewer fields, which allows more efficient packet processing. One notable departure from IPv4 is absence of the header checksum that has been used by routers to detect errors in the packet header.

Below are descriptions of the header fields:
- o *Traffic Class* and *Flow Label* are designed to support quality of service (QoS). *Traffic Class* prioritize traffic. The functional specs of *Flow Label* are still evolving.
- o *Payload length* indicates the length of the IPv6 payload (data field).
- o *Next header* indicates the type of PDU (e.g., protocol) in the data field.
- o *Hop limit* represents the maximum number of routers a packet is allowed to pass and is equivalent to *time-to-live* (TTL) in IPv4
- o *Source address* identifies the IPv6 address of a source node.
- o *Destination address* identifies the IPv6 address of a destination node.

Version 6 (= 0110)	Traffic Class (8 bits)	Flow Label (20 bits)	
Payload Length (16 bits)		Next Header (8bits)	Hop Limit (8 bits)
Source IP address (128 bits)			
Destination IP address (128 bits)			
Next Header or Payload (Data Field): Variable in size			

Figure 10.12 IPv6 Packet

10.4.3 IP Addressing

The IPv6 address uses 128 bits or 32 hexadecimal digits (e.g., 0089:A0CD:0234:EF98:0000:000F:0D0B:0F20) in which each represents 4 binary bits. Hexadecimal digits are not case sensitive (e.g., A0CD is equivalent to a0cd). With 128 bits, IPv6 affords enormous address space (trillion times of IPv4 space) eclipsing IP shortage for a long time to come. Out of 128 bits, the first 64 bits represent a network address and the remaining 64 bits are for a host address within a particular network.

Exercise 10-3: IPv4 uses subnet masks such as 255.255.255.0 to indicate the subnet portion of a 32 bit IP address. Do we also need to use subnet masks in IPv6?

Subnet Address Bits

IPv6 also adopts hierarchical IP addressing in which the 64 network address bits are further divided into:
- o 23 bits for the regional registry prefix
- o 9 bits for the ISP prefix
- o 16 bits for the site prefix necessary for global routing
- o 16 bits for the subnet prefix

Just as with IPv4, IPv6 packet routing also relies on the longest matching of the subnet prefix.

Exercise 10-4: Search the Internet and find prefix ranges allocated to all regional registries including AfriNIC, ARIN, APNIC, LACNIC and RIPE NCC.

Host Address Bits

As for the 64-bit host address part, three options are available in assigning host addresses.
- o The host address can be manually configured in a computer.
- o The host address can be dynamically provided by such protocol as DHCPv6.
- o Unique to IPv6, there is a third IP addressing option called EUI-64. EUI stands for *Extended Unique Identifier*. With EUI-64, the 64 bit host address of a computer can be automatically derived from its 48 bit MAC address. This approach, however, exposes a computer's MAC to the world, raising major privacy concerns.

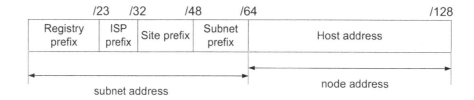

Figure 10.13 IPv6 address structure

There are also private and loopback IP address ranges. For example, the loopback for IPv6 is 0:0:0:0:0:0:0:1 (or "::1" in abbreviation), equivalent to 127.0.0.1/8 for IPv4. If necessary, additional loopback addresses can be defined by an organization for internal usage.

10.4.4 Address Abbreviation

IPv6 addresses are long and can be shortened according to two abbreviation rules.

Rule 1: *Leading zeros* within each block of hexadecimal values separated by colons (:) can be omitted. For example, following two addresses are equivalent.

0089:A0CD:0234:EF98:0000:000F:0D0B:0000
89:A0CD:234:EF98:0:F:D0B:0

Rule 2: A group of consecutive zeros can be substituted by a double colon. For example, the following addresses are all equivalent.

0089:A0CD:0234:0000:0000:0000:0D0B:0F20
89:A0CD:234:0:0:0:D0B:F20
89:A0CD:234::D0B:F20

This trick of removing all 0s is allowed 'only once' for a reason. For example,
0089::A0CD:0234::0D0B:0F20 can be interpreted either
0089:0000:A0CD:0234:0000:0000:0D0B:0F20 or
0089:0000:0000:A0CD:0234:0000:0D0B:0F20.

Exercise 10-5

1. Use the address abbreviation rules to reduce the following IP addresses to the smallest possible.
   a) AD89:00C0:0204:0000:0000:ABC0:000B:0020
   b) 0000:0000:0000:0D89:0EC0:0204:00FB:0A20
   c) 0000:0D89:00C0:0204:0000:0000:000B:0000

2. Restore the following IP addresses to their non-abbreviated ones.
   a) 89:CD:4::B:20
   b) B:FD:3:F98:0::D0B:F20
   c) B:1:3:8:0::B:0

10.4.5 IPv6 vs. IPv4 Standards

Besides the massive address space, the IPv6 standard improves IPv4 on many fronts. The protocol details of IPv6 are still evolving and some of the key differences are highlighted here.

Features	IPv4	IPv6 (IPng)
Network security	Using a security protocol is an option.	IPsec is mandatory for packet encryption, sender authentication, and data integrity.
Quality of Service	Relies on the Diff-Serv field	Provision of more refined QoS becomes available through the Traffic Class and Flow Label fields.
Packet size	Up to 64KB in payload	Can be larger than 64KB in payload. Packets greater than 64KB are called jumbograms. Jumbograms can be theoretically as large as 4 GB.
Methods of packet	Unicasting, multicasting, and	Broadcasting is not available. Instead,

distribution	broadcasting are possible.	multicasting will be used extensively.
Network address translation (NAT)	Heavily used due to shortage of IP address space and weak security. Improving network security with NAT is losing its effectiveness as most security attacks are targeted at the application and transport layer functions. This makes the role of NAT in security increasingly marginal. Think of phishing through emails as an example.	IPv6 is designed so that NAT is unnecessary and this makes it easier to implement advanced network applications such as virtual private networks (VPNs). Despite, there is also possibility that NAT may return in IPv6 as vendors start to support it.
Address resolution protocol (ARP)	Used for mapping between IP and physical (MAC) addresses.	IPv6 is designed so that ARP is not necessary. Instead, ICMPv6 packets perform functions similar to ARP for IPv6.

Table 10.3 Comparison: IPv4 vs. IPv6

10.4.6 Approaches of IP Transition

The transition from IPv4 to IPv6 will be rather gradual. Currently, some networks and their nodes purely depend on IPv4 while many others support both IPv4 and IPv6. To ensure coexistence of IPv4 and IPv6 for the foreseeable future, several technical solutions have been introduced. Among them are *dual IP stacks*, *tunneling*, and *direct address conversion*.

Dual IP Stacks within a Node

With the dual IP stack approach, the operating system of a node (e.g., computer and router) supports both IPv4 and IPv6 concurrently. For example, Figure 10.14 demonstrates a scenario in which dual stack routers (R4, R5, and R6) provides address mapping between IPv4 and IPv6 networks to enable the transition. Running dual IP stacks is a popular approach as operating systems of hosts and network nodes support them.

Direct Address Conversion

With this solution, IPv4 packets can be turned into IPv6 packets and vice versa. For this IPv4 addresses of 32 bits can be directly converted into IPv6 addresses of 128bits with a little bit of a trick. For the conversion, a 32 bit IPv4 address is preceded by 80 first zero bits and then 16 one bits. For example, the IP address of 123.45.67.89 can be translated into:

0000:0000:0000:0000:0000:ffff:123.45.67.89 or
0:0:0:0:0:ffff:123.45.67.89 or
::ffff:123.45.67.89.

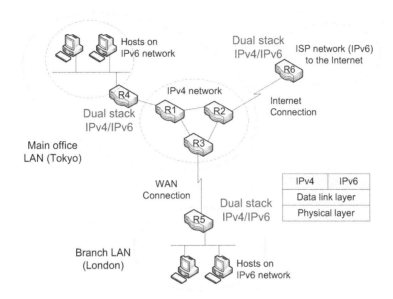

Figure 10.14 Scenarios of dual stack routers

Packet Tunneling

Tunneling has been introduced as well. For example, if a destination network is running on IPv6 but the local network is still on IPv4, then the local host can produce an IPv6 packet and encapsulate it within an IPv4 packet for delivery. Depending on the situation, the reverse can happen when an IPv4 packet is produced and encapsulated within an IPv6 packet for transportation.

As another scenario, tunneling can be used by dual stack routers (Figure 10.14) for packet delivery. For example, if the source and destination hosts are all on IPv6 networks but a packet needs to pass through an IPv4 network, the dual stack router can encapsulate/de-encapsulate the IPv6 packet by adding/dropping an IPv4 header (see Figure 10.15).

IPv6 Header	IPv4Header	IPv4 Data

IPv4 Header	IPv6Header	IPv6 Data

Figure 10.15 Packet tunneling

345

10.5 CLIENT-SERVER SYSTEMS

In the Internet, the majority of applications run in the client-server relationship in which clients take advantage of server resources. These programs run at the application layer. Figure 10.16 demonstrates the client-server relationship in which the IIS web server exchanges web pages with web-browser clients running on different operating system platforms.

In the remaining section, three client-server protocols (HTTP, DNS, and DHCP) defined at the application layer are explained in more detail as they represent standards absolutely fundamental for the modern Internet and the web to function.

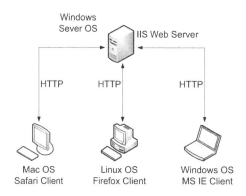

Figure 10.16 Client and server models

10.5.1 Hypertext Transfer Protocol (HTTP)

The web browser and the web server rely on HTTP for communication. For demonstration, let's assume that the main webpage, *www.president-news.org*, is composed of 3 files: a text file and two image files (a banner and a president photo), and the three files are all stored in the web server. The three files are:

    File #1: index.html (the main text page)
    File #2: banner.jpg (a photo)
    File #3: president.jpg (a photo)
This means that all three files have to be downloaded for web browsers to construct the complete webpage and present it to web surfers.

When a web surfer enters *http://www.president-news.org* into a browser, it uses HTTP to produce a request (i.e., an application PDU) that contains a simple header and no data field. In the header, GET is the keyword that indicates file request. HTTP/1.1 represents the HTTP version the browser wants to use for communication with the target server. On receiving the browser request, the *www.president-news.org* server returns a HTTP response composed of a header and data fields. The header contains information including the server program (e.g., Apache, Microsoft's IIS), content-type (e.g., text, image), and data size. The data field includes actual content (e.g., index.html) requested by the browser. Below is a partial display of the browser request and server response.

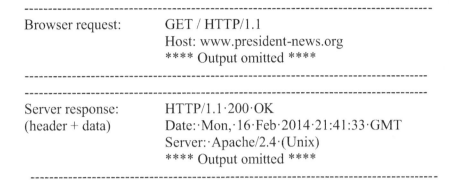

```
------------------------------------------------------------------------
Browser request:        GET / HTTP/1.1
                        Host: www.president-news.org
                        **** Output omitted ****

------------------------------------------------------------------------

------------------------------------------------------------------------
Server response:        HTTP/1.1·200·OK
(header + data)         Date:·Mon,·16·Feb·2014·21:41:33·GMT
                        Server:·Apache/2.4·(Unix)
                        **** Output omitted ****

------------------------------------------------------------------------
```

To download the 3 files, the request-response cycle above is repeated three times between the browser and the web server (Figure 10.17).

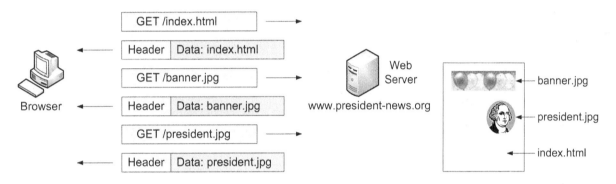

Figure 10.17 A process view to download three files

Exercise 10-6: You can observe the syntax of HTTP request/response messages through a HTTP viewer site such as *http://www.rexswain.com/httpview.html* or a viewer program such as *http://www.httpwatch.com*. From *http://www.rexswain.com/httpview.html,* access a web site of your choice and answer the following questions.

1. What are information items included in the request header?
2. As for the server response:
   a) The response message is divided into two parts of _____ and _____
   b) What does the value 200 included in the first line mean? (Search the Internet)
   c) What version of HTTP is used by both the browser and the server?
   d) What is the name of the web server program?
   e) What operating system is running on the web server machine?
   f) What is the total size (in bytes) of the response message?
   g) What is the size (in bytes) of the message header?
   h) What is the size (in bytes) of the content (data)?
   i) What is the content type?

10.5.2 Domain Name System (DNS)

Domain and Name Resolution

The *domain* such as *indianna.edu* defines a boundary within which an organization (e.g., university) manages or controls its network resources. Within the boundary, hosts are labelled with human-readable *domain names* such as *www.indiana.edu* (for web server) paired with IP addresses. Routers, however, do not understand domain names and route packets only based on their corresponding IP addresses.

The mapping process, termed *name resolution*, between domain names and their IP addresses is handled by DNS servers. For name resolution, thus, each DNS server maintains a database of domain names and their IP addresses, and the list is continuously updated either manually or automatically. With the rapid growth of host devices attached to the network, automatic or dynamic updates of DNS databases are popular these days. Name resolution can be both forward (e.g., www.facebook.com => 12.34.56.78) and backward (e.g., 12.34.56.78 => www.facebook.com), although DNS usage is mostly for the forward resolution.

Domain Hierarchy

The domain name itself is formed in a hierarchical structure composed of *top-level, second-level,* and *lower level* domains. *Top level domains (TLDs)* include *generic TLDs (or gTLDs)* such as *.com, .edu, .gov*, and *.org*, and *country code TLDs (ccTLDs)* such as *.jp* (for Japan) and *.uk* (for United Kingdom). Second-level domains are sub-domains of top level domains. For example, in *texas.edu, texas* is its second-level domain. A majority of the second-level domains represent organizations, schools, and businesses.

Internet Assigned Numbers Authority (IANA) of ICANN is responsible for managing top-level domains as well as allocating IP address space. Specifically, it manages generic (*gTLD*) and country code (*ccTLD*) top-level domains, and delegates their control to *domain name registrars* (e.g., Network Solutions Co.) who process domain name applications from businesses and individuals. There are a number of ICANN-accredited registrars in the world (refer to *www.icann.org* for the list). Businesses and individuals who want Internet presence are required to register second-level domain names through the registrars. For country code TLDs, the domain registry is generally controlled by each country's government.

On receiving a second-level domain name, an organization can freely create lower-level domain names. As an example, think of a hypothetical web server with the domain name, *www.cba.sdsu.edu*. The naming indicates that the web server host belongs to the *edu* top-level, *sdsu* (university) second-level, and *cba* (college of business) third-level domains.

The difference between *URL* (Uniform Resource Locator) and domain names needs to be clarified. In general, when a domain name is preceded by a protocol such as *http, https* or *ftp*, it becomes a URL. Therefore:

URL = protocol + domain name

For example, *http://www.yale.edu* becomes a URL in which *www.yale.edu* is a domain name and browsers communicate with the web server using HTTP.

DNS Architecture

For name resolution, DNS servers in the world are in two types: *local DNS* and *root DNS* servers. Organizations and ISPs have their own *local DNS* servers for local service provision. For instance, a university has at least one DNS computer to serve local inquires. The DNS server maintains a database of local domain names and their IP addresses, and also cached information of frequently visited external sites.

The name resolution is initially attempted by local DNS servers. If the local server is unable to resolve an inquiry from a host, it is forwarded to a root DNS server. The root server does not have the answer either, but it knows which DNS 'authority' server can answer the inquiry (Figure 10.18). The authority server finally returns the domain name's IP address to the requesting host.

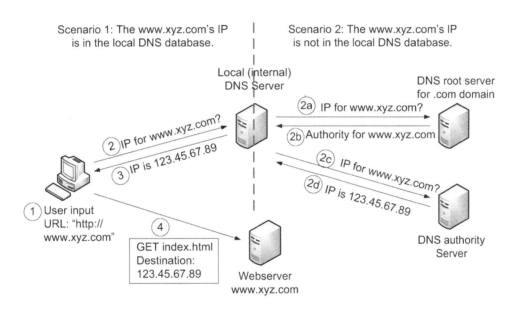

Figure 10.18 Obtaining the IP address of a domain name

~~~~~~

Exercise 10-7

1. At the command prompt of your computer (assuming Windows), enter "*C:\>ipconfig /all*" to find out the IP addresses of local DNS servers.

2. The host maintains in its cache DNS information on previously visited sites. Find out the paired list of domain names and IPs using the command "*C:\>ipconfig /displaydns*".

3. What is the main benefit of storing DNS information in cache?

349

4. Clear the name resolution table with "*C:\>ipconfig /flushdns*" and confirm the clearance with "*C:\>ipconfig /displaydns*". There may be only one entry of *localhost* paired with 127.0.0.1 (loopback IP) after the flush. If your computer displays "*The requested operation requires elevation*", complete the following procedure: go to *All Programs*, *Accessories*; right click *Command Prompt*; and click *Run as administrator*.

5. Assuming that the DNS list is empty, visit a website of your university. Then, observe additions of TCP connections with "*C:\>netstat –n*" at the command prompt. Also, display the name resolution table with "*C:>ipconfig /displaydns*". Can you explain why several DNS entries are added after visiting just one site?

6. In the screenshot below, the inquiry with "*C:/nslookup www.sdsu.edu*" was returned with 130.191.8.198. Then, the 'nslookup' program must have sent the query to a _____ server.

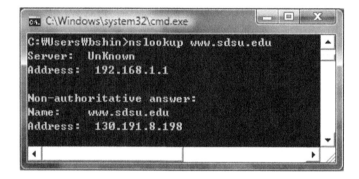

Figure 10.19 Sample *nslookup* inquiry

Host DNS File

The operating system of a host computer has a DNS file that can be manually configured for name resolution. In Windows, the file is *hosts* and available at *C:\windows\system32\drivers\etc*. The file is automatically loaded into memory during boot. Its initial entries only include loopback addresses that redirect packets to itself (refer to Section 5.6.1). The loopback addresses automatically entered into the file are:

"127.0.0.1 localhost" (for IPv4)
"::1   localhost" (for IPv6)

When a user enters a target domain name into an application (e.g., browser), the computer first searches its own *hosts* file. If the mapping information is not found in the hosts file, then the computer sends an inquiry to the default local DNS server as in Figure 10.18. The well-constructed *hosts* entries can offer significant benefits in several fronts:
- Web-access speed improves by bypassing DNS servers.
- A newly developed system can be tested without an entry in local DNS servers.
- Privacy and security can be enhanced by blocking unwanted sites from downloading

annoying ads and banners, and tracking user behaviors (see Exercise 10-8).

On the other hand, the *hosts* file also has been subject to security attacks in which malicious programs (e.g., Trojan) secretly changed the *hosts* file entries of infected computers to redirect user inquiries to malignant websites.

Exercise 10-8: Windows OS

1. Which Windows command can be used at the command prompt to check whether the IP address of your computer's DNS server has been changed into a suspicious address?
2. Open the *hosts* file in *Notepad*. Add 3 hypothetical DNS entries into the hosts file just for practice (Do not save the file).

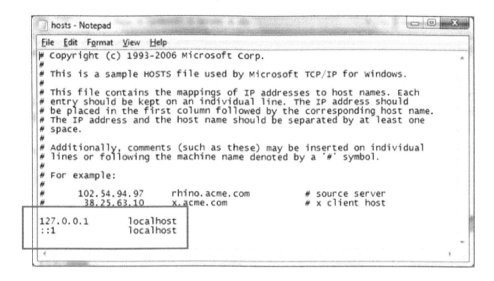

Figure 10.20 Demonstration of *hosts* file in Windows

3. Entering "*127.0.0.1 ad.doubleclick.net*" into the host file results in blocking of all ad/banner files from *ad.doubleclick.net* (DoubleClick advertising server) and their displays on your browser. It also has an effect of preventing the ad server from tracking your movements (e.g., other visited websites) through cookies. Explain why? Understand that there are many other ad servers on the Internet.

10.5.3 Dynamic Host Configuration Protocol (DHCP)

DHCP (Dynamic Host Configuration Protocol) allocates temporary IP addresses to requesting hosts. The DHCP server may be running on a dedicated computer or router. When a client station is powered on, its built-in procedure broadcasts an IP request to reach the DHCP server that maintains a range of temporary IP addresses. On receiving the request, the DHCP server leases an IP address to the requesting station for a limited time (e.g., 1 day). For example, with "*C:>ipconfig*

/all" for Windows or "*C:>ifconfig /all*" for Unix/Linux at the command prompt, the lease information including *Lease Obtained* and *Lease Expires* is displayed (Figure 10.21). The leased IP is returned to the DHCP server if the host is shut down or taken off from the network. The client station may issue a renew request to the DHCP server before its expiration. Besides, with *Autoconfiguration Enabled* (see Figure 10.21), the workstation can use a pre-assigned IP address for *internal networking* only (thus, not for Internet navigation) just in case the DHCP request fails and the computer is forced to wait until the DHCP service is restored.

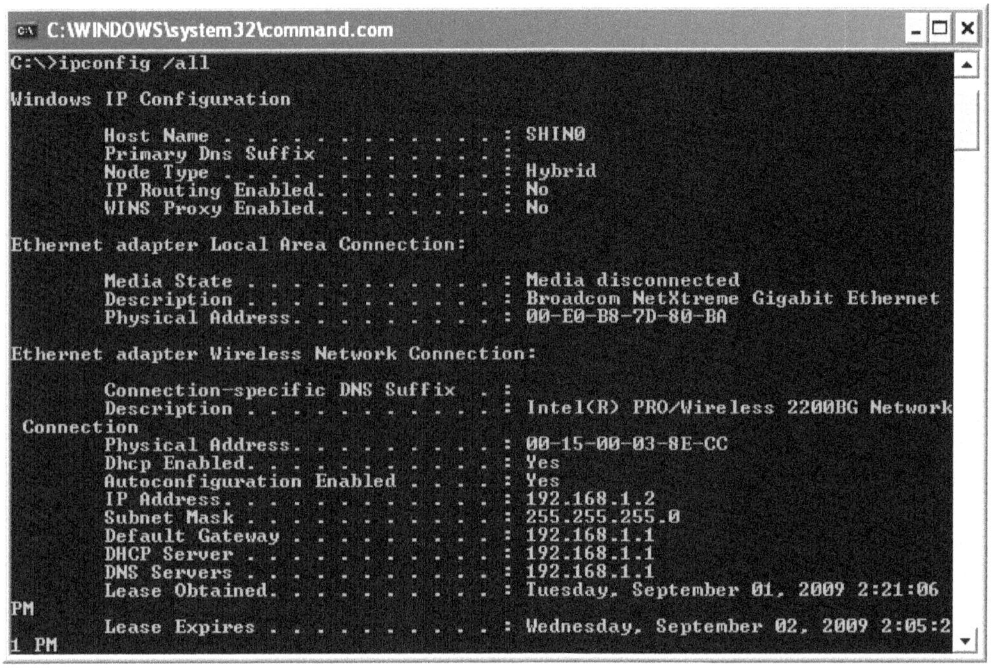

Figure 10.21 IP configuration screenshot (Windows)

The Process View

The following describes the acquisition procedure of a temporary IP address:

(1) On a cold start, a workstation initially broadcasts an IP request that contains its own MAC address and computer name (see Figure 10.22). Given the initial absence of its own IP address, the request packet contains the destination address of 255.255.255.255 (broadcasting) and the source address of 0.0.0.0.

When the workstation and the DHCP server are separated by a router, the broadcast is stopped by the router. In this case, there are two different solutions possible. First, the router can have its own DHCP server programmed to respond to DHCP requests. Alternatively, the router can be instructed to turn the broadcast packet into a unicast packet and relay it to the target DHCP server.

(2) On receiving the request, the DHCP server offers a dynamic IP address to the workstation.

Such information as the IP's subnet mask, default gateway, DNS server address, and lease period in hours/days/weeks is provided as well. The DHCP standard also defines additional rules of engagement when more than one IP address are offered to the workstation by different DHCP servers.

Figure 10.22 Computer name example (Windows)

(3) After the station is given a temporary IP address, the DHCP server passes the host station's information to a DNS server for its dynamic database update (see Figure 10.23).

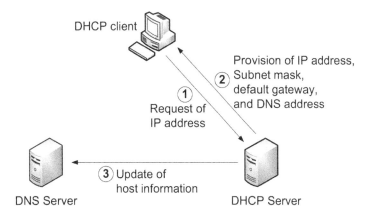

Figure 10.23 DHCP and dynamic IP assignment

10.6 SERVER VIRTUALIZATION

In this section, the client-server model explained is further extended to explain *server virtualization.* Virtualization has become a dominant computing paradigm these days being adopted virtually everywhere, especially in the form of *server virtualization* because of significant financial and non-financial benefits it affords to adopting organizations. These include reduced cost of computing, and increased flexibility and effectiveness in allocating system resources. Because of its enormous importance in enterprise computing and significant implications on the planning and deployment of corporate networks, server virtualization is explained in this section.

10.6.1 Traditional Computing Model

The traditional model of enterprise computing without virtualization is shown in Figure 10.24. In that approach, a physical server is equipped with a server operating system and is generally dedicated to a particular server application (e.g., file server, email server, web server, database server). In that setup, hardware resources including CPU, memory, and storage are utilized by the single OS and dedicated application. The traditional approach, however, poses a host of problems when a company has to operate 100s or even 1000s of server machines.

Here is a list of most obvious challenges an enterprise has to deal with on a daily basis by operating a large number of server machines that host dedicated server applications:

- High setup, operation, and maintenance costs:
  - ➢ Setup costs including hardware acquisition, operating system licensing, and installations
  - ➢ Operational costs as servers take up floor space and consume much power for cooling and operation
  - ➢ Maintenance costs such as performance monitoring and tuning of each server, and the replacement of ones that have reached the end of their life cycle
  - ➢ Upgrade and update costs including updates of software patches for operating systems and applications
  - ➢ Infrastructure costs such as deployment of high speed networks and intermediary devices
- Low utilization of existing servers: Dedicating a physical machine to a server application results in limited utilization of available hardware resources (e.g., CPU, memory, storage).

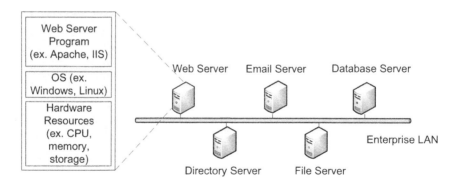

Figure 10.24 Traditional approach in deploying server hosts

10.6.2 Virtualization Concept

Many of the problems explained above can be resolved or alleviated if there is a technological solution that:

- Reduces the number of physical machines without sacrificing overall processing capacity necessary to run the server applications
- Makes better use of existing server resources

Virtualization is a technological solution that enables one physical machine to house multiple virtual machines (VMs), each of which behaves just like a standalone computer with its own operating system. This creates an environment where several *independent* server applications run in parallel on a single physical host (see Figure 10.25). With virtualization, therefore, the number of computers necessary to run the server applications is reduced significantly. As a result, the utilization of each physical server is much enhanced, curtailing waste of server resources and still handling equivalent amount of workloads.

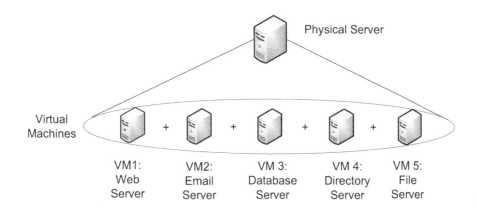

Figure 10.25 Server virtualization

10.6.3 Virtualization Approaches

Based on the general understanding of virtualization, this section explains two different technical approaches available to create virtual machines (VMs) on a physical machine: hosted-virtualization and hypervisor-based virtualization.

Hosted Virtualization

In this mode, the host machine has its own server OS (e.g., Windows, Linux) just as with the traditional server system. Then the virtualization software (e.g., VMware, VirtualBox) is installed on top of the host OS and subsequently multiple VMs each with its own OS are created on top of the virtualization software. Remember that each VM thus created becomes a totally independent (logical) server machine with its own OS, application(s), own IP and MAC addresses. Figure 10.26, for example, demonstrates a scenario in which five VM servers are running in parallel on one physical machine. Evidently, the more powerful the physical machine is, the more VMs can be created concurrently without having performance bottlenecks.

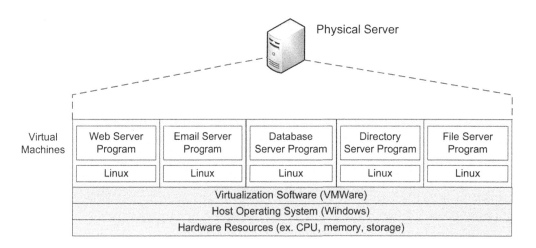

Figure 10.26 Hosted server virtualization

Hypervisor-based Virtualization

In this solution, the host machine does not need to have its own host OS (see Figure 10.27 for a scenario). Instead, the so-called *hypervisor* program (or VM manager) is installed in the hardware so that multiple VMs can run on top of it sharing available hardware resources. Although shared environment, each VM has its own OS and acts as if it has its own dedicated processor, memory and other resources. In this environment, the hypervisor ensures that conflicts do not occur in resource sharing between VMs. Its main advantage over the hosted-virtualization approach is performance enhancement because it skips the host OS layer that mediates processing between hardware elements (e.g., CPU, storage) and VMs.

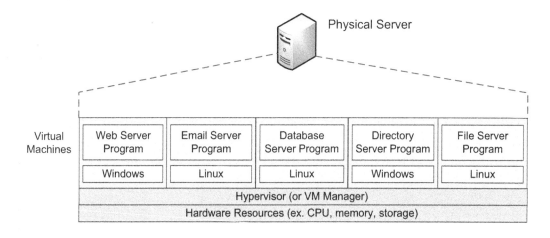

Figure 10.27 Hypervisor-based server virtualization

356

10.6.4 Shared Infrastructure

Although the explanation thus far has focused on the *'one physical host to multiple VMs'* relationship, the virtualization technology has progressed much to realize *shared infrastructure* in which hardware resources of server computers are pooled and managed as a whole (e.g., 32 CPUs, 7000 TB storage, and 2000 GB RAM). The resources in the inventory are controlled by the VM manager program and dynamically allocated to different server applications over the network. In this shared dynamic environment, physical computers are almost completely transparent to VMs and to system users.

For instance, an application (e.g., database) running on a VM can use hardware resources available from other computers. Also, the VM can be easily moved from one physical host to another (e.g., a form of drag and drop through the management program) when a situation rises (e.g., A physical host needs to be retired or shut down for regular maintenance and upgrades). With the centralized inventory management of computing resources, the workload of physical machines can be easily redistributed (see Figure 10.28).

Managing resources of physical machines as a commonly shared inventory is an essential technology for cloud computing. Cloud computing has become a dominant IT service paradigm in which various hardware (e.g., storage) and software (e.g., ERP) resources owned by service providers (e.g., Google, Amazon) are offered to business clients over the computer network. A service provider manages thousands of physical machines whose resources are utilized by a number of business customers. It is not difficult to see that virtualization is a fundamental technology solution for cloud service providers to effectively utilize available computing resources.

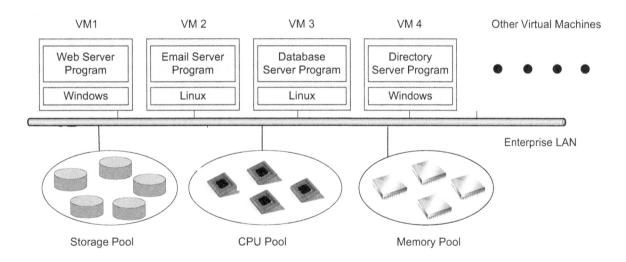

Figure 10.28 Virtualization with shared infrastructure

10.6.5 Summary: Benefits Realized

Virtualization offers benefits to enterprises and many of them have been explained in terms of cost savings and better utilization of infrastructure resources. The benefits of virtualization are revisited in more detail.

- The number of physical servers necessary to deliver equivalent tasks at hand can be reduced significantly, resulting in considerable savings of capital and operational costs.

- In the VM environment, the number of servers a person can manage increases order of magnitude. For example, operational time necessary for server building and application loading dramatically shrinks. The same efficiency applies to server maintenance and updates.

- VMs can be easily moved from one physical machine to another and therefore the disruption of computing service due to maintenance and IT outages is reduced.

- With one physical machine housing multiple VMs, there are reduced needs for physical cabling of computers to the network and network management.

- Lastly, virtualization results in much better usage of existing computer resources by optimizing their utilization. For example, even relatively outdated hardware resources can become a part of the production infrastructure.

KEY TERMS

authentication
autoconfiguration
autonomous systems (AS)
cloud computing
country code TLD (ccTLD)
data confidentiality (privacy)
data integrity
DHCP
Domain Name System (DNS)
dual IP stacks
Dynamic Host Configuration
Protocol (DHCP)
EUI-64
FTP over SSL (FTPS)
generic TLD (gTLD)
hosted virtualization
Hypertext Transfer Protocol
(HTTP)

hypervisor-based virtualization
Internet Corporation for
Assigned Names and Numbers
(ICANN)
internet exchange point (IXP)
internet service provider (ISP)
IP Security (IPSec)
IPng
IPv6
local DNS server
local ISP
national ISP
network access point (NAP)
packet tunneling
peering
Point-of-Presence (POP)
regional ISP
remote-access VPN

root DNS server
routing domain
Secure Socket Layer (SSL)
shared infrastructure
site-to-site VPN
SMTP over SSL (SMTPS)
top-level domain (TLD)
Transport Layer Security
(TLS)
transport mode
tunnel mode
tunneling
uniform resource locator
(URL)
virtual machine (VM)
virtual machine manager
virtualization
virtual private network (VPN)

CHAPTER REVIEW QUESTIONS

1. Choose an INCORRECT statement regarding DHCP.
   A) It is a protocol used to obtain temporary IP addresses.
   B) When a user computer is powered on, it broadcasts the DHCP request.
   C) A router may be programmed to provide DHCP service to requesting hosts.
   D) When an IP is assigned to a host, the information is updated to a DNS server.
   E) Many web servers obtain their IP addresses from DHCP servers.

2. Which is a top level domain name?
   A) .com
   B) whitehouse.gov
   C) www.stanford.edu
   D) sdsu.edu/mis
   E) microsoft.com

3. Which is NOT in the first 64 network address bits of IPv6?
   A) regional registry prefix
   B) ISP prefix
   C) site prefix necessary for global routing
   D) subnet prefix
   E) time to live (TTL) prefix

4. Which is CORRECT about the ISP?
   A) Companies and individuals can access the Internet without ISPs.
   B) National ISP networks form the Internet backbone.
   C) The Internet is owned by the US government.
   D) ISPs interconnect each other through network service points.
   E) Tier 1 ISPs are regional or local ISPs.

5. _____ represents an arrangement of direct links between ISPs to bypass Network Access Points.
   A) Pairing
   B) Channeling
   C) Exchanging

D) Hopping
E) Peering

6. The _____ is a junction point that joins ISP networks together to enable packet routing over the Internet.
   A) gateway
   B) internet switching point
   C) internet exchange point
   D) internet service point
   E) internet portal

7. Which INCORRECTLY describes IPv6 addressing?
   A) An address is composed of two parts: 64-bit network ID and 64-bit host ID.
   B) Host addresses can be configured manually.
   C) IPv6 supports broadcasting of IP packets as IPv4 does.
   D) Host addresses can be dynamically provided through the DHCP service.
   E) The 64 bit host ID of a computer can be derived from its 48 bit MAC address.

8. Benefits of VPN do NOT include:
   A) VPN performance is not affected by Internet congestion.
   B) VPN offers flexibility in forming and terminating secure connections over the Internet.
   C) VPN affords bandwidth scalability in which the data rate between a client and an ISP can grow.
   D) VPN supports anytime, anywhere, and any-to-any accessibility.
   E) VPN is cost effective in forming WAN links.

9. Which VPN requires additional purchase and installation of security software in user computers?
   A) SSL in the tunnel mode
   B) IPSec in the transport mode
   C) IPSec in the tunnel mode

D) IPSec in the site-to-site mode

E) SSL in the regular mode

10. Which statement describes the IPv6 standard?
A) Using a security protocol will become an option.
B) Each packet's payload should be less than 50 KB.
C) IPv6 packets have a simpler header structure than IPv4 packets.
D) Unicasting, multicasting, and broadcasting are supported by IPv6.
E) SSL is a security protocol preferred by IPv6.

11. Which is CORRECTLY paired between a VPN standard and its operational layer?
A) IPSec: internet, SSL: data link
B) IPSec: internet, SSL: application
C) IPSec: transport, SSL: data link
D) IPSec: transport, SSL: application
E) IPSec: internet, SSL: transport

12. _____ represents the process of encapsulating a packet within another packet and is heavily used for VPN.
A) Binding
B) Packing
C) Tunneling
D) Bonding
E) Trunking

13. Below message must have been generated at the _____ layer:
"GET / /HTTP 1.1
Host: www.whitehouse.gov"
A) application
B) transport
C) internet
D) data link
E) physical

14. The transition from IPv4 to IPv6 will be rather gradual and one approach that allows their coexistence is direct address conversion. In that approach, 123.45.67.89 (IPv4) becomes _____ for IPv6:
A) 0000:0000:0000:0000:0000:ffff:123.45.67.89
B) 1111: 1111: 1111: 1111: 1111:ffff:123.45.67.89
C) 123.45.67.89: 0000:0000:0000:0000:0000:0000
D) 1111: 1111: 1111: 1111: 1111:0000:123.45.67.89
E) 123.45.67.89:1111: 1111: 1111: 1111: 1111:ffff

15. Choose a WRONG statement regarding Domain Name Service (DNS).
A) The top level domain includes university names.
B) The second level domain is also called sub-domain.
C) Obtaining a second level domain name, an organization can freely create lower-level domain names.
D) The country code is a top-level domain.
E) The uniform resource locater (URL) combines a protocol and a domain name.

16. Which is an INCORRECT statement on server virtualization?
A) The virtual machine installed in a host computer has its own operating system.
B) The number of servers an IT professional can manage declines with server virtualization.
C) The number of physical servers necessary to deliver equivalent amount of computing is reduced.
D) The need for physical cabling of server computers to the network decreases.
E) IT service disruption due to maintenance and outages is reduced.

17. _____ is a popular security standard built into web browsers.
A) SSH (Secure shell)
B) PPTP (point-to-point tunneling protocol)
C) SSL (Secure socket layer)

D) SET (Secure electronic transaction)

E) IPSec (IP security)

18. The following information should be kept in

"127.0.0.1   localhost" (for IPv4)

"::1   localhost" (for IPv6)

A) local DNS servers

B) root DNS servers

C) DNS authority servers

D) host computers

E) DHCP servers

19. Which describes the transport mode of IPSec?

A) IPSec servers are placed at the boundary of local sites.

B) Hosts internal to a site are not aware of IPSec servers.

C) When a packet in transition is in a corporate network, it remains unencrypted.

D) It is a popular choice for implementing intranet-based site-to-site VPNs.

E) The data field of an IP packet is protected by encryption, but not the IP header.

20. Choose a CORRECT statement regarding VPN standards.

A) SSL offers the most secure VPN solution among available standards.

B) The IPSec's tunnel mode is more cost effective to implement than the transport mode.

C) Implementing the IPSec's tunnel mode requires software installation in each computer.

D) IPSec's security software is embedded in web browsers.

E) When SSL is combined with HTTP, the mutual authentication of both client and server is mandated.

CHAPTER 11 CYBERSECURITY: THREATS

11.1 INTRODUCTION

As computer networks have become the backbone of society, as more valuable information and data are stored electronically and transported over networks, and as more financial and non-financial transactions are carried out in the form of electronic commerce, attacks on computer systems and system users have become more organized, diversified, sophisticated, destructive, and difficult to detect and prevent. Cybersecurity - largely intended for the protection of *information, data*, and *people* - is a very broad and continuously changing field with numerous technological (e.g., networks, computers, programs) and non-technological (e.g., rules and processes, business and government policy, training and education) issues entangled.

Many cybersecurity threats comprise computer networks one way or another these days. It is also known that the vast majority of security breaches occurring at organizations are intentionally or unintentionally perpetrated by their own employees who may be disgruntled, inadequately prepared (e.g., gullible employees, lack of education and training), or motivated to expose information/data for personal benefits (e.g., financial gains). Given the breadth of cybersecurity issues, two chapters are designated to explain fundamental concepts associated with the technological side of cybersecurity (e.g., networks, programs). This does not mean that non-technological subjects (e.g., protection rules and processes) are less important. In fact, they are equally, if not more, important than technological issues.

This chapter introduces prevalent types of cybersecurity attacks committed by attackers primarily over the computer network to attain malignant goals such as information/data theft and system break-in. Some attacks such as *viruses* and *denial of service* are designed to disrupt the target network and its computers. However, the majority of attacks perpetrated these days intend to steal (or snoop) private and sensitive information, sometimes for fun and other times for financial gains. For information theft, many different technical approaches have been mobilized, sometimes in isolation and other times in concert with others. The following represents common cybersecurity attacks today's system users and corporations face.

- Malicious codes (malware)
- Password cracking
- Spoofing
- Denial of service attack
- Packet sniffing
- Port scanning
- Social engineering and phishing
- Man-in-the-middle attack
- Spam
- Zero-day attack
- WiFi threats

Although most of them are carried out over the computer network, they differ in their malignancy. Some attacks cause more severe damages on the victim than others directly or indirectly, which include financial losses, stolen confidential data, tarnished firm reputation, dropped share price, and weakened customer confidence. Also, some attacks (e.g., malware development) are more technologically-intensive than others (e.g., port scanning).

11.2 MALICIOUS CODES: MALWARE

Malware, the combination of the words, **mal**icious and soft**ware**, represents a type of software code designed to cause destructive damages to infected systems and subsequently system users. Malware generally does not damage the hardware portion of computers and intermediary devices. Rather, the damage (e.g., destruction, corruption, theft) is inflicted on data, files, and software stored/installed in network nodes. Among the main malware types are *viruses, worms*, *Trojan horses* (or *Trojans*), and *bots*. There are also other malware types such as *adware* that displays uninvited advertisements and *spyware* that steals personal information (e.g., keystroke loggers) and monitors/tracks system usage. In fact, it is difficult to clearly define the nature and scope of each malware type, partly because of their evolving nature. For instance, to some people, the virus is a type of malware with its own unique functional features and thus different from other malware types. To others, the virus represents a broad concept that refers to any evil code designed to disrupt the target network, system or system usage. In this section, the malware types are explained based on their narrower definitions.

11.2.1 Virus

The virus is an executable program and, if infected, can result in various effects ranging from mild annoyance to more serious damages to user data or programs installed in a system. As a result of virus infliction, the system can crash or lock up leading to the denial of system service; files and directories can be manipulated; hard disk data can be erased; and the system can behave erratic or slow down significantly.

The virus spreads to other computers mostly by attaching itself to or becoming a part of a benign executable program (let's call it a host program). When the host program is executed, the virus code is executed as well infecting the system. System users, however, do not notice the infection because generally the host program behaves normally after its execution.

There are several channels (e.g., CD-ROM, USB memory stick) through which host programs hiding or infected with viruses can be copied or transferred from one system to another. With the ubiquity of computer networks especially the Internet, the majority of them spread through network applications such as email, web sites (e.g., social networking), and instant messaging these days.

11.2.2 Worm

The worm is a program designed to replicate itself and spread to other computers over the network without human intervention. The self-replication capability without being attached to another program is what makes it different from viruses. In other words, the worm becomes a stand-alone, self-sustaining program that propagates by itself. To do that, it frequently takes advantage of known/unknown vulnerabilities of a target operating system or relies on social engineering (e.g., a benign-looking email with an executable worm attached) to trick system users into its execution.

Just as with viruses, worms can result in various types of damages if infected. Some do not necessarily damage the components of infected (or relaying) systems. Because of self-replications and resulting bandwidth consumption, one of their destructive effects is disrupted network performance. As many worms exploit design flaws in operating systems, it is critical to regularly install OS patches to protect networks and computer systems.

~~~~~~

Example: Sobig Worm

Sobig was a worm architected to replicate by itself and also a part of its code was designed to execute the Trojan function. Sobig was initially sent to numerous email accounts as an attachment from a spam network. It used various subjects such as *Re: Approved* and *Re: Thank you!*. When gullible users clicked on the attachment with such file names as *details.pif* and *application.pif*, the program was executed. The worm was designed to search the infected machine to find email addresses. Then, it emailed the worm program to all email addresses recovered from the infected machine, resulting in a large scale replication and spread of automatically generated emails.

Also, the worm planted a Trojan in the affected computers to initiate contacts with shadowy servers in order to obtain the URL of a Trojan web server. Once they obtained the URL, these computers visited the Trojan web server and downloaded another Trojan program. When the Trojan program was secretly installed, the infected computer became a proxy server through which spammers could send spam without being traced.

~~~~~~

11.2.3 Trojan

The Trojan, named after the wooden horse from the Greek myth, is a malicious code hidden behind a program or web page that looks legitimate. Downloaded from a website or sent in an email attachment, the evil code is secretly triggered when the benign looking program is executed or downloaded web pages are presented on web browsers. The attachment to an innocent looking program gives a resemblance to the virus. Trojans, however, differ from viruses or worms as they are not designed to infect other files/programs or self-replicate. The majority of Trojans are designed to create a backdoor so that attackers obtain sneak access to a target system -- locally or remotely -- by bypassing the normal authentication and login procedure. Different approaches have been taken to install the malicious code into a target system. As a popular approach, a hacker can hack into an ordinary web server or FTP server and alter the legitimate program in order to plant a Trojan, which will result in a backdoor if downloaded and installed by a user computer. Some well-known download sites including Linux distribution sites have fallen to this type of attack. As another popular approach, a Trojan inserts an undocumented password into the password file of a target system.

With the sneaky establishment of a backdoor, an attacker can literally turn an infected computer into a stealth server that gives almost complete control to him/her through a telnet or HTTP session.

With the Trojan in place, the attacker can exercise a host of activities. Among them are: uploading and downloading of files, planting malware for subsequent DDOS (distributed denial of service) attack to a target victim, stealing passwords and other sensitive information, installing spyware for keystroke monitoring, and gathering email addresses for spam distribution. Also, some Trojans created backdoors so that email spammers can access the infected systems and send junk emails from them.

Example: *FreeVideo Player* Trojan

Once there was a website whose visitors were told that they needed to install a FreeVideo player *codec* to view certain videos. As a computer program, the codec compresses and decompresses audio and video files. It shrinks movies, videos, or music files too large to transfer quickly over the Internet. When clicked for downloading, this installed the FreeVideo player, benign looking but with a Trojan hidden. One of the things the Trojan did was to change the IP address of the victim computer's DNS setup so that DNS inquiries are sent to the rogue DNS server controlled by the attacker(s) located in a third country. The name resolution by the rogue DNS server re-directed system users to dangerous web sites infested with malware. Although the FreeVideo player could be removed through the regular un-installation procedure, this did not roll back the DNS setting. A learned lesson is that the border firewall of an organization should filter all DNS queries not directed to the official DNS server internally arranged. Also, computer users should beware of software downloading from questionable sites and they need to check DNS entries to ensure that inquiries are sent to the local DNS server.

11.2.4 Bot

The *bot* is a secret program planted by a cybercriminal to turn innocent computers into zombies. The bot program, once it successfully finds a home within a victim computer, has capability to report back to the criminal master and listens to his/her commands. The bot also has a built-in program logic that goes to other computers (as spiders) over the network, find their weak spots, infect and turn them into zombies, and report the 'successful landing' back to their evil master. The collection of zombies thus formed is called a *botnet* and they can be collectively 'remote controlled' by an evil master. That is, bots of a botnet can act in a coordinated manner, executing routines according to commands coming from the master. For this large-scale coordination, the attacker sets up one or more "command and control" servers -- generally harbored in compromised computers -- running the *Internet Relay Chat* (IRC) protocol and remotely control a large number of infected machines. The remote control capability is what differentiates the bot program from other malware types.

Once a botnet is up, the criminal or organized crime ring can perpetrate evil activities such as spreading spam emails, stealing data and personal information, triggering DDOS attacks, attempting phishing, spreading new malware, and hacking websites. In particular, the botnet has become a perfect channel to mass spread spam emails. It is said that there are thousands of botnets in the Internet space. Well-known examples include Grum, Bobax, Rustock, Cutwail, and Bagle. Taking down the botnets is difficult and has only short term effects because getting them up again

366

is relatively easy thanks to such programs as pay-per-install and botnet renting in the underground marketplace. They can be shut down permanently only when their operators are arrested.

As a case in point, the Cutwail botnet is considered one of the largest botnets in terms of the number of compromised hosts. It was estimated that somewhere around 1.5 to 2 million personal computers were infected and the botnet had a capacity of flooding the Internet with over 7 billion spam emails a day. IT security researchers found that the Cutwail's botnet engine and infrastructure have been rented to spam advertisers who are willing to pay for mass advertisement.

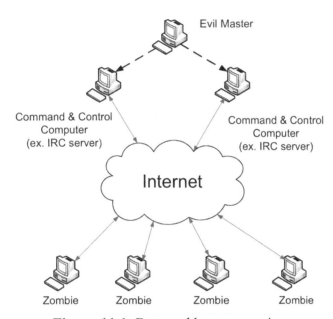

Figure 11.1 Bots and botnet creation

11.2.5 Malware Issues

As is the Sobig case, malware increasingly combines more than one functional element (e.g., Trojan + worm) in its payload -- software code embedded in malware designed to cause damages to the infected system on execution. Such functional combinations have two key implications on defenders. First, its execution can cause maximum damages, making the attack more effective to the perpetrator but more costly to victims. Second, the functional combination increases the chance of neutralizing the defender's defense system.

Malware attacks user systems both at the application level (i.e., application layer) and the operating systems level (i.e., transport and internet layers). At the application level, the most prevalent attack is the installation of evil application codes designed to cause various types of damages (e.g., deleting files, stealing user data). At the OS level, attacks can modify or replace OS files. For example, planting a Trojan to open a backdoor and modifying a password file in order to gain a stealthy access to a target computer are such attacks.

To prevent a computer from falling to a victim of the vicious code, it is crucial to regularly install

367

patches issued by OS vendors, use anti-virus/anti-spyware software, harden it with a host-based firewall, deploy a border firewall, and back-up files regularly. Also, on downloading software (e.g., freeware, open source program) from the Internet, its integrity should be checked first using a hash function (e.g., MD5, SHA-1), known as an act of *fingerprinting*. For fingerprinting, web sites offer one or more hash values along with downloadable software. A prudent IT professional checks the hash value(s) by visiting two or more mirror sites to ensure that downloaded software has not been tainted. Downloaded software should not be put into production before its thorough integrity testing.

11.3 PASSWORD CRACKING

The password is the most prevalent form of user authentication. An individual typically uses a number of passwords to access different websites, and their safe maintenance and usage has become a challenge. User passwords can be stolen in many different ways, including trial-and-error (guesswork), social engineering, phishing, login spoofing, keystroke logging with malware, and password cracking. Among them, password cracking is explained in this section.

Password cracking uses software tools and the brute processing capacity of a computer to obtain or steal user passwords. For example, the operating system of a computer has a designated file that stores user passwords encrypted by such standard as DES (Data Encryption Standard) or hashed by such hash function as MD5 (Message Digest 5), which generates a one-way 128-bit hash value from a user password. Linux, for instance, keeps encrypted passwords and their related information (e.g., password expiration) in the '*/etc/shadow*' file that is readable only with the root (or system) access privilege. In Windows, passwords are hashed and stored in the *C:\Windows\System32\Config\SAM* file that remains invisible to system users. To steal passwords, an attacker can legally or illegally access a target computer system and copy the password file to work on his/her own terms with password cracking software. Password cracking software can break an encryption using two different approaches: *brute force* attack and *dictionary* approach. Before their explanation, the hash function as a popular technology utilized to encrypt passwords is briefly reviewed.

11.3.1 Hash Function

A hash algorithm such as MD5 and SHA-1 takes an input (e.g., password, plaintext) of any length and produces a fixed-length hash value known as a *message digest*. For example, MD5 and SHA-1 produce unique 128 bit and 160 bit hash values regardless of the input size. A hash value thus generated cannot be reversed to restore the original input, making the hash function a one-way function. Table 11.1 demonstrates select input values and their corresponding outcomes in hex produced by MD5.

The hash function is extensively used and among the applications are: a cryptographic tool to conceal user passwords of a computer system; to conduct digital fingerprinting (see Section 11.2.5); to produce digital signatures (see Figure 12.7); and to perform transmission error control in the form of error detection and correction.

Inputs (e.g., passwords)	Outputs (hash values in hexadecimal)
Stealth →	899db408cba5858a0f1701a2caef2628
she →	1a699ad5e06aa8a6db3bcf9cfb2f00f2
I am a student. →	2f1f75e8bb00643cb05aed57f7bdb4a8

Table 11.1 Production of hash values with MD5

Exercise 11-1: Find a website with online hash value calculators (e.g., MD5 and SHA-1) and enter texts of varying sizes (e.g., a word, a sentence, a paragraph) to observe results.

11.3.2 Brute Force Method

The *brute force approach* breaks an encrypted or hashed password by trying every possible alphanumeric combination exhaustively in an automated fashion using the computer's brute force. For example, if the password size is 64-bit (or 8 characters) or less, there are 2^{64} possible binary combinations -- remember that computers only understand 0s and 1s. The brute force software encrypts/hashes each combination and compares its encrypted/hashed value with the one stored in the password file to find a match. The recovery time of a password using an ordinary computer that can process half a million passwords per second is summarized in Table 11.2.

Characters included	Password length		
	6 characters (48 bits)	7 characters (56 bits)	9 characters (72 bits)
Lowercase letters only	10 minutes	4 hours	4 months
Lowercase and uppercase letters	10 hours	23 days	178 years
All ASCII characters -- letters, numbers, and special characters	18 days	4 years	44,530 years

Table 11.2 Password cracking with brute force (source: businessweek.com)

Exercise 11-2: Discuss at least two important lessons learned from Table 11.2

11.3.3 Dictionary Method

Unlike the brute force approach, the *dictionary* method attempts to recover a password by linking an electronic dictionary file that contains a list of words to password cracking software. This technique is effective because most people come up with passwords made up of certain dictionary terms easy to remember. The software program encrypts each dictionary word or combined words using an encryption function, and compares the result with the encrypted password. In doing so, the cracker can subject each word to a list of altering rules such as alternating uppercase and lowercase letters. Several password hacking tools are available on-line. These programs are necessary evils because system administrators also need them to recover passwords that might have been misplaced.

11.4 SPOOFING

Spoofing, synonymous with *masquerading,* is defined as pretending (or faking) to be someone or something. There are many different forms of spoofing in cybersecurity. Among them, source address spoofing, email spoofing, and web spoofing are demonstrated. DHCP spoofing is also explained later as an example of the man-in-the-middle (MITM) attack.

11.4.1 Source Address Spoofing

IP Spoofing

IP spoofing is one of the most common types of on-line camouflage in which the source IP address of a packet is replaced with a fake one to mask the sender's true identity. Not surprisingly, IP spoofing has been heavily utilized by attackers to coordinate the *Denial of Service* (DOS) attack or to spread spam emails. Two popular methods utilized to hide the source IP are explained here to demonstrate their relative easiness: IP spoofing software and IP proxy server. First, there are software tools that can manipulate the source address of an IP packet and some of them are freely available on the Internet.

Second, IP spoofing can be done by establishing a proxy server. The proxy server can be set up by a firm to improve network performance and also to serve security functions: keeping internal computers anonymous by hiding their IPs; filtering access to restricted Internet sites; scanning inbound/outbound traffic; and caching frequently visited web pages to accelerate their downloading.

The IP proxy function is also offered by third party websites so that ordinary web surfers can keep personal privacy using camouflaged IPs while surfing the Internet. However, the proxy service poses problems as well. For instance, an employee of a company can use the proxy function to bypass the firewall that keeps him/her from visiting rogue or distractive (e.g., social networking) websites. Also, imagine that an attacker turns an innocent computer into a stealth proxy server by secretly planting the IP spoofing function. The attacker, then, can mount an attack on target systems via the compromised host without revealing his/her own identity.

***

Exercise 11-3: Search a web-based proxy service site on the Internet. Experience how you can use the website to spoof your computer's IP address while visiting different websites. Think about pros and cons of utilizing such spoofing service.

***

MAC Spoofing

The MAC address, although permanently imprinted on a network interface card (NIC), can also be spoofed with a software tool that does network address translation. The permanent MAC address on a NIC, however, does not change because of the spoofing. MAC spoofing is generally not as damaging as IP spoofing because the usage of a MAC address is limited to a particular subnet.

MAC spoofing can be abused to disrupt a network or degrade network performance. For example, an attacker can mount an attack on Ethernet switches. As explained, a switch uses its switch table to relay Ethernet frames based on their destination MAC addresses. A switch stores a certain number (e.g., 4096) of MAC entries. An attacker can use a software tool that rapidly generates Ethernet frames with spoofed MAC addresses and releases them to a network. On receiving the fabricated frames, a switch updates their bogus MAC addresses into its switch table and, sooner or later, its table will be filled to the capacity. The maxed out table prevents the switch from updating other legitimate entries. Also, all aged out legitimate MAC entries will be continuously replaced by spoofed MAC entries. From that moment, whenever a frame arrives with a destination MAC address not in the switch table, the switch floods (for broadcasting) the frame to the network. Imagine that this will happen to all interconnected switches of a subnet as a chain event of the MAC spoofing. This will surely result in heavy consumption of network bandwidth, subsequently degrading network performance.

11.4.2 Email Spoofing

With email spoofing, an email sender can disguise/fake its originating email address. Not surprisingly, spammers heavily rely on email spoofing to mask spam sources. Email spoofing can have serious consequences on legitimate e-mail users. For example, imagine a situation in which a spammer floods networks with spoofed emails using an innocent person's email address as the sender. Then, the victim's e-mail inbox will be filled with *undeliverable* emails. Also, the spoof victim may receive angry e-mails from spam recipients or ISPs may terminate his/her email account. Email spoofing can also be done for legitimate reasons (e.g., to represent a company or university where a sender is employed) by changing the settings of a standard email program. To support such legitimate usage, popular online email services (e.g., Yahoo mail, Gmail) offer the email spoofing function.

11.4.3 Web (or HTTP) Spoofing

Web spoofing happens when a person is tricked into communications with a copycat site, not the original website. The bogus website can be infested with malware that gather personal information including user logins and passwords, or perpetrate other evil activities. The fake website closely resembles the original site in design and oftentimes uses a similar URL address making it difficult to tell them apart. As a matter of fact, replicating a genuine website has become so easy because of software tools.

Different tricks have been in use to entice people to spoofed websites. Most notably, spoofed spam that contains a hyperlink to a copycat site can be sent to potential victims. Traditional spam contains messages that are applicable to a broader group of people. However, spam emails are increasingly customized to target victims because spammers can find so much personal information (e.g., high school a person attended) from Internet sites, especially through social networking sites. This fraudulent process of tricking people itself is an example of phishing, the most prevalent form of social engineering (see Section 11.8). Once a user is phished, he/she will end up in a spoofed website.

Besides spam, there are other ways to trick innocent computer users into a spoofed website. Among them are:
- The DNS setup of a user computer (revisit Figure 10.20) can be changed when it falls to a victim of malware.
- The database of a legitimate DNS server can be changed to link a legitimate website URL to the IP address of a spoofed website.
- The hyperlink within a legitimate web server page can be changed to connect to the URL of a spoofed web page.

11.5 DENIAL OF SERVICE

With the Denial-of-Service (DOS) attack, one or more attackers generate enough traffic targeting a particular server -- primarily web server these days -- of a corporation so that the overwhelmed system becomes either unavailable to ordinary users or its service response slows to a crawl. Oftentimes, DOS attacks are politically or ideologically charged these days. With much consumption of network bandwidth, the DOS attack can also debilitate the performance of target networks. For example, there was a report that the average bandwidth consumed by DOS attacks was about 5Gbps and some attacks exceeded 10Gbps.

11.5.1 Pinging and SYN Requests

Among the popular message types used for the DOS attack are *ICMP-based Pinging* and *SYN* requests:

Pinging

A typical form of the DOS attack floods a target server with requests for communications. For example, ping requests produced by the ICMP protocol can be concentrated on a target server. When the server's CPU time is spent on responding to the fraudulent ICMP inquiries, this can significantly undermine the server's capacity to react to other legitimate communications. Due to this risk, the majority of servers on the Internet disable the ping response function these days.

SYN Requests

Flooding the target server with bogus SYN requests to pretend handshaking attempts is another popular form of the DOS attack. The attacker can use a software tool to rapidly produce SYN messages, each carrying a spoofed source IP address, targeting a victim server. The victim server responds with a SYN/ACK and waits for the return of an ACK from the spoofed IP address (see Figure 2.14), which will not happen. This results in the consumption of server resources and limits other regular connections.

Distributed DOS

DOS does not physically harm or infect the target system or network. However, when it takes advantage of flaws in system design (e.g., defects in server OS), the consequence can be more malignant (e.g., server crash). To produce enough traffic and to camouflage attack sources, most DOS attacks are executed in the form of distributed DOS attack (or DDOS) for which evil programs are planted in a number of compromised computers (i.e., zombies) and they launch attacks to a target server at once. The attackers use one or more 'command and control' hosts, frequently called *handlers,* to coordinate attacks on target computers. Chances are that the handlers themselves are also victimized computers. This relationship similar to Figure 11.1 makes it difficult to pinpoint the original source of DDOS attacks. Not surprisingly, the *botnet* explained earlier becomes a perfect platform for such large-scale DDOS attacks.

[**Video Tour 11-1**] Visualization of DDOS attacks

Example: MyDoom

MyDoom was probably one of the most destructive computer worms, affecting computers running Windows OS. It was designed to propagate mainly through email attachments with a deceptive transmission error message on the subject line such as *Mail Delivery System* or *Mail Transaction Failed.* The attached payload triggered three different attacks if activated -- worm, DDOS, and Trojan.

1. It was a worm that generated mass emails. For this, when the mail attachment was activated by a susceptible system user, it located email addresses stored in the infected system and re-sent the worm to the recovered email addresses. This resulted in the worm's effective replications. The warm was also known to copy itself to the file-sharing folder of a popular P2P application for mass spreading.
2. The infected computer systems were instructed to mount a DDOS attack on a particular target website.
3. It also created backdoors on the victim computers by opening a range of TCP ports, which allowed the victims to be remotely accessed and controlled.

It was reported that about one in five emails was attributable to MyDoom when it was most active.

11.5.2 MAC Address Flooding

MAC address flooding is a form of *Denial of Service* (DOS) attack on switches, which disrupts or disables normal switch operations. This form of attack is not as prevalent as DDOS over the Internet, but can pose a serious threat to an enterprise network. The mechanism of switch learning that dynamically updates MAC addresses into the switch table was explained previously (see Section 3.5.3). For MAC address flooding, an attacker can use a program that generates a large number of Ethernet frames with bogus source and destination MAC addresses and send them to a connected switch. On receiving the fabricated frames, the switch surely has no entries of them in its switch table. As a result, the bogus MAC addresses and their connecting ports are updated in the switch table while the frames are flooded to all switch ports.

As a switch table can hold only up to a certain number of entries (e.g., 8000 entries), the switch table will soon max out with both fictitious and legitimate MAC addresses. In that situation, any additional frame -- either legitimate or forged -- arriving with a destination MAC address not in the switch table should be broadcasted. Also, whenever a switch table entry is aged out, it can be replaced by a forged MAC address from the attacker. This form of attack imposes a heavy process burden on the target switch and also the excessive broadcasting degenerates network throughput. Besides, the attacker can capture and view the content (e.g., usernames and passwords) of legitimate frames broadcasted by the victim switch. You should be able to see that MAC address flooding and MAC spoofing go hand-in-hand.

It was emphasized (see Section 3.5.5) that an organization should take preventive measures to lower the chance of such attacks. These include (1) allowing only one or more legitimate MAC addresses of user stations on a switch port; (2) automatic shutdown of a switch port if an unauthorized computer attempts to join it; and (3) shutting off all unused switch ports.

11.6 PACKET SNIFFING

As an attempt to steal information contained in packets, packet sniffing is equivalent to the wire-tapping of telephone lines. Packet sniffing can be especially problematic in wireless networks that broadcast packets. The old-fashioned hub-based network that broadcasts packets is highly vulnerable to packet sniffing as well. On the switched Ethernet (Ethernet relying on switches), packets are better protected from sniffing because of the point-to-point mode of communications between hosts, and broadcasting is used only when it is necessary or inevitable.

Many applications produce data in clear text, making them vulnerable to interceptions. For example, FTP (port 20, 21), Telnet (port 23), SMTP (port 25), POP3 (port 110), IMAP (port 143), and HTTP (port 80) all transmit their data and authentication information in plain text, although more secure siblings (e.g., FTPS for FTP, HTTPS for HTTP, SSH for Telnet) that incorporate SSL encryption are replacing the non-secure protocols. Simply put, exchanging sensitive data in clear text is an invitation for trouble.

Packet Sniffing with Wireshark

Various packet sniffing tools have been in use by practitioners for diagnosis and analysis of network traffic. Among the well-known applications is Wireshark (formerly Ethereal). As a GUI tool, it can sniff PDUs of popular protocols such as Ethernet and WiFi. In particular, by setting a computer's NIC to the *promiscuous mode* (see Section 3.3) rather than the regular mode, Wireshark can capture more packets. The NIC's default setup is to retrieve only the frames with a matching destination MAC address and to drop all the other non-matching frames. However, with the *promiscuous-mode* option activated by Wireshark, a computer's NIC turns off the default setting and copies all arriving frames regardless of their destination addresses. When frames are broadcasted in WiFi, therefore, Wireshark captures them all in the *promiscuous mode*. In the switched Ethernet, however, Wireshark is unable to sniff non-broadcasting frames even in the *promiscuous-mode* mode.

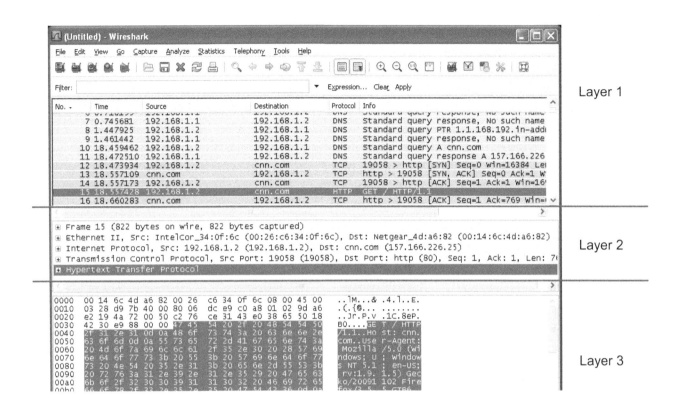

Figure 11.2 Demonstration: Wireshark screenshot.

Figure 11.2 illustrates a screenshot of Wireshark in which the entire window is divided into three layers. The top layer lists captured PDUs; the middle layer displays protocols used for a particular PDU; and the bottom layer shows its actual content in the header and data fields in both hex and plain text. Currently, the top layer highlights message #15 (i.e., http request to *www.cnn.com*). The second layer lists standard protocols (i.e., Ethernet, IP, TCP, and HTTP) used in sending the http request. The third layer displays actual content of PDUs produced by the second layer protocols. Given that HTTP is highlighted in the second layer, the third layer displays the actual HTTP request message.

11.7 PORT SCANNING

The port is an entrance through which application messages leave and arrive (see Section 2.7.3) and attackers want to know which entrance is open for business and can become a target. Some of the well-known ports are listed in Table 2.2. Port scanning is an act of probing the ports of a target host in an automated fashion using software tools. With port scanning, an attacker can obtain valuable information about the target host including:

- Open (or listening) ports waiting for connections
- Service/program currently running on a particular port
- Port accessibility (e.g., possibility of anonymous logins)
- Authentication requirement for a network service
- Target computer's operating system

As a key reconnaissance activity to locate ways into computer systems, port scanning often takes place at the early stage of an attack in order to determine a target system or to gather preliminary information on a target system. For instance, port scanners can send SYN packets to a system and watch SYN-ACK responses to determine its *listening* ports and thus vulnerable to hacking. Port scanning tools can scan both connection-oriented TCP and connection-less UDP ports.

Port Scanning with Zenmap

Zenmap, formally Nmap, is demonstrated in its scanning functions. As a popular utility program, it is designed to help network professionals in exploring, tracking, and securing networks. Zenmap is able to scan a particular target host or an entire network via its command line interface or graphical user interface. It can sweep one or more networks entirely to search hosts that are currently up and determine their system details such as open ports and operating system. Although a very powerful utility tool for network management and security auditing, it can be easily abused by wrong hands when they try to learn about target systems or networks and to locate their vulnerabilities.

As an example, Figure 11.3 demonstrates my home network (192.168.1.0/24) and its scanning results using the Zenmap's *ping scan* function. The screenshot shows the command issued (*Nmap –sP 192.168.1.0/24*) and a summary of the search results in terms of host addresses and their MAC addresses. The home network's IP assignment at the time of scanning is summarized below:

- 192.168.1.1: The home network's default gateway
- 192.168.1.2: A phone adaptor for VoIP over the Internet
- 192.168.1.4: A laptop with Zenmap installed
- 192.168.1.5: Apple's iPad

~~~~~~

Exercise 11-4: Based on the demonstration above, let us try a few scanning options of Zenmap.

1. Set up a network for experiment: Use your home network that has at least one router (e.g., a wireless access router that bundles switch, access point, and router functions – see Figure 8.21) and two hosts. If necessary, two or more students can team up to do this project.

2. Go to the command prompt of your computer and find out the following information:
   - IPv4 address of the hosts:
   - Physical (MAC) address of the hosts:

- Subnet masks:
- IP address of the default gateway:
- IP address of the local DNS server:
- IP address of the local DHCP server:

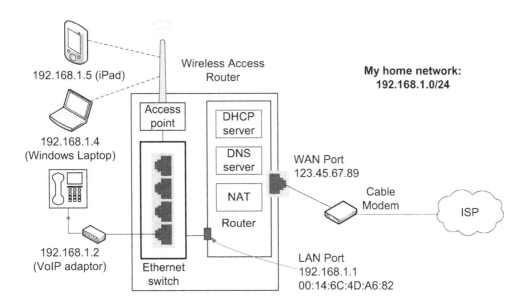

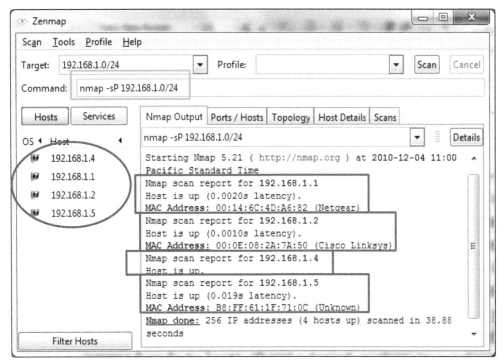

Figure 11.3 Zenmap's *ping scan* of a home network

3. Download Zenmap from http://nmap.org/ and install it in your computer.

4. Survey the home network using *Ping scan*: Ping scan sends an ICMP echo request to every host address of a subnet and any responding host is considered up and running. Assuming that your home network is 192.168.1.0/24, issue '*Nmap –sP 192.168.1.0/24*' (*s* and *P* in the '*-sP*' flag mean *scan* and *Ping* respectively). Then, answer the following questions:

   a) How many IP addresses are scanned by the Ping scan? Explain why.
   b) What IP addresses are found 'up' and what are their corresponding MAC addresses?

Oftentimes, hosts are instructed to ignore ICMP pinging to prevent probing. In this case, probing packets can be sent to a particular port (e.g., 80 for HTTP) of every possible host IP address. With the probing packets destined to reach TCP port 80 (i.e., web server port), chances are that the border router/firewall is instructed not to filter them. Meanwhile, on receiving the packets, computers respond with the TCP's RST (reset the connection) flag as the socket does not exist or closed. Assuming that the home network is 192.168.1.0/24, the command to issue packets to port 80 of all possible hosts in the network is '*Nmap -sP -PT80 192.168.1.0/24.*'

   c) Does it end up with identical results as the ordinary ping scan above?

5. Surveying host ports with *TCP SYN port scan*: An intruder can find potential target hosts with *ping scan* above. Once a target host is determined, the attacker's next move is to identify its vulnerable port(s) through port scanning. Among many different ways of port scanning available on Zenmap, we try *TCP SYN scan*. With the option, Zenmap sends a SYN packet to each port -- the first packet in the three-way TCP handshaking process (review Section 2.7.2). An open port of the target host may respond with SYN/ACK bits flagged. On receiving the SYN/ACK packet, Zenmap sends RST (for reset) rather than ACK to abruptly terminate the 3-way handshaking, but learns that the particular port is listening and open for business. If the SYN packet is sent to a closed port, then the target host responds back with RST, indicating Zenmap that the target host is not listening on the particular port. This port scan is also called *stealth scan* as the 3-way handshaking with open ports is never completed because of the abrupt termination by the attacker, enabling him/her to survey open ports without leaving a trace.

Assuming that the target host's IP is 192.168.1.1, issue the command '*Nmap -sS 192.168.1.1*' for *TCP SYN port scan* (or *stealth scan*).
   a) What information is obtained about the target host with *TCP SYN port scan*?
   b) Zenmap categorizes port status into several types. How many ports are *open* (i.e., inviting for a connection) and *closed* (i.e., rejecting a connection)?

6. Zenmap accepts various *profiles* in addition to text commands (see Figure 11.3). Among them, the '*intense scan*' option tries to capture all information gathered by previously introduced commands. Assuming the target host's IP is 192.168.1.2, enter the IP address into the *Target* field and then choose *intense scan* from the *Profile* options. Observe the automatic formation of the corresponding text command in the *Command* field. Summarize what additional information is gathered by choosing *intense scan*.

11.8 SOCIAL ENGINEERING

Social engineering represents a collection of non-technological approaches designed to manipulate people in an effort to obtain unauthorized access to a target system or to steal private and oftentimes confidential information. For this, perpetrators find clever ways to earn trust from people exploiting their gullibility. Basically, computer users become vulnerable, and it is much easier for attackers to cheat people to obtain sensitive information (e.g., passwords) than hack into a hardened system.

Among various social engineering tactics, the biggest threat is phishing, an act of sending e-mails in an attempt to scam users into surrendering private information for such evil doing as identity theft. A majority of phishing emails carry one or more clickable links or web addresses. Figure 11.4 illustrates clickable phishing emails sent to the author to steal the password of an email account. Not surprisingly, the senders' emails and IP addresses were all spoofed.

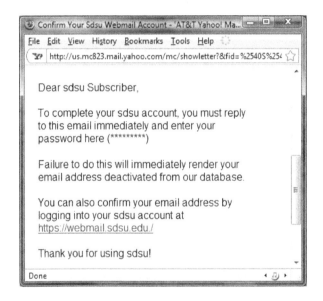

Figure 11.4 Sample phishing emails

It is said that roughly 1 out of every 400 emails is a phishing attack these days. Attackers appear to prefer education institutions whose networks are generally more open than tightly controlled enterprise networks, and students may be more trusting. According to a study, one in every 150 emails is a phishing attack targeting educational institutes. Phishing emails are frequently sent out at night, on weekends, and over holidays to make it more difficult for timely response.

In executing social engineering, perpetrators use clever tactics rather than simply lying in an attempt to buy in or manipulate people's trust. For example, an attacker may cite direct or contextual information about the target system (e.g., server name) or a user (e.g., victim's name), or come up with a realistic scenario to trick a person to release the necessary information. To carry out social engineering, therefore, attackers can do comprehensive reconnaissance of a target and the Internet has become the richest source in finding relevant information (e.g., from business names and addresses to telephone numbers and emails of people). Not surprisingly, security professionals agree that Google's search power has more intrusion potential than any hacking technology. To make online searches more effective, sites such as Google offer both basic and advanced search functions so that parameters can be further elaborated.

Malignant hackers use social engineering along with industrial espionage, snail mail theft, identity theft, and malware to obtain information or to invade a system/network. Security experts agree that social engineering, especially phishing, has become a more serious threat than high-tech driven attacks.

Exercise 11-5: Determining phishing emails from legitimate ones can be difficult. Let's do a "phishing test" that challenges you to tell phishing emails from ordinary ones. Visit the site www.sonicwall.com and search "SonicWALL Phishing IQ Test." Go through the test questions.

11.9 MAN-IN-THE-MIDDLE (MITM)

MITM occurs when an attacker is able to intercept IP packets exchanged between two computer systems and relay (or substitute) them as a middle man. The two communicating parties have no idea of the session hijacking and believe that they are talking to real partners. The attacker may perpetrate it to steal sensitive data or to obtain credentials (e.g., password) in order to intrude into a protected network. Among many different technical approaches, let me demonstrate how a bogus DHCP server can be set up for the MITM attack. Another form of MITM in the WiFi setting is explained later.

MITM with Bogus DHCP Server

A rogue computer located within a subnet can act as a DHCP server providing temporary IP addresses to requesting clients located in the same subnet. When the 'real' DHCP server is not in the same subnet, the request for a dynamic IP has to be relayed to another subnet by a router. In this case, the response from the 'real' DHCP server can take longer than the response from the rogue server, and subsequently the requesting client can choose an IP address and other additional information (e.g., DNS address, subnet mask, and default gateway) the rogue server provides. This is DHCP spoofing!

Now, imagine that the default gateway address offered by the rogue DHCP server is identical to its own IP address. All packets from the victim station will be directed to the rogue computer disguised as a legitimate gateway to the external network, enabling it to view the packets before forwarding them to the real gateway. This is a form of MITM!

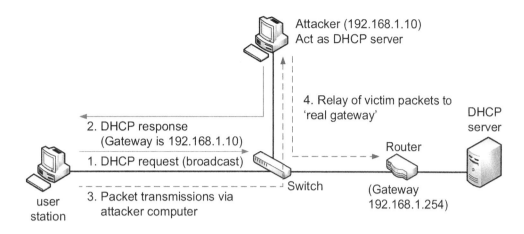

Figure 11.5 DHCP Spoofing and MITM

11.10 SPAM

Spam primarily represents unsolicited commercial emails and more of a nuisance than anything unless it hides harmful and executable malware. Spam is different from the emails computer users opt in to receive, oftentimes as a result of marketing promotions by senders. Spammers generally hide the source with email spoofing and IP spoofing. The original SMTP protocol does not require any form of sender authentication, making spoofing easy. Spammers also use malware-infected PCs (i.e., zombies) to send junk emails containing spoofed source email addresses. It is said that, in 2013, around 70% of all emails were spam, which represents a significant decrease over the 90% of spam reported in 2008.

As a spam-related technology, spam spiders -- also known as spam bots or harvesting bots -- are computer programs that can gather email addresses from various online sources including websites, mailing list archives, message boards, and online forums, and bring them back to their evil master for spamming.

11.11 ZERO-DAY ATTACK

Software programs including operating systems have vulnerabilities that their developers are simply unaware of. In the past, security holes have been reported in numerous applications including web browsers, database programs, multimedia players or plug-ins, office productivity applications, mobile apps, and operating systems. The security holes make it much easier for attackers to inflict damages, most notably by planting malware on targeted systems through the holes. Not surprisingly, cybercriminals are energized to uncover software flaws before vendors find them.

The zero-day attack is an act of exploiting software vulnerabilities that have not been adequately patched by vendors. The zero-day attack is, thus, carried out by attackers before a software company finds vulnerabilities in its products and distributes security fixes. As cybercriminals do not publish the discovery of security flaws in software, determining how long they have been abused is difficult. For example, there was an occasion in which a vulnerability of a popular browser was discovered more than 5 years after its release. When an attacker finds a defect in software, s(he) develops something (i.e., malware) to exploit the weakness and distribute it through such channels as web browsers and emails. Once a victim computer is affected, this will result in damages intended by the malicious attacker (e.g., downloading files to unknown locations).

[Video Tour 11-2] A PC being infected with malware by just visiting a website because of zero-day vulnerability of a web browser

11.12 WIFI THREATS

WiFi networks are easily exposed to various security threats and it is imperative to protect them from such vulnerabilities with adequate security policy and defense mechanisms. Although advanced spread spectrum technologies could make it somewhat harder to intercept WiFi frames, standards publish the spreading codes so that vendors can develop inter-operable WiFi products. This publicity pretty much erases the benefit of spread spectrum technologies in providing security. Some of the threats WiFi networks face today are listed here.

Wardriving

With a utility tool, anyone can capture broadcasted WiFi frames while driving or walking around areas with WiFi signals. Such practice has been popularized in the name of wardriving. Information obtained with wardriving can be exploited (e.g., free Internet access). When such wardriving tool is in the wrong hands (e.g., drive-by attackers), this poses a great deal of security risks.

Denial of service

In WiFi, the source of denial of service can be both intentional (e.g., a hacker's malicious attack) and unintentional (e.g., signal interferences). For example, an attacker may insert bogus frames into a WiFi network to keep legitimate users from accessing it or set up his/her wireless NIC (or WNIC) to send a continuous stream of *clear-to-send* (CTS) frames pretending to be an AP. The CTS frames force all client computers to wait and they are continuously denied network access, resulting in denial of service. To execute this type of attack, the attacker has to gain WiFi access one way or another through tricks such as evil twin AP (see below).

Rogue AP

The rogue AP generally means an AP installed by an employee of a corporation for personal usage without obtaining a formal permission. The rogue AP installed by a non-IT professional can result in inadequate security configuration. This invites trouble when it grants outsiders access to the enterprise network and ultimately to internal resources (see Figure 11.6). Due to the risks, an organization should adopt a policy that restricts unauthorized employees from installing an AP at their own discretion and also deploy a monitoring system that detects such rogue APs.

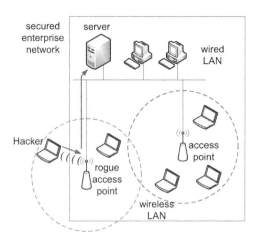

Figure 11.6 Dangers of rogue AP installed by an employee

Man-in-the-middle (MITM)

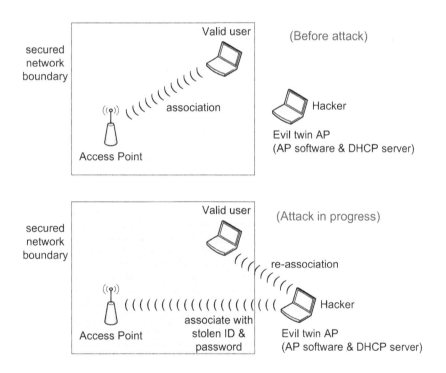

Figure 11.7 MITM with evil twin AP

MITM is among the well-known hacking techniques used by intruders to break into WiFi networks. To begin with, a hacker can use a packet sniffing tool to monitor frames passed between employee computers and APs of a company to capture such information as IP addresses and SSID. Then, the hacker can set up a fake AP that operates at a higher power outside the target organization's physical boundary, but close enough so that the fake AP's signals are pick up by the computers inside. Such AP becomes a different type of rouge AP known as an *evil twin* AP. With the close proximity between the *evil twin* AP and internal stations, they can re-associate themselves with the malignant *evil twin*. With the re-association, the *evil twin* is able to steal the clients' access credentials such as the user name and password. Now the attacker has authentication information necessary to access the corporate network and do damages.

KEY TERMS

Adware
bot
botnet
brute force attack
denial of service (DOS)
DHCP spoofing
dictionary attack
digital signature
distributed denial of service (DDOS)
email spoofing
evil twin wireless access point
fingerprinting
hash function
HTTP spoofing
intense scan

IP spoofing
keystroke logger
MAC address flooding
MAC spoofing
malware
man-in-the-middle (MITM)
masquerading
message digest
packet sniffing
password cracking
payload
phishing
ping scan
port scanning
promiscuous mode
proxy server

rogue wireless access point
social engineering
spam
spoofing
spyware
SYN port scan
Trojan horse
virus
wardriving
web spoofing
Wireshark
worm
Zenmap
zero-day attack

CHAPTER REVIEW QUESTIONS

1. A video player infected with malware was downloaded. When it was installed, the _____ was activated and changed my computer's default DNS setup to direct all DNS inquires to the rogue DNS server maintained by a criminal group.
A) worm
B) Trojan horse
C) macro
D) virus
E) backdoor

2. A malignant hacker sends an email with an attachment that, if activated by an unsuspecting user, searches up to 50 other email addresses stored in the victim's system and relays the same infection code to the email addresses. This must be a _____.
A) worm
B) Trojan horse
C) zombie
D) virus
E) spam

3. Flooding the _____ is a popular approach to trigger denial of service on a target server. Assume that the ICMP protocol on the target server has been disabled.

A) ARP request
B) traceroute message
C) SYN request
D) telnet message
E) DNS request

4. Which attack or pre-attack CAN be done without planting malware or gaining access to a victim's computer or network?
A) worm
B) Trojan
C) denial-of-service
D) port scanning
E) MAC address flooding

5. When an IP packet with a spurious source IP address is crafted in an attempt to bypass a firm's firewall, it is a form of _____.
A) phishing
B) sniffing
C) spoofing
D) fingerprinting
E) backdooring

6. When a computer's NIC (network interface card) is in the *promiscuous* mode, it can perform _____ better.
A) brute force attack
B) denial of service attack
C) dictionary attack
D) packet sniffing
E) IP address spoofing

7. Denial of Service (DOS) attacks are intended to compromise a system's _____.
A) confidentiality
B) availability
C) integrity
D) privacy
E) authenticity

8. Every possible combination of alphanumeric characters can be applied to crack the password of a system. This is a form of _____.

A) brute force attack
B) backdooring
C) dictionary attack
D) packet sniffing
E) hash attack

9. Below email is an example of _____:
A) phishing
B) sniffing
C) man-in-the-middle-attack
D) cracking
E) scanning

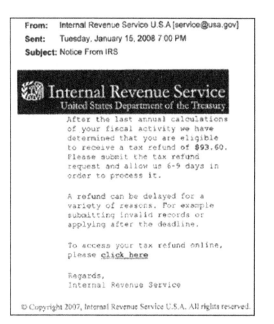

From: Internal Revenue Service U.S.A [service@usa.gov]
Sent: Tuesday, January 15, 2008 7:00 PM
Subject: Notice From IRS

Internal Revenue Service
United States Department of the Treasury

After the last annual calculations of your fiscal activity we have determined that you are eligible to receive a tax refund of $93.60. Please submit the tax refund request and allow us 6-9 days in order to process it.

A refund can be delayed for a variety of reasons. For example submitting invalid records or applying after the deadline.

To access your tax refund online, please click here

Regards,
Internal Revenue Service

© Copyright 2007, Internal Revenue Service U.S.A. All rights reserved.

10. The evil twin AP is a form of _____.
A) man-in-the-middle attack
B) war-driving attack
C) zombie AP attack
D) denial of service attack
E) port scanning attack

11. Which represents a security hazard a corporate employee can create unintentionally?
A) evil twin AP
B) rogue AP
C) master AP
D) war driving AP
E) drive-by hacker AP

12. Wireshark is probably the most popular tool for _____?
A) port scanning
B) packet sniffing
C) man-in-the-middle-attack
D) social engineering
E) spam generating

13. Which may be the LEAST relevant approach to steal someone's password?
A) social engineering
B) port scanning
C) phishing
D) brute force attack
E) keystroke logging

14. Phishing is a form of _____ attack.
A) social engineering
B) port scanning
C) packet sniffing
D) fingerprinting
E) man-in-the-middle

15. Which is NOT a well-known security threat for the WiFi LAN?
A) rogue access point
B) evil twin
C) wardriving
D) denial of service
E) fingerprinting

16. The _____ is a password cracking method that relies on a computer's powerful processing capability.
A) worm
B) social engineering
C) dictionary attack
D) packet sniffing
E) port scanning

17. When an attacker's computer sets up his/her WNIC to broadcast a continuous stream of CTS (clear-to-send) frames, this should result in:
A) man-in-the-middle attack
B) wardriving attack
C) zombie AP attack
D) denial of service attack
E) port scanning attack

18. The hash function is used to derive a _____ from an original message.
A) message digest
B) digital certificate
C) session key
D) public key
E) private key

19. Choose an INCORRECT statement regarding spoofing.
A) Spoofing and masquerading are used synonymously.
B) MAC spoofing is damaging because it shuts down WiFi NICs.
C) IP spoofing is used to conceal the sources of *Denial of Service* (DOS) attacks.
D) Email spoofing is used much by spammers.
E) Phishing becomes an effective tool for web spoofing.

20. When an attacker sets up a DHCP server to steal user information (e.g., password), it is a type of _____ security threat.
A) man-in-the-middle
B) rogue access point
C) evil twin
D) wardriving
E) denial of service

CHAPTER 12 CYBERSECURITY: DEFENSES

12.1 INTRODUCTION

The previous chapter explained common threats that network and computer users face. In this chapter, various defensive measures available to counter the cybersecurity threats and to protect workplaces are explained. In fact, there is no single magic bullet that deters or prevents attacks, and both technological and non-technological (e.g., education and training, security and information assurance policy, security auditing) approaches should be mobilized in combination to mitigate risks. On a related note, security experts have been preaching the *defense-in-depth* principle in which attackers are forced to break multiple lines of defense to be able to penetrate a protected area or a system. For *defense-in-depth*, not only should the entire enterprise network and its subnetworks be protected by several defense mechanisms, but every host should also be hardened by having frequent backups, timely software patches for applications and operating systems, host firewalls, and other authentication and access control reinforcements. This chapter places much focus on technological solutions available to defend networks and computer systems from the rampant security threats. The learning objectives of this chapter are:

- Requirements of cybersecurity and technological solutions
- Firewall and demilitarized zone (DMZ)
- Access control list (ACL)
- Cryptography system
- Digital signatures
- Digital certificates
- WiFi LAN security standards

12.2 DEFENSE REQUIREMENTS AND SOLUTIONS

12.2.1 Security Requirements

In planning and deploying defense measures of cybersecurity, there are fundamental security requirements that need to be perfected: *confidentiality* (*privacy*), *data integrity*, *authentication*, and *access control & authorization*. Although brought up oftentimes throughout the chapters, they are re-visited here.

Confidentiality (Privacy)

Confidentiality means that data in storage or in transit should be readable only by the intended party and must be protected from eavesdropping and snooping. To satisfy this condition, various encryption technologies have been in use. Cryptography protects the confidentially of messages from such threats as packet sniffing and man-in-the-middle attack (MITM).

Data Integrity

Data integrity ensures that data are not changed -- insertion, deletion, or substitution --

accidentally or manipulated maliciously by unauthorized parties. If the data change or tampering takes place, this should be detected by communicating parties. *Frame Check Sequence* (FCS) added at the end of each frame for error detection has been a general approach to detect the data moderation. However, when sensitive information is to be exchanged over the network or downloaded (e.g., open source software) from the Internet, a stronger detection mechanism should be in place to ensure its integrity.

Authentication

Authentication means that the identity of communicating parties and data sources need to be validated. Among various communication sources subject to authentication are:
- People trying to access controlled resources
- Software applications initiating correspondence with other applications
- Servers running online stores to sell products/services to customers
- Intermediary nodes (e.g., routers, switches) that forward network traffic.

Authentication becomes an effective weapon against man-in-the-middle attack and various types of spoofing.

Access Control/Authorization

Access control and *authorization* refer to the process of granting/denying the access of (1) a network; (2) computer systems attached to a network; and (3) resources such as files, directories, and programs available from a computer system. The main requirements are:
- The access policy should be in place at both organizational and sub-organizational (e.g., department) levels and should be enforced through such measures as Access Control List (ACL).
- The invasion of a network and systems by malware should be detected and thwarted.
- A person or user group should be granted limited access to system resources (e.g., data, files and directories of a server) depending on his/her status and qualification. This is a key element of user *identity management* and *directory service* designed to manage accessibility of shared resources.

12.2.2 Technology Solutions

There are a number of technological solutions and protocols designed to improve cybersecurity. Key technologies being widely used to protect networks, computer systems, and data communications are summarized in Table 12.1. It can be seen that *cryptography* and its applied technologies such as *digital signatures* and *digital certificates* (to be explained) play a critical role in supporting the security requirements. There are also other defense measures (e.g., anti-virus, anti-spyware, passwords and passphrases) readers are already familiar with through daily usage. In the remainder of this chapter, the focus is placed on the technological elements of firewall, access control list (ACL), cryptography, digital certificate, and digital signature. Then, standard protocols that take advantage of the technologies are explained.

Security requirements	Popular Technologies
Data Confidentiality	• Cryptography
Data integrity	• Checksum/frame check sequence (FCS) • Digital signatures
Access control/ Authorization	• Access Control List(ACL) • Anti-virus and anti-spyware • Intrusion detection and prevention system • Directory server
Authentication	• Passwords and passphrases • Digital signatures and digital certificates • Smart cards and biometric solutions (e.g., voice and face recognition). • Security tokens

Table 12.1 Security requirements and technology solutions

12.3 FIREWALL

The firewall represents software and/or hardware designed to protect networks and computer systems from intruders by controlling services allowed for inbound (or ingress) and outbound (or egress) traffic; and by monitoring patterns of data flows and of network/system usage by local and remote users. Some of the firewall functions are supported by the router's operating system (e.g., access control list) as well (see Section 12.4).

An organization should set up firewalls as part of the multiple lines of defense strategy:
- A dedicated border firewall filters out unwanted packets at the entry point to a corporate network.
- Each segmented internal network can install its own firewall with an access control tailored to business needs.
- Each enterprise server and workstation should install its own firewall to further fortify host security. Defining protection rules customized for a particular host is relatively easy and they can protect the system, even when the border firewall deployed to safeguard the entire organization or sub-organization is compromised. Hardening each host is crucial, especially with wireless networks becoming a major threat to cybersecurity.

12.3.1 Firewall and DMZ

Figure 12.1 demonstrates an approach designed to guard a corporation from outsiders with border firewalls. For this, the corporate network can be divided into two segments: a *production network* and a *Demilitarized Zone* (or DMZ) *network*. The production network is an internal network that needs secure protections from external threats. The DMZ network, as part of the enterprise network, houses servers -- particularly email and web servers -- that are more exposed to the Internet and thus more vulnerable to attacks than other corporate systems. The two network segments can be separated physically (e.g., separate LAN cabling) or logically (e.g., different subnets). In the case of Figure 12.1, the border router/firewall is dividing the corporate network into two subnets.

Mini-Case: Firewall Router and DMZ

This mini-case is derived from a real company with over $30 million in revenue to demonstrate the firewall router and DMZ, deployed to protect the main production network. The firewall router joins three subnets; one for the Internet connection, one for the main production network, and one for the DMZ network. The production network (192.168.10.0/24) and DMZ (192.168.20.0/24) are given private subnet IDs and the firewall interface with 128.31.10.5, assigned by an ISP, enables access to the Internet. The Internet access line relies on T-1 with bandwidth of 1.54 Mbps. The firm maintains internal DNS servers to provide name resolutions for internal hosts. For Internet routing, packets are sent to the default gateway that is the firewall's LAN port (192.168.10.254).

The firewall router drops IP packets incoming from the Internet unless they are a part of ongoing correspondence initiated by internal hosts -- this is called stateful filtering, explained in the next section. However, certain packets such as e-mails to the SMTP server (192.168.20.241) and HTTP requests to the web server (192.168.20.242) are allowed into the DMZ. Overall, the firewall screen packets based on information in the internet layer (e.g., IP address-based filtering), transport layer (e.g., port-based filtering), and application layer (e.g., malware removal, web content-based filtering).

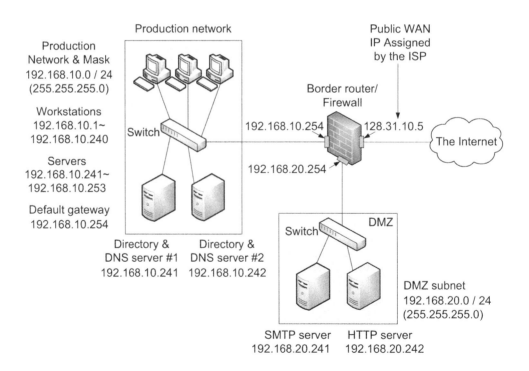

Figure 12.1 Border router firewall and DMZ

The firewall router also performs network address translation (NAT) between the production network and the Internet, and between the DMZ and the Internet. For example, all packets from the production network carry the source address of 128.31.10.5 after NAT. The corresponding responses from the Internet, therefore, contain the destination address of 128.31.10.5 before its translation back into original IP addresses by the firewall router.

When an email arrives from the Internet, the firewall performs packet filtering and forwards it to the SMTP server (192.168.20.241) in DMZ. The SMTP server removes any virus and spam, and forwards the screened emails to the production network's email server. This two email server approach adds an extra security to the internal email system.

Separating Firewall and Border Router

Very often, corporations choose to maintain a dedicated firewall device separated from the border router for several reasons.

a. The corporate network is large and needs a dedicated firewall to take a big load off the router. Also, with its capacity to examine PDUs all the way up to the application layer, a dedicated firewall can be better positioned than a border router to deter sophisticated attacks.

b. A firewall may not support the connectivity (e.g., serial port) necessary for the Internet link. When a firewall does not come with a built-in support for T-1/E-1, Frame Relay, or other high speed WAN connections, it has to rely on a router for such connectivity.

c. Routers support protocols necessary for external packet routing. For example, when two autonomous systems (see Section 10.2.3) are interconnected, their border routers use such exterior gateway protocol as Border Gateway Protocol (BGP) to advertise information necessary for adding routing table entries (see Chapter 6). A firewall, however, may not support the exterior gateway protocol. Possible approaches of their separation are shown in Figure 12.2 in which the second one maintains two connections to the Internet for improved accessibility.

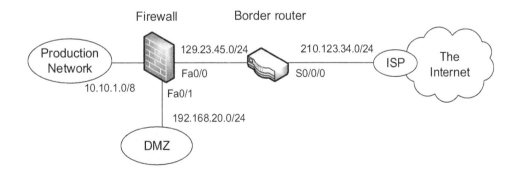

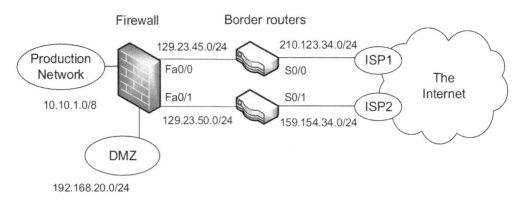

Figure 12.2 Separating firewall and border router(s)

12.3.2 Firewall Functions and Management

Firewall Functions

Firewalls are customizable and commercial products afford selective combinations of security functions in order to better protect networks. A firewall's packet filtering generally relies on information relevant to the internet, transport, and application layers. Listed below are some of the key functions.

- Packet inspection of IP, TCP, UDP, and ICMP protocol data units (PDUs) by applying predefined filtering rules – intrusion prevention
- Inspection of application layer PDUs for email and web content filtering, URL filtering, and malware screening – intrusion prevention
- Intrusion detection to discover potential or on-going attacks such as denial-of-service. This complements the firewall's intrusion prevention capability.
- Network address translation (NAT) to hide internal IP addresses (see Section 5.6.4)
- Implementation of a VPN (virtual private network) gateway for secure tunneling of remote connections over the Internet (see Section 10.3.4)

Managing Firewall

The effectiveness of firewalls in protecting corporate networks requires adequate configuration and management. For this:

- The firewall's packet filtering rules should be synchronized with a firm's security policy that reflects its business requirements. In fact, the business requirements change continuously and the changes should be reflected in the firewall's programming. As a simple example, if a firm decides to introduce a telecommuting program for employees, filtering rules in the firewall should be adjusted to allow remote access to corporate systems (e.g., databases) via VPN connections.

- To ensure that firewall management, corporate security policy, and business requirements are in sync, security audits should be conducted regularly.

- There are general principles of security management that should be closely followed. For example, vulnerabilities in the firewall's operating system should be patched immediately -- in addition to patching workstations and servers -- and TCP/UDP ports that are either unnecessary or subject to threats should be disabled.

- The filtering rules should be developed for ingress (inbound) and egress (outbound) traffic respectively. Ingress filtering is important for obvious reasons -- intrusion prevention and detection. Egress filtering is also critical because:
  o Internal resources and data must be protected from unauthorized copy or stealing over the network.
  o Egress packets with evil codes such as viruses and worms should be stopped from spreading outside the network.
  o Internal systems should be guarded from being exploited (e.g., DDOS attacks by Trojans).

12.3.3 Stateless vs. Stateful Filtering

In terms of the screening process, filtering rules in the list are applied to each arriving packet in sequence from top to bottom. If a matching rule is found, then the rest of screening rules are skipped and the matching statement (e.g., either *permit* or *deny*) decides the fate of a packet. Generally, if no matching rule is found for a packet, it is dropped (i.e., default *deny*) by the firewall. Packet filtering rules are divided into two types: those of *stateless* filtering and of *stateful* filtering.

Stateless Filtering

Stateless filtering is a rather static form of screening in which the firewall examines each packet as an isolated case. For example, a border firewall may be configured to drop (or reject) IP packets outright when they meet any of the following conditions:

- If source IP = 172.16.*.* to 172.31.*.* or 192.168.*.* (Private IP range)
- If TCP destination port = 21 (FTP connection attempt)
- If TCP destination port = 23 (Telnet connection attempt)

Also, the border firewall may be set up to allow IP packets when they satisfy any of the following criteria:

- If destination IP = 161.154.23.59 and TCP port = 80 (Web server connection)
- If destination IP = 161.154.23.59 and TCP port = 25 (Email server connection)

Such stateless packet filtering has limitations. Above all, with the relative easiness of IP spoofing, decision making of incoming packets based on their IP addresses is risky. Also, stateless filtering is not effective in detecting or preventing intrusions as each packet is inspected independently from other inbound or outbound packets.

Stateful Filtering

With stateful filtering, the firewall reviews each packet in the context of previous engagements (e.g., a session), making the packet screening much more effective than stateless filtering. For this, firewalls should maintain *state* information such as TCP sessions and active UDP correspondence in their state table. If arriving packets are consistent with the information stored in the state table, they are allowed to enter networks. Otherwise, they are dropped (i.e., default deny). The following rules demonstrate stateful filtering.

- If a packet's source and destination sockets are in the state table, *pass*.
  Comment: If a packet is a continuation of a previously established session, pass it without further filtering.
- If a packet's source and destination sockets are not in the state table or the packet is not a connection-opening attempt, *drop*.
  Comment: Drop any packet if it is not a part of an ongoing session or if it does not carry a handshaking message.

Although stateful filtering is more powerful than stateless filtering in locating intrusion attempts, both approaches are used in combination to make the screening process more effective.

Exercise 12-1

In this exercise, you will be designing a relatively simple stateless rule-set for a firewall, similar to the example in Figure 12.3.

Rule Name	Direction	Event Name	Protocol	Source Port	Destination Port
Allow HTTP in	inbound	Allow http in	TCP	80	*
Allow HTTPS in	inbound	Allow https in	TCP	443	*
Allow ICMP in	inbound	Allow icmp in	ICMP	*	*
Allow SMTP in	inbound	Allow smtp in	TCP	25	*
Allow POP3 in	inbound	Allow pop3 in	TCP	110	*
....	....	....	....	....	.....

- The "Rule Name" is the name you choose to call a rule.
- The "Direction" is either *inbound* or *outbound*.
- The "Event Name" specifies whether the rule is a(n) *allow* or *deny* rule.
- The "Protocol" column specifies a protocol to which a rule is applied.
- The "Source Port" causes a rule to apply to a specific source port of a packet.
- The "Destination Port" causes a rule to apply to a specific destination port of a packet.

Figure 12.3 A sample packet filtering list

For example, the first rule is named as "Allow HTTP In" and "allows" all inbound HTTP protocol data units (PDUs) when they are encapsulated within a TCP segment containing 80 as the source port and 'any' destination port number. You can guess that they are inbounding packets containing web server responses to web browser requests from internal hosts. It is important to remember that the order of rules is critical in correctly filtering disqualified packets. Having the same set of rules entered in different orders can result in contrary filtering outcomes.

Scenario (XYZ Company)

The XYZ Company has hired you to improve security of their corporate network. They have purchased a firewall that can perform packet inspections. Your job is to configure a static rule set in the firewall that reflects XYZ's business needs. Use best practices to lockdown firewall security as much as possible without blocking legitimate traffic. In developing a static rule set, you are required to develop both outbound (egress) and inbound (ingress) screening rules.

XYZ's business requirements are translated into the following rules.
1) The XYZ company has several remote offices that access the web server placed in the corporate network. Remote office 1 accesses the XYZ's web server on port 80, from the source port of 8724. Remote office 2 accesses the XYZ' web server on port 80, from the source port of 7323.

2) The XYZ Company wants to restrict its employees' ability to send ICMP messages from inside its network to the Internet.

3) XYZ needs to allow its employees to check their e-mails on port 110. The company's email server uses POP3 and is located within its corporate network.

4) XYZ has an SMTP email server operating in its corporate network. The mail server sends and receives emails using the SMTP's default port.

5) XYZ wants to deny all other traffic coming into its corporate network.

12.4 ACCESS CONTROL LIST

Ordinary routers also come with built-in capacity to maintain the *Access Control List* (ACL), a collection of packet filtering rules. With the ACL, a router grants or denies IP packets based on the header information of the transport and internet layer PDUs. More specifically, the ACL-based filtering primarily relies on:
- Source and destination IP addresses
- Source and destination TCP/UDP port numbers
- Packet protocol (e.g., ICMP, UDP)
- ICMP message types (e.g., ping, traceroute)
The screening rules in the ACL are generally stateless. The static nature of ACL rules and their

dependence on IP address and port information for packet filtering limit a router's effectiveness as a serious device for network protection.

12.4.1 How Many ACLs?

For better customization of filtering rules, an ACL is created for each router port in use. Also, just as with the dedicated firewall, an ACL list should be developed for ingress (inbound) and egress (outbound) traffic respectively. For example, if a border router is using two WAN ports (S0/0/0 and S0/0/1), then 4 customized ACLs should be created to filter packets. The list of active ACLs are:
- ACLs for interface S0/0/0
    1. ACL for inbound traffic (ACL#1)
    2. ACL for outbound traffic (ACL#2)
- ACLs for interface S0/0/1
    3. ACL for inbound traffic (ACL#3)
    4. ACL for outbound traffic (ACL#4)

12.4.2 ACL Filtering vs. Packet Routing

When the border router performs both ACL-based packet filtering and packet routing, it becomes a natural question regarding which decision should be done first for a particular packet: filtering decision or routing decision? In general, there is a difference between inbound (arriving) and outbound (departing) packets:

- For an inbound packet, its filtering decision is performed before the routing decision. This action is intended to stop any harmful packet at the door before it has any chance of getting into the internal network. Thus, the order is:
    1. A packet arriving at a router interface is screened against the rules of inbound ACL.
    2. Once the packet is permitted to pass, its forwarding path is determined referring to the routing table.
    3. The packet is released through the corresponding exit interface for forwarding.

- For an outbound packet, its routing decision is performed prior to the filtering decision. That way, an outbound packet is screened against the ACL tailored to a particular exit interface. Thus, the order is:
    1. The exit port (or interface) of an IP packet is determined first referring to the routing table.
    2. The packet is then filtered according to the egress ACL rules customized for the exit port.
    3. If the filtering decision is 'pass', the packet is released through the exit port.

12.5 CRYPTOGRAPHY

Cryptography is a procedure that transforms a message into an unreadable code. The technology is highly versatile and heavily utilized to attain security requirements of confidentiality, integrity, and authentication.

12.5.1 Cryptography System

Basic Elements

A cryptography system is composed of four elements: plaintext, ciphertext, cipher, and key.

- The *plaintext* is an original unencrypted message in various formats including text, voice, data, and video. The *ciphertext* is an encrypted plaintext and therefore unreadable unless decrypted.

- The *cipher* is an encryption algorithm used to convert plaintexts to ciphertexts and vice versa. *Transposition* that simply reorders the letters of a message and *substitution* that replaces one character with another are simple examples of the cipher. Today's cipher standards (e.g., DES, RC4, RSA) are more complicated and they are divided into two types: *stream ciphers* and *block ciphers*. The stream cipher encrypts a message bit by bit (i.e., bit-level encryption) and the block cipher does the encryption per block of a certain size (e.g., 128 bit block). The majority of standard ciphers are block ciphers.

- The *key* represents a value the cipher utilizes to encrypt/decrypt a message. A ciphertext is, therefore, compromised when a third party obtains the 'secret' encryption key one way or another. The cryptography system uses a fixed key size. These days, a key size of at least 100 bits is recommended to safeguard encrypted messages. For example, web browsers use at least 128 bits for secure communications. With the advancement of computers in their processing speeds, it takes less time to recover secret keys and longer keys will be necessary soon.

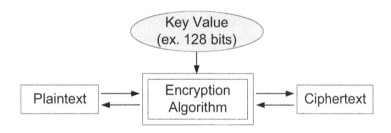

Figure 12.4 Components of cryptography

How It Works

A super simple example is used to demonstrate the relationship among the four cryptography elements -- assuming that only one secret key is used. For this, think of the following scenario:
- Two parties exchange confidential information.
- The plaintext is 34105.
- Both parties know that the secret key value is 3.
- Encryption algorithm (cipher) is "To add the key value to each plaintext digit".

Applying the key value and encryption algorithm to the plaintext results in the ciphertext of 67438. Its decryption requires a reverse process -- subtract 3 from each digit of the ciphertext. Even if somebody intercepts the ciphertext, the interceptor is unable to obtain the plaintext unless he/she knows the key value. Of course, in reality, encryption keys are much longer and algorithms (ciphers) are more complicated in order to make encryptions difficult to break.

Keys can be generated randomly by encryption software or derived from user passwords or passphrases. As an example of the password/passphrase-derived key, a password (or passphrase) is entered into an AP and client hosts during the initial setup of a WiFi home network. Then, the password is used to derive a secret key that is necessary to encrypt data. Table 11.1 demonstrates how a variable size, user password is converted into a fixed-size key value by a built-in algorithm (e.g., MD5 hash function).

12.5.2 Symmetric-Key Cryptography

Cryptography standards use either *symmetric* or *asymmetric* keys. With the symmetric-key cryptography system such as DES (Data Encryption Standard), 3DES, AES (Advanced Encryption Standard), RC4, Blowfish, and IDEA (International Data Encryption Algorithm), a *secret key* is shared by communicating parties to encrypt and decrypt data. The key, therefore, should remain confidential to protect encrypted data. A drawback of the secret key-based encryption is that, when multiple parties need to exchange data over the network using one secret key, its distribution and subsequent management becomes problematic. A distinctive advantage of the symmetric key system is its fast throughput in encrypting and decrypting data, putting less process burden on network nodes.

As a type of secret symmetric-key, the *session* key is used widely for secure exchange of data during a particular session (e.g., TCP session) only. For example, browser-enabled online transactions (e.g., online banking, electronic commerce) rely on session keys to encrypt and decrypt exchanged data. For this, randomized and symmetric session keys are created by web browsers and then shared with web servers for secure client-server communications.

12.5.3 Asymmetric-Key Cryptography

How It Works

The asymmetric cryptography system such as RSA uses a *private* and *public* key pair. This means that it takes 2 *private* and *public* key pairs (i.e., one pair for each communicating party) when asymmetric cryptography is used for secure data exchange over the network. The private key is kept by the owner and not shared with anybody else. Meanwhile his/her public key information is available to public just like phone numbers in the telephone directory. To maintain the confidentiality of a message, the sender encrypts it with the receiver's public key, and then the receiver decrypts it with his/her own private key.

With asymmetric cryptography, a message encrypted with a public key cannot be decrypted with the same public key. Likewise, a plaintext encrypted with a private key cannot be decrypted with the same private key. If a sender uses his/her own private key to encrypt a message, then the receiver can decrypt the ciphertext using the sender's public key, although this practice defeats the purpose of keeping message confidentiality because anybody can decrypt the ciphertext (This can be used to authenticate the sender, though).

Pros and Cons

The asymmetric-key system has its own share of pros and cons. Among key advantages are:
- With no need for secret key sharing, there is little chance that the private key is exposed, making asymmetric encryption significantly more secure than the symmetric counterpart.
- The public key of a person (or a system) does not need to be distributed through secure channels. This also means that the private and public key pair of the person (or the system) does not need to be replaced frequently out of security concerns.
- The owner of a private-public key pair can use his/her private key to produce *electronic autographs* (or *digital signatures*) for authentication. The digital signature takes advantage of the fact that only one person in the world owns a particular private key. This makes the asymmetric key system an effective vehicle in ensuring message confidentiality and in undertaking sender authentication.

The asymmetric key system has disadvantages as well. Above all, it has a much longer key size than the symmetric system. For example, RSA, one of the most popular asymmetric systems use 1024 or 2048 bit keys, compared to 128 or 256 bit symmetric keys. The longer key makes the encryption and decryption of a message much slower than the symmetric-key system. For example, it is said that RSA takes at least 100 times more computations than DES (Data Encryption Standard), the leading symmetric cryptography system.

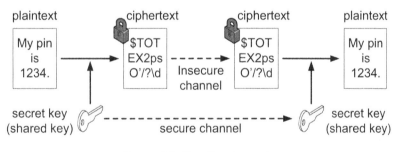

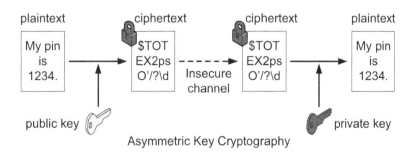

Figure 12.5 Symmetric-key vs. asymmetric-key cryptography

12.5.4 Hybrid Approach

Because of strengths and weaknesses inherent to both symmetric and asymmetric encryption technologies, they are often used in tandem to complement each other's weaknesses and to make the most of their strengths. Because the main problem of asymmetric encryption is its slow performance compared to the symmetric counterpart, a hybrid solution is used often for which:

- The symmetric key (e.g., session key) encryption is utilized for encrypting/decrypting lengthy messages to ensure their *confidentiality*.
- The asymmetric key encryption is applied in order to exchange the symmetric key in a secure manner; to *authenticate* communicating parties and exchanged messages; and to check message *integrity*.

Let's take a look at a scenario regarding how both symmetric and asymmetric encryption systems can work in concert. Imagine a situation in which a confidential document should be exchanged between two parties over the Internet. Then:

1. The sender can encrypt the document using a symmetric session key, which is not processing intensive.
2. If the receiver does not have the symmetric session key already, the sender encrypts it with the receiver's public key. Encrypting a relatively short session key (e.g., 128 bits) with the public key does not bear much process burden on the computer.
3. Both the symmetric-key encrypted document (ciphertext) and the asymmetric-key encrypted session key are dispatched to the receiver.
4. On their arrival, the receiver decrypts the encrypted session key using his/her own private key.
5. The decrypted session key is then used to decode the ciphertext back to the original document.

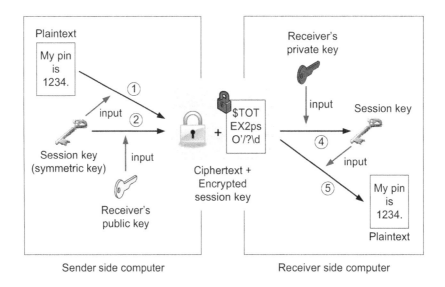

Figure 12.6 Hybrid usage of symmetric and asymmetric cryptography

As you can see, the hybrid solution is intended to make the most of the two different cryptographic systems to securely and effectively exchange messages and the overall procedure is summarized in Figure 12.6.

Pretty Good Privacy (PGP) is a popular commercial software product that adopts the hybrid (asymmetric + symmetric) technology to protect texts, files, directories, and e-mails primarily on the Windows platform. *GNU Privacy Guard (GPG)* is the PGP's open source version freely available and also interoperable with PGP.

12.6 DIGITAL SIGNATURES

The digital signature is a high-tech solution for 'message' and 'sender' authentication. In computer networks, user authentication is commonly done through the verification of passwords or passphrases. However, passwords can be accidentally revealed, forgotten, or even worse, stolen in various manners as previously explained. For this reason, a more reliable authentication process/technology is required oftentimes between communicating parties. This is where the *digital signature* (or *electronic autograph*) comes in as the electronic equivalence of the hand-written signature. Figure 12.7 demonstrates a scenario on how the *digital signature* works to authenticate engaging parties and exchanged messages. In that scenario, it is assumed that each party has his/her own public-private key pair.

On the sender side:

1. A sender's computer uses a hash function (e.g., MD5) to compute a hash value (e.g., 128 bits for MD5) from the original message to be transported. The hash value is also called a *message digest* as it is derived from the source message.
2. The *message digest* is encrypted with the sender's private key. The output becomes a sender's *digital signature* because it can be created only by the sender's private key – making it perfect for sender *authentication*. Observe that the digital signature changes with the original message.
3. The original message and digital signature is then encrypted with a symmetric session key generated by the sender's computer.
4. The session key itself is encrypted with the receiver's public key.
5. The encrypted *original message, digital signature,* and *session key* are dispatched to the receiver's computer over the Internet.

On the receiver side: On accepting the encrypted units from the sender,

6. The encrypted session key is first decrypted by the receiver's own private key (reverse step 4).
7. Using the restored session key, the original message and digital signature are decrypted (reverse step 3). Thus, message *confidentiality* has been achieved.
8. The restored digital signature is decrypted by sender's public key and the original message digest is obtained (reverse step 2).
9. The receiver hashes -- using the same hashing function -- the original message to generate his/her own message digest.

10. The receiver compares the delivered message digest (i.e., hash value) with the locally-produced one. Their matching confirms that the original message has not been tampered, confirmation of *message integrity*. The matching also validates that the sender indeed owns the public-private key pair -- confirmation of *sender authentication*.

This somewhat complex process, summarized in Figure 12.7, is automatically executed by computer systems.

Sender's computer

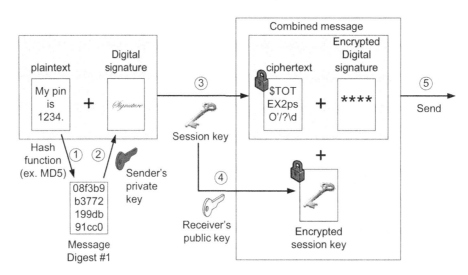

Receiver's computer

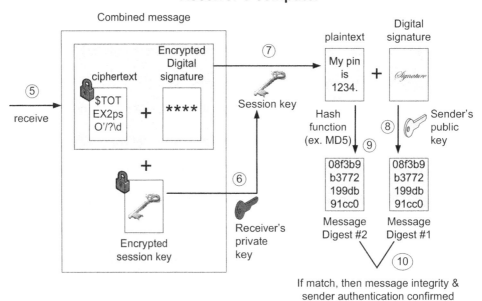

Figure 12.7   Usage of a digital signature

12.7 DIGITAL CERTIFICATES

12.7.1 Digital Certificates

The *digital certificate* is a digital equivalent of the ID card and is used in conjunction with the asymmetric encryption system. More specifically, the digital certificate verifies the holder of a particular *public key* (not private key) and has become an extremely popular means to authenticate parties communicating over the network. By certifying the true owner of a public key, it is intended to safeguard innocent people/systems from falling victim to high-tech scamming. Remember that a digital certificate is not an indicator of the owner's integrity since malicious hackers or con artists can certainly own a digital certificate. The certificate simply validates who the real owner of a particular public key is.

Digital certificates are sold by *certificate authorities* (CAs) through the *public key infrastructure* (or simply PKI) servers. The PKI represents a set of software (e.g., digital certificate), hardware (e.g., server), and procedures designed to protect online users based on the public-private key encryption system. The PKI's main responsibility is to create, distribute, and manage digital certificates in order to safeguard people's data and financial transactions over the public network. A firm may choose to set up its own PKI server to issue digital certificates to employees instead of purchasing them from a *certificate authority* as a trusted third party.

Figure 12.8 Information items of X.509 and its simplified view (Chrome)

The digital certificate contains such information as the owner of a particular public key, certificate's serial number, certificate's expiration, the issuer (i.e., certificate authority), and the certificate authority's digital signature in order to prevent spoofing. X.509 from *International*

403

Telecommunications Union (ITU) is a widely accepted standard of the digital certificate. Figure 12.8 lists key information items contained in the X.509 standard. Remember that the digital certificate does not contain the private key of a person.

12.7.2 Certificate Authorities

Certificate Authorities (CAs) are both public and private institutes that sell digital certificates and therefore a digital certificate is only as good as its CA. In other words, if a CA is not a reliable or trusted business, digital certificates issued by the CA cannot be trusted either. There are a number of highly trusted commercial CAs including VeriSign, Microsoft, and America Online and web browsers list trusted CAs. CAs can revoke a person's digital certificate for various reasons including its expiration, compromised private key, and policy violation. Revoked certificates are placed in the *certificate revocation list (CRL)*. The verifier (e.g., user computer) of a digital certificate must check with its issuer to determine if the certificate is on the CRL list. Without the CRL check, the integrity of a digital certificate is not guaranteed.

Figure 12.9 demonstrates a scenario of how the digital certificate is used by a verifier for the authentication of an applicant who initiates communication (e.g., e-commerce transactions) over the network. In this scenario, the applicant and the verifier can be a user computer and a server (e.g., online store or bank) respectively. Alternatively, the applicant can be a server and the verifier is a client computer. In fact, in today's online environment, client computers (with web browsers) mostly become verifiers that check servers' authenticity through their digital certificates.

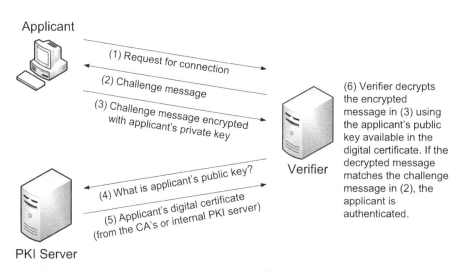

Figure 12.9   Scenario: digital certificate-based authentication

Example: Certificate authorities trusted by web browsers

Web browsers, on the client side, maintain a list of certificate authorities they trust. Figure 12.10 demonstrates the list of CAs trusted by Firefox and Google Chrome. The digital certificate assures a server web site's authenticity and, thus, plays an important role in protecting consumers when they engage in e-commerce transactions.

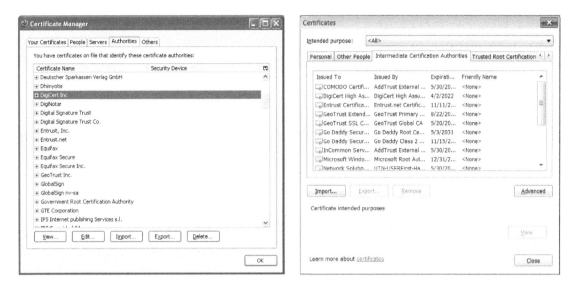

Figure 12.10 Trusted CAs: Firefox (left) and Chrome browsers

If a web browser, triggered by a user input, attempts engagement with a web server (e.g., amazon.com), the web server returns its digital certificate to the browser for server authentication. Then, the browser validates it by contacting the CA's PKI server that issued the certificate and by examining the certificate revocation list (CRL). If a CA itself is not recognized by a browser (e.g., see Figure 12.11a) or if there is a problem with a presented certificate (e.g., expired or revoked certificate, revocation information not available -- see Figure 12.11b), the browser alerts the user. On facing such a warning, it is generally safer not to click through the website unless the user positively identifies and trusts the server site.

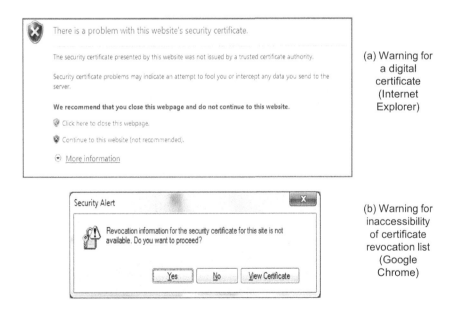

(a) Warning for a digital certificate (Internet Explorer)

(b) Warning for inaccessibility of certificate revocation list (Google Chrome)

Figure 12.11 Sample warnings associated with digital certificates

12.8 SECURITY PROTOCOLS

The cryptography, digital signature, and digital certificate technologies perform their intended functions as a part of security protocols. Many different security protocols have been introduced, each with its own strengths and weaknesses. For example, the transport layer's SSL protocol has been the de facto standard used to protect HTTP-based transactions (HTTP + SSL = HTTPS) (see Section 10.3.7). IPSec (IP security) in the Internet layer was also explained (see Section 10.3.6) as a protocol particularly important for VPN and IPv6. Some of the popular security protocols defined in each layer are:

- Application layer: S/MIME, PGP
- Transport layer: SSL
- Internet layer: IPSec
- Data link layer: WPA, WPA2

Cybersecurity is strengthened when a defense system employs protocols to cover multiple layers. However, as a tradeoff, this results in compromised performance of computer systems and the network due to the increased processing burden. IT professionals, therefore, should find a sweet spot that balances the associated benefits and risks while planning for cybersecurity. In the rest of this section, data link layer protocols designed to guard the ubiquitous WiFi LANs are explained in more detail.

12.8.1 WiFi Security Standards

Three security standards have been introduced for WiFi networks.
- Wired Equivalent Privacy (WEP)
- WiFi Protected Access (WPA)
- IEEE 802.11i (also known as WPA2)

Wired Equivalent Privacy (WEP)

WEP, the first generation and legacy standard introduced in 1997, was intended to offer WiFi security comparable to that of wired networks, although it has been proved otherwise. Both the AP and the associated client stations share a secret key that is manually entered into them for client authentication and encryption of exchanged data. WEP delivers the level of security that can deter casual snooping. However, the shared secret key can be revealed using software tools that perform such discovery methods as brute force search or dictionary-based search (refer to Section 11.3). WEP is especially vulnerable if it uses short encryption keys such as 40 bits -- instead of at least 128 bits. Due to the inherent risks, WEP has been replaced by WPA and then WPA2. Simply speaking, setting up WiFi LANs with WEP should be avoided.

WiFi Protected Access (WPA and WPA2)

WPA and WPA2 offer much stronger security than WEP. With WPA and WPA2, WiFi nodes initially use the same pre-shared key -- just as WEP does -- entered into both the AP and the user stations. As pre-shared keys are oftentimes derived from user-provided passwords/passphrases, they must be long and complicated. Unlike WEP that uses fixed pre-shared keys, those of WAP/WPA2 are dynamically changed by APs. That is, the WAP/WAP2-enabled AP produces a new pre-shared key after a specific time interval (e.g., every 10 minutes) or after exchanging a certain number of frames. This dynamic and periodic alteration of key values makes WAP/WAP2-guarded networks more difficult to penetrate than WEP-based ones.

WPA is not an official IEEE standard as it was intended to be an interim solution for transition from WEP to WPA2 – the IEEE 802.11i standard offering government-grade security. The network in compliance with IEEE 802.11i is known as a Robust Security Network (RSN) as it allows WiFi access only to authorized users. One key difference between WPA and WPA2 is the choice of encryption technology, making WPA2 more secure than WAP. As a temporary solution, WAP relies on the same encryption technology as WEP and, thus, a wireless NIC that supports WEP can be updated to WPA without replacing the WNIC. The backwards compatibility was a reason for having WPA as an interim solution. WAP2, meanwhile, is not upgradeable from WEP or WPA, and should be built into a WNIC. Although WPA2 offers a higher security assurance, WPA still remains a viable solution for WiFi users if strong passphrases/passwords (e.g., 13 characters or more) are used to withstand password cracking attempts.

Enterprise Mode vs. Personal Mode

WPA and WPA2 can be implemented in two different modes: *enterprise mode* and *personal mode*. Their differences are listed below.

1. Personal mode (also known as Pre-shared Key or PSK Mode).
   - Designed to offer WiFi security for homes and small offices
   - Supports either *WPA-Personal* (or *PSK-WPA*) or *WPA2-Personal* (or *PSK-WPA2*)
   - The AP is responsible for the authentication of client stations and key management (e.g., dynamic creation of new keys).

2. Enterprise mode
   - Designed to offer WiFi security for corporations
   - Supports either *WPA enterprise* or *WPA2 enterprise*
   - Uses a *central server* (refer to Figure 8.17) for authentication and key management
   - The central server ensures consistency in client authentication.
   - The central control of authentication reduces cybersecurity risks resulting from mismanaged APs.

~~~~~~

Example: WiFi Security in Windows OS

As an example, WiFi security options available on Windows OS are examined. Figure 12.12a shows a screenshot in which users can choose different authentication options including: open authentication, shared key authentication with WEP, WPA (i.e., WPA-Personal and WPA-Enterprise), and WPA2 (i.e., WPA2-Personal and WPA2-Enterprise). The network security key -

- password -- entered by a user in Figure 12.12b is used to derive a pre-shared key when the WPA2-personal standard is chosen. Figure 12.12b also indicates that AES (Advanced Encryption Standard) is an encryption technology option available under the WPA2-Personal mode.

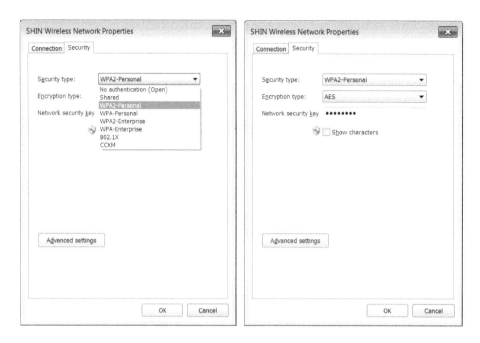

(a) Security standards   (b) Network key (i.e., password)

Figure 12.12 WiFi security standards (Windows)

Table 12.2 summarizes the WiFi security standards and their technical differences in authenticating network nodes and providing data confidentiality. Although not a security standard, the *Open* (i.e., no shared key) option is also included in the summary table.

Exercise 12-2: Answer below questions.

1. What are differences between WEP and WPA/WPA2?
2. What are differences between the personal (or PSK) mode and the enterprise mode of WPA/WPA2?
3. How does WPA2 differ from WPA?
4. What is the WEP's critical problem?
5. What information is exchanged during open authentication?
6. What is RADIUS?
7. What is a popular approach to derive a pre-shared key in WEP/WPA-Personal/WPA2-Personal?
8. With the pre-shared key (PSK) approach, which network nodes are configured with a password/passphrase?

9. What are the two key functions of WiFi security standards such as WEP and WPA?

Security Standards	Authentication of a station	Message privacy	Note
Open (no shared key)	Use SSID and clear text	No message encryption	No meaningful security measure
WEP (with pre-shared key)	The same password is entered into both client stations and the AP. Client stations are authenticated by the pre-shared key derived from the password.	The pre-shared key is used to encrypt messages. The pre-shared key remains the same, making it vulnerable to decipher attacks.	Avoid WEP and use at least WPA.
WPA-Personal	The same password is entered into both client stations and the AP. Client stations are authenticated by the pre-shared key derived from the password.	Once authenticated, the shared key changes periodically according to the pre-set time interval. Messages are encrypted with the continuously changing key, resulting in better confidentiality than WEP.	Mostly (not Fully) compliant to IEEE802.11i security requirements Should use a longer and evasive password for better defense from possible attacks.
WPA-Enterprise	Client stations are authenticated by an authentication server via such protocol as RADIUS.		
WPA2-Personal & WPA2-Enterprise	Works similar to WPA-Personal and WPA Enterprise, but there are some differences between them (e.g., preferred authentication protocol). Wireless NICs supporting only WEP/WPA are not upgradeable to WPA2.		Fully compliant to IEEE802.11i security requirements Achieves Robust Security Network (RSN)

Table 12.2 Summary of WiFi security standards

KEY TERMS

3DES
access control

access control list (ACL)

Advanced Encryption Standard (AES)

anti-virus
anti-spyware
asymmetric-key encryption
authentication
authorization
biometric solution
block cipher
Blowfish
border firewall
certificate authority
certificate revocation list
(CRL)
checksum
cipher/ciphertext
confidentiality/privacy
content filtering
cryptography
Data Encryption Standard
(DES)
data integrity
defense in depth
demilitarized zone (DMZ)
digital certificate
digital signature

egress filtering
encryption key
fingerprinting
firewall
frame check sequence (FCS)
GNU Privacy Guard (GPG)
hash function
IEEE802.11i
ingress filtering
International Data Encryption
Algorithm (IDEA)
intrusion detection
intrusion prevention
message digest
packet filtering
passphrase
password
personal mode
plaintext
pre-shared key (PSK)
Pretty Good Privacy (PGP)
private key
production network
public key

public key infrastructure (PKI)
RC4
Robust Security Network
(RSN)
RSA
secret key
session key
smart card
stateful filtering
stateless filtering
stream cipher
symmetric-key encryption
URL filtering
WiFi Protected Access (WPA)
WiFi Protected Access2
(WPA2)
Wired Equivalent Privacy
(WEP)
WPA-Enterprise
WPA- Personal
WPA2-Enterprise
WPA2- Personal
X.509

CHAPTER REVIEW QUESTIONS

1. Which is considered a stateful firewall filtering rule?
A) If source and destination sockets are in the connection table, then PASS the packet.
B) If protocol = TCP and destination port number = 25, then PASS the packet.
C) If IP address = 10.47.122.79, protocol = TCP, and destination port number = 80, then PASS the packet.
D) If protocol = UDP, then DROP the packet.
E) If protocol = ICMP, then DROP the packet.

2. The router's Access Control List examines PDUs of the following protocols EXCEPT (choose the least relevant):

A) IP
B) TCP
C) UDP
D) DNS
E) ICMP

3. Which is CORRECTLY paired in terms of security requirements and technology solutions?
A) data confidentiality --- access control list
B) data integrity --- anti-spyware
C) access control --- frame check sequence
D) authentication --- digital signature
E) access control --- cryptography

4. Choose a CORRECT statement on the WPA standard.

410

A) WPA provides the most advanced WiFi security.
B) WPA comes only in the enterprise mode that uses central authentication servers.
C) Its encryption key in a WiFi network changes periodically.
D) WPA's official standard is IEEE802.11i.
E) WPA is as weak as WEP in protecting WiFi networks.

5. The PKI (Public key infrastructure) is maintained and operated by _____.
A) governments
B) certificate authorities
C) Internet engineering task force
D) Internet service providers
E) WAN service providers

6. When a digital signature is used for authentication, a session key can be utilized concurrently to:
A) generate a message digest by the sender.
B) encrypt the original message and digital signature.
C) generate a digital signature by the sender.
D) generate a digital signature by the receiver.
E) generate a message digest by the receiver.

7. Choose an ACCURATE statement on asymmetric vs. symmetric key encryption.
A) In asymmetric key encryption, both parties encrypt and decrypt messages with the same single key.
B) In symmetric key encryption, each party should have two keys -- a public key and a private key.
C) In asymmetric key encryption, only one key must be shared between communicating parties.
D) Symmetric keys are longer than asymmetric keys.
E) Asymmetric key encryption is slower than symmetric key encryption.

8. An applicant is sending an encrypted message with her/his digital signature appended. To authenticate the sender, the verifier (message receiver) uses the _____.
A) private key of the verifier
B) public key of the verifier
C) private key of the applicant
D) public key of the applicant
E) session key

9. The Public Key Infrastructure (PKI) and X.509 are necessary elements of the _____ technology.
A) digital signature
B) digital certificate
C) public key encryption
D) symmetric key encryption
E) message digest

10. The *digital certificate*:
A) is an alternative authentication method when encryption is unavailable.
B) validates the owner of a particular public key.
C) transports a private key to the owner.
D) is a method to securely exchange session keys.
E) is an electronic receipt of an online transaction.

11. The digital signature attached to a message can authenticate:
A) both the message sender and message itself
B) the message sender only
C) the message only
D) both the message sender and receiver
E) both the message receiver and message itself

12. _____ is a security standard developed for 802.11 WiFi LANs.
A) Wired equivalent privacy (WEP)
B) Secure socket layer (SSL)
C) Packet acknowledgments

D) Service set identifier(SSID)
E) Pretty good privacy (PGP)

13. Improving host security through anti-virus software and a firewall is _____.
A) host firewalling
B) host self-defense
C) host hardening
D) host patching
E) host demilitarizing

14. When a person has a 20MB message to transmit electronically, how can she add a digital signature for sender authentication?
A) By scanning her handwriting signature
B) By encrypting the message with her own public key
C) By encrypting the message with her own private key
D) By encrypting the message digest with her own public key
E) By encrypting the message digest with her own private key

15. Which is NOT a technology solution for user or message authentication?
A) digital signature
B) digital certificate
C) password/passphrase
D) voice recognition
E) access control list

16. Cryptography can be a tool for:
A) confidentiality and authentication
B) authentication and integrity
C) integrity and confidentiality
D) confidentiality, authentication, and integrity
E) confidentiality

17. Which is CORRECT in describing the DMZ?
A) The DMZ and production networks generally belong to a single subnet.

B) SMTP email and HTTP web servers are frequently placed in the DMZ.
C) The DMZ and production networks should be physically separated.
D) Servers in the DMZ should use public IP addresses.
E) The border router is unable to perform network address translation when the DNZ is set up.

18. Firewalls can undertake the following functions EXCEPT:
A) packet inspection and filtering
B) network address translation
C) detection of denial-of-service attacks
D) packet filtering based on application layer information such as web content and URL addresses
E) provision of digital certificates

19. The WPA standard has one major advantage over WAP2. What can it be?
A) WPA offers stronger authentication than WPA2.
B) WPA offers better quality of service than WPA2.
C) Wireless NICs that support WEP can be upgraded to WPA, but not to WPA2.
D) WPA has been standardized by IEEE but WPA2 has not.
E) WPA is supported by more WiFi standards including 802.11g and 802.11n than WPA2.

20. Which information may NOT be included in a digital certificate?
A) Owner's private key
B) Issuer company
C) Expiration date
D) Name of its owner
E) Owner's public key

GLOSSARY

Access control list (ACL): ACL contains packet filtering rules based on such information as IP addresses and source/destination TCP/UDP ports. The rules are applied to ingress (inbounding) and egress (outbounding) packets to improve network security.

Access link: The link that provides connectivity between a host and an intermediary device.

Access port: The switch port that provides hosts with direct connectivity to a network.

Ad hoc mode (in WiFi): Also called as peer-to-peer mode, two or more wireless hosts exchange data/messages directly without going through an access point.

Add-drop multiplexer (ADM): The technology component that inserts and removes traffic to/from the SONET ring.

Address Resolution Protocol (ARP): The protocol used by hosts and routers to obtain the MAC address of a network node or router interface/port based on its IP address.

Advanced Mobile Phone Service (AMPS): A 1st generation cellular technology that was purely analog and introduced primarily for voice communications.

Aggregate throughput: An actual, total data rate that can be pushed through a LAN switch at any moment. The majority of LAN switches have aggregative throughput that is slower than forwarding rate (i.e., combined data rate of all switch ports) due to their internal architecture.

Amplitude: The strength (i.e., the highest point) of a signal represented by such metric as voltage.

Analog signaling: Signaling method in which properties (i.e., amplitude, frequency, phase, and wavelength) of continuously varying electromagnetic waves are used to convey bit stream data.

Association (in WiFi): The binding required between a WiFi host and an access point before data exchange.

Asymmetric switch: A switch with ports that support different speeds (e.g., 100Mbps and 1 Gbps). The asymmetric switching is necessary when there is traffic concentration on one or more ports due to server connectivity or network design.

Asymmetric-key cryptography: The cryptography system that uses a private and public key pair for data encryption and decryption.

Asynchronous transfer mode (ATM): A WAN technology that supports faster connections than popular Frame Relay. ATM speed is defined in terms of optical carrier (OC) that has the base speed of about 52Mbps. With the high speed connectivity, it has been largely adopted for the service carrier's backbone platform.

Asynchronous transmission: A data transmission method in which one character (7 or 8 bits in ASCII) is transported at a time over the network. For this, each character is added by the start (indicating the start point), stop (indicating the ending point), and parity (for error detection) bits.

Attenuation: Gradual weakening of the strength or intensity of a signal (e.g., electronic, light, or radio signal) traveling over a cable or through the air.

Authentication server: The server system designated to authenticate WiFi clients and/or to authorize remote access through dial-in and virtual private network

Authentication: Validation of the true identity of communicating parties and of the source of data transported over the network.

Autonomous system (AS): A network that is under the control of one entity (e.g., university, enterprise, or ISP) and, thus, uses a consistent packet routing policy

Autonomous System Number (ASN): The unique identifier of an autonomous system, which is assigned by Internet Assigned Numbers Authority (IANA).

Backbone cabling subsystem: Also termed vertical or riser cabling, it interconnects wiring closets on different floors and the equipment room of a building.

Bandwidth: The frequency range of a communication channel or a medium (e.g., cable) calculated as the difference between its highest and lowest frequencies supported.

Baseband transmission: The mode of transmission in which a signal uses the full bandwidth of a medium or its channel to transport data. It utilizes digital signaling method and today's wired networks mainly take advantage of the approach.

Base Station (BS): A cell of a cellular system has a base station that communicates with mobile hosts, mostly cellphones, using high-frequency radio signals. With antenna, transmitter, receiver, and controller devices, the base station is mounted on a cell tower and connected to a MTSO through a fixed line.

Basic service set (BSS): The smallest building block of a WiFi LAN. In the ad hoc mode, it takes minimum two stations. In the infrastructure mode, it needs at least one host station and one access point.

Basic service set identifier (BSSID): Each BSS has a 48 bit BSSID to uniquely distinguish a BSS from other BSS. In the infrastructure mode, the BSSID of a basic service set is the access point's MAC address.

Block cipher: The *cipher* is an encryption algorithm used to convert plaintext to secretive ciphertext. There are two types of ciphers: *stream ciphers* and *block ciphers*. The block cipher encrypts data per block of certain size (e.g., 128 bit block).

Bonding: see link aggregation

Border Gateway Protocol (BGP): One popular Exterior Gateway Protocol used by border routers of an autonomous system in order to develop their routing table entries necessary for inter-domain routing of IP packets.

Bot: It is a secret program planted by a cybercriminal to turn innocent computers into zombies. Once successfully finds a home within a victim computer, it has capability to report back to the criminal master and listens to his/her commands. The remote control capability is what differentiates the bot program from other malware types.

Botnet: The collection of zombies formed by a bot is called a *botnet* and they can be collectively 'remote controlled' by its evil master. That is, bots of a botnet can act in a coordinated manner, executing routines following commands from the master.

Bridge & bridge table: The bridge is a layer 2 device designed to divide a network into smaller, manageable segments and to control the flow of unnecessary traffic from one segment to another. For this, the bridge examines the MAC address of every frame arriving at its port, and either passes or filters it referring to the bridge table.

Bridge Protocol Data Unit (BPDU): In Ethernet, the Spanning Tree Protocol/Rapid Spanning Tree Protocol exchanges BPDUs that contain information used to determine redundant paths between any two nodes.

Broadband transmission: The mode of transmission in which several frequency channels are created within a medium (e.g., cable) to concurrently transport multiple analog signals coming from different data sources.

Broadcast domain: It defines the limiting boundary of data/message broadcasting. The router generally does not relay broadcasted messages and thus becomes a divider between broadcast domains.

Brute force attack (in password cracking): This approach breaks the encrypted or hashed password by trying every possible key/password exhaustively in an automated fashion using a computer's brute force.

Building entrance subsystem: It is the junction point of the external and internal cabling of a building. As a building's entrance facility, it connects the building's network to the campus backbone or to a WAN/Internet service carrier.

Carrier Ethernet: The carrier's WAN service platform running on the Ethernet technology. It is a natural progression of Metro-Ethernet.

Carrier Sense Multiple Access/Collision Avoidance (CSMA/CA): The media access control standard for the WiFi LAN.

Cell switching: ATM's packet switching technology is called cell switching as ATM frames are called cells.

Cell: The name of ATM frames that contain 48 octets of payload (data) and 5 octets of header (there is no trailer), making each cell 53 octets (bytes) long.

Central Office (CO): Also called as point-of-presence (POP), it is a local facility that connects client LANs to the carrier's WAN infrastructure.

Certificate Authority (CA): An organization/authority that, as a trusted third party, issues digital certificates to business and individual clients, and oversee issued certificates.

Certificate Revocation List (CRL): The certificate authority can revoke the digital certificate of a person/business for various reasons including its expiration, compromised private key, and policy violation. Revoked certificates are placed in the CA's certificate revocation list (CRL) for public viewing.

Challenge Handshake Authentication Protocol (CHAP): The three-way authentication and handshaking standard used by Point-to-Point Protocol (PPP).

Channel Service Unit/Data Service Unit (CSU/DSU): The physical layer device that converts a digital signal generated by the customer premise equipment (e.g., border router) into another digital signal format used by a WAN link.

Circuit switching: In this mode of data transmission, the end-to-end circuit with reserved capacity is created beforehand between communicating parties, and the dedicated circuit capacity is exclusively used by the parties.

Classful IP: With the classful IP, the network ID part is a multiple (i.e., 8 bits, 16 bits, or 24 bits) of an octet that translates into class A, class B, or class C network respectively.

Classless IP: With the classless IP, the network ID part is not necessarily a multiple of an octet.

Code Division Multiple Access (CDMA): As one of the *random access* standards, radio signals carrying data are scattered across a frequency range by the "spread spectrum" technology.

Code Division Multiple Access 2000 (CDMA2000): It is an advanced version of CDMA.

Collision domain: A network segment within which only a single host is allowed to transmit data because multiple, concurrent data transmissions from different host stations result in collisions.

Common carriers: Telephone companies (telcos), Internet Service Providers (ISPs), and cable companies that offer voice and data services to business and individual customers.

Connection-less protocol: A protocol that does not require handshaking (or session establishment) prior to data exchange.

Connection-oriented protocol: A protocol that requires handshaking (or session establishment) prior to data exchange.

Control frames (in WiFi): Frames of acknowledgment and request-to-send/clear-to-send

(RTS/CTS), which are critical to control/manage the integrity of communications over WiFi.

Crossover cable: The cable is designed to connect similar devices (e.g., switch and switch). For this, it directly connects transmitting pins (1 and 2) on one end to the receiving pins (3 and 6) of the other end and vice versa.

Cryptography: Technology that transforms a plaintext (i.e., original unencrypted message) into an unreadable ciphertext (i.e., encrypted plaintext). The cryptography system is composed of four elements: plaintext, ciphertext, cipher (i.e., encryption algorithm), and key value.

Customer premises equipment (CPE): Network nodes, including modems, CSU/DSUs, routers, and host stations, that are placed at the client site in forming WAN connections.

Cut-through switching: A switching method in which a switch does not wait until the entire frame becomes available in the queue before its forwarding. Instead, it begins relaying the frame as soon as necessary information such as the destination MAC address becomes available.

Data confidentiality (or data privacy): A requirement that data in transit or in storage should be protected from eavesdropping.

Data Encryption Standard (DES): Introduced by IBM in 1977, it is a symmetric encryption standard that uses block cipher for message encryption. To make encryption more secure, the advanced version called 3DES or Triple DES has been in usage as its successor.

Data frames (in WiFi): Frames that carry actual user data (e.g., emails)

Data integrity: Assurance that packets in transit are not changed accidentally or manipulated by unauthorized parties. If the moderation takes place, it should be detected.

Data Link Connection Identifier (DLCI): The 10 bit virtual circuit identifier used to deliver Frame Relay frames to the destination router over the WAN connection.

Data VLANs: VLANs designed to transport computer-generated data such as emails and web pages. The majority of VLANs belong to this category.

Datagram: It is the connection-less mode of packet switching in which the end-to-end delivery path of a message is not determined in advance, but dynamically decided by the intermediary nodes.

Default route: The route used by a router when it cannot find the destination network of an incoming IP packet from the entries of its routing table.

Default VLAN: Switch ports that are not assigned to any other specific VLANs belong to the default VLAN. That is, when a switch is in the out-of-the box condition and thus its ports are not configured, all the switch ports belong to the default VLAN.

Demarcation point: The junction point where CPE (customer premise equipment) meets SPF (service provider facility) for WAN connectivity. The cabling junction box is placed at the customer premise and becomes a dividing point of network operation and maintenance responsibility.

Demilitarized zone (DMZ): The DMZ is an enterprise network segment that houses servers such as email and web to provide public access service and, therefore, is more vulnerable to cyber-attacks. It is physically and/or logically separated from the main production network by one or more firewalls.

Denial of Service (DOS): It indicates the situation in which a server (mainly web server) cannot offer its normal service to legitimate/authorized users caused by debilitating amount of incoming traffic and/or system crash. Many DOS attacks are executed in the form of DDOS (distributed DOS attack) for which zombie programs are planted in a number of innocent computers and they launch attacks to a target server at once.

Dense Wave Division Multiplexing (DWDM): A multiplexing technology used to concurrently place a number of light signals in one fiber strand to multiply the transmission throughput.

Dictionary method (in password cracking): An attempt to break a password by automatically trying various combinations of dictionary terms. This is possible by linking an electronic dictionary file that contains dictionary words to a password cracking software.

Digital Certificate: It is the traditional ID card's digital equivalence and is used in conjunction with the asymmetric encryption system to verify the holder of a particular public key (not private key).

Digital Signal (DS): A standard digital speed hierarchy introduced when cabling options for computer networks were mainly copper wires such as twisted pairs and coaxial cables. The DS0 at 64Kbps is the basis of the DS hierarchy and higher DS levels are multiples of 64Kbps.

Digital Signature: It is an electronic equivalence of the hand-written signature and is produced by encrypting the message digest (also known as hash value) of a message with the sender's private key. This encrypted hash value becomes a unique electronic signature because it can be produced only with the particular private key.

Directed broadcasting: Broadcasting a packet to a subnet that is different from the sender's subnet.

Directly connected routes (in routing table): All IP addresses of subnetworks physically connected to the interfaces (or ports) of a router are entered to its routing table as directly connected routes.

Distributed DOS attack (DDOS): see DOS

Domain Name System (DNS): A mechanism that provides mapping between domain names (unofficial addresses) and IP addresses (official addresses). The mapping is called name resolution.

Domain: It defines the boundary within which an organization or an organizational unit controls its network resources.

Dynamic Host Configuration Protocol (DHCP): A protocol used for temporary assignment of IP addresses to requesting clients.

Dynamic routes (in routing table): They are entries added to a router's routing table. The entries are automatically derived from the information periodically advertised by the dynamic routing protocol activated in routers.

Dynamic routing protocol: A protocol that enables the automated addition and update of the routing table entries by exchanging information with other routers.

E-Carrier: An international digital leased line service hierarchy introduced by ITU-T. The different service grades (e.g., E-1, E-2, E-3) are multiples of the basic digital signal (DS0) speed, 64Kbps. For example, E-1 leased line at 2.048 Mbps is designed to transport data equivalent to 30 DS0 channels.

Encoding: A term commonly represents the conversion process from non-binary contents (e.g., sound, alphanumeric characters) to binary bit steams in the application layer. Decoding is the reverse process. Another form of encoding/decoding takes place in the physical layer to convert bit streams into digital/analog signals and vice versa.

Equipment room subsystem: The equipment room houses core switches, routers, and telecom equipment such as private branch exchanges (PBX). The equipment room may be located on the first floor of a building. Sometimes, it is placed on a higher floor to better protect the facility from possible threats such as flooding.

Error control: It is a measure to detect and correct errors (e.g., change or loss of data) that may take place during data transmissions. A popular error control mechanism is acknowledgement (ACK).

Evil twin access point: A hacker can set up an access point called evil twin that operates at a high power outside the target firm's physical boundary, but close enough to its employees. With strong signals, an employee computer's WNIC can re-associate itself to the evil twin, allowing it to steal the employee's credentials (e.g., passwords).

Extended service set (ESS): An ESS is composed of multiple basic service sets (BSS), each with a wireless access point and associated host stations.

Exterior Gateway Protocol (EGP): The routing protocol is activated in border routers to exchange routing table information and thus to support inter-domain (i.e., between autonomous systems) routing of packets. Border Gateway Protocol (BGP) is the most well-known EGP.

Federal Communications Commission (FCC): The US government's independent regulatory agency that plays a key role in overseeing the country's telecommunications policy. Among the well-known responsibilities are the promotion of competition in communication services and the usage of radio spectrum.

File Transfer Protocol (FTP): A popular standard protocol developed for TCP/IP to transport files over the network. Its weakness has been the lack of security as files are not encrypted. For improved data security, FTPS that runs FTP over SSL (secure socket layer) is also used.

Fingerprinting: It is an act or technique of identifying suspicious, threat elements. For example, on downloading software (e.g., freeware, open source program) from the Internet, its integrity can be checked using a hash function (e.g., MD5, SHA-1).

Firewall: A software and/or hardware device designed to protect a computer network from cyber threats by controlling inbound and outbound traffic and by monitoring the patterns of data transmissions.

Fixed port switch: The switch device that comes with a fixed number of ports and, thus, no expandability.

Flash memory: A type of memory that is faster in reading files than the conventional hard drive disks and also does not lose the content even when it loses power.

Flow control: It is used to regulate data flow between two hosts with different processing capacity so that one is not overwhelmed by the other. The key mechanism of flow control is through the Window Size field, which basically tells the other party how much data can be transmitted without receiving an acknowledgement.

Forwarding rate: It represents the combined data rate of all switch ports. For instance, a switch with five 100 Mbps ports has the forwarding rate of 500 Mbps.

Frame check sequence: The FCS of a frame contains an error checking code (called Cyclic Redundancy Check or CRC code), which is used by the receiver station to detect a transmission error.

Frame relay: One of popular PSDN services as it covers the speed range most enterprises demand at competitive pricing.

Frame: It is a designated name for PDUs produced in the data link layer.

Frequency: It represents the number of cycles a wave (e.g., radio wave) has in every second. When a wave has one cycle per second, for example, its frequency is 1 Hertz (or Hz).

Frequency Division Multiplexing (FDM): A multiplexing method in which the available bandwidth of a line (or a channel) is divided into several frequency ranges and a data source is assigned to one of the available frequency ranges so that multiple data sources share the line (or channel) capacity.

Frequency Division Multiple Access (FDMA): It divides an available frequency band within a cell into smaller frequency channels, each of which is allocated to a user. This conceptually resembles to Frequency Division Multiplexing

Full-duplex mode: The mode in which data flow both directions simultaneously between two communicating nodes.

Global System for Mobile Communications (GSM): It is one of the most popular 2G cellular standards.

Half-duplex mode: The communication mode in which only one party is allowed to transmit data at a time, and the other party should wait until its turn.

Hash algorithm (function): The hash algorithm such as MD5 and SHA-1 takes a message of any length as input and produces a fixed-length string as output, called message digest. The hash value (message digest) thus generated cannot restore the original message, making it a one way function. The hash value is frequently used for digital fingerprinting.

Horizontal cabling subsystem: It connects wall plates in the work area to the patch panel in the wiring closet of a floor. It is permanent cabling pre-installed behind the wall.

Host name: When a domain name is paired with one or more IP addresses, it is frequently called as a host name, making the domain name and the host name practically interchangeable.

Host: The production source of information/data such as networking-enabled computers and smartphones that accept user inputs, process them, and generate outputs. Often times, hosts are also called end devices, end systems, end nodes, end stations, or end points.

Hub: The hub is a pure physical layer device that accepts incoming messages, regenerates their signal strength and shape, and repeats transmissions. Because of the hub's relay function, it is also called a multiport repeater.

Hypertext Transfer Protocol (HTTP): The application layer protocol used to enable communications between the web browser and the web server.

Infrastructure mode (in WiFi): It is the setup in which the WiFi LAN coexists with the wired LAN (mainly Ethernet) and wireless access points provide connectivity between them.

Inter-domain routing: Packet routing across different domains (or autonomous systems)

Interior Gateway Protocol (IGP): Protocols (e.g., RIP, OSPF, IS-IS) through which routers share information to develop/update routing table entries necessary for packet routing decisions within the boundary of an autonomous system.

Intermediary devices: see networking devices

Intermediate Distribution Facility (IDF): A wiring (or telecommunications) closet that keeps intermediary devices such as switches. It connects to Main Distribution Facility (MDF) and other IDFs via backbone cabling.

Internet Assigned Numbers Authority (IANA): The organization that oversees the global allocation of IP address space. IANA delegates available IP address space to Regional Internet Registries.

Internet Control Message Protocol (ICMP): An internet layer protocol used to exchange supervisory (e.g., ping, traceroute) IP packets. The supervisory packets play an important role in diagnosing connectivity between two network nodes.

Internet Engineering Task Force (IETF): The organization, as an international community of network designers, operators, vendors, and researchers, is responsible for developing TCP/IP standards.

Internet Exchange Point (IXP): Frequently called a network access point (NAP), it interconnects ISP networks. For this, it operates a high-speed LAN running on such standard as 10 Gigabit Ethernet.

Internet Group Management Protocol (IGMP): A protocol designed for IP multicasting. Multicasting over the Internet is possible when routers are multicasting enabled.

Internet of Things (or IoT): It represents a phenomenon in which numerous devices (e.g., cars, appliances, gadgets, electronics, mobile devices) automatically detect each other and communicate seamlessly to perform a host of routine and innovative tasks over the wired and wireless networks.

Inter-VLAN routing: The process of forwarding data between VLANs.

Intra-domain routing: Also call as internal routing, this is about routing IP packets within a domain (or autonomous system).

Intrusion Prevention System (IPS): The security system/appliances designed to detect threats mainly coming from outside and prevent (e.g., remove packets) them from affecting the internal network.

IP masquerading: see network address translation (NAT)

IP Security (IPSec): A standard introduced by Internet Engineering Task Force (IETF) to implement virtual private networks (VPN). As the most secure VPN protocol, it ensures data authentication, integrity, and confidentiality.

ISM bands: The license-free radio frequency bands and 900 MHz, 2.4GHz and 5.0 GHz bands are among them.

Label Information Base (LIB): MPLS-enabled routers maintain a LIB table that contains a list of label numbers and exit ports (interfaces), and refer to the table information to forward IP packets.

Label switching router: It is a MPLS-enabled router that can route IP packets based on label information instead of IP addresses.

Limited broadcasting: It is when a node broadcasts a packet to all other nodes within the same subnetwork. 255.255.255.255 is the destination IP address for limited broadcasting.

Link aggregation (also called port trunking or bonding): Two or more physical links between two network nodes (e.g., a server and a switch, two switches) can be combined to multiply transmission capacity as one logical link.

Link Aggregation Control Protocol (LACP): The link aggregation technology standardized as IEEE 802.1AX.

Local Area Network (LAN): The network that covers a relatively confined area such as a building or a single floor of a building.

Localhost: The domain name of the loopback IP address such as 127.0.0.1.

Logical Link Control (LLC): Standardized as IEEE802.2, it is an interface between the internet layer and the MAC sub-layer.

Long-Term Evolution (LTE): 4G cellular system that has received global acceptance, which include support from all US carriers.

Loopback IP address: A special IP address a host can use to send a message addressed to itself. Packets with a loopback address as the destination are, therefore, directed back to the sender before leaving its network card (or NIC).

MAC address: It is a physical address permanently printed on the network card (NIC) of a device and therefore cannot be changed (although it can be spoofed or masked).

Malware: Various types of software codes designed to cause malicious damages to infected systems and system users. Among the prevalent ones are viruses, worms, Trojan Horses, bots, adwares and spywares.

Managed switch: The switch that allows manual configuration of switch functions through the interface with its operating system.

Management frame (in WiFi): Management frames (e.g., authentication and association/de-association frames) in WiFi are exchanged between nodes an access point and clients to establish and maintain connections through the authentication and association process.

Management VLAN: This VLAN transports network management information such as automated updates of VLAN information and remote IP address assignment.

Man-in-the-middle attack (MITM): A form of attack in which a hacker is able to hijack a session and relay (or substitute) data as a middle man. This way, an attacker can steal sensitive data or obtain credentials (e.g., password) in order to intrude a protected network.

Masquerading: see spoofing

Media Access Control (MAC): A mechanism developed to avoid message collisions in shared media (e.g., hub-based Ethernet, WiFi) and to remedy if collisions take place. It is built into the host computer's network card (or NIC).

Medium Dependent Interface Crossover (MDIX): With this technology, a switch port can detect the type of cabling and connected device, and make necessary adjustments in terms of crossover versus straight-through mode.

Message Digest 5 (MD5): A popular hash algorithm that produces hash values (or message digest).

Metro-Ethernet: With the ubiquity of Ethernet LANs, common carriers have been offering Metropolitan Area Network services running on the Ethernet technology, thus metro-Ethernet.

Metropolitan Area Network (MAN): It is a network designed to cover good-sized cities and thus considerably larger than LANs or campus networks in scope. The MAN service available from common carriers offers Internet access or can interconnect LANs.

Mobile Terminal Switching Office (MTSO): In a cellular system, the MTSO performs fully automated functions essential for cellular service provision including call setup and termination, call routing, handoffs, roaming, and monitoring calls for billing.

Modal dispersion: When light pulses travel in different modes (i.e., angles) inside an optical fiber, their arrival becomes irregular. This modal dispersion become worse as the transmission distance gets longer, a potential problem in maintaining the integrity of exchanged data.

Modem: Stands for modulator & demodulator. Modulation converts a computer's digital bit streams into analog signals for transmission and demodulation reverses the process (i.e., from analog to digital).

Modular switch: The switch that comes with slots that can accommodate line cards (or modules), each with multiple ports.

Modulation: The process of altering the characteristics of analog signals to encode data. In other words, the values of frequency, amplitude, and phase are adequately varied (or modulated) for an analog signal to convey digital data.

Multicasting: Multicasting of a message results in its concurrent delivery to a selected group of destinations.

Multi-mode fibers: Optical fibers with a core diameter around 50/62.5 microns. With the significantly larger diameter than single mode fibers, multi-mode fibers allow light signals traverse the core in different angles (thus multi-modes).

Multiple Inputs Multiple Outputs (MIMO): The WiFi technology that transmits multiple, concurrent bit streams in contrast to the single bit stream of legacy standards (e.g., IEEE802.11g).

Multiprotocol Label Switching (MPLS): It is a popular WAN technology designed to bypass the traditional routing of IP packets in order to accelerate their delivery. MPLS-enabled routers perform switching (instead of routing) to move IP packets fast.

Name resolution: The mapping between a domain name and an IP address

Network access point (NAP): see Internet Exchange Point (IXP)

Network address translation (NAT): Address conversion (or mapping) between private and public IPs. Many firms adopt private IPs for internal nodes and they are translated into one or more public IPs by the border router or firewall when IP packets are routed outside the company boundary. As the practice shields internal hosts from external viewing it is also called as network masquerading or IP masquerading.

Network interface card (NIC): To be network enabled, a host is equipped with at least one NIC, an electronic circuit board. Also called as adaptor or LAN card, it is installed in networks nodes (e.g., host station, routers) and plugged into their bus. The NIC implements data link and physical layer functions.

Network interface device (NID): The junction point where CPE (customer premise equipment) meets SPF (service provider facility). At a house, it is generally placed on the outside wall so that a service technician can access it for maintenance and troubleshooting.

Network masquerading: see network address translation (NAT)

Network node: A broad concept that includes hosts and intermediary (or networking) devices.

Network topology: The physical layout of a network, which represents the design approach utilized to interconnect intermediary devices and hosts. Different topologies including bus, star, ring, mesh, tree (hierarchy), and hybrid have been in use.

Networking devices: Hardware devices (with built-in software components) that conduct activities necessary to move data between end stations. Also called as intermediary devices, they include bridges, switches, routers, modems, firewalls, multiplexers, CSU/DSU, and wireless access points.

Non-blocking switch: When the aggregate throughput of a switch can match its forwarding rate, the switch is non-blocking because all ports can achieve their highest transmission speeds simultaneously without being constrained by the switch's internal architecture. In reality, most switches are blocking.

On/Off signaling: As a digital signaling method, it is used for bit transmissions over optical fibers. With on/off signaling, the light source (e.g., laser) rapidly switches between on and off to send data according to the clocked cycle time.

Open authentication: In WiFi, it uses SSID for authentication. As SSID is exchanged in clear text, it is easy to intercept with a software tool and therefore open authentication is not a serious form of authentication.

Open Systems Interconnection (OSI): A standard architecture (also framework or reference model) introduced by ISO (International Organization for Standardization) of United Nations. It defines 7 function layers (i.e., application, presentation, session, transport, network, and data link layers).

Optical Carrier (OC): OC is the North America standard that defines various channel speeds on optical fibers. With their huge bandwidth, the basic channel speed of OC starts at 51.84 Mbps (OC-1) and higher OC speeds are multiples of OC-1.

Orthogonal Frequency Division Multiple Access (OFDMA): OFDMA is a multi-user version of OFDM (Orthogonal Frequency Division Multiplexing), which itself is an advanced form of FDM (Frequency Division Multiplexing). The 4G standard, LTE, uses OFDMA.

Packet filtering: Firewalls or routers use filtering rules to grant or deny inbounding and outgoing packets. Many of the rules are applied to the transport and internet layer information (e.g., IP addresses, source and destination ports).

Packet sniffing: In computer networking, it is equivalent to the wire-tapping of telephone lines in an attempt to steal information. The packet sniffing can be especially problematic in wireless networks that inevitably broadcast data.

Packet switching: In this mode, messages are digitized and packaged into a stream of relatively short (generally a few hundred to thousand bytes) and discrete units called packets, and each packet gets transported one by one.

Packet: The protocol data unit (PDU) produced at the internet layer

Password Authentication Protocol (PAP): A two-way authentication and handshaking standard available for Point-to-Point Protocol (PPP).

Patch cable (or patch cord): The UTP or optical fiber cord used to interconnect network nodes co-located (e.g., mounted on a rack).

Patch panel: A panel that is generally rack mounted and comes with a number of jacks to provide connectivity between network nodes (e.g., host stations in the work area and intermediary devices).

Peering: The arrangement in which Internet service providers (ISPs) directly exchange data bypassing IXPs (or NAPs) to improve accessibility to the Internet and to obtain other benefits such as network redundancy.

Peer-to-peer mode (in WiFi): see ad hoc mode

Peer-to-peer networking: Although most applications are running on the client/server paradigm these days, peer-to-peer is an alternative computing model in which there are no dedicated clients or servers, and each participating host behaves as both a client and a server in sharing services/resources.

Personal Area Network (PAN): It is a small network whose coverage is typically a few (up to 10) meters. It has been popularized with the introduction of such wireless standards as Bluetooth, WiFi Direct, Zigbee, and more recently NFC (Near Field Communication).

Phase: It represents the relative position of a signal point on a waveform cycle and is measured by the angular degree within the cycle.

Phishing: As a representative social engineering technique, it is an act of sending e-mails in an attempt to scam users into surrendering private information for such evil doing as identity theft. Most phishing emails carry one or more clickable links.

Ping: A utility program that sends echo requests to the target node using the ICMP protocol to check its availability and link connectivity. It is a very useful and important tool in testing and troubleshooting network links and nodes.

Point of Presence (POP): see Central Office

Point-to-Point Protocol (PPP): A popular data link layer protocol for leased WAN links. PPP frames can be transported over various physical links including twisted pairs, optical fibers, and radio waves.

Port (not as a hardware device): It identifies a particular application, service, or process (e.g., HTTP) implicated in the exchange of data between two hosts. A 16-bit number, commonly known as the port number is used for the identification.

Port density (port as a hardware device): Number of physical ports available on a switch

Port scanning: An act of probing the ports of a host in an automated fashion using one or more software tools to obtain information about the target host

Port mirroring: Managed switches come with a *mirror port* for network management. Frames going through some or all regular ports of a switch can be copied to its mirror port so that network traffic can be monitored by the computer attached to the mirror port.

Power over Ethernet (PoE): PoE enables a switch to use Ethernet LAN cables not only to transmit data signals but also to supply electric power to connecting nodes such as wireless access points (APs), VoIP phones, and web cameras. Using PoE enabled switches, the planning and deployment of these network nodes becomes more flexible without being constrained by the access to power sources.

Preamble: In the synchronous data transmission mode that moves data in blocks (e.g., frames), the preamble is used for the synchronization of data processing speed between communicating nodes.

Pre-shared key authentication: It is a popular solution to authenticate a wireless client station. For this, a secret key should be manually configured on both the access point and client stations. The pre-shared key may be derived from a user passphrase/password stored in the client stations and the access point.

Pretty Good Privacy (PGP): It is a popular commercial software product that adopts the hybrid (asymmetric + symmetric cryptography) approach to protect texts, files, directories, and e-mails primarily on the Windows platform.

Private IP: IP addresses intended for internal use only (e.g., within an organization or a home), and not for routing over the Internet. The border router does not allow packets with private IPs go beyond the organization's network boundary unless they are translated into public IPs.

Promiscuous mode: When the NIC of a host station is in the promiscuous mode, it copies all arriving frames and processes them even if there is mismatch between their destination MAC addresses and the NIC's MAC address.

Protocol data unit (PDU): The discrete message unit produced in each layer (except physical layer). The PDUs of data link, internet, and transport layers are called frames, packets, and segments/datagrams respectively.

Protocol: A protocol (e.g., HTTP) specifies a meticulously defined collection of communication rules that have to be complied by applications. The rules are largely divided into those regarding the format of a message (syntactic rules) and those concerned with the meaning/interpretation of the message (semantic rules).

Proxy server: It is set up by an organization to improve network performance and also to serve security functions: keeping internal computers anonymous by hiding their IPs; filtering access to restricted Internet sites; scanning inbound/outbound traffic; and caching frequently visited web pages to accelerate their downloading.

Public Key Infrastructure (PKI): It is a collection of hardware, software, policies, and procedures managed by the certificate authority to create, issue, monitor, and revoke digital certificates. A private enterprise may also setup its own PKI to issue digital certificates to its employees.

Public Switched Data Network (PSDN): A common carrier's WAN platform that runs on the packet switching technology and offers WAN connection services (e.g., Frame Relay) to mostly business clients. PSDN is generally shown to customers as a cloud because the carrier fully controls its operation and maintenance.

Quality of Service (QoS): When a carrier offers QoS provision for a service, network performance is guaranteed especially for real-time and mission-critical applications, regardless of the circumstance (e.g., traffic congestion). For this, the carrier can use such measures as message prioritization and the reservation of link capacity.

Radio spectrum: Radio waves are heavily utilized to offer advanced communication services. The radio's frequency spectrum ranges 30 Hz through 300 GHz, and different frequency ranges have been allocated to various commercial and non-commercial services including satellites, cellular systems, and WiFi.

Regional Internet Registry (RIR): RIR is an organization responsible for the management of IP address space for a region (e.g., North America). Large ISPs obtain IP address blocks from a RIR and divide them into smaller chunks to allocate them to small ISPs, business firms, and schools.

Repeater mode (WiFi): In the repeater mode, an access point becomes a repeater that relays radio signals to another access point in order to extend the range of a WiFi LAN. In this mode, however, the relay of frames can result in a considerable loss of throughput.

Request for Comments (RFC): The documentation of a particular TCP/IP-related project. Some RFCs become TCP/IP standards after going through the maturation stages and final ratification by IETF. The list of working groups and RFCs is available on the IETF's website (www.IETF.org).

Request to Send/Clear to Send (RTS/CTS): As a form of handshaking between an access point and a host station, RTS/CTS is designed to provide additional assurance to avoid transmission collisions, especially due to the hidden node problem in which client stations associated with an access point may not be able to sense others' presence.

Robust Security Network (RSN): see Wi-Fi Protected Access 2 (WPA2)

Rogue access point: It is an access point installed by an employee of a company without authorization. The rogue access point without adequate security configuration is an invitation for trouble when it grants attackers an unauthorized, easy entry point to the enterprise network.

Routing: Packet forwarding through multiple subnetworks joined by routers and the router's internet layer protocol is responsible for the activity. Packet routing can have multiple delivery paths between two network nodes, making routing decisions more complicated than switching for which there is only a single delivery path between any two network nodes.

Secure Socket Layer (SSL): A security protocol developed by Netscape Co. to provide a relatively secure means for communication, information access, and e-commerce transactions (ex. online banking). It has become a popular protocol to implement virtual private networks (or VPN) over the Internet.

Segment (as Protocol Data Unit): The name of PDU produced by TCP in the transport layer

Service level agreement (SLA): It specifies detailed contract terms and conditions of WAN or Internet access service (e.g., throughput) both a carrier/ISP and a client agreed upon.

Service provider facility (SPF): The SPF enables WAN connectivity between remote client sites and includes: (1) carrier's Central Office (CO)/Point of Presence (POP); (2) local access lines that link customer premises equipment (CPE) to the CO/POP; and (3) WAN backbone network.

Service set identifier (SSID): It is the identifier of a WiFi network and is configured in the access point(s).

Signalling: Frames produced in the host are in 1s and 0s and they should be encoded into light or electronic signals for delivery over the network. The conversion process is called signalling.

Simple Mail Transfer Protocol (SMTP): A standard protocol developed to exchange emails over the network. More specifically, SMTP is used for delivering emails between email servers and also uploading emails from user hosts to email servers. To download emails from servers to user hosts, other protocols such as POP3 or IMAP are used.

Simple Network Management Protocol (SNMP): A standard protocol introduced to manage network nodes such as routers, switches, bridges, IP phones, printers, copiers, and access points. The network nodes subject to the monitoring and administration are called managed devices.

Simplex: In simplex transmission, messages flow one direction only. Radio and TV broadcasting are good examples. This mode also exists between the computer and its input devices (e.g., keyboard, mouse).

Single Input Single Output (SISO): The wireless technology that supports one data stream between two nodes (e.g., client host and access point) on either 2.4GHz or 5.0GHz band. The legacy WiFi standards (i.e., 802.11a, 802.11b, and 802.11g) use SISO.

Single mode fiber: Optical fiber that is very thin in its core with diameter typically less than 10 microns (1 micron is one millionth of a meter). With the narrow core, light signals travel in a straight line, allowing one mode of transmissions.

Social engineering: A collection of non-technological (mostly psychological) tricks such as pretexting, impersonation, and phishing used to manipulate or fraud people in an effort to obtain unauthorized access to a target system, or steal private and oftentimes confidential information.

Socket: It is the combination of an IP address and a port number assigned to an application/service. A socket = an IP address: a port number

Spam: It represents an unsolicited email and becomes more of a nuisance unless it hides an executable malicious code. Spam is different from emails that receivers opt in to receive, oftentimes as a part of marketing promotion by senders. Spammers generally hide their origin with email spoofing.

Spanning Tree Protocol (STP)/ Rapid Spanning Tree Protocol (RSTP): The protocols (IEEE802.1D and IEEE802.1w standards) that identify redundant paths between any two end points within a switched network and performs their de-activation and re-activation as needed.

Spoofing: Also called masquerading, it is an act of faking to be someone or something to hide the real identity. There are many different forms of spoofing in cyberspace including IP and MAC address spoofing, email address spoofing, and web page spoofing.

Spread spectrum: It represents a collection of advanced modulation techniques heavily used for today's wireless networking. Among them ones are Direct Sequence Spread Spectrum (DSSS) and Orthogonal Frequency Division Multiplexing (OFDM). WiFi standards including 802.11g and 802.11n rely on OFDM.

Stackable switch: Some switches can be stacked on top of the other and they, as a whole, function just like one big switch with many ports. For this, the stacked switches are joined together by high-speed cables in daisy chain.

Standard architecture: A framework that broadly defines necessary network functions in a multi-layer structure

Start frame delimiter: The field that indicates the starting point of a frame

Stateful packet filtering: The packet filtering method in which the firewall (or the router) reviews each arriving packet in the context of previous communications. For this, the firewall/router should maintain state information such as TCP sessions and active UDP communications in the state table.

Stateless packet filtering: A packet filtering method in which the firewall (or the router) reviews each arriving packet as an isolated case. Stateless packet filtering is not effective in detecting or preventing intrusions.

Static route: It represents a routing path manually added to the routing table and remains there unless manually changed or dropped.

Store-and-forward switching: A switching method in which the switch waits until the entire frame becomes available before switching (or forwarding). While waiting, the frame is kept at the queue/buffer assigned to a particular incoming/outgoing port or at a common memory space shared by all ports.

Straight-through cable: An Ethernet patch cable in which the transmission pins 1 and 2 on both ends of the cord are directly connected and so does the receiving pins 3 and 6. The straight-through cable is designed to connect dissimilar devices (e.g., router and switch).

Stream cipher: Bit-level encryption method in which a message is encrypted one bit at a time.

Structured cabling system: The structured cabling system of a building includes cabling, voice and data network components, and other building system components (e.g., safety alarms, lights, security access, energy systems), implemented according to the standard principles of high-performance cabling. The structured cabling system divides the cabling infrastructure of a building into six segments called subsystems.

Structured cabling: Network cabling executed in accordance with the published standards is referred to as structured cabling. The standards define recommended practices on all aspects of cabling including cabling types, effective transmission distances, modular connectors and termination, installation requirements, and testing methods of installed cable.

Sub-interface: It is a virtual interface tied to a physical interface (e.g., Fa0/1) of a router. One router interface may be configured with multiple sub-interfaces. That is, a single router port can connect multiple subnets or virtual circuits (advanced concept!).

Subnet mask: The combination of 0s and 1s used to indicate the subnet ID of an IP address. Many practitioners use two terms -- network mask and subnet mask -- interchangeably, just as network and subnet are mixed-used.

Subnet: A single network within which the delivery of data between any two nodes is through one or more intra-networking devices such as switches and wireless access points. The data link layer is responsible for moving data within a subnet.

Subnetting: The process of creating subnets within an organization

Supernetting: With supernetting, multiple subnets are combined (or summarized) into a larger subnet. It is also known as classless inter-domain routing (CIDR).

Switch table: The switch table stores MAC addresses and exit ports of directly and indirectly connected hosts. When a frame arrives at a port, the switch refers to its switch table to decide the frame's exit port.

Switched Ethernet: An Ethernet LAN running on switches

Switching: Delivery of frames within a subnet for intra-networking. In a LAN, the switching decision relies on MAC addresses. There should be one active delivery path between the source and the destination, and this makes switching simpler than routing that may have multiple possible paths between two nodes.

Symmetric switch: A switch whose ports come with the same transmission speed such as 100Mbps. The switch is ideal when network traffic is evenly distributed through all switch ports.

Symmetric-key encryption: The encryption method (e.g., DES, 3DES) that uses the same key to encrypt and decrypt data.

Synchronous Optical Network (SONET): It is a North American standard for high speed leased line service offered on optical fiber infrastructure. The capacity of SONET lines is defined according to the optical carrier (OC) hierarchy in which OC1 is 51.84 Mbps and higher grades are multiples of the OC1 speed.

Synchronous transmission: A data transmission method in which each message unit such as the Ethernet frame is essentially a long string of characters. It includes a data field and a header/trailer that contains overhead information necessary to move the data.

Synchronous Transport Module (STM): The international standard of digital speed hierarchy introduced by ITU-T for optical fibers. In North America, the Optical Carrier (OC) hierarchy is used in place of STM. STM-1, as the base data rate, is 155.52 Mbps, three times of OC-1 speed.

T-Carrier: A digital leased line hierarchy in North America, which includes T-1, T-2, and T-3. The leased line speed is based on the multiples of digital signal (DS) hierarchy. For example, T-1 leased line (1.54Mbps) can accommodate 24 DS0 (64kbps) channels.

TCP/IP: A standard architecture (or reference model) introduced by IETF (Internet Engineering Tasks Force) for the Internet. It defines 4 function layers (i.e., application, transport, internet, and subnet layers) and comes with several protocols in each layer. The majority of popular standards in the application, transport, and network (internet) layers belong to the TCP/IP protocol suite.

Time Division Multiplexing (TDM): A multiplexing method that uses the entire line (or channel) bandwidth to transport a single data stream that combines (or multiplexes) inputs from several data sources. For the multiplexing, data inputs are interleaved one after the other.

Time Division Multiple Access (TDMA): It divides an available frequency band into smaller frequency channels, and then further divides each frequency channel into several time slots (e.g., 3 slots) and each time slot is allocated to an individual.

Traceroute: As a utility program running on ICMP, it shows the routing path to a target node and the roundtrip delay (latency) of packets. This tracing is possible as each router along the way responds to the Traceroute request.

Traffic engineering: With traffic engineering, the data delivery path between two locations can be pre-planned for balanced usage of network resources (e.g., links, routers). This approach can address problems of the traditional packet routing in which the routing path is decided by such factors as the shortest delivery path and network bandwidth, which may result in uneven utilization of network resources.

Traffic load balancing: see traffic engineering

Translational bridge: The bridge device designed to interconnect network segments running on different data link standards (e.g., Ethernet and WiFi). The translational bridge should convert the format of frames before they cross from one segment to another. The wireless access point is the most prevalent example.

Transmission Control Protocol (TCP): The transport layer protocol that is responsible for the provision of message integrity, session management, and port management. It is a connection-oriented protocol.

Transparent bridge: The bridge device designed to interconnect network segments running the same data link technology (e.g., Ethernet).

Trojan horse: A malicious code hiding within a legitimate program downloaded from a website or sent in email attachment. The majority of Trojans are designed to create a backdoor so that attackers obtain a sneak access to a target system (locally or remotely) by bypassing the normal authentication and login procedure.

Trunk link: The link that interconnects intermediary devices (e.g., router-router, router-switch, switch-switch), which results in the extension of network span. The trunk link is a point-to-point connection and can carry traffic from more than one access links.

Trunk port (in Ethernet): A switch port designated to connect to a port of another switch and the cable link itself becomes a trunk link. The trunk port of an Ethernet switch transports frames coming from different VLANs.

Trunking: see link aggregation

Tunnelling: It is the process of encapsulating an encrypted and/or authenticated packet within another packet for secure delivery.

Unicasting: The mode of message transmission in which there is a single source and a single destination. Here, the destination may be co-located with the source within the same subnetwork (thus requires intra-networking) or separated by multiple subnetworks (thus requires internetworking).

Uniform Resource Locater (URL): When a domain name (e.g., www.sdsu.edu) is preceded by a protocol such as http, https and ftp, it becomes a URL. As an URL example, http://www.sdsu.edu.

Universal Mobile Telecommunications Systems (UMTS): a 3G cellular system

User Datagram Protocol (UDP): The connection-less, transport layer protocol. UDP is an unreliable protocol that does not perform flow control and error control. UDP is an ideal transport protocol for real time data produced by voice over IP, video conferencing, online gaming, and multimedia streaming that cannot afford delays.

Virtual Channel Identifier (VCI): A component of the ATM's (Asynchronous Transfer Mode) virtual circuit identifier. When a VCI is combined with a virtual path identifier (VPI), the two becomes a particular virtual circuit number. So, VC = VPI + VCI.

Virtual circuit: A logically defined end-to-end path of a WAN link between two locations. The virtual circuit is either permanent (PVC) or switched (SVC). With PVC, a virtual circuit remains static. With SVC, a virtual circuit is dynamically setup at the beginning of a communication session and lasts only until the session ends. Generally, carriers use PVC because it lessens process burden on WAN switches.

Virtual LAN (VLAN): Hosts (or end points) attached to the switched Ethernet can be logically divided into groups (or segments), each logical segment becoming a VLAN. With the creation of VLANs, the switched LAN normally as one broadcast domain is further divided into multiple broadcast domains defined by different applications, workgroups, or organization units.

Virtual Path Identifier (VPI): see Virtual Channel Identifier (VCI)

Virtual private network (VPN): Technology that protects packets in transit through the advanced encryption in order to secure WAN connections over the Internet.

Virus: An executable program that often causes malicious damages to the infected system. For example, the system can crash or lock up, files and directories can be manipulated, the hard disk data can be erased, the system can behave erratic or slows down significantly, or it may even damage hardware.

VLAN tagging: It is the process of adding VLAN information to regular Ethernet frames. When a switched Ethernet has VLANs, frames from user stations are tagged with VLAN information by switches so that frames coming from different VLANs can be transported over the same trunk link without losing their VLAN identity.

Voice VLAN: A VLAN dedicated for voice over IP calls. The voice VLAN moves digitized voice and signalling information (e.g., call setup, dial tone, caller id) over the computer network. Given the time-sensitivity of voice calls, voice VLAN traffic is given a higher priority than data VLAN traffic to minimize call delays.

Voltage signaling: The signaling method used by traditional copper wires such as twisted pairs and coaxial cables to transport source data. Different voltage states in which each state sustains the same signal strength during a clock-cycle are used to represent bit data. At the end of each clock cycle, the voltage state may change abruptly to another voltage state to reflect another bit or bit combination.

Wardriving (in WiFi): With a utility tool, anyone can capture broadcasted WiFi data while driving or walking around areas with WiFi signals. When the wardriving practice is abused by wrong hands such as drive-by hackers, this poses security risks.

Wavelength: The distance between two adjacent peaks of a wave. Wavelength is inversely proportional to frequency. Depending on the frequency of an analog signal, its wavelength can be the length of a football field or of a molecular.

Wide Area Network (WAN): A network that spans across a state, a nation, or an international territory. A business organization creates its own private WANs by interconnecting its distributed LANs relying on the WAN service from common carriers.

Wi-Fi Protected Access (WPA): A WiFi security standard. WPA offers a stronger security than WEP by dynamically changing the key, which makes the key recovery attack much more difficult than when using a static key. WPA was intended to be more of an interim solution before WPA2 and therefore WPA is not an official IEEE standard.

Wi-Fi Protected Access 2 (WPA2): WPA2 is an official security standard known as IEEE 802.11i that meets government grade security. The network with all technical components complying with IEEE 802.11i is called Robust Security Network (RSN), allowing only authorized users to access a network. One key difference between WPA and WPA2 is their encryption technology.

Wire speed: The maximum data rate (speed) of a port

Wired Equivalent Privacy (WEP): The first generation and legacy security technology introduced in 1997 for WiFi LANs. Although intended to offer advanced security comparable to the traditional wired networks, its vulnerability was quickly discovered. The access point and associated stations share the same key that remains unchanged.

Wireless Access Points (WAP or AP): Access points are equipped with their own WNIC and bridging software to enable message forwarding between two different LAN standards. It provides connectivity mainly between Ethernet and WiFi by translating their frames.

Wireless access router: It combines switch, router, and wireless access point functions altogether for the relatively simple home networking.

Wireless mesh network (Wi-Mesh): It uses the WiFi standard to cover considerably larger territories such as a metropolitan area. It uniqueness is that access points -- frequently called mesh points -- can route data and therefore do not need to be tied to a wired LAN. IEEE issued 802.11s as the Wi-Mesh standard.

Wireshark: A popular packet sniffing software

Wiring closet subsystem: The wiring closet subsystem located on a building floor houses equipment (e.g., workgroup switches) that provides network accessibility to host stations in the adjacent work area via horizontal cabling. It also becomes a junction point to backbone cabling.

Work area subsystem: The subsystem covers structured cabling between the wall plates of a room and various voice/data end points including PC stations, telephones, and network printers.

Worm: A program designed to replicate itself and spread to other computers without human interventions. It does not necessarily damage the components of infected (or relaying) systems. Because of the self-replication and resulting bandwidth consumption, one of its main consequences is disrupted network performance.

X.509: The popular digital certificate standard from International Telecommunications Union (ITU)

Zero-day attack: It is an act of exploiting software vulnerabilities that have not been adequately patched by vendors. It is, thus, carried out by attackers before a software company finds vulnerabilities in its products and distributes security fixes.

Acronyms

ABR	Available Bit Rate
ACK	Acknowledgment
ACL	Access Control List
ADM	Add-Drop Multiplexer
ADSL	Asymmetric Digital Subscriber Line
AMPS	Advanced Mobile Phone Service
ARP	Address Resolution Protocol
AS	Autonomous Systems
ASN	Autonomous System Number
ATM	Asynchronous Transfer Mode
BGP	Border Gateway Protocol
BPDU	Bridge Protocol Data Unit
Bps	bits per second
BS	Base Station
BSS	Basic Service Set
BSSID	Basic Service Set Identifier
CA	Certificate Authority
CAT5	Category 5
CBR	Constant Bit Rate
ccTLD	Country Code TLD
CDMA	Code Division Multiple Access
CDMA2000	Code Division Multiple Access2000
CHAP	Challenge Handshake Authentication Protocol
CIDR	Classless Inter-domain Routing
CLI	Command Line Interface
CO	Central Office
CPE	Customer Premises Equipment
CRC	Cyclic Redundancy Check
CRL	Certificate Revocation List
CSMA/CA	Carrier Sense Multiple Access/Collision Avoidance
CSMA/CD	Carrier Sense Multiple Access/ Collision Detection
CSU/DSU	Channel Service Unit/Data Service Unit
DDOS	Distributed Denial of Service
DES	Data Encryption Standard
DHCP	Dynamic Host Configuration Protocol
DLCI	Data Link Connection Identifier
DMZ	Demilitarized Zone
DNS	Domain Name System
DOS	Denial of Service
DS	Digital Signal
DSL	Digital Subscriber Line
DSSS	Direct Sequence Spread Spectrum
DWDM	Dense Wave Division Multiplexing
EGP	Exterior Gateway Protocol

EIGRP	Enhanced Interior Gateway Routing Protocol
ESS	Extended Service Set
FCC	Federal Communications Commission
FCS	Frame Check Sequence
FDM	Frequency Division Multiplexing
FDMA	Frequency Division Multiple Access
FHSS	Frequency Hopping Spread Spectrum
FRAD	Frame Relay Access Device
FTP	File Transfer Protocol
FTPS	FTP over SSL
GPS	Global Positioning System
GSM	Global System for Mobile Communications
gTLD	Generic TLD
GUI	Graphical User Interface
HDLC	High-level Data Link Control
HEX	Hexadecimal
HTTP	Hypertext Transfer Protocol
HTTPS	Hypertext Transfer Protocol over SSL (Secure Socket Layer)
IANA	Internet Assigned Numbers Authority
ICANN	Internet Corporation for Assigned Names and Numbers
ICMP	Internet Control Message Protocol
ICT	Information and communication technology
IDF	Intermediate Distribution Frame (or Facility)
IEEE	Institute of Electrical and Electronics Engineers
IETF	Internet Engineering Task Force
IGMP	Internet Group Management Protocol
IGP	Interior Gateway Protocol
IoT	Internet of Things
IP	Internet Protocol
IPng	IP Next Generation
IPS	Intrusion Prevention System
IPSec	IP Security
IRC	Internet Relay Chat
IS-IS	Intermediate System to Intermediate System
ISM Band	Industry, Scientific, and Medical Band
ISO	International Organization for Standardization
ISP	Internet Service Provider
ITU	International Telecommunication Union
IXP	Internet Exchange Point
LACP	Link Aggregation Control Protocol
LAN	Local Area Network
LIB	Label Information Base
LLC	Logical Link Control
LSR	Label Switching Router
LTE	Long-Term Evolution
MAC	Media Access Control

MAN	Metropolitan Area Network
MBWA	Mobile Broadband Wireless Access
MD5	Message Digest 5
MDF	Main Distribution Frame (or Facility)
MDIX	Medium Dependent Interface Crossover
MIMO	Multiple Inputs, Multiple Outputs
MITM	Man-in-the-middle
MLS	Multi-Layer Switch
Modem	Modulator Demodulator
MPLS	Multi-Protocol Label Switching
MTSO	Mobile Terminal Switching Office
NAP	Network Access Point
NAPT	Network Address Port Translation
NAT	Network Address Translation
NIC	Network Interface Card
NID	Network Interface Device
OC	Optical Carrier
OFDM	Orthogonal Frequency Division Multiplexing
OFDMA	Orthogonal Frequency Division Multiple Access
OSI	Open Systems Interconnection
OSPF	Open Shortest Path First
OUI	Organizational Unique Identifier
P2P	Peer-to-Peer
PAN	Personal Area Network
PAP	Password Authentication Protocol
PAT	Port Address Translation
PBX	Private Branch Exchanges
PCM	Pulse Code Modulation
PDA	Personal Data Assistants
PDU	Protocol Data Unit
PGP	Pretty Good Privacy
PKI	Public Key Infrastructure
PMP	Portable Multimedia Players
PoE	Power over Ethernet
POP	Point of Presence
POP3	Post Office Protocol 3
POTS	Plain Old Telephone Service
PPP	Point-to-Point Protocol
PPTP	Point-to-Point Tunneling Protocol
PSDN	Public Switched Data Network
PSK	Pre-Shared Key
PSTN	Public Switched Telephone Network
PVC	Permanent Virtual Circuit
QoS	Quality of Service
RADIUS	Remote Authentication Dial in User Service
RAM	Random Access Memory

RFC	Request for Comments
RIP	Routing Information Protocol
RIR	Regional Internet Registry
ROM	Read Only Memory
RSN	Robust Security Network
RSTP	Rapid Spanning Tree Protocol
RTS/CTS	Request to Send/Clear to Send
S/MIME	Secure/Multipurpose Internet Mail Extensions
SCS	Structured Cabling System
SDH	Synchronous Digital Hierarchy
SDSL	Symmetric DSL
SHA	Secure Hash Algorithm
SISO	Single Input, Single Output
SLA	Service Level Agreement
SMTP	Simple Mail Transfer Protocol
SMTPS	SMTP over SSL
SNMP	Simple Network Management Protocol
SONET	Synchronous Optical Network
SPF	Service Provider Facility
SSH	Secure Shell
SSID	Service Set Identifier
SSL/TLS	Secure Socket layer/Transport Layer Security
STDM	Statistical Time Division Multiplexing
STM	Synchronous Transport Module
STP	Shielded Twisted Pair
STP	Spanning Tree Protocol
SVC	Switched Virtual Circuit
TACACS+	Terminal Access Controller Access-Control System Plus
TCI	Tag Control Information
TCP	Transmission Control Protocol
TDM	Time Division Multiplexing
TDMA	Time Division Multiple Access
TLD	Top level domain
TLS	Transport Layer Security
TPID	Tag Protocol Identifier
TTL	Time to Live
UBR	Unspecified Bit Rate
UDP	User Datagram Protocol
UMTS	Universal Mobile Telecommunications Systems
URL	Uniform Resource Locater
UTP	Unshielded Twisted Pair
VBR	Variable Bit Rate
VCI	Virtual Channel Identifier
VLAN	Virtual LAN
VM	Virtual Machine
VPI	Virtual Path Identifier

VPN	Virtual Private Network
WAN	Wide Area Network
WAP	Wireless Access Points
WEP	Wired Equivalent Privacy
WIC	WAN Interface Card
WIFI	Wireless LAN
WNIC	Wireless Network Interface Card
WPA	Wi-Fi Protected Access
WPA2	Wi-Fi Protected Access 2

INDEX

A

ABR (Available bit rate)   311-12, 320, 433

Access control   170, 173, 269, 387-9, 409-10

Access control list   104-5, 388-9, 395, 409-10, 412-13, 433

Access layer   217-18, 220

Access links   6-7, 33-4, 116, 134, 138, 143, 225, 231, 305, 321, 323, 413, 429

Access ports   230-2, 234, 239, 242-4, 250, 413

Acknowledgement   41, 52-4, 67, 261, 284, 286, 418

Ad hoc mode   255, 258, 272, 286, 413-14, 423

Add-Drop Multiplexer *see* ADM

ADM (Add-Drop Multiplexer)   299-300, 320, 413, 433

Advertise   89, 183, 203, 208

Advertisements   200-1, 203-4, 207

Adwares   364, 384, 421

Aggregate throughput aging time   104

Amplitude   112-15, 140, 413, 421

Amplitude modulation   113-14, 143

Analog signaling   43, 110, 112-17, 121, 134, 142, 413

Anti-spyware   388-9, 410

Application data   39, 47, 52, 55, 93-4

Application layer   38-9, 41, 59-60, 63, 67-8, 103, 109, 186, 286, 335-6, 346, 367, 390-2, 417

Applications   2, 7-9, 37-9, 57-8, 60-2, 64, 66-8, 71-2, 151-3, 155, 293, 312, 335, 360, 428-9

Architecture, internal   79, 413, 422

ARP (Address Resolution Protocol)   68-9, 71, 94-5, 103-6, 153, 160, 184, 208, 221, 226, 239, 309, 344, 413, 433

ASN (autonomous system number)   205, 207, 325, 329-30, 414, 433

Association   247, 254, 256, 264, 269, 271, 286, 383, 413, 421

Asymmetric switch   85, 104, 413

Asynchronous Transfer Mode *see* ATM

Asynchronous Transmissions   119

ATM (Asynchronous Transfer Mode)   287, 292-3, 305, 310-12, 314, 320-1, 323, 413, 429, 433

Attenuation   126-7, 131, 140, 142, 413

Authentication   256-7, 264, 269-71, 285, 301, 323, 337, 339, 387-9, 396, 399, 404, 407, 409-13, 421-2

Authentication frames   264, 269-70

Authentication server   271, 409, 411, 413

Authorization   271, 387-9, 425

Autonomous system number *see* ASN

Autonomous systems   199-200, 205, 207, 325-6, 329-30, 358, 391, 413-14, 418-20, 433

Auxiliary port   105

Available bit rate *see* ABR

B

Backbone cabling   135, 137-8, 140, 419, 431

Bands   265, 268, 284

Bandwidth   24, 34, 116-18, 121, 125-6, 128, 140, 187-8, 201, 207, 222-3, 266-7, 274, 276, 285

Baseband   109, 117-18, 134, 142

Basic service set *see* BSS

Basic Service Set Identifier *see* BSSIDs

BGP (Border Gateway Protocol)   186, 200, 205, 207-8, 329-30, 391, 414, 418, 433

Binary   26, 28, 147, 163-4

Block ciphers   397, 410, 414

Block switch ports   221

Bluetooth   15, 253, 255, 264, 266, 285, 423

Bonding   85, 104, 213, 222-3, 248, 276, 360, 414, 420

Border Gateway Protocol *see* BGP

Border router firewall and DMZ   390

BPDUs (Bridge Protocol Data Units) 222, 247, 251, 414, 433

Bps 23, 32, 117

Bridge Protocol Data Units *see* BPDUs

Bridge table 75-7, 104, 107, 414

Bridges 5, 71, 75-7, 102-7, 241-2, 312, 414, 422, 426

Broadband 17, 117-18, 134, 139, 142

Broadband modem 278, 283

Broadcast domains 89, 99, 102-4, 106, 153-4, 172, 225, 227, 230, 232, 238-9, 249, 414, 429

Broadcast IP address 180

Broadcast storms 221, 247

Broadcasting 9-10, 12, 35, 74, 78, 98, 101-3, 151, 153, 165-7, 176, 215-16, 226-8, 343-4, 359-60

Brute Force Method 369

BSS (basic service set) 254, 256, 258-61, 267-8, 274, 276, 283-5, 316, 414, 418, 433

BSSIDs (Basic Service Set Identifier) 258-9, 268, 272, 283, 414, 433

Building entrance 141

Bus topology 12

C

Cable modem 91, 115, 117, 278-9, 281, 289, 377

Campus network 34, 86, 131, 139, 142, 217, 257, 329, 421

Capacity 5, 8, 23, 35, 74, 117, 124, 261, 298, 303, 313, 367, 371, 391, 419

Carrier network 18, 116, 289, 295, 298, 305, 333

Carrier Sense Multiple Access *see* CSMA

Carriers 17-19, 26, 115, 121, 287-9, 293-4, 298-9, 302-8, 312, 314, 316, 319-20, 322-3, 332-3, 425

CBR (Constant bit rate) 311-12, 320, 323, 433

CcTLDs 348, 358

Cell 256-7, 261, 267, 283, 311, 316-17, 320-2, 414-15, 419

Central office (CO) 121-2, 139, 289-90, 298-9, 303-5, 316, 320-1, 415, 423, 425-6, 433

Central Offices 290, 298-9, 303-5, 316, 320, 423, 425, 433

Challenge Handshake Authentication Protocol *see* CHAP

Channel bonding 276, 283-4

Channel capacity 24, 34, 121, 261, 266, 273

Channels 11, 34, 115-18, 120-1, 125, 261, 266-8, 272-7, 283, 286, 298-300, 317, 399, 418-19, 428

CHAP (Challenge Handshake Authentication Protocol) 301-2, 320, 323, 415, 433

CIDR (classless inter-domain routing) 168, 175, 427, 433

Cipher 397-8, 414, 416

Ciphertext 397-400, 402, 416

Circuit 11, 67, 120, 291-2, 298, 318-21, 415

Classful IP scheme 148, 340

Classless inter-domain routing *see* CIDR

Classless IP 150-1, 178, 415

Clear-to-Send *see* CTS

CLI (Command Line Interface) 32, 72, 104, 376, 433

CLIENT-SERVER SYSTEMS 325, 346

Cloud 292, 303-4, 306-8, 310, 312, 315, 323, 425

CO *see* central office

Collision domains 99-101, 103-4, 108, 213, 260, 415

Collisions 74-5, 99-104, 214, 260-2, 284, 286, 415, 421

Command Line Interface *see* CLI

Confidentiality 335, 385, 387, 396, 398, 400, 412, 420

Console port 72-4, 89-90, 105

Constant bit rate *see* CBR

Control frames 263-4, 283, 286, 415

Copper wires 6, 13, 34, 117, 124, 126, 128, 131, 139, 417

Core layers 217-20, 247, 249-50

Country code 348, 360

Full-duplex mode   5, 11, 35, 78, 105, 134, 419

G

Gateway   99, 105, 139, 174, 195-6, 207, 328, 359, 381, 392
Generic
Gigabit Ethernet   79-80, 134, 138-9, 217, 223-4, 291, 328, 420
Graphical User Interface *see* GUI
GTLDs   348, 358
GUI (Graphical User Interface)   72, 104, 376, 434

H

Handshaking   41, 53-6, 62, 67, 261, 372, 415, 423, 425
Hash function   203, 368, 386, 401-2, 418
HDLC (High-level Data Link Control)   434
Header   40, 48-9, 53, 63, 67-8, 98, 119, 200, 214, 263, 304, 311-12, 315, 341, 346-7
Hexadecimal   26, 28, 77, 107, 215, 369, 434
Hierarchical design   216, 219, 225
Hop count   187-90, 207, 209
Horizontal cabling subsystem   136, 139, 141, 419
Host computers   38-9, 60, 62, 68, 81, 157, 170-1, 195, 221, 231, 249-50, 350, 360-1
Host identification   145, 176, 178
Https   57, 146, 335, 338, 348, 374, 394, 406, 429, 434
Hub-and-spoke   13-14, 33, 322
Hubs   5, 7, 11, 33, 35, 43, 71-2, 74-8, 99-108, 214, 220, 249, 419
Hypertext Transfer Protocol   39, 53, 105, 346, 419, 434

I

IANA (Internet Assigned Numbers Authority)   145-6, 174-5, 178, 325, 329, 340, 348, 414, 419, 434
ICANN (Internet Corporation for Assigned Names and Numbers)   178, 325, 348, 358, 434
ICMP (Internet Control Message Protocol)   37, 39, 48-9, 51, 66, 68-9, 106, 329, 394-5, 410, 419, 428, 434
IDF (intermediate distribution facility)   135, 139, 224, 419, 434
IEEE   30, 80, 88, 178, 213-14, 216, 221, 223, 253-4, 256, 273, 277, 284-6, 412, 420
IETF (Internet Engineering Task Force)   37, 57, 66, 175, 200, 314, 325, 335, 338, 340, 419-20, 425, 428, 434
IGMP (Internet Group Management Protocol)   156, 175, 420, 434
IGP (interior gateway protocols)   199, 207, 330, 419, 434
Infrastructure mode   254-5, 257-8, 285-6, 414, 419
Ingress   389, 393, 395-6, 413
Inquiry   98, 349-50, 366
Intense scan option   378
Interior gateway protocols *see* IGP
Intermediary devices   2, 5-7, 11, 13, 15, 25, 28-30, 33-5, 38, 45-7, 62-4, 71-4, 98-9, 105-7, 170-1
Intermediate distribution facility *see* IDF
Intermediate system   199, 207-8, 434
International Telecommunications Union (ITU)   299, 404, 431, 434
Internet   20, 37-9, 41, 63, 66-8, 183, 213, 286, 321, 325, 359-60, 392, 424, 428
Internet   17-19, 21-2, 37-9, 64, 115-16, 153-8, 172-6, 278-80, 287-8, 292-4, 325-38, 345-8, 359, 366-8, 388-92
Internet Assigned Numbers Authority *see* IANA
Internet Control Message Protocol *see* ICMP
Internet Corporation for Assigned Names and Numbers *see* ICANN
Internet Engineering Task Force *see* IETF

447

Published by Montezuma Publishing.

Please direct comments regarding this product to:

Montezuma Publishing
Aztec Shops Ltd.
San Diego State University
San Diego, California 92182-1701
619-594-7552

or email: *orders@montezumapublishing.com*

website: www.montezumapublishing.com

Production Credits
    Production mastering by: Gianna Punzalan
    Quality control by: Scott Leyland

ISBN-10:   0-7442-8855-X
ISBN-13: 978-0-7442-8855-1

This anthology contains copyrighted material requiring payment of royalties to the publisher of $13.75.

CPSIA information can be obtained
at www.ICGtesting.com
Printed in the USA
BVOW05s1652020917
493537BV00011BA/90/P